Men Doing Feminism

Men Doing Feminism

Edited by Tom Digby

ROUTLEDGE

New York and London

Published in 1998 by

Routledge
29 West 35th Street
New York, NY 10001

Published in Great Britain by

Routledge
11 New Fetter Lane
London EC4P 4EE

Copyright © 1998 by Routledge

Printed in the United States of America on acid free paper
Typography: Jack Donner

Library of Congress Cataloging-in-Publication Data

Men doing feminism / edited by Tom Digby.
     p.   cm. (Thinking Gender)
  Includes bibliographical references and index.
  ISBN 0–415–91625–9 (cloth). — ISBN 0–415–91626–7 (pbk.)
    1. Men—United States—Attitudes. 2. Men—United States—Psychology. 3. Feminism—United States. 4. Sex role—United States. I. Digby, Tom, 1945– . II. Series.
HQ1090.3M44 1998
305.32—dc21   97–39468
                                                                                                                          CIP

For Luna—a philosopher, no matter what

Contents

Part 2: Feminist Theory *in* Men's Lives

Acknowledgments

My first and greatest debt is quite obviously to the contributors. Working with them contributed immensely to my growth as a feminist and as a philosopher. I thank them for their patience, their energy, and their enthusiasm for this project.

Paradoxically, for several years after I began to study and teach feminist theory, I didn't think the relationship between men and feminism was an interesting subject. Sandra Harding convinced me otherwise. Sandra's support and encouragement gave me the confidence to take on this project. While I knew that others could do it better, Linda Nicholson and Maureen MacGrogan kept that realization from standing in my way. Linda's guidance and friendship throughout the process of producing this anthology have been invaluable; I now realize why she has been such an extraordinarily successful series editor. It is an immense honor for me to have this book included in the *Thinking Gender* series, which has played a pivotal role in feminist theory and has been a profound influence on the intellectual life of every feminist theorist I know.

Susan Bordo, during several weeks of extensive, and intensive, emailing at the beginning of the project, helped me see what this volume could be, even if it doesn't entirely measure up to the aspirations she gave me. The fact that Susan continued to believe in me and the project, no matter what, carried me past many a discouraging moment.

Through many hours of warm, supportive, and stimulating conversation, Sandra Bartky, Laurence Thomas, Jim Sterba, Cheryl Hughes, Tamar March, Gretchen Breese, Jennifer Miller, Amy Crafts, Fran Chelland, and Judy Jones have, as I think this collection shows, kept me from succumbing to the provinciality of rural New England; they have also proved to be such friends as make for a fulfilling life, regardless of any other circumstances. As I have indicated in the Introduction, it was Phyllis Kenevan who made me a feminist philosopher, rather than just a feminist, and rather than just a philosopher, although she did have important assistance during that crucial period from Valerie Broin, Sherry Walton, and Wendy Williams.

Innumerable students during the past fifteen years of teaching feminism have contributed to my thinking and my personal growth as a feminist, including Corinth Matera, Galo Grijalva, Steve Stoltz, Christina Klucznik, Aaronelizabeth Turner, Michelle Connelly, David Voight, Rob DuMars, Rob Schwartz, Robert Chan, Ben Churchill, Esti Feller, Patrick Dunagan, Aishwarya Lakshmi, Kim Firth, Ceti Boundy, Michelle Cotler, Karen Allison, Aysin Karaduman, William P. Kelley, Kurt Steiner, Julie Cobb, Aimee Armata, and many others whose presence in my memory or address book has momentarily lapsed. For assistance in critiquing most of the chapters, I am indebted to the students in my "Men Doing Feminism" seminar at New England College: Amanda Gilbert, Brenda Johnson, Sascha Wlodyka, Jared Rich, Amanda Kaplan, and Steffi Churchill.

I am deeply grateful to William Germano, my editor at Routledge, for the wit, intelligence, intuitiveness, and grace with which he handled this project. He was ably assisted by associate editors Alexandria Giardino and Laska Jimsen, and editorial assistant Nick Syrett, all of whom were indispensible in getting the book ready for press. I greatly appreciate Marie Leahy's good humor and enthusiasm for marketing the volume. Anthony Mancini's production work speaks for itself; he clearly knows how to make beautiful books. In the final weeks before going to press, production editor Lai Moy deployed the perfect blend of diplomacy and discipline to insure that the book got into print on schedule.

Above all, my gratitude goes to poet, performance artist, and philosopher Elvia F. Herrera. In its early stages she was a virtual co-editor of this book, and even when her own work took her energies in other directions, she continued to be a profound influence on its shape and content. Her friendship has made me a better person, philosopher, and feminist.

Foreword

Sandra Bartky

The Second Wave feminism of the late sixties and seventies emerged and grew strong and confident in an environment where men were largely excluded. While intersections of race and class inflected this environment in important ways, and while there was sometimes acceptance of an "exceptional" male, an undercurrent of separatism characterized much of feminism. Consciousness-raising groups were for women only; women debated and enacted forms of political struggle with one another, but against men, at least against male-dominated institutions and practices. Women's studies programs were first imagined and later established and taught almost exclusively by women, typically in the face of hostility from male-dominated university administrators. Now all of these separatist tendencies seemed at the time to be eminently sensible and desirable. The discoveries we made about the nature and extent of our sometimes blatant but often disguised oppression could not and would not have been made "in the presence of the oppressor." Given the central role played by the raising of consciousness in women-only venues, and given the closeness of theory and experience, it seemed obvious that men had no role to play in the development of feminist theory or feminist politics. Anyhow, we told each other, "all men oppress all women." Only a fool or traitor would make common cause with the enemy in what we knew would be a Protean struggle.

While I no longer accept the overgeneralized claim that "all men oppress all women," I still believe that patriarchy, like racism, is a lethal, and, unless we act with some dispatch, quite possibly a terminal illness of the social body. I still believe that a movement for the liberation of women should be led by women and answerable to them. Moreover, it seems clear to me that many women want and need their own spaces and places; such spaces—and the organizations to which they have given birth—are life-enhancing, indeed life-saving for many women. In particular, lesbian separatists have invented new ways for women to be together, both socially and sexually; they have also made indispensable contributions to feminist theory.

Nevertheless, I feel that the profoundly separatist moment that animated radical feminist organizing twenty-five years ago is a moment that is passing. The reasons for this are manifold. First of all, we have discovered in the course of over two decades of feminist agitation that many men have been stalwart, committed, and politically effective allies, while many women, even some self-styled feminists (the proverbial wolves in sheep's clothing), often with the financial support of rich conservative foundations, have made crude and uninformed criticisms of feminism, trivialized our ideas, distorted what we say almost beyond recognition, and called for the defunding of women's studies programs. Second, younger feminists appear not to have the same need for separation of the genders that feminists of my generation needed so badly. I do not think that this is a result of "false consciousness" on the part of younger women. We are at a different historical moment now: many of the insights that my feminist generation wrested with such difficulty out of the confusion of our lives, insights that needed a protective space in which to come to consciousness and then to word, are now accepted by younger feminists as obvious, even self-evident.

We have learned from reading men's writings that the imposition of male gender identity can be as painful and as shot through with ambiguity and confusion as the imposition of feminine identity. In this way, and in many other ways (as this volume demonstrates) men have made important contributions to feminist theory. For many men, the pain inflicted by the imposition of male gender identity serves as an entirely comprehensible motive for their active support of the women's movement. There is also at play here a matter of simple justice: many men have integrated feminist values and a profound commitment to the feminist movement into their lives, their personal relationships with both men and women, their relationships with children, their romantic involvements, their work, and, if they are academics, their research and teaching. These men deserve a place at our table: they have listened and learned from us; there is much that we can learn from them. There are also practical political reasons for abandoning a thoroughly separatist politics. Given the antiquity, power, depth, and breadth of patriarchy, I doubt that women alone can overthrow it. We need "gender traitors," and lots of them, to effect a thoroughgoing reform of our institutions and a wholesale movement to a new plateau of consciousness. *Men*

Doing Feminism is not the first volume in which gender traitors have spoken, but it is surely one of the best.

In a climate of conservatism, many men have been organizing around gender issues in ways that are clearly regressive: the re-establishment of solid male dominance in the family seems to be part of the appeal of the Nation of Islam; it is even more clearly a factor in the rapid growth of the Promise Keepers. Nothing on this scale is happening among feminist men; nevertheless, there is a progressive men's movement: some of the contributors to this volume are active in it, organizing and reaching out to other men. We need to cheer on our brothers in this effort. Indeed, more broadly, we need to think about what forms genuine political solidarity between men and women should take in a movement aimed at the liberation of women. The essays in this volume take important steps in that direction.

The charge of "opportunism" that is brought routinely against men who become involved in feminism is, in my view, misconceived and perhaps cruel. Few men benefit professionally, not just in academia but in most work environments, from too close an alliance with feminism; such alliances tend more to discredit a man than to advance his career. Coming out for feminism regularly earns a man not only the distrust of many feminist women, but the scorn of "manly" men, who charge him with having been "pussywhipped." A final reason for rejecting the forms taken by separatism in earlier years: an argument by analogy. I think that there are many white people who find racism profoundly repellent and who have given much time, effort, energy, and money to combat it. Some have devoted their lives to this struggle; a few have laid down their lives for it. People act from a variety of motives, but common to whites who struggle against racism is the desire no longer to be complicit in a system of oppression. Whatever privileges may accrue to them, they do not want. It must be acknowledged, however, that to be white and repelled by racism is by no means to be free of it: those of us who have grown up in a racist culture know how insidious are the forms that it can take, even within ourselves.

What I believe to be true of anti-racist whites (I include myself), I believe to be true of many men. There are men who do not want to be oppressors any longer: they too are repelled by a system that, unbidden, has bestowed privileges upon them which they have not earned, and which it denies to women. They do not want to be complicit in the subordination of half of humanity. They do not always succeed: just as a political stand against racism does not automatically free whites from some forms of racism, so the decision to struggle against sexism does not automatically extinguish in men a lifetime of sexist conditioning. But to the extent that men do engage in profeminist struggle, they deserve support.

The essays in *Men Doing Feminism* offer evidence that there are men who envision an egalitarian society and are willing to fight for it. Some of these essays record the struggle that men fight within themselves to identify and root out the tenacious bonds that tie them to an unjust social order. Some make arresting contributions to feminist theory. Many of these essays use personal narrative to develop their ideas in a way that reminds the reader of women's consciousness-raising. Theory and practice are interwoven in a way that normally escapes academic philosophy. The diversity of voices here avoids the narrowness of perspective that plagued much earlier feminist writing: there are straight men, gay men, transsexuals, black men, and white men. Several women's responses to male feminism have been included, giving the collection as a whole a dialogic quality, but also showing that there is important, even compelling, work that women can do in theorizing the increasing participation by men in feminist change.

Second Wave feminism did not beam its messages primarily to men, but I find it serendipitous that many men have received them nonetheless. *Men Doing Feminism* gives me hope.

Introduction

Tom Digby

Despite the long history of men's involvement in feminism, I've learned over the years that telling someone, anyone, that I am a feminist is bound to have a startling effect. The responses vary, but they usually involve questions, such as "What do you mean?," often accompanied by some stuttered expressions of doubt about whether it is possible for a man to be a feminist, perhaps whether it is even logically possible. If my interlocutor is male, there is typically an immediate loss of eye contact, an abrupt effort to change the subject, and often a move toward parting company as quickly as possible. Most men and some women respond to my self-characterization with acute embarrassment, but with a difference: with women it's as if I had just announced that I like to wear fuzzy animal slippers, while with men, it's as if I had just said that I am a turnip. That is, women's embarrassment seems to center on how my being a feminist diminishes my manliness, while men seem to think I'm crazy. Some women—and I've encountered this primarily in academic contexts—respond with suspicion, presumably about my motives.

It's not hard to find explanations for why the very idea of a feminist man is likely to be met with some form of incredulity. For example, some women are inclined by the manifold ways in which they have found feminism to be empowering to them *as women* not to see feminism as a sociopolitical stance which could be espoused or rejected by anyone, male or female. If feminism is seen primarily as a source of empowerment for individual women, men claiming to be feminists are incomprehensible at best, and interlopers at worst.

Even if feminism is understood primarily in terms of sociopolitical positions and practices, there are good reasons for wondering about male feminists. The feminist movement has given most people, whether they are feminists or not, a heightened awareness of male power and privilege. Given all the advantages of being a man in a society where men dominate politics, business, education, law, religion, and most other areas of life, a man who says he is a feminist is perplexing. Why would a man advocate change that is inimical to his own interests? It's quite understandable why the suspicious academics I mentioned go beyond wondering to doubt, tending to see male feminism as a subterfuge for the pursuit of some typical male interest. (As a suspicious academic myself, I have to say they're sometimes right.)

Skepticism about feminist men also derives from the fact that most men are socialized into *identities* that are hostile to feminism.[1] That is, they are socialized as *men*, and so long as manhood is defined not just as different from, but as opposite and opposed to womanhood, the notion of a feminist man may strain most folks' imaginations. Especially insofar as male dominance is considered integral to manhood (however tacitly in recent years), it is difficult not to think that male feminism is, as David Kahane suggests in the title of his essay for this volume, an oxymoron.

Thus, in contemporary North America at least, what are generally assumed to be male interests and male identities (which may vary significantly from the actual interests and identities of particular men) contribute to the widespread perception that the relation between feminism and men is necessarily antagonistic. Men are expected to resist feminism, and feminists are often assumed to hate men.[2]

This presumed oppositionality between men and feminism is rooted in the gender binary that is typical of patriarchal cultures, according to which every (or almost every)[3] human being is rigorously confined within one of two mutually exclusive categories, man or woman. While in contemporary North America this gender binary is beginning to crumble around the edges of popular culture and high theory, and is under assault from (some) "transgender warriors" (to borrow Leslie Feinberg's expression), it is unavoidably the case that to the extent a culture is patriarchal, it must strive to maintain the integrity and oppositionality of the gender binary. That is to say, to the extent that men as a group are to be dominant over women as a group, every (or almost every) person will have to be overdetermined as a member of one and only one of those groups, and the two groups will have to be understood as fundamentally oppositional to each other.[4] Any diminution of the oppositionality of the gender binary undermines dominance, and any loosening of the binary undercuts gender oppositionality—either way the dominance of men as a group over women as a group is weakened. Within such a context, male feminists are both a problem and a puzzle. By opposing male dominance, they disrupt gender oppositionality, but also, as some of the papers in this collection illustrate, in both their writings and their lives they have the potential to blur and muddle the gender binary itself. So to the extent patriarchy continues to prevail in any society, men in that society who say they are feminists are likely to be asked, "What do you mean?" by women and men, and are likely to be treated as traitors by many men, and with suspicion by some women.

"Why are you a feminist?" is another question I often get when I say that I am one. For me, this is an easier question to answer. I take it as an invitation to launch into a critique of male domination and the suffering it causes women, or a paean to feminist theory as an influence on my philosophical development, or an explanation of how patriarchy harms men as well as women, depending on the circumstances and mood. For me, it is as easy to explain why I am a feminist as it is to explain why I am an antiracist, or why I oppose economic injustice—in all three cases, I can choose among several justifications and explanations that I find persuasive.

There is a third kind of question, however, that I find more difficult: "How did you become a feminist?," or sometimes more blatantly, "What happened to you?" Either way, the query reflects a tacit understanding that a feminist man is an anomaly, and like all anomalies, requires a causal explanation. It's an understandable line of questioning, which for many years stumped me. I could only shrug my shoulders and ask back, "Who knows?" But as these questions continued to be repeated over the years, I had no choice but to think about possible answers pretty often. The answers I developed involved stories about my life, for I take the questions to be about the process of development that led me to become a feminist. At first the stories I told were accounts of my philosophical development, for it was in that context, especially under the tutelage of one of my dissertation advisors, Phyllis Kenevan, that feminism came to be central to my intellectual and political identity.

Eventually my narratives began to navigate further back into my past, all the way to my childhood. I grew up in an extremely conservative environment which was permeated with sexist values, attitudes, and practices. My family life was no exception to that, but included circumstances which inadvertently prepared me for the feminist interventions that were to occur later in my life.

My father is a wonderful human being, has been an exceedingly loving parent, and clearly has always aspired to be the best father possible. Fathers with such aspirations, during the time I was growing up, conceived of themselves first and foremost as providers, and my father excelled at that. We always had a nice home, plenty of food, new clothes on a regular basis, more toys than we needed, and when the time came for college, even though it must have been a strain, my father paid for everything unflinchingly. But like most superfathers of that period, mine tended to see childcare, including play, as primarily the responsibility of mothers or other women. Thus, the biggest influence on my character development in my early years was probably my mother, who is one of the most caring and empathetic persons I've ever known.

Many mothers under such circumstances feel they themselves must take on the responsibility of insuring that their boys become men—i.e., unlike themselves; instead, my mother was more concerned that I become a good *person*. And while I wasn't conscious of it then, I must have tacitly identified with her as much as with my father. Sure, I wanted to have the status, power, and respect that my father had, but my mother may have been just as important in shaping the kind of person I became, not just as my primary caregiver, but also as a role model. I continued to identify rather powerfully with her well into adulthood, which surely contributes to the sense that I now have, looking back, that in some important respects I have been "woman-identified" from childhood.

To the extent that my father was also a role model, he was a kinder, gentler version than is the case with many fathers. While he did become much more involved in my life during my teen years, introducing me to some quite manly pursuits, such as hunting, fishing, and long horseback rides in the woods, he never initiated me into the cult of Real Manhood. He never set up tests, or exploited my discomfort or suffering, in order to goad me into proving that I was a real man. In fact, when I survey my memories of my father, I now have the sense that he has always been rather disdainful of men who are constantly trying to prove their manhood. With some men such disdain is a way of displaying their own surplus of manliness; I think it was something else with my father, especially given his gentle, non-aggressive demeanor. I think he just saw men's efforts to prove their manhood as rather silly.[5]

Today I am profoundly grateful to my father for not having imposed on me an arduous manhood regimen. But during childhood this omission disadvantaged me in some respects; for example, it resulted in a fairly regular feeling of awkwardness whenever I felt pressured by peers to participate in team sports, where I lacked the bravado, aggressiveness, and athletic skill that fathers are "supposed" to instill in their sons. The result was that I often felt like an outsider, a status that was little altered by my achievements in individual athletic activities.

Paradoxically, it was just this outsider relationship to other boys that resulted in my serving as campaign manager for a girl who ran for student body president in junior high school. No girl had ever run for this office, and she needed a boy to compensate for her gender disadvantage, in particular to give a speech for her at the election assembly. I've always assumed that other boys had turned her down, not wanting to be seen as betraying their gender. While that concerned me also, as an outsider I couldn't pass up this opportunity to be seen as someone of importance. And, perhaps secondarily, I really was bothered by the unfairness of the discriminatory attitudes my candidate faced. My opportunistic proto-feminism paid off. I gave a rousing speech (that her mother helped me write), she won (her speech was even better), and during the next year or so I enjoyed a halo effect, getting elected to several student leadership positions and attracting girlfriends. I thus learned two important lessons: (1) that there were means other than team sports to bolster my masculine status, and (2) that gender loyalty was not crucial to being a successful heterosexual.

This was clearly not a trajectory that was to lead inexorably to my becoming a feminist. Yet both of those lessons did enrich and complicate an ambivalence toward the cult of Real Manhood that had begun in my early childhood. That ambivalence may have created a sort of "readiness" for the feminist interventions in my life that were to occur in the 1970s and early 1980s. One such intervention was the breakup of my first marriage, during which I came to realize that sexism could be implicit as well as explicit, as well as just how damaging even unintentional sexism could be to women and to heterosexual relationships. I also began to become aware of how sexism damages men themselves. Just as crucial as those realizations were extended discussions of feminist theory and practice with Phyllis Kenevan, Sherry Walton, Wendy Williams, and Valerie Broin, which resulted in a degree of intellectual excitement comparable only to my initial discovery of philosophy in college. Soon I came to feel a profound commitment to feminist movement, energized by both feminist hope and feminist anger. Indeed, for several years during the 1980s, using the buzzword of the time, I explicitly thought of myself as "woman-identified." I still consider feminism to be the most important defining characteristic of my philosophical and personal life.

I would surmise that every feminist man has a similar story (articulated or not) of the origins of his feminism that is particular to his life. My assumption that every man who has become a feminist has done so along a unique path has been confirmed every time I've discussed the matter with another male feminist. That's significant, in my view, because it urges on every one of us theorists who would try to understand male feminism a wariness of generalizations that lead either to sweeping cynicism or unqualified approbation. Understanding the diverse paths by which men come to be feminists may help dissolve suspicions when they are gratuitous, and when they are well-founded, refine them into more useful, focused, and systematic cautions. Essentialism is just as problematic here as it is elsewhere in feminism.

That may be the only theme of this volume as a whole. Surveying the possibilities for men's feminist theorizing, teaching, and living from a variety of perspectives, these essays mark places for men in feminism, but they also put up warning signs, map difficult terrain, and point to uncharted territories.

Part I, on feminist theory from men's lives, begins with Susan Bordo's "My Father the Feminist," in which she tells us of a man who was anything but feminist in his self-conception and in his ideological commitments, but whose life as a father had powerful feminist effects. Bordo's essay, particularly her concluding narrative of her father's last moments, gives me much-needed optimism about the potential for moving men in a feminist direction, and more generally, a sense that there are possibilities for feminist change that cannot be anticipated, and that's why I chose it to lead off this collection.

Patrick D. Hopkins' essay, "How Feminism Made a Man out of Me," opens with two narratives. In the first, he is taught how to be a "real man" in a high school class called "Christian Family Living," but his gender-contrarianism survives, and he becomes a feminist instead. Familiar with conservative resistance to feminism, he manages to get all the way through college before encountering *feminist* resistance to his feminism. Prior to graduate school, Hopkins' feminism may have diminished his manliness, but in the second narrative, he finds his manhood suddenly restored as he takes a graduate course on "Radical Lesbian Feminism." In his theorizing about the two narratives, Hopkins rejects the essentialism that he sees lying behind the notion that feminism is for women only, and argues for notions of subjectivity and experience that allow anyone to do feminism: "In fact, what seems to be important about being a feminist is not that someone perceives and understands as a woman, but that they perceive and understand *as a feminist.*"

In "Who's Afraid of Men Doing Feminism?," Michael Kimmel describes his experiences on the lecture circuit, where he focuses on getting men interested and involved in feminist issues. Most of his audience members respond enthusiastically, but there are two groups who don't. First, there are the "angry-white-men-in-training": "These young men are defensive, angry, and fully resistant to anything that remotely hints of feminism." The second kind of criticism, which comes typically from a minority of the feminist women in the audience, Kimmel finds more troubling: "Their followup questions and the ensuing discussion unravel quickly to what one might call 'patriarchy-baiting,' trying to find some reaction, some slip-up, some element of defensiveness, some point of weakness which will reveal my own patriarchal biases. These are inevitably revealed, to which their response is a loudly triumphant 'Ahah, we knew it!' and a quieter, but no less pronounced sigh of relief. All men are the same, and that 'same' is patriarchal." The defensiveness of the first group derives from a tendency to see a pro-feminist man like Kimmel as denying their individual experiences of disempowerment (such as being subject to the control of parents, professors, administrators, and coaches), while simultaneously threatening their sense of entitlement as men. The second group's response to Kimmel is more complex, but involves both essentialist assumptions and an acute—and accurate—awareness that men, including feminist men, inevitably benefit from patriarchal privilege. Kimmel proceeds to articulate an approach to male feminism that is responsive to the fears of both groups.

In "On Your Knees: Carnal Knowledge, Masculine Dissolution, Doing Feminism," Brian Pronger explores how constructs of masculine desire, including masculine eroticizations of spatial domination, particularly in sports, are barriers to doing feminism. Utilizing Deleuze and Guattari's concepts of desire and the power of deterritorialization, he considers how through deep reflective erotic practices that demand the giving of space, rather than taking it, men can enjoyably give up masculinity, and how this dissolution of masculinity frees men to do feminism.

While many of the ways that a man's feminism should affect his relations with women are obvious, it's often less clear how his feminism should affect his relations with other men. Richard Schmitt's essay, "Profeminist Men and Their Friends," begins with a narrative contrasting his and his woman partner's relations with their friends. He explains how becoming profeminist can actually de-center a man's friendships with other men, and argues that profeminist men must forge new ways of being friends with each other, not just because it will enrich their lives, but for political reasons: it is a crucial element in the struggle against patriarchy.

In the opening of "Tracing a Ghostly Memory in My Throat: Reflections on Ftm Feminist Voice and Agency," C. Jacob Hale describes the responses of some feminist philosophers to his transition from teaching feminist philosophy as a woman to teaching it as a female-toward-male transsexual. Many of these responses involved erasures of the concrete specificity of his life, forcing him into one or another category that would then justify a particular appraisal of the appropriateness of his teaching feminist philosophy. In response to those erasures and the silencing of transsexual voices by medical and legal "authorities," Hale charts an "epistemological subject position from which some ftms can engage productively in feminist theorizing and practice." He shows how this subject position gives some ftms certain advantages over non-transsexual men in the project of unsettling and re-forming the categories of manhood, manliness, and masculinity, but also how there can be problems faced by ftms in undertaking some other feminist projects. Hale concludes with a discussion of how political goals specific to ftms often dovetail with feminist political goals, proposing that "if those of us who are working to end the cultural rape of all flesh do not strengthen such alliances we will either leave in place structures of gender oppression or fail to restructure the world in ways which accord with our moral and political values."

Teaching college courses as a male feminist inevitably raises a host of issues and concerns, especially if your students are all, or mostly all, women. Thomas Wartenberg, who teaches at Mt. Holyoke College, recounts how this experience has changed his approach to teaching in "Teaching Women Philosophy (as a Feminist Man)," where he argues for recognizing the feminist political dimensions of reading philosophical texts. This is not just a matter of finding blatant sexism in the texts, but also of uncovering ways that texts tacitly create communities, partly through a logic of exclusion, keeping members of some groups out of the community. In an epilogue to his previously published essay, Wartenberg notes that for a man to engage in this kind of feminist teaching practice conveys the message that the struggle against sexism and other forms of oppression is not just for the oppressed themselves, but also for their allies. Thus, he says, "As a male teacher of philosophy to women, my gender . . . functions as a resource as well as a problem for my feminist teaching practice."

For Michael Awkward the use of personal narrative, in particular writing as an autobiographical "I," has a particular political value for feminist men, as he explains in "A Black Man's Place in Black Feminist Criticism":

> in male feminist acts, to identify the writing self as biologically male is to emphasize the desire not to be ideologically male; it is to explore the process of rejecting the phallocentric perspectives by which men traditionally have justified the subjugation of women.

Awkward expresses skepticism toward suggestions that men, feminist or otherwise, represent a threat to feminism, because feminism is "an incomparably productive, influential, and resilient ideology and institution." He also rejects the claim that men cannot be feminists as essentialist. He says, however, that the "feminist" label is less important to him than commiting himself to the struggle against patriarchal values:

> What is most important to me is that my work contribute, in however small a way, to the project whose goal is the dismantling of the phallocentric rule by which black females and, I am sure, countless other Afro-American sons have been injuriously "touched."

Engaging the work of Hortense Spillers, Awkward proposes "the distinctive nature of the Afro-American male's connection to the 'female,'" and espouses a black womanism that requires both black females and males to recognize gender inequities and to work for change as comrades. He relates his own movement in such a direction to his "having been raised by a mother who, like too many women of too many generations, was the victim of male physical and psychological brutality." The stories his mother told him about this brutality unsettled his relationship to masculinity, prompting him to pursue "a gendered self-definition" in opposition to traditional maleness. In the concluding section of his essay, Awkward writes of certain ways the male feminist project can go awry, in particular by reducing women to "protective maternal womb[s]," and by attempting other kinds of erasure and control. "A black male feminism," Awkward insists, must be "self-reflective enough to avoid, at all costs, the types of patronizing, marginalizing gestures that have traditionally characterized Afro-American male intellectuals' response to black womanhood."

Part II, on feminism *in* men's lives, begins with Sandra Harding's "Can Men Be Subjects of Feminist Thought?" Given the many contributions men have made to feminist theory and activism, Harding finds the reluctance of some feminist theorists (men as well as women) to answer affirmatively the question in her title surprising. She asks, "Are we really supposed to assume that our enthusiastic men students and colleagues are unable to think for themselves and come up with original feminist understandings, just as our women students and colleagues learn to do? Are men only supposed to parrot what women feminists say?" In response to the skeptics, she provides a sweeping, powerful, and systematic exploration of the possibilities for the development of male feminist subjectivities and male feminist theorizing within Liberal, Marxist, Radical, Socialist, and other more recent "public agenda feminist theoretical approaches." This approach puts the issues in the context of both the history of political thought and contemporary feminist theories that have guided or influenced feminist demands for changes in institutions and policies. Harding concludes that "feminist thought is disadvantaged by a lack of contributions from men's feminist subjectivities." Her essay thus not only scouts places for men to do feminist theory, but also demonstrates the need for them to do it.

Complementing Harding's essay, Harry Brod espouses "a view in which men bring valuable resources to their feminism in so far as they are men." In "To Be A Man, Or Not To Be A Man—That Is The Feminist Question," he argues, against theorists like Brian Pronger (above), that for men to do feminism they need not "leave their masculinity behind." Brod draws on two stories of Hillel to support the view that for men to do feminism effectively they must be "male affirmative," i.e., they must have "a positive vision of themselves as men," which is altogether consistent with critiquing male-hegemonic behavior and attitudes. Further, while feminist men should be motivated by a desire for feminist justice, the realization that "feminist transformation will enhance our lives" is a source of sustaining energy. Brod opposes efforts to portray men as inherently prone to rape or violence:

> they paint a bleak picture of male beings incapable of change, beings who must be simply opposed or written off, rather than beings who must be challenged to change and whose change must be facilitated. Anti-male images must be resisted, precisely in the name of feminism. Such images, no matter the intentions of those who present them, ultimately situate themselves on deeply conservative terrain, and I do not believe any progressive movement can successfully move on this terrain.

Not only is a male-affirmative feminism more progressive, says Brod, it also helps overcome a resistance men have to feminism when they view it as anti-male. He ends his essay with a discussion of the matter of terminology: Should men who advocate feminism be called feminists, pro-feminists, or pro-feminists? Brod finds each term appropriate in different contexts, concluding with the overall point that "positive transformation requires a positive vision, and therefore for men to do feminism requires positive visions of both men and feminism."

David J. Kahane and Joy James take decidedly warier stances toward men who would be feminists. In "Male Feminism as Oxymoron," Kahane says that "men have to face the extent to which fighting patriarchy means fighting themselves," and since that struggle is not likely ever to be complete, feminist men are prone to engage in "various forms of bad faith and self-deception." Insisting that he is skeptical, but not pessimistic about men doing feminism, Kahane engages the work of Sandra Harding to consider how male experience militates against the kind of feminist knowledge that is transformative. He describes four types of men who fall short of adequate forms of male feminist knowledge: the *poseur*, the insider, the humanist, and the self-flagellator. "Recognizing these pitfalls," he says, "we can explore ways of moving beyond them, to more creditable and sustainable forms of male feminist engagement." Kahane offers practical guidance and caveats for men who would be feminists, but still concludes that "only in a profoundly transformed world will male feminism be something other than an oxymoron."

Reminding us of earlier gender asymmetries in the civil rights movement, Joy James provocatively problematizes contemporary relations between black women and black and other antiracist male feminists. Her essay, "Antiracist (Pro)Feminisms and Coalition Politics: 'No Justice, No Peace,'" explores the work of four of these men: Michael Awkward, Lewis Gordon, Devon Carbado, and Richard Delgado. While James is encouraged by Awkward's forthright embrace of feminism, she is troubled by his naivete regarding the possible dangers to feminism presented by the increasing numbers of male feminists. When Awkward pronounces the end of the Father's rule, James raises questions about the gender-hybrid feminist son whom she sees waiting in the wings. James is similarly ambivalent about Lewis Gordon's phenomenological description of antiblack racism, where white masculinity is seen as pure Presence, so that the black man "embodies femininity even more than the white woman" and the white woman has within her a "secret abundance of blackness." James wonders, "what are black women in this antiblack world?" And if there is a femininity shared by black men and black women, "based on the racialized epidermal in a racist society," how are we to understand the domestic violence that comes between them (just as it comes between white women and men)? On the other hand, James questions Devon Carbado's privileging of black women over black men; she calls for a more expansive paradigm that would take into account the broader context of gender politics. Finally, after an examination of Richard Delgado's discussion of coalition politics in a fictional narrative, James asks: "With the growing appearance of the articulate male feminist, what sustains coalitions between male and female feminists?. . . . Equally important, when do coalition politics become caretaking politics for subaltern women indebted to the patronage of feminist men?" James concludes with some questions and suggestions for male feminists, and expresses "an appreciation for the work of profeminists and a cautious concern that a growing feminist discourse need not always signal a shift in power relations."

Judith K. Gardiner's essay, "Feminism and the Future of Fathering," serves as a critical intervention in feminist discussions of fathering since the publication of Nancy Chodorow's *The Reproduction of Mothering.* Gardiner discusses a variety of theories that have been influenced by, or have responded to, Chodorow, as well as some relevant empirical data. She concludes that shared parenting often has unforeseen results, sometimes opposite to what has been expected by many theorists. Thus, changes in the roles of fathers cannot alone produce the sorts of sweeping changes in the construction of gender that some writers have claimed it could. Gardiner says that fathering must be understood both in its diversity and in terms of its multifaceted, complicated interrelationships with a variety of other cultural factors. She ends her paper by proposing that "to stop the patriarchal reproduction of mothering, . . . we need to assist a new postproduction of fathering."

Gary Lemons and James P. Sterba both offer strongly optimistic views of the possibilities for male feminism. In "A New Response to Angry Black Male Anti-Feminists: Reclaiming Feminist Forefathers, Becoming Womanist Sons," Lemons urges black men to respond to black male antifeminists (in the academy and in popular culture) by placing themselves in alliance with black women in their struggles against sexism and misogyny. He cites valuable historical antecedents for this pro-womanist stance, including the writings and work of Frederick Douglass, W.E.B. DuBois, and many other black male thinkers and activists of the nineteenth and early twentieth centuries who supported woman suffrage. They offer a sharp contrast with gangsta rap lyrics in which "black females occupy the status of 'bitch' and 'ho'—served up in a sexist minstrel show of black male supremacist, masturbatory fantasy." Lemons offers a sustained "critical remembrance" of Douglass and DuBois, joining them in the conclusion that the struggle against racism requires a struggle against sexism.

James P. Sterba answers both questions in his title, "Is Feminism Good for Men, and Are Men Good for Feminism?," affirmatively. Sterba espouses "a gender-free society where basic rights and duties are not assigned on the basis of a person's biological sex." He details the kinds of changes that such an androgynous society would require in the areas of the family, economic relations, and violence against women. While he acknowledges the general advantanges men have presently, Sterba argues that the changes he advocates would benefit men as well as women. For example, it is likely that if men become less prone to engage in violence against women, they will also be less likely to engage in violence against other men, so there will be fewer male victims of violence. Further, Sterba proposes, feminism is morally good for men. He also shows how men are good for feminism. For example, given present conditions of male dominance, often there are situations in academia and elsewhere where there is either no woman present or no woman with sufficient institutional power to argue the case for feminist policies—better to have a feminist man make that argument than for it not to be made at all. Also, often it is the case that if a man advocates for feminism it is more unsettling than when a woman does so, making it more likely that feminist results can be obtained. Men have a particularly valuable contribution to make, Sterba thinks, in the battle against hard-core pornography, for they are better equipped to understand how it operates to reinforce sexist and misogynistic attitudes and practice.

The next two chapters deal with ambiguities and complexities of male feminism in everyday life. Henry Rubin draws on his experiences as a female-to-male transsexual feminist theorist to explore issues that are difficult and complicated for non-transsexual feminist men as well. To illuminate his relation to feminist theory, before and after his transition, Rubin begins "Reading Like a (Transsexual) Man" with a description of the shift in feminist theory from the identity-paradigm to the action-paradigm. He finds the shift equivocally implemented in the way some feminists think about him as a female-to-male transsexual. Residues of the identity-paradigm result in erasures of him either as a man or as a feminist. The reality of the lives of feminist (transsexual) men involves them in a tension between a desire to be "real men" and a desire for feminist social justice, a tension within which a perverse male identity can be activated that can be used to generate male feminist knowledge. Rubin recounts how prior to his transition his interest in feminism focused solely on the subject of gender construction: "At the same time, I was repelled by the work that theorized social injustice because these highlighted my continued vulnerabilities in a gender order that presumed I was a woman." This changed after he became a man, enabling him to become a better feminist. Still, he lives within that tension between his feminism and his desire to be a real man, a life that he shares with the reader through some vivid narratives, such as the following:

> I like going to parties thrown by my gorgeous hunk of a gay male friend;
> I get cruised there. It makes me feel like I am authentic. Sometimes though,
> I worry that I am giving off some sign that will reveal my past or that will
> (more frighteningly) mean that I am gay. Like most heterosexual guys, I
> have a panic response, one that verges on homophobia. I go home from
> parties disturbed by, as much as I took pleasure in, those cruisy eyes.
> Uncertainty about my status produces a defensive stance.

While they may experience it differently, Rubin maintains that for both transsexual and non-transsexual male feminists that tension between feminism and manhood can be a fertile ground for engendering perverse identities that can be used for feminist purposes.

Laurence Mordekhai Thomas' essay, "Feminist Ambiguity in Heterosexual Lives: Reflections on Andrea Dworkin," offers an explanation for why sexual egalitarianism has not been better realized in U.S. society. A significant factor must be, he proposes, that among heterosexuals men continue to see sexual intercourse with women as affirming their manhood, and women continue to hang on to the power associated with being gatekeepers to that important source of manhood affirmation. Thomas relates this to broader issues of homophobia, men's reluctance to express feelings, and men's dependence on women for emotional support. He concludes with a call for moral courage to change the ways heterosexual men and women relate to each other, which will be necessary in order to bring an end to sexism in general.

Larry May concludes the book on a strongly positive note in "A Progressive Male Standpoint." In this essay, he develops "an egalitarian theoretical and practical position from which men can critically assess male experience and traditional male roles." A man who takes up a progressive male standpoint is able to use it to generate the kind of knowledge that makes a political difference, in particular in the direction of eliminating gender inequality. May develops a model of a progressive male standpoint with four dimensions:

> First, there is a striving for knowledge or understanding based on experience, especially personal experience of traditional male roles and activities. Second, there is a critical reflection on that experience in light of the possible harms to women, as well as men, of assuming traditional male roles and engaging in traditional male activities. Third, there is a moral motivation to change at least some aspects of traditional male roles and activities. And finally, there are practical proposals for changes in traditional male roles that are regarded as believable by other men.

May proposes that a progressive male standpoint containing all four of these elements can serve as the basis for a moral reconceptualization of masculinity.

Clearly, there is no single point of view common to all of the authors who have written for this book, other than a profound commitment to feminism. Rather, there are eighteen voices here, all starting new conversations about men and feminism. My hope and expectation is that these conversations, joined by many more voices, will substantially contribute to feminist social change.[6]

Notes

1. David Kahane has helped me appreciate the importance of this point.
2. See Tom Digby, "Do Feminists Hate Men?: Feminism, Antifeminism, and Gender Oppositionality," forthcoming in *Journal of Social Philosophy*.
3. See Gilbert Herdt, *Third Sex, Third Gender: Beyond Sexual Dimorphism in Culture and History* (Cambridge, MA: Zone, 1994) for discussions of a variety of patriarchal cultures in which a limited number of exceptions to the gender binary exist alongside it, in some cases obliquely reinforcing it. For a discussion of berdache traditions in particular, see Walter L. Williams, *The Spirit and the Flesh: Sexual Diversity in American Indian Culture* (Boston: Beacon, 1986).
4. As I write, NBC has, with considerable fanfare, begun a week of special programs on "The Sex Wars: The Tension Between Men and Women" (October 19–26, 1997), and John Gray has begun broadcasting infomercials promoting a videotape series based on his long-time bestseller, *Men Are from Mars, Women Are from Venus*.
5. Elvia Herrera and Laurel Davis have each suggested to me that class privilege may be at work in my father's eschewal of rigorous manhood training and tests for his sons. I agree that higher class status can sometimes ease the pressures on men to prove their manhood, even if it does not consistently do this.
6. I am profoundly grateful to my new colleagues at Springfield College, Laurel Davis, Dan Fraizer, and Susan Joel, as well as to Elvia Herrera and David Kahane, for their helpful comments on this Introduction. In the past few years, Elvia and David have become my personal feminist gadflies; both have influenced my thinking and my feminism more than they know.

Part I

Feminist Theory *from* Men's Lives

Chapter 1

My Father the Feminist

Susan Bordo

I.

Most of the images of Judaism that I grew up with were strongly patriarchal. Some of these images came from popular culture: Charlton
Heston on the mountaintop, Immutable Commandments in his arms.
Some of them came from Christian renderings of Judaism, to which all
Jews are subjected in this culture: the stern, unforgiving God of the
"Old" Testament versus Jesus, God of Love. Some of them came from
my slender understanding of the (undeniably) patriarchal laws and institutions of Judaism. But most of them derived from childish analogy with
my father; he was a stubborn patriarch and he was Jewish, so Judaism
must be stubbornly patriarchal, too.

My father made most important decisions for our family: where we
would live, how we would spend our money, what we would do on the
weekends. In *Manhood in the Making*, anthropologist David Gilmore
describes Jewish-American culture as "one of the few in which women
virtually dominate men."[1] This information would have come as a big
surprise to my mother. My father's preferences shaped our lives. Because
he didn't like my mother's relatives, we rarely saw them. Because he
didn't swim or enjoy the beach, our trips to the Jersey shore (essential for
deliverance from the sweltering heat of the Newark tenement in which
we lived) were for walking the boardwalk, loading our stomachs with
hot dogs and knishes and playing Pokerino. I'd look over the wooden
railing at the rambunctious, physical crowd on the beach, diving into
waves, cavorting like human creatures, and feel myself exiled, my body
developing into something non-American and graceless. Because my
father adored the racetrack, we spent our family vacation at a shabby
boardinghouse in Saratoga Springs, New York. Over breakfast, he would
dope out the morning line with his cronies while we kids hung out on the

stoop, trying to avoid the acrid cigar smoke and odd, sweaty cooking smells from the kosher kitchen, hoping not to be caught and trapped into conversation with an old person. At the track in the afternoon, we would pick through the sad, discarded tickets that littered the pavement, looking for carelessly castaway "place" or "show" winners, restlessly marking time until he had placed his final bets and we could leave.

My father had been popular and successful during his Brooklyn youth. He was a track star and a straight-A student, but somehow managed—through his keen iconoclastic wit, feisty spirit, and willingness to take a dare—to win the respect and affection of members of the Jewish Mafia and their "dolls," with whom he hung out on occasion. I grew up hearing stories of his romantic exploits and brushes with danger. There were two parts to the story of how the gorgeous, thrill-seeking girlfriend of Louis Lepke ("Bugsy") Buchalter, head of Murder, Inc. had taken a shine to my father. In the first part, my father takes her up on the roof, where the two get drunk and presumably have sex (although he always left that detail out); he then falls asleep, and wakes up to see her walking stark naked along the edge of the roof. In the sequel, Bugsy—having found out about her dangerous and near-fatal liaison with my father—sends word out that he wants a meeting with my father at a specified hour later that day. Not knowing what might happen, my father arranges to have a gun purchased and brought to him by a flunky-pal. The established meeting time approaches and no gun has appeared; my father is getting very nervous. Bugsy arrives, and still no gun; my father is beside himself. They exchange a few Damon Runyonesque words (dialogue I unfortunately cannot remember). The tension builds. Suddenly, the flunky arrives, out of breath, and thrusts a crumpled brown paper bag into my father's hands. In it is the gun, in pieces, unassembled. Buchalter bursts into laughter, and lets my father go with just a warning.

Did these incidents actually happen? Told to me by a plump, balding forty-five-year-old man, these tales belonged to a time and place as distant as Camelot and as unavailable to factual confirmation. (My mother never disputed my father's accounts, but she never confirmed them, either.) There were photographs which suggested that the stories could be true; ones showing my father as well-built and as dashingly handsome as John Garfield, the tough, Jewish street-kid who became a Hollywood star. Whatever the literal truth of the stories, my father had thrived in his dual role of a promising scholar and street-smart adventurer. It was the more sober, unromantic requirements of provider-manliness that let my father down. The Depression forced him to abandon his dreams of college and a career in journalism. After the war, my father returned from the South Pacific to his wife and small daughter, my older sister, and a job as a poorly-paid employee of wealthier relatives: selling candy "on the road" for the family business. The job was not entirely unrewarding. He enjoyed making sales and loved traveling to exotic places like New Orleans, where he ate and drank in fancy restaurants, swapping stories with the pleasure-loving southern brokers who reveled in "Yosh's warmth and wit." But coming home from these trips was always a return to his subordinate status in the company, and what he increasingly came to experience as a "failed" life. He identified with Willie Loman.

When men did "wrong" by his wife and daughters, however, my father's boyhood skills could re-surface. An abusive gym teacher was told on no uncertain terms that if he called me "fatty" one more time he was going to have the shit kicked out of him. The summer after my first year at college—a year in which my main accomplishment was that I had "gone all the way" on my eighteenth birthday—I dared to close my bedroom door with a boy inside the room. He was the boy with whom I had celebrated my birthday. My father had suspicions, which I subtly encouraged, that I had come home changed. He pounded on the door, threatening to break it down if we did not come out. These scenes left me confused about what I admired and wanted in a man. It was embarrassing for a modern girl to have her father behave like a caveman. But these were the proofs of love my father offered, and they had an archetypal zing that I couldn't deny.

Contemporary theorists distinguish between the penis (a part of male anatomy that can be soft as well as hard, that pees far more often than it penetrates, and that was once probably wiped by a mommy) and the "phallus": everything cultural that advances or is symbolic of the unity, mastery, immutable logic, law, and authority that have been associated with male dominance in Western cultures. My father spent much of his later life pining for the street-"phallus" that he embodied so brilliantly as a youth, and—like many working class and minority-men—often looked to the women in his life for proofs of the respect that he couldn't get from the dominant culture. Along with his sample cases of candy, he carried the requirements and failures of his "manliness" heavily with him. Monthly payments and investments in the future were somehow demeaning to him, as though reliance on banks and other bureaucracies threatened his autonomy; as a consequence, he never owned a house and died without life insurance. He refused to "let" my mother work outside the home, although we had little money and nothing in the bank; all three daughters paid their ways through college. Although he was pleasure-loving, generous and expansive, his shame over not having done better in life was a low-lying cloud perpetually threatening to erupt into a storm of bitterness. Any small insult to his authority or any minor wound to his pride could set it off. His eyes would darken and his mouth would set, almost in a snarl; often, he would leave rooms and houses, slamming the door behind him and managing to convey, with impressive believability, the possibility that he might never return. He always returned, as I remember.

Our nuclear family had little to do with the institutions of Judaism, religious or social. My mother, born in Poland, had come from an orthodox family; her own mother had remained fiercely observant to the end of her life, keeping kosher, lighting candles, faithful to Yiddish. My father, brought up on Hollywood and hot dogs, regarded the religiosity of my mother's family as an Old World encumbrance, and—remember—he made the rules. We did not belong to a temple, nor attend Hebrew school. We did not have a tree at Christmas (my father drew the line on what he took to be *goyish* paraphernalia, or symbols of Christianity), yet we exchanged presents on Christmas morning. Father's parents had just arrived in America when he was born. They were more worldly than my mother's clan and remained steeped in tradition. He had no patience with my maternal grandmother's rigid adherence to Jewish law, but loss invariably brought out something deeply planted in his own body: on *Yom Kippur* he *davened* in Yiddish; at my mother's funeral, he tore at his shirt (an Old World symbol of grief). He regarded his WASP brokers and their blonde wives as classy and my mother's relations as peasants; but he adored taking the family on a weekend afternoon to the Brownsville section of Brooklyn, which even into the 1950s was an Old World Jewish ghetto of pushcarts, live chickens, and Yiddish theater.

My father's Jewishness was rent with contradictions. He was by nature rebellious and skeptical of orthodoxies. But like Job he was in continual conversation with Jehovah about the trials and sorrows of his life; his sense of personal injustice was cosmic. In *Avalon*, Barry Levinson's film memoir of growing up in an immigrant Jewish family, Levinson presents an incident that nearly jolted me out of my seat in recognition. The film follows the changing lives of a family of brothers who arrived in Baltimore early in the twentieth century, and depicts with nice ambivalence, the losing struggle of family cohesiveness against the fragmenting attractions of individualism, consumerism, suburbia, and mass-media culture. In the film, mealtime is a metaphor for this struggle, as extended-family gatherings around the dinner table give way over the years to frozen dinners taken on trays to the living room, where TV is the only real dinner companion. In a pivotal scene, the eldest brother of the clan—at his point in the film he is about seventy years old—arrives for Thanksgiving dinner to find that the turkey has already been carved by his younger brother. It had been the unquestioned family custom for the assembled clan to wait for the eldest brother's arrival before carving the turkey, and he had always made them wait, in a yearly ritual testing the waters of respect and authority. This time, screaming kids and growling stomachs won out over symbolic fealties to the patriarch. The eldest brother, injured beyond repair, swears never to speak to his younger brother again. *And doesn't.*

When the needs of others collided with and overruled my father's expectations of how things should be, his overwhelming tendency was to interpret this as lack of respect; his retaliation, although rarely physical, could be as harsh, irrevocable, and consequential as Zeus's. Throughout my childhood, my father constructed numerous small tests of loyalty and devotion. Love me, love my cigar. My father sometimes said this jokingly, but we all knew he meant business. We knew, too, that much more than his freedom to smoke was at stake. Our willingness to tolerate burning eyes and gagging throats was a measure of our love for him. Once, at age twenty-nine, I made the mistake of requesting that he smoke his cigar outside the airless basement apartment that I was living in as a graduate student. He blew up at me with a fury that surpassed the considerable furies I had witnessed throughout my childhood. My half-brother, my father's son by an earlier marriage, made the fatal mistake of siding with his own wife against my father in an ugly (and to me, still obscure) exchange of insults and injuries. I know that my father's generosity—a badge of pride with him—had been called into question and that terrible words were spoken and written, words that cut my father to the quick. It was a genuine crisis, an awful fight. But when my father declared that Gary was henceforth cut out of his life, I could hardly take that threat seriously. I was wrong. My father died a decade later without ever having spoken again to his son.

II.

Traditional Judaism *is* patriarchal. It would be an anomaly within dominant Western cultural traditions if it were not. But there is an element within Jewish paternalism that seeds its own deconstruction. While trying to cram as much learning about Judaism as I could into one weekend of preparation for writing this essay, I found this amazing story "from the time of the Romans" in a book about Bar Mitzvah—the Jewish ceremony signifying a boy's becoming a man:

> A group of rabbis were arguing an issue of religious law. Rabbi Eliezer ben Hyrcanus offered an opinion. It was rejected. Rabbi Eliezer protested the decision. "I am right and I can prove it. If my opinion is correct, let the stream outside this study house flow backward."
>
> The stream began to flow backward.
>
> Rabbi Joshua ben Hananiah, who led the majority, said, "A stream doesn't prove anything."
>
> Rabbi Eliezer continued, "If my opinion is correct, let the walls of the study house prove it."

> The walls started leaning toward them.
>
> Rabbi Joshua held firm, and told the walls to go back to their place.
>
> Finally, Rabbi Eliezer said, "Let Heaven itself bear witness that my opinion is the correct one."
>
> A voice came from out of the sky. "Why do you reject Rabbi Eliezer's opinion? He is right in every case."
>
> To which Rabbi Joshua responded, "The Torah is not in heaven. We pay no attention to voices."[2]

Pay no attention to God's voice? I read this story aloud to the Protestant man with whom I live and his mouth fell open. But then, so did mine. The association of Jewish scholarship with radical and ongoing disputation and debate is not new to me, of course. I have no schooling in Judaism, but I know that Jews consider the Torah—God's covenant with Israel, given to Moses at Mount Sinai—a much more extensive and flexible body of literature than the classic pictorial version of Ten Commandments indelibly burned in stone. Far from ten straightforward commandments, the Torah includes not only "all the rules, obligations, history, poetry, and literature contained in the first five books of the Bible" but also "all subsequent interpretations and adaptations."[3] The latter, known as the Talmud, is the subject of continuous interpretation and contestation among scholars and theologians.

Within popular culture, too, the Jew's enjoyment of and limitless capacity for tenacious argumentation has been a motif of many Yiddish jokes and humorous self-depictions of Jewish life. In *Avalon*, the family engages in a running debate about the most efficient route from New York to Brooklyn, jousting with each other in the same combative, stubborn style as Rabbi Eliezer and Rabbi Joshua. The implication is that if we don't have something serious to debate, we will invent a dispute around something trivial, just to satisfy the itch for argument. The same idea figures as well in less affectionate, arguably anti-Semitic depictions, such as Mousorgsky's musical sketch, in *Pictures at an Exhibition*, of "Two Jews, One Rich and the Other Poor." In that sketch, two musical voices yammer at each other argumentatively, one bossy and the other whining ("kvetching," as Jews would say), stubbornly unable to come to agreement.

The Eliezer/Joshua story, however, is not about how Jews love to argue. Eric Kimmel reads the story as signifying that "the Torah is a living document . . . not the property of mystical fanatics. Reason and logic could be used to adapt its teachings to changing times and conditions."[4] In my opinion, this reading does not go far enough; the message of the story is far more radical than an authorization of temporal human "adaptation" of eternal teaching. It is a parable about where to look for truth. In the narrative, a contest is staged, ostensibly between two competing human interpretations (Rabbi Eliezer's and Rabbi Joshua's), but *actually* between human argumentation and Immutable Law as two genres of knowledge. The dramatic way in which this contest is depicted is extraordinary. First, the physical world confirms Rabbi Eliezer's opinion, producing miraculous occurrences (the stream flows backward, the walls lean) that we *expect* to function in the story as proofs of the authority of the one who has called them up. Readers of the Bible are used to the sea parting for the righteous, not for the errant or the erring. So Eliezer seems positioned, by narrative convention, to be the ultimate victor of the debate. This victory seems inevitable when God himself comes out on Eliezer's side. But in this story, remarkably, even God's opinion is "put in its place," subordinated to the authority of human reason. Rabbi Joshua has the final word. It is by adjudicating scholarly conversation on its own terms—that is, by evaluating the rigor and validity of the respective arguments, *not* by seeking external validation from God—that we decide which opinion is right.

Nothing is written in stone. Not even, presumably, the authority of patriarchal laws and institutions. Come up with a good argument against them, and then we'll see. This is indeed what I grew up believing. So apparently, too, did many of the young Jewish women who formed the core of "second wave" feminist politics in the late sixties and early seventies. We thought we had an unanswerable argument, its logic evident, its claims for justice compelling; many of us were sincerely baffled when husbands and boyfriends just didn't "get it." Even today, although I have learned that reason doesn't always win the day, I am unable to let go of my faith. I write memos after department meetings, working into the night. I make early morning phone calls: "I'm not sure I fully explained what I meant yesterday. Do you have a minute?" I obsessively revise my academic papers, endlessly honing, elaborating, pruning, clarifying. I feed on the hope that if I can articulate my ideas with precision—anticipating objections, neutralizing potential misunderstanding—I can make feminism convincing.

How did I, growing up with my patriarchal father, come to believe this? Isaac Bashevis Singer's short story, "Yentl the Yeshiva Boy" describes a family situation that is not uncommon in Jewish families, especially in families without sons:

> [Yentl's father,] Reb Todros . . . had studied Torah with his daughter as if she were a son. He told Yentl to lock the doors and drape the windows, then together they pored over the Pentateuch, the Mishnah, the Gemara, and the Commentaries. She had proved so apt a pupil that her father used to say:

"Yentl—you have the soul of a man."

"So why was I born a woman?"

"Even Heaven makes mistakes."[5]

Letty Cottin Pogrebin, in her angry and honest account of her feelings about her own father, describes a modern-day version of the same:

> He put me through my paces as if he were a rabbi, which he could have been, and as if I were a boy, which I should have been to please him, although he never said it. I adored him for treating me like a son and taking me seriously. He drilled and polished my Hebrew recitation until I was the kind of virtuoso performer that synagogue legends were made of back in 1952, when girls, as a rule, did not do that sort of thing. But I did whatever my father valued. More than anything, I wanted his approval because he was my mentor and I saw myself as his intellectual heir. There was no son to make that claim. . . . Clearly, his legacy was mine if I proved myself worthy of it. Even when I was very young, he made me feel important just by talking to me. He spoke didactically but never condescendingly the way he sometimes addressed my mother and aunts. He talked to me as if I could be trusted to get it on first learning.[6]

Within traditional Judaism, it is sons, of course, who are the preferred recipients of the father's wisdom and knowledge, the sons who are taught the arts of reason and argument. But even within traditional Judaism, a father's recognition of a daughter's ability and his own desire to have a challenging conversational partner (or a good listener) can overcome convention. My own father, unlike Letty Cottin Pogrebin's, did not instruct us in Torah or train us to be intellectual gladiators in any formal way. By the time I was an adolescent, he was usually too exhausted and depressed to engage in extended conversation with us. But there had been a time when my father did not return from work sullen and withdrawn, eager only for his schnapps and an evening in front of the television. There had been a time when he still saw himself as a scholar and teacher of his children, a source of wisdom, a communicator of knowledge, values, and ideas. These memories were, for a long time, overshadowed by my anger at the way he had bullied my mother and ignored her needs. She died at the age of sixty-three, largely of neglect—in the last instance by doctors, but more fundamentally by my father. Forbidden to have any real life beyond waiting for my father to return from his trips, my mother had become sedentary and depressed, increasingly non-vital, her body an invitation to decay. I never hated him, but I blamed him for her decline. It was a long time before I was in the mood to recover any positive childhood memories.

Then one day about eight years ago I noticed how my father, at that point nearly eighty-years old, long-since remarried and the inheritor of several grandchildren by his wife, talked to his young granddaughter. He conversed. Really. No baby-talk nor condescending monosyllables of faked comprehension and distracted nods. Father's gaze was steady and focused. He listened attentively and questioned when he didn't understand. He spoke in full, grammatical sentences. He created the impression that this conversation—about the rights and wrongs of a minor disagreement that the child had just had with her brother—was as complex and thought-provoking as a discussion about the pros and cons of nuclear disarmament. I watched this conversation, an equal dialogue transpiring between an elderly man and a five-year-old girl, and I suddenly knew—did not exactly remember, but *knew*—that he had once had such conversations with me.

Later in his life, when his daughters were all grown up and professionally successful, my father might feign suffering over our unconventional lifestyles and failure to conform to traditional feminine ideals. But actually he was extremely proud of his brainy girls. "My daughters," he'd moan, shaking his head mournfully but barely suppressing his laughter, "They can't dance. They can't sing. All they can do is think." But smart thinking and good talking was what he admired most of all. Everyone in the neighborhood knew that Yosh was smart; it was the one part of his identity that never really failed him. He was a spellbinding storyteller, an avid reader, and an acute analyst of political affairs. His razor-sharp wit could turn his depressive, self-indulgent moods (and ours) around with the snap of a droll and surprisingly sophisticated and self-aware comment. Yosh liked to use his humor as a sneak attack on our expectations of him, and against threatening rifts, and he was deft at it. A master Scrabble player, he could do the Sunday *New York Times* crossword puzzle in one morning in ink.

Much like Letty Cottin Pogrebin, I grew up believing that my father was passing his legacy on to me. In my father's case, however, that legacy was a lack to be filled, ambitions to be carried through to their rightful conclusion. I was almost desperate that my father understand that he was responsible for my becoming a scholar, and then a writer. I thought that this would somehow heal his hurt. It did not. However, he kept the note I had slipped between the pages of my bound dissertation:

To my darling daddy—Do you have any idea how important you have been in bringing me to where I am now? I don't think you do. When I was a little girl, I knew that I had the smartest, wittiest, most exciting daddy of everyone—a daddy who could tell wonderful stories, who could delight people with words . . . It was you who taught me about the excitement of ideas, who made the world seem a fascinating place. It was you who brought my imagination and intellect to life, who made me begin to dream that someday I too would be able to charm through words and stories. It was you who turned me on to movies, books, images—who made me feel that no matter how bad things got, one could always depend on the imagination for comfort and inspiration. Now, these things I learned from *you*, these talents and dreams that *you* nurtured in me, are bearing fruit. I know, with every fiber of my being, that *you* are responsible for the writer that I am becoming. You were my first, best inspiration, and you put me on the road. I love you very, very much. You are my darling, darling daddy. Susan. (P.S. Estelle can read this, but please do not show it to anyone else.)

III.

Contemporary theorists like Daniel Boyarin have admirably tried to construct positive images of Jewish masculinity out of the Jewish man's supposed lack of phallic, aggressive manliness. That "lack" typically figured by his stereotypical bookishness, inferiority, and mildness has been dominantly represented as a condition of castration in the numerous racist tracts, cartoons, movies, and jokes depicting the Jewish man as passive, weak, squirrely, and bossed around by his wife (as in the Gilmore quote cited earlier). Boyarin, while accepting that Jewish masculinity may indeed have "feminine" strains, wants us to view those strains as active resistance to phallic ideals rather than involuntary deprivation of them. Focusing (tendentiously, as he himself admits) on certain Talmudic narratives, he tries to show that, far from pining for the phallus, "Jewish culture rejects the phallus as a representation of male sexuality and thus imagines the possibility of a nonphallic male sexuality."[7]

"Jewish culture rejects the phallus . . ." As a textual strategy, fine. Boyarin's deconstructive reading of the Talmud gives us a utopian moment, a way of accessing, as he puts it, "a model for a gentle, nurturing masculinity . . . a male who could be so comfortable with his little, fleshy penis that he would not have to grow it into 'the Phallus,' a sort of velvet John."[8] How many Jewish men have actually felt his way? I am sure there are some, perhaps many. Jewish men, like black men and others whose race or ethnicity has often been branded with a unitary, stereotypical identity, are in fact a highly diverse population. But I certainly didn't see much resistance to the phallus in my father's life or in the lives of the Jewish men that I grew up with in the fifties and sixties. Many of them were intellectuals and poets, but, like Mailer, Roth, and other post-war Jewish writers, they used their minds as weapons and flexed their words like muscles. The last thing they could endure was to be seen as soft and they set about defeating those stereotypes with a vengeance.

Boyarin does note that alongside the utopian, feminist elements that Jewish culture offers as a reconstruction of male subjectivity, there are also those elements that merely dress phallic masculinity in the clothes of the scholar, enjoining men to the "gladiatorial combat of Torah study," showing them how to kill with the voice rather than the spear.

Now *that* reminds me of the Jewish boys I grew up with. These boys were coming of age, of course, in an era when intellectual bad-boy machismo was particularly rampant, and rapidly taking over cultural politics. In the early sixties, civil rights leaders were our heroes and the ethics of nonviolence was our political philosophy; by the late sixties, Mark Rudd, Stokely Carmichael and other brash politicos had endowed protest with an aggressively martial, phallic cast. I wouldn't presume to generalize about "Jewish masculinity" on the basis of my father's life, or the cultural style of the young men I grew up with in Newark. I do know something, however, about gender transformation in the twentieth century, and it seems to me that what traditional Jewish culture has provided that has been most useful to that transformation is *not* resistance to the phallus. What has been most subversive is Jewish culture's unique valuing of *intellectual* forms of phallic power—the taste for disputation and radical critique, tenacity in argument, or muscular reason—that are easily transferable to women, and (as described in the preceding section of this piece) that many Jewish fathers have indeed handed over unstintingly and with great pride to their daughters. For all our often justified anger at our fathers, Letty Cottin Pogrebin and I grew up to be feminist gladiators under their tutelage.

There is a high price to be paid, of course, for this phallic legacy. In both the Singer story and Pogrebin's reminiscence, the girl blessed with her father's respect and instruction is chosen because she is not like other, real women. Like them, she has a female body; but unlike them, she has the soul or mind of a man. She may *look* like a daughter, but actually she is the desired son—in drag. Male mentors, when I was growing up, often complimented me in this way. In graduate school, one of my teachers told me how surprised he was to discover that my (blind-graded) comprehensive examination had been written by a woman, because it had been so rigorously argued. He thought this praise would please me.

By the time I entered graduate school, I knew enough to be offended by my teacher's remark. When I was younger, I was flattered to be told that I was as smart as a boy. I don't recall my father ever saying this. But he certainly acted as though my sisters and I were of a radically different order than my mother. She was good at Scrabble, too, but judging from the extreme gallantry with which my father complimented my mother on this, that skill was one of "heaven's mistakes," an anomaly, a singular and isolated intellectual talent in a soul made for other things. I valued those things: warmth and sympathy, cooking and cleaning, taking care of us, accompanying him to the track, getting her hair done and being taken out to dinner, being good humored when teased. But I grew up believing that I had inherited my father's brain. To have acknowledged any mental kinship with my mother would have been to align myself with those who are not invited into conversation about ideas, who are spoken to condescendingly, and whose opinions are not sought. In fact, in many ways my mother was a far deeper and more perceptive thinker than my father. Like many women (and other groups whose survival depends upon staying in the good graces of the more powerful), she was adept at "psyching" things out, at discerning motivation, need, and mood. She was not educated in clarifying the surfaces of things, but she knew how to look behind and under, and see in the dark. It was she, not my father, who taught me suspicion of the "clear" and "self-evident," who taught me to dig beneath appearances.

For women, the mantle of intellect—when we are invited to put it on— has always been a two-sided garment, with one side beautiful, clean-pressed, and smooth to the touch, but with the other side woven through with hidden thorns. Many philosophers, theologians, and scientists have believed that women simply do not have the reasoning powers of men. In their case, what you see is what you get. Others present a more complex picture, both providing arguments that have been used by women in their fight for equality with men while at the same time requiring, like Yentl's father, that women (and men) disidentify with and discard all things "womanly" in the process. Some have argued—Descartes, for example— that reason is "naturally" equally possessed by all. An implication of such arguments is that only law and custom stand in the way of women's full exercise of rationality; not surprisingly, many elite seventeenth and eighteenth-century women took to Cartesianism with avidity.[9]

But at the same time as Cartesianism opened doors for women, it defined a style of good thinking that shut out other kinds of intelligence. Indeed, this was the very argument of the dissertation in which I had placed that tribute to my father. I had written the note to him, but dedicated the dissertation to both of them—to my mother in remembrance. Actually, my mother's empathic intelligence was the study's muse. Criticizing some of the changes brought about by modernity, I wrote:

The seventeenth century saw the death, too, of another sort of "feminine principle" . . . [a] cluster of epistemological values, often associated with feminine consciousness . . . If the key terms in the Cartesian hierarchy of epistemological values are clarity and distinctness—qualities which mark each object off from the other and from the knower—the key term in this alternative scheme of values might be designated as *sympathy*. "Sympathetic" understanding of the object is that which understands it . . . as James Hillman describes it, through "merging with" and "marrying" it. To merge with or marry that which is to be known means, for Hillman, "letting interior movement replace clarity, interior closeness replace objectivity." It means granting personal or intuitive response a positive intellectual value . . . allow[ing] the variety of [the object's] meanings to unfold without coercion or too-focused interrogation.[10]

My point was not that sympathetic thinking should take the place of scientific detachment, but that understanding the world fully requires both. My mother's empathic, psychological intelligence, I now know, is as much a part of how my reason functions as my father's intellectual acuity, and I am profoundly grateful for that. I pass that mix down to my students, in whose philosophical intelligence I hope to see it mesh in still more integrated and creative form.

IV.

My father was not a feminist. He rolled his eyes skyward when I lectured my stepmother's son on the sexual politics of Passover seders, which ended (as theirs always did) with the women clearing the table and the men watching football in the den. My father worried about my politics, too. He lay awake for two nights because he had let it slip to a fundamentalist broker that he had a daughter who was a feminist; he was afraid the broker would dispatch right-to-lifers to throw bombs in my window. My father did not have enlightened ideas about men and women. But those conversations I saw him have with his granddaughter and that I know he had with me when I was a little girl tell a different story. I know with absolute certainty that they were the foundations for my feminist self. I am also struck by how different those conversations were from so many other conversations I've had all my life with men—conversations at parties, on dates, at conferences, with men of correct politics and liberal views, men who supported abortion rights (my father never knew that I had had an abortion), believed Anita Hill (my father's first sympathies in such cases always went to the beleaguered man), and taught *Gender Trouble* in their classes (my father believed the differences between men and women were created by God). I think of how many times those liberal men have seemed to look through me as I spoke, or nodded distractedly, or didn't let me get a word in edgewise.

During the Anita Hill–Clarence Thomas hearings I received a call from my father, then about eighty years old, wanting to find out my views. This was in itself an unusual occurrence. I suspected what he really wanted was to tell me his views and challenge me to love him in spite of them. He didn't believe Hill, he told me. He clearly identified with

Clarence Thomas and his struggle as a black man to get respect from this culture. And, like many men (and some women) he was genuinely puzzled by the fact that Hill had continued to work for Thomas after he had allegedly harassed her. "Why didn't she just quit? Why did she follow him to the EEOC?" he challenged me.

My first impulse was to want to scream or make some excuse to get off the phone. Those questions were an incessant mantra in the media, and few people seemed to be able to truly hear the answers that were given. My father often shared the editorial perspectives of his favorite male journalists and talking-heads, and none of them "got it" at all. What chance was there of this conversation having a happy resolution, of ending in anything other than making me feel crazy? I decided to give it a try anyway. As my father aged, I was inclined to grab whatever opportunities I could to communicate with him. And I had some answers. I had been harassed myself, knew many other women who also had been harassed, and understood that mixture of intimidation, pragmatics, and training in feminine comportment that keeps one from making a fuss. I swallowed hard, girded my loins like a gladiator, and tried to explain it all to my father—beginning with my own harassment and how it had made me feel. After a few minutes, I suddenly sensed that he was listening with an attentiveness that I hadn't experienced since I was a little girl, when he would fix his blue eyes on me and ask me to slow down and explain some muddled childhood notion. He asked me questions. He listened to my answers. By the end of our phone conversation, my eighty-year-old Jewish father had remarkably gotten it. In the midst of that time, when so many of us had begun to doubt that there would ever be any progress made past the stereotypes of lying temptresses and women scorned, when we had begun to despair of the possibilities of communication between men and women, of women's experiences being taken seriously, my father had handed me a sweet wildcard of hope.

Notes

1. David Gimore, *Manhood in the Making* (New Haven: Yale University Press, 1990), p. 127.
2. Eric A. Kimmel, *Bar Mitzvah* (New York: Puffin Books, 1995), p. 27.
3. Ibid., p. 25.
4. Ibid., p. 27.
5. Isaac Bashevis Singer, *The Collected Stories of Isaac Bashevis Singer* (New York: Farrar, Straus & Giroux, 1982), p. 149.
6. "I Don't Like to Write About My Father," in *Nice Jewish Girls: Growing up in America*, ed. Merlene Adler Marks (New York: Penguin, 1996), pp. 261–77, quote on p. 263.
7. "Homotopia: The Feminized Jewish Man and the Lives of Women in Late Antiquity," *Differences*, 7.2 (1995), pp. 41–81, p. 54.

8. Ibid., p. 69. In "Reading the Male Body," (in *The Male Body*, edited by Laurence Goldstein, Ann Arbor: University of Michigan Press, 1994, pp. 265–306). I offer the figure of the aroused (rather than erect) penis in much the same spirit as Boyarin plumbs the Torah for ideas that could nourish a re-visioned masculinity. My point was to provide a concrete image that encourages other ways of thinking about bodies than the dominant dualisms (for example, that one is *either* "hard"-phallic or "soft"-feminine), and which might open up the imaginations of readers to considering their own experience, expectations, assumptions in new ways. When the "erect" penis is imagined in terms of its capacity for *feeling* (arousal) rather than its readiness to "perform" and penetrate, I argue, it is neither "feminine" nor phallic.

9. Ibid., p. 67.

10. See Susan Bordo editor, *Re-reading the Canon: Feminist Interpretations of Descartes* (University Park: Penn State Press, 1998) for essays exploring feminist responses to Descartes and Cartesianism.

11. *The Flight to Objectivity: Essays on Cartesianism and Culture* (New York: SUNY Press, 1987), p. 102.

Chapter 2

How Feminism Made a Man Out of Me: The Proper Subject of Feminism and the Problem of Men

Patrick D. Hopkins

1. A Course On Applied Sexual Difference I

Through accidents of birth and geography both damaging and richly enlightening I attended a conservative, and in many respects fundamentalist, Christian high school. Along with English, math, history, and Bible, all students were required to take a course called Christian Family Living. This course was geared to teach adolescents how Christian families (and evangelically, of course, this meant all families) should be run, preparing them for dating, marriage, sex, childraising, and in large part rescuing them from the examples of their own, mostly broken, homes. While other religious classes studied biblical history or points of conservative doctrine, however, Christian Family Living turned out primarily to be a training course in a conservative Christian ideology of gender. In fact, the very notion of "family" itself depended almost entirely on beliefs about the divine purpose of sexual difference and scripturally derived gender roles.

Contrary to some extreme stereotypes, the conservative Christian view taught here was not that women were inferior to men, nor that women were created to serve men. Women and men, we learned, were equal in value, worth, respect, and intelligence—claims shored up by the fact that our teacher was a woman of powerful presence who entertained no simple-minded claims that men were "better" or "smarter" than women. However (and it is the "however" that does in fact lead to clear sex-based hierarchies), the scriptures taught that men and women were destined for different roles in social, spiritual, and familial life, and (though not apparent in scripture) we were also taught that men and women differed psychologically—a "fact" which both reflected and reinforced teachings on distinct social and familial sex roles.

Let me separate for the moment these two aspects of my formal train-ing in gender—the doctrinal and psychological. The empirical, psycho-logical claims taught were not so much used to explain why there should be hierarchical differences between women's and men's roles in families—that was established by doctrine, independent of contingent facts (for example, the doctrinal position that men should be the head of house-hold). Instead, information on female and male psychology was imparted to help us predict, control, and shape our own and others' behavior in doctrinally appropriate ways. These basic psychological differences are ones any historically informed reader might imagine. Quite specifically and explicitly, we were taught that women were more emotional, more verbal, more in need of security, love, and attention, more interested in their physical appearance, more interested in family than individual suc-cess, naturally maternal, less logical, less sexual, less aggressive, less lead-erly, and in general, people whose self-esteem was (properly) wrapped up in relationships and doing for others. Men, we were explicitly taught, were more individualistic, more aggressive, more independent, more in need of social stature, more leaderly, more rational and yet paradoxically far more controlled by a forceful sex drive, less interested in their physi-cal appearance, less naturally parental, less emotional, less socially adept, and in general, people whose self-esteem was based on their social success and being effective leaders.[1]

Doctrinally speaking, the ahistorical, literalist interpretation of scrip-ture required men to be the spiritual, social, and economic leaders within the governing structure of both church and family. A clear spiritual hier-archy existed in which men submitted themselves to God through Christ, women submitted themselves to God through their husbands, and chil-dren submitted themselves to God through their parents. These specific doctrinal claims did not, for most school staff, necessarily extend to civil arrangements, and the separation of civil and spiritual–familial realms led to some odd consequences, revealing the sheer insidiousness of a worldview constructed so much around gender.

For example, it may surprise some readers to learn that we were explicitly taught that a woman could be an effective President of the United States.[2] However, such individual aspirations would have to be subordinated to one's place in the gender structure of the family. So, while a female head of state was permissible, only a single woman could become President. A married woman would have to submit to the authority of her husband, thus making him the ultimate, unelected, executive authority. Obviously this would produce a serious conflict. Since her first duty is to her husband (as a way of submitting to God), a married female President could never fulfill both national and familial obligations.

Another example is that a woman could work outside the home and have a successful, high-paid career—but only if her children were old enough to be in school, and only if she made less money than her husband. The first requirement stood because it was the wife's responsibility to take care of the children (which would be intrinsically more rewarding anyway, due to her natural maternal instincts). The second requirement stood not due to any specific doctrine but because of the psychological differences between men and women; a wife making more money than her husband would damage his self-esteem as family head and provider, while her self-esteem, dependent on being a good wife and mother, would not suffer from making less money or stalling a career. It was therefore, her responsibility to turn down promotions should they push her salary past that of her husband's.

The connection between women's responsibilities and male psychology also got cashed out in regards to sex. We were specifically taught that girls and women had the power to control their sex drive—including the ability virtually to shut it on or off at will. Boys and men, on the other hand, lacked such ability, and although they were clearly held morally responsible for their own behaviors, they were much more susceptible to sexual impulse, more likely to get caught up in the moment, lose perspective and conviction. Because of these sexual differences, females were primarily responsible for making certain that dating situations did not result in sexual immorality. It was their responsibility to see that males did not get overstimulated, their responsibility to resist physical contact or suggestive behavior that might inflame their suitors.

These sorts of rules, jointly informed by doctrine and psychology, extended even to evangelism. As a Christian, any woman or girl was obligated to witness to unbelievers in an effort to convert them and lead them to salvation. However, when a female witnessed the gospel to a male, and saw that he was genuinely interested in spiritual guidance and teaching, she was obliged to seek out an adult male Christian to convince the potential convert—this was because if she were to lead an unbelieving man entirely through the process of conversion, she would then establish herself as his spiritual guide, an improper spiritual leadership position for a woman. Even salvation itself, it turns out, must be subordinated at times to the ideology of gender.[3]

These were only a few of the specific rules taught. Others, sometimes more subtle, sometimes more fuzzy, were in the air, a gender-conscious arrangement always present. Boys were required to do all the lifting and moving of desks and chairs. After-school work programs sent boys to the stables and hayfields and girls to the crafts building to learn quilting and sewing, with few exceptions.[4] We were taught the evil of the mysterious and utterly irrational Equal Rights Amendment, which would force men and women to use the same public bathrooms and force our daughters, sisters, and mothers into infantry combat.

I chafed under this ideology and what seemed to me its unjust and arbitrary practices. And in fact, without encouragement, I resisted it in various ways.[5] In Christian Family Living, we were all assigned to read and report on three or four books each semester. The books were all Christian inspirational teachings on how to be a good wife or husband, on sexual morality, and on how to raise children using Christian principles. While the vast majority of the class simply read the book and regurgitated the principles therein (whether or not they agreed with them) I inevitably felt compelled to criticize. I was especially drawn to books written by women (and directed to women) discussing the successful application of Christian principles in their own marriages, how they managed their husband's testy male psychologies in an effort to strengthen him as head of the family, how they experienced the joy of submitting to their husbands as a greater act of obedience to God, and how they felt sorrow for the angry feminists of secular humanist society who rejected their satisfying God-given roles in the pursuit of power. I hated these books and, although I was only fifteen or sixteen at the time with no training whatsoever in critical thinking or debate, I denounced their conclusions in every report I turned in—to the dismay, but admitted fair-mindedness of my teacher. Even when I felt I had no doctrinal way to refute the authors' claims (being very much a believer) something deeply and thoroughly in me rebelled. I challenged the universality of the claims, I challenged the truth of the psychological claims, I challenged everything I could—short of the literalist legitimacy of the scripture itself.

I resisted in other small ways as well. I wrote history term papers on Indira Ghandhi and Golda Meir as important world leaders. When directing our junior class play I changed the sex of several of the characters, making the police chief and the scientist female. As class president I put female class members in charge of committees. I criticized my female friends for hanging out with boys who insulted each other with sexist slurs.[6] No doubt all these efforts seem pitiful and minuscule by any standard of political resistance feminist activists are familiar with, and in the big scheme of things no doubt they are—but for a teenager within the confines of this small, insulated, patriarchal religious community, they were activities that felt like resistance, that felt subversive. At any rate, I knew what I felt, knew what I wanted to think—that the universal claims about female and male psychologies were just plain false or at least greatly exaggerated, that interpretations of scripture were fixed by preexisting sexist attitudes. I hated the idea (heretically, even if it did come from God) that men should have power over women simply by virtue of their sex. And I wasn't just repelled by the treatment of women. I hated the idea that boys and men were expected to do all the physical labor, that they were to be chivalrous, opening doors and giving up seats, that maternalism and emotion were so often or completely denied to them. In short, I hated the obsession with sexual distinction.

Interestingly, at times in this class and in other situations where I voiced my thoughts—advocating equality in the family, or insisting that girls should also have to help with some physical labor, or suggesting that some women might do well in combat military roles—the response was to look at me blankly and say "You sound like some kind of feminist" or "Are you for women's lib?" In this context, these responses were quasi-accusations that simply meant "You are expressing beliefs that are inconsistent with being a Christian." It was similar to being accused of liberalism, secularism, materialism, or atheism.

Whatever its instructional intent, "sounding like a feminist" or a supporter of "women's lib" suited me in many respects. In supporting "equality," I did not merely argue for the elevation of women, or the leveling of sex roles. I failed to accept my own obligations as a man, as an eventual head of household, spiritual leader of my family, and protector of wife and children. I was, in effect, rejecting my masculine duties, my native responsibilities. Resisting my spiritual obligations as a man, however, cohered with a complex of attitudes and behaviors I already had, for by many of the standards of behavior at the time I was not sufficiently masculine—and what's more, I didn't much care. I had never fit into the stereotypical and overly-valued ideal of masculinity—in all the cliché but culturally very consequential ways. I preferred piano to football, eschewed basketball for drama, wrote short stories in English instead of rebuilding motors in shop, glommed onto Boy George and Annie Lennox as my favored 1980s cultural pop icons while other boys preferred Mr. T and Rambo. All simple silly things, no doubt, but which nonetheless elicited inane name-calling from students (sissy, fag, homo, etc.) and resulted in compulsory baseball and mechanical drawing classes ordered by adults. Masculinity, it seems, is not something that *merely* comes *naturally* to boys, nor femininity *naturally* to girls.[7] There is a vast array of cultural sanctions, motivations, pressures, practices, and picayune distinctions that train children in behaviors and beliefs "appropriate" to their sex—and in my case, formal instruction in the guise of Christian Family Living. Sexual difference is worrisomely produced, it seems, even while touted as simply "there." Even though my masculinity should have been an automatic property of my being male, they nonetheless struggled to make a man out of me.

2. A Course On Applied Sexual Difference II

In many respects, graduate school was dimensions away from my high school setting—urban, affluent, low on religious conservatives, and academically competitive. By the time I arrived at graduate school, I already considered myself officially a feminist, having been introduced to feminist theory and history as an undergraduate. This is not to say that such an introduction was very formal. My undergraduate school was in many ways an extension of my high school's culture and experience—conservative, though nominally secular, a place where you could get accused of being a liberal and a feminist just for uttering support for equality or abortion rights.[8] While there was a Women's Studies program, the program was tiny and rarely offered any courses other than an historical introduction. Education in feminist theory came from books and graduate student friends in the English department—the most knowledgeable and informed of which happened to be male, so much so that when other students asked about feminist theory, professors often directed them to him.

At any rate, when I applied to graduate school I expressly stated my interest in feminist theory, an interest which I found in no ways incongruent with my being a man (which I had never been terribly successful at or invested in anyway). Having been the village feminist in both high school and often in undergraduate school, I saw studying feminist theory, writing feminist theory, and teaching feminist theory as a simple extension of my interests and my self-perception. So it was with no hesitation, no cognitive dissonance, and no sense of being out-of-place that in my very first semester of graduate school I signed up for a course in Radical Lesbian Feminism.

As one might expect I was the only male in class. I knew this going in, of course, and it didn't give me the slightest bother. I had often been in all or virtually all-female groups and been entirely comfortable there—from staying on the girls' side of the playground during elementary school recess, to working in the kitchen at family reunions,[9] from group piano classes in junior high school, to mall-shopping with friends, and to weekend nights spent dancing at lesbian bars during college. In fact, even in some of these situations I had been considered "the feminist," spending my time explaining, arguing, and even proselytizing for feminism. But this class was a different situation.

Predominantly, the class was taken by senior women's studies majors—and if my own high school experience had been one of being unsuccessfully trained in a conservative, religious ideology of gender—most of the students in this class had spent their college years being successfully trained in another ideology of gender variably self-described as *radical, lesbian, separatist,* and *woman-identified.*[10] This ideology, like the conservative Christian one I was familiar with, also maintained a rigid focus on sexual difference, fundamentally distinguishing between women and men in psychology, spirituality, world-view, and moral perception.[11] Of course, while the conservative ideology valorized a certain kind of traditional masculinity for men and labored to instill it in adolescent boys, this cultural feminist ideology vilified masculinity (which was a nebulous collection of traits involving rationality, objectivity, and a propensity to dominate others) and spent a great deal of time ardently seeking out the essentialist taint of masculinity and male-centeredness wherever it might be found, attempting to eliminate it from a gynocentric, radical, lesbian-feminist consciousness, language, and politics.

Now, conceptually speaking, this was not entirely new to me. I had read, been acquainted with, or had explicated the work of Mary Daly, Sarah Hoagland, Jeffner Allen, Marilyn Frye, Andrea Dworkin, Catherine MacKinnon, Z. Budapest and various separatist manifestoes—though it was true that none of the feminists I had met before had actually identified themselves with this kind of cultural feminism.[12] What I found fascinating about the class then (and for my purposes here) was not the novelty of this re-polarized feminism, but the sheer contextual difference in the understanding of masculinity, of "thinking as and being a man" and "thinking as and being a woman."

For the first time, simply being the kind of body I was made me masculine—indeed too masculine. Whether interpreted biologically or as an unavoidable social construction, my *maleness* or *being a man* was assumed to be central to who I was, how I would think, and constitutive of where my energy would go. Having always been comfortable as "one of the girls" (or as college friends dubbed me, an "honorary lesbian"), having always traversed the hyperbolic gender poles of my culture, having walked the liminal line of gender performance, having never been man enough to satisfy peers or conservative teachers, it was strange suddenly, unambiguously, uncomplicatedly, to be a man, to be seen as a representation of men—and strange too for what this meant practically. There were feminist meetings I could not attend, a women's resource center on campus I could not visit, class essays I had no *right* to comment on, courses I would not be considered to teach. Moves that in other contexts had been seen as in the service of feminism were now interpreted as male-oriented—appeals to scientific research, to liberal notions of equal rights or equal power, concerns about logical contradiction or standards of proof. I was also told I could not be considered a *feminist*, but only a *profeminist man* because feminism required that one have women's experiences—something that presumably no man could. Strange then, to go from being accused of feminism by anti-feminists, to being stripped of the feminist label by feminists.[13]

Incapable of being a feminist, my contributions to the class were often received with a sense of coming from "outside." Sometimes class conversations elicited by a question I asked or a comment I made were cut short because someone felt they were investing too much energy in a "man's interests." In fact, one of the key elements of the self-described separatist aspect of this feminism (which was represented as the truest or most thoroughgoing feminism) was that feminists (always women) were obligated to put their "energy" into other women, not allowing it to be stolen by men. At times, this led to what seemed odd results. It was considered no conflict with principles, for example, to claim that feminists would have a greater obligation to "support" or "invest energy" in a Phyllis Schlafly rather than in any profeminist man (an explicitly stated position).

This did not mean, of course, that all women were considered supporters of feminist ideals or goals—they clearly were not. In fact, the search for masculinity or "male-oriented thinking" often extended to women. Women, it was claimed, were often duped or trained into giving their support to men, some to the point that they could be considered "male-identified women" (there didn't seem be a category of "female-identified men" however—a category more familiar to me in the form of the "sissy" or "homo" taunts of male peers). This concept lead to constant self-examination among the female students—a perpetual scrutiny of their ideas and behaviors in an effort to locate and excise any "male-identified" language, thoughts, biases, or attitudes.[14] Sometimes this search spiraled in ways that made it seem male-identification and male values might never be excised because they infused every logically possible position. For example, in a discussion of the androcentric valorization of physical power and strength and the sexist perception that women are always physically weak, the question arose how women might resist this patriarchal stereotype. One suggestion was to look to female body-builders for guidance because they reject the male characterization of women as weak, pretty, and in need of male protection. Female body-builders developed their own strength and resisted the male values of femininity. However, it was put forth, the obsession with strength and physical prowess is actually an internalization of male values and female bodybuilders alter their bodies to match a masculine ideal of strength. But, it was claimed, maybe it didn't have to be a masculine ideal. Maybe women could make their own ideal of body, health, and physicality that didn't rely on traditional male values. But, perhaps the very notion of ownership of one's body was male in itself. But, perhaps the very concern about male values was a male value that limited women's self-definition. But, perhaps the notion of self-definition was a male value because it relied on individualism and the idea of a discrete self while feminists should focus on interrelationships and community. But, perhaps this was just acceding to the male ideal of women as giving up themselves to others and community.

Masculinity, it seemed, perfused every corner of the world, threatened every pure motive. In many ways, masculinity played the role for these particular cultural feminists that secularism did for Christian devouts. It was ubiquitous, insidious, infinitely locatable and Manichaeanly motivating.

But whereas secularism was evident only in behavior and attitude, masculinity was an inevitable possession and consequence of being male. And while the religious conservatives made the self-referentially problematic assumption that since I *was* a man I should behave *like* a man, and thus paradoxically trained me in what they said was *natural*,[15] the cultural feminists assumed that since I *was* a man, anything I said or did was automatically male or masculine. Cultural feminism seemed to do by fiat what Christian Family Living tried to do with education—stop me from being a feminist and make a man out of me.

3. The Problem of Men (The Problem of Women?)

Both of these idiosyncratic experiences were lessons in the powerful organizing categories of gender. In both cases—though in different ways—my sex was interpreted as a limitation. Sometimes it was a descriptive limitation, constraining the possible ways I might think, act, feel, understand, and *be*. Sometimes, it was a prescriptive limitation constraining and generating behavioral norms and ideals that I was morally and socially compelled to reach. Whatever the specifics, in both cases the governing factor was an ideology of gender, a practice of gender, a set of compulsory gender performances, a set of gendered inclusions and exclusions.

When I was first asked to write about the issue of men in feminism—confronted by the very characterization of men's relationship to feminism as an "issue" in need of attention—an image came to mind, an image topographical, political, almost military in character. Somewhere in the cultural landscape is feminism. Somewhere else, perhaps all around but nonetheless outside, are men. The status of the border between them is in dispute.

Perhaps as productive of this image as derivative are the standard questions surrounding the issue of men and feminism: Can men be feminists? Should men be feminists? Can men be supportive of feminist projects or do they drain away energy and reshape the politics back around themselves? Can men be trustworthy allies for feminists? Can men think and write and feel as feminists? Can or should they facilitate or organize or lead feminist political actions? Should they take women's studies classes? Teach women's studies? Write in women's studies? Lesbian studies? Should they stick to profeminist studies of masculinity and political projects aimed at changing men?

But if these questions tend to generate an image of women inside feminism and men outside, that image was immediately countered by my own experience of being the village feminist, of reading, writing, and teaching feminism.[16] It was immediately countered by my history, in which women were often anti-feminist and in fact even the leaders, teachers, and writers of anti-feminism; a history in which men were sometimes feminists even introducing, explaining, writing, and teaching feminist theory; a history in which some few feminists seemed to mirror the essentialist practices of the very patriarchal enemies they deplored. In short, all these questions were countered by a sensitivity to the influence notions of gender have over the entire conceptual set-up of the "problem of men."

One of those influences regards assumptions not so much about men as about women. While the questions of men's relationship to feminism are explicitly concerned with men, they seem to assume that women do *not* have a problematic relationship with feminism. Insert "women" where "men" appears in these questions and note that problems of inclusion and exclusion seem to melt away. Categorically speaking, at least, being classified as a woman seems to be ₍nough to set the theoretical problems of inclusion in feminism aside—the question Can women be feminists? is answered in the transparent affirmative, or not entertained at all.[17]

The primary assumption here, which shapes the problem of men in feminism as a problem, seems be that feminism is about women. The very subject of feminism seems to be *women*—or in more universalist terms, perhaps *Woman*. As such, the very substance of feminism appears to be the political, ethical, psychological, spiritual, and experiential expression of women, for women. Feminism in this way is treated as if it is the property and projection of the collective *Woman* and as such any woman who wishes to become part of it may do so, because it is already hers. In some sense, even those women who do not wish to become part of it—complicit apoliticals, right-wing women, anti-feminist crusaders, or fundamentalist activists—are still included under the aegis of feminism. Being about women and for women, it speaks even on behalf of those women (as women) who oppose it, taking account of their experience and interests, offering support, raising consciousness—it is perpetually open to them.

It is not surprising that if feminism is conceived of as *about women* and *for women,* the question turns up whether feminism can or should only be *by women.* Men, then, are a problem. Not being women (in standard binary form), they are simply not what feminism is about and not the group to which feminism gives voice, not the group whose experience is the core of feminism.

And here is where much of the debate over men and feminism gets located. Are men unable to *do* feminism? Are they incapable of acting, writing, studying, teaching, thinking, and feeling *for and about women?* Lacking the essential quality for *doing* feminism—women's experience— are men simply epistemically or emotionally unequipped? This is at the core of the common criticism among women's studies students that men should not teach women's studies courses because they do not have and cannot understand women's experiences, cannot relate to women's experiences—again, the assumption here being that women's studies and feminism have the same subject, women.[18] On the face of it then, masculinity is an impediment, a potentially theoretical as well as practical obstacle to being a feminist and doing feminism.[19]

No doubt many readers so far will see this explication as utterly uninformative and obvious. Of course feminism is about and for women. Of course men's lack of women's experience is an obstacle to doing feminism. However, it is useful to explicate what many would think obvious in order to point out that there are problems with these assumptions. It is not at all unproblematic to think that the core subject of feminism is women, and it is not at all clear that thinking of masculinity as an impediment to doing feminism is very useful.

This is why I began with my two narratives. The immediate object lesson to be learned from those accounts is not so much about any specific proposition that was expounded, or about the positions of any particular group, but rather about the contextual relativity of what counts as *masculinity,* and what counts as *feminist,* with an eye toward rationales of exclusion. Both of these concepts—masculinity and the proper subject of feminism—are worth looking at more closely.

4. The Problems of Masculinity

One understanding of the idea that masculinity is an impediment to being a feminist is that masculine traits and attitudes, characteristic of men, are obstacles to embodying feminist ideals, to enacting feminist principles or values. Typically such masculine characteristics are thought to include a tendency to dominate others, a tendency toward violence, an excessive reliance on rationality and narrowly construed objectivity, overindependence, a distaste for emotion, sexual aggressiveness, and an excessive concern with contractual thinking in moral matters and personal relationships. Trained or predisposed to masculinity, men have a hard time unlearning these behavioral and emotional patterns and as such are often unable to replace them with feminist traits and values. The problem with this picture is threefold.

First: Masculinity is variable, contextual, and multiply defined. What counts as *masculine* depends on the gender order in place and can shift from context to context. In my own experience, appealing to notions of formal equality, emphasizing individualism, and de-emphasizing difference was interpreted in my radical feminist graduate course as typical signs of masculinity—of a pathological reliance on male values of sameness, contractual thinking, and devaluating personal relationships. In my Christian Family Living class, however, these same appeals were seen as neither here nor there in terms of the masculine/feminine divide but were interpreted as secular attacks on proper doctrinally and psychologically grounded sex roles, and therefore tainted by feminist ideas. In liberal feminist contexts, like local NOW (National Organization for Women) meetings, the very same appeals were seen as part and parcel of basic feminist principles and opposed to oppressive hierarchies of difference.

Now this is not to say that there is not some general agreement among various cultural groups that some traits are masculine and some are feminine—however differently those traits may be valued. Some agreement may very well exist. Certain aspects of a gender ideology may be shared among otherwise disparate groups. But even when there is tacit or explicit agreement on what counts as masculine and feminine, it is not clear that these divisions merely depend on the actual behavior or predilections of men and women. Most binary sexual difference ideologies seem to contain categories for classifying members of one sex who act like the other sex—and more often than not these categories are criminal ones, either legal or cultural or both. For example, when observing a boy playing with dolls, rarely is it the case that the observer simply realizes "Oh, then playing with dolls is included among the list of masculine behaviors because a boy is currently exhibiting this behavior." Instead, boys who act "femininely" get classified as "sissies," "homos," or "faggots"—and not surprisingly, categories encompassing the "feminine" boy are most unpleasant. Similarly, it is not unusual for girls or women who are assertive, play rugby, or are unconcerned with cosmetics, to be categorized as "tomboys," "butches," "dykes," or "ballbreakers." And these classificatory schema are not limited to patriarchal culture. Among some cultural feminists, the same sort of phenomenon occurs when a woman's actual behavior fails to cohere with the ideals of difference that are supposed to mark a woman's distinct perspective and attitude. A woman who ruthlessly climbs the corporate ladder, struggles to become a military combat pilot, or perhaps teaches Christian Family Living is considered a "male-identified" woman. So at least in some cases, the distinction between masculine and feminine precedes and constrains the observations of actual persons and actual behaviors. This seems at least to interfere with the notion that "masculinity" or "masculine values" are very illuminating concepts, seeing as how masculine women and feminine men abound. Worries about masculinity and femininity usually end up in attempts to train people into, or out of, masculinity and femininity—which calls into question their initial descriptive accuracy.

Second: Even if "masculinity" were clear, it is not clear that "being masculine" is in and of itself any indication that some trait or practice is at odds with feminism. Sometimes, the worry about whether some practice is "male-identified" ends up eliminating a number of useful tools for feminist practice. For example, at least for a while it was common among feminist groups to insist on consensus decision-making procedures. Consensus was supposed to be an antidote to the masculine power hierarchies present in most political groups, and so procedures such as majority voting and offices such as president were eliminated. While consensus is perfectly appropriate for small groups, however, it fails in large groups because it cannot accommodate the chaotic expansion of interests combined with the power of the individual to veto the collective. Consequently, in every larger group with which I have been familiar (say, more than ten or so people) consensus decision-making failed. Either no consensus was ever reached and the discussions continued interminably, or individuals who could not get their pet positions supported self-selected out of the group eventually leaving a much more homogenous and workable collective, or if consensus was reached it was concerning some very general and watered down position. What this meant was that very little got done—protests failed to be organized, reproductive rights marches failed to get off the ground, lesbian support groups failed to get administration approval, conference speakers failed to get selected, and so on. In short, a more effective procedure for actualizing feminist goals was abandoned because of its apparent masculinity.

Third: Along this same line, it is not clear (even if "masculinity" were) that masculinity should not also belong to women as much as men. Let me extend a point made by Judith Butler. Butler writes:

> . . . parodic categories serve the purposes of denaturalizing sex itself. When the neighborhood gay restaurant closes for vacation, the owners put out a sign, explaining that "she's overworked and needs a rest." This very gay appropriation of the feminine works to multiply possible sites of application of the term, to reveal the arbitrary relation between the signifier and the signified, and to destabilize and mobilize the sign. Is this a colonizing "appropriation" of the feminine? My sense is no. That accusation assumes that the feminine belongs to women, an assumption surely suspect.[20]

Similarly, we can ask if masculinity (whatever counts as that) should be the sole possession of men? Why should masculinity not be freely available to women and to feminists should it serve a useful goal? This does not suggest that anything goes, that anything traditionally or even recently associated with masculinity should now be appropriated by women or by feminists, but instead that the sheer worry about whether some practice is masculine or "male-identified" is useless. If some behavior, attitude, practice, or perspective is harmful (say non-consensual sexual aggression, or a reactive tendency toward violence, or an obsession with domination) then presumably we should be able to spell out why it is harmful without merely pointing to its gendered associations. After all, a female sexual offender is not bad because she acted like a man, but because she hurt someone. Similarly, if a hierarchical style of management is likely to produce the best results for a particular feminist goal, then that management strategy should not be unavailable simply because it is "masculine." An historically associated femininity or masculinity is simply not enough, and perhaps not relevant at all, to deny or recommend some practice or attitude for feminist use.[21]

5. Experience and the Subjects of Feminism

Another understanding of the notion that masculinity is an impediment to feminism focuses less on psychological objections than on epistemological ones. The idea is that men, regardless of their beliefs, attitudes, and behavioral characteristics, cannot be feminists because they don't know what it is like to be a woman, that is, they lack women's experience. Rosi Braidotti evinces this idea, writing:

> What the heterosexual men are lacking intellectually—the peculiar blindness to sexual difference for which the term *sexism* is an inadequate assessment—is a reflection of their position in history. They have not inherited a world of oppression and exclusion based on their sexed corporal being; they do not have the lived experience of oppression because of their sex. Thus, most of them fail to grasp the specificity of feminism in terms of its articulation of theory and practice, of thought and life.[22]

When this reliance on similarity of experience as a grounding or requirement for feminist apprehension is coupled with the assumption that the subject of feminism is women as such, the epistemic and proprietary exclusion of men from the feminist circle is complete. Braidotti protests:

> Somewhere along the line I am viscerally opposed to the whole idea: men aren't and shouldn't be IN feminism: the feminist space is not theirs and not for them to see.[23]

Stephen Heath succinctly captures the position:

> Men have a necessary relation to feminism . . . and that relation is also necessarily one of a certain exclusion—the point after all is that this is a matter

for women, that it is their voices and actions that must determine the change and redefinition. Their voices and actions, not ours: no matter how "sincere," "sympathetic" or whatever, we are always also in a male position which brings with it all the implications of domination and appropriation, everything precisely that is being challenged, that has to be altered. Women are the subjects of feminism, its initiators, its makers, its force; the move and the join from being a woman to being a feminist is the grasp of that subjecthood.[24]

Now my criticisms here have nothing to do with the import of men's sincerity, sympathy, or other psychological states, but rather with the sheer claim that the subject of feminism is women and furthermore, that the essence of the transformation into a feminist is found in a woman apprehending that subjecthood. The problems with these views are at least twofold.

First: There is considerable trouble for the idea that we can or should ground feminism in a concept of Woman or of women's experience. The critical work in this area is extensive, and it would be prohibitively long and complicated to give a comprehensive examination of the problem.[25] However, I will briefly encapsulate the argument.

Early radical feminism began to distinguish itself from other liberation movements associated with the Left by claiming that women were not oppressed simply as incidental members of racial or class groups, but were oppressed *as women.* In recognizing that women were marginalized and maltreated in a variety of different contexts because they were women, it became apparent that what was needed was a political movement that addressed the specific oppression of women. However, if a movement about women's oppression was to be genuinely distinct from other liberation movements, then it needed some theoretical base. Just as class liberation had Marxism, women's liberation needed a theory. But one of the main purposes of theories backing political movements is to explain how a particular group of people form a definable and locatable group at all, and as such how individuals who are members of that group are oppressed as members. An early concern, then, was what united women as a group. What was the basis of women's connection and collective oppression? As Judith Grant explains it, this concern from the very start led to the invention of the core concept of Woman as a universal category.[26]

As it turns out, early feminism (and contemporary feminism for that matter) had difficulty with any objective definition of women's oppression and connection. Class oppression could more or less be defined in terms of economics. Racial oppression could more or less be defined in terms of the treatment of people of specific skin color.[27] But women were scattered throughout both recognized oppressed and oppressor groups. Of course, individual women were oppressed, but there were also white women, rich women, aristocratic women, working women, and leisure class women. How then were women as women oppressed? Eventually, feminists discarded the search for any "objective" definition of women's oppression and settled on defining oppression differently—subjectively. As such, feminism began to rely centrally on *experience*. Women defined their own oppression as they experienced it—which also set up the basis for considering objectivity as a predominantly male value contrasted to subjectivity, a feminist or women's value. This reliance on experience was itself the theoretical glue that was to hold the category of Woman together. As Grant writes: "The idea of experience was necessary because of the need for some kind of evidence that women were oppressed. That is, it was necessary to prove that the category Woman existed because if women did not have something in common, the full analytic value of the major foundational category of feminist theory would disappear."[28]

The problem with the category of Woman and the idea of experience that held it together was that it didn't work very well. The assumption had been that some core experience would be more or less common to all women, but it wasn't—at least not to the extent that it had a completely unifying effect. Women had a wide variety of experiences based on their relative positions in other economic, racial, religious, and education groups, on personal relationships, on individual beliefs and commitments, and on idiosyncratic sensibilities. Some women felt they were not oppressed. Some women experienced oppression by other women. Some women experienced oppression by not being allowed to work, some by virtue of having to work. Some women assumed that mothering or a maternal sensibility was a universally shared experience, while other women never had or desired to have maternal instincts and sensibilities, and even others argued that motherhood and maternal labor was the very source of all their oppression. Some women sought liberation through communist ideals, some sought liberation through corporate capitalist powermongering. Some women attributed oppression to male dominated religions and sought to remake the idea of God, some women experienced liberation and freedom through accepting and submitting to their secondary or tertiary positions in familial and religious hierarchies. Some women fought for abortion rights, some were radical pro-life activists. Some were lesbian, some were homophobic. Some women were anti-pornography activists, some women were sadomasochist pornographers. Some women made feminism the new core of their very being, some women became outspoken anti-feminist crusaders.

This sort of variability prevented the concept of experience from doing the full work it was supposed to do. It could not give voice to a common essence of women's oppression, nor could it unite women as an oppressed group. So, in an effort to explain and criticize the experiences of women who did not feel they were oppressed, and who rejected or actively fought against feminism, the notion of "false consciousness" developed. This was basically the idea that some women were so steeped in patriarchal ideology they could not see their own oppression. They could not see that the limitations placed on them and their very understanding of women were the result of male domination. Such women were often referred to as *male-identified* and were in need of *consciousness raising.*

While this notion of false consciousness is reasonable and no doubt harmonizes with the intuition that someone can be deceived about their own experiences, it was in direct conceptual conflict with the reliance on women's experience as way to unite and connect all women and to define women's oppression. Any notion of "false consciousness" presupposes a "true consciousness," an accurate understanding of one's own experiences. But this leads back to a previously rejected objectivity, relying on some objective notion of what counts as oppression in order to interpret experience.[29] Women's experiences, which were supposed to be the only authoritative source of truth about women's oppression, were just being read and re-read through a pre-established feminist conclusion.

The upshot of all these problems, bluntly stated, is that women's subjective interpretation of their experiences cannot be the ground of feminist theory, as Judith Grant writes, ". . . if for no other reason than that it is impossible to discern those experiences authentically, and that attempting to do so has resulted in the imputing of experiences to some imagined universal Woman or group of women."[30] Joan Scott makes a parallel point about the use of "experience" as authority in historical research. She writes: "Experience is at once always already an interpretation and is in need of interpretation. What counts as experience is neither self-evident nor straightforward; it is always contested, always therefore political."[31]

If experience does not provide a solid theoretical basis for feminism, however, it is not at all clear that men can be excluded from being feminists or doing feminism because they lack an already suspect and inessential "experience." This is not to say that certain experiences cannot lead one to feminism, nor that certain experiences cannot shed crucial light on particular practices, but it is to say that what constitutes being a feminist is not an essentially female perspective on those female experiences.

Second: The other problem with relying on women's subjective experience as a ground and requisite for feminism, however, lies not merely in its conceptual coherence (which is significant enough) but also with its political efficacy and relevance for transforming society. Grant makes the point that "The test of a good feminist theory seems to no longer be, Will this help in the liberation of women? but rather, Does this reflect the female experience? These are two very different questions."[32] Indeed they are. A focus on women's experience and difference shapes feminism as primarily an identity extended from and dependent on the presumed identity of Woman, rather than primarily a set of beliefs and moral and political positions about women's liberation and the broader normative implications of gender categories. This identity focus is misleading. After all, having a woman's experience and perceiving as a woman isn't what makes a woman a feminist—plenty of them aren't. So then what does make a woman a feminist? Presumably, her beliefs, actions, political positions, and critical perspective.

To test the force of this idea, while writing this paper I went around my building (housing various humanities departments) and asked several self-identified feminists this question: "What is the difference between a woman and a feminist?" After a strange look or two, every response began more or less with "Well, feminists believe that . . ." or "Feminists take the position that . . ." followed by a varying list of political and moral positions. While making this very unscientific survey, I also noticed a sign attached to the door of the Women's Studies office that began with the phrase: "I'm not a feminist, but . . ." and then listed a number of questions about beliefs and positions such as: "Can a woman not marry or not have children and be happy? Should women be in positions of responsibility in government and in business? Should men take equal responsibility for housework and child rearing? Should women have an equal voice in politics?" This list was followed by the statement: "If you agree with the above items, you probably *are* a feminist!"

Now, what items should and should not be on these lists are, of course, up for debate. But the point is that these explanations and this poster suggest that what makes a feminist is belief, action, and position, not the subjective assessment of one's experience combined with a revelatory appreciation of one's objective gender identity.[33]

In fact, what seems to be important about being a feminist is not that someone perceives and understands *as a woman,* but that they perceive and understand *as a feminist.* As Grant writes: ". . . antifeminist women do not see feminism as being in their interests. This simply means that human relations look different when viewed through a feminist lens, but not necessarily simply from the perspective of women."[34] It is this feminist lens, this set of beliefs, suspicions, politics, actions, and critical views, that seems to be crucial for feminism, not gender identity, not one's sex. And what this feminist lens focuses on is not women per se, but on gender and its cultural treatment—on the limitations of gender, the constraints of gender, the production of gender, the normative implications of gender, the sexism and oppression that depends on particular gender orders and their valuations. Of course, this in no way means that women as women are ever ignored. A woman may no doubt experience oppression as a woman, be singled out as a woman, and treated horribly and unjustly by virtue of her perceived membership in that group. However, that singling out and that grouping are dependent on a hegemonic ideology of gender. Her oppression, the very core of the sexism that cuts at her, is dependent on the virulent sex system in which she finds herself.[35] But a feminist perspective on this is a perspective on gender, sexism, and oppression. A feminist intervention into this process is an attempt to change culture, to change gender ideology, in such a way that women are no longer oppressed. And of course, a change in gender ideology not only changes the classification and treatment of women but the classification and treatment of men. Therefore, what seems to be the ground of feminist praxis (and theory) is a critical assessment of and attack on ideologies of gender that lead to certain people being classified into certain groups and oppressed.

But if feminism is (or should be considered) a critical strategy, set of beliefs, and set of political positions and actions, then presumably there is no reason why men might not also be able to form this critical strategy or possess such beliefs and take such positions. Men, like anyone else, are feminists if they believe and do what feminists believe and do. If one still wants to argue that a woman and a man could have the same beliefs, actions, goals, and positions, but only the woman could be a feminist, then this is just an arbitrary weighting given to gender and as such should be subjected to the scrutiny of gender criticism itself.

Of course, focusing on beliefs and positions rather than identity and experience leads to the question of what beliefs and positions are necessary for feminism. No doubt there will continue to be debate about this, but we could start with an oft repeated position such as: Gender *by itself* should have no normative implications for who has power over whom— implying that men should not have power over women, simply because they are women. Given some minimal position statement like this, many people of many sexes are feminist.

6. Just Do Feminism

My conclusion then is that feminism should be about gender and the structures of sexism and oppression that arise from hierarchical evaluations of gender, not about the problematic ahistorical category of woman per se. Of course, all women, as categorized and treated differently by a gender ideology are themselves still subjects of feminism—as are men. Further, feminism should be characterized by adherence to a basic set of beliefs and political positions—which are aptly, if not uncomplicatedly, captured by most typical minimalist claims of eliminating gender-based power. There will still be vast diversity in how that plays out, but the core of feminism would be *feminist* positions, not *women's* experiences. As a result of this characterization, men can be feminists.[36]

Now, someone might suggest here that a feminism focused on gender and gender-based oppression rather than on women per se would be better called by another name, leaving *feminism* for those who prefer to locate feminism in the heart of women's lives and female sexual difference. Perhaps my position would better be called *genderism* or *anti-genderism* or *critical gender theory* or something to that effect. I suppose in some sense I would not be conceptually opposed to this, especially if there is fierce resistance to the notion that feminism is about gender ideology and not grounded on the universal category of Woman. But it seems unnecessary. Nothing about my characterization of feminism threatens to impede the liberation of women—provided liberation is not understood in terms of releasing or magnifying the "essential qualities" of women. And in fact, I expect that at least some feminists seem to have little or no problem with my analysis and suggestions. I think they will agree with Alison Jaggar, quoted on the back cover of a recent book on masculinity and feminist theory, when she writes: "The insights resulting from the authors' use of gender as a category for critical analysis demonstrate incisively that feminist philosophy is no longer by, about, or even for women only."[37]

Feminism, it turns out, is something we all can do.

Notes

I want to thank Tom Digby, Jennifer McCrickerd, Perry Stevens, and David Powell for their very helpful comments and suggestions on earlier drafts of this paper.

1. I should point out that in my four years of high school, Christian Family Living was taught by the same woman and it is entirely possible that at least some of the things she taught were her own intuitions, beliefs, or assessments of particular experiences. Other instructors might emphasize or de-emphasize other aspects of these psychological claims. In any event, class did not revolve entirely around lectures. We read books (still sold in Christian bookstores today—I went out and checked while writing this paper), listened to audio-tapes by prominent conservative Christian activists still popular today (such as James Dobson), and had guest speakers who made the national circuit of conservative Christian churches and schools. While no doubt some content of the class would be different now, I think it is safe to claim that the general tenor of the class represented mainstream conservative Christian ideology.

2. Since the U.S. Presidency is arguably the most powerful position in the world, it is often used as a "test case" to find out what one thinks about the psychological abilities of some class of individuals. It is worth noting, however, that not everyone at my school agreed that women were capable of being President. Some claimed, just as the stereotype might suggest, that PMS might pre-

vent a woman from being President because she might lose control at some critical point during her cycle, becoming irrational.

3. These sorts of concerns are also behind the rule in many conservative churches that exclude women from teaching Sunday school classes in which "saved" males are present—even if the males are only young boys.

4. The school was also partly a boarding institution with approximately three-fourths of the students living and working on campus.

5. It is not entirely evident, even to me, where my nascent feminism came from. It might have been due to observing my parents' relatively egalitarian marriage, from egalitarian moral messages on television, from following the adventures of numerous female heroes in my beloved science fiction and fantasy books, or who knows?—even genetics.

6. The slur I was most intrigued and disgusted by was simply "girl." Several male students in the class called each other "girls" as insults—something male coaches also did when criticizing their players. For an analysis of this phenomenon, see my paper "Gender Treachery: Homophobia, Masculinity and Threatened Identities" in *Rethinking Masculinity: Philosophical Explorations In Light of Feminism*, 2nd ed., edited by Larry May, Robert Strikwerda and Patrick D. Hopkins (Lanham, MD: Rowman & Littlefield, 1996), pp. 95–115; reprinted in *Free Spirits: Feminist Philosophers on Culture*, edited by K. Mehuron and G. Persecepe (New York: Prentice-Hall, 1994), pp. 419–433.

7. By saying this, I do not mean to suggest that children are merely neurological tabula rasa on whom culture can inscribe any gendered behavior. It may very well be the case that girls and boys are born with statistical tendencies toward certain kinds of behavior. But whatever these statistical biobehavioral differences might be, they cannot account for the actual resultant differences, or beliefs about differences, when so much of a child's developmental period is spent being rewarded and punished for acting like girls or boys.

8. Which lead some people to the not unfamiliar phenomenon of prefacing such beliefs by saying: "Now, I'm not a feminist, but . . ."

9. In the South, at least, it is common at family reunions for women to prepare all the food and work in the kitchen while the men sit in the living room or on the porch talking about hunting and football. When the food is ready, typically the men and children are served first and the women make up their plates afterward. This is changing somewhat, particularly as female teenagers fail to see the logic in this arrangement and get in line right along with the men. In any event, I preferred to work in the kitchen with the women both because it galled me that they did all the preparation and because their conversations were so much more interesting than the men's.

10. These nominal categories are themselves debated, of course. While these students variably called themselves "radical," "lesbian," and "separatist" feminists, they would also be labeled by other feminists as "cultural feminists" or by some, less charitably, as "fundamentalist feminists." It is important to note here, as I did with my Christian teachers, that these particular students, schooled in this particular program, cannot be said to represent all feminisms that are called "separatist" or "radical." There are significant differences between feminists about what "radical" means and what "separatist" means. There are, however, family resemblances among these positions, at least some of which were characteristic of these women's studies students. For the lack of a better term I shall

usually use "cultural feminism" to refer to this family of ideas, though sometimes will defer to individuals' self-description as "radical" or "separatist."

11. It was not always clear if these differences were attributed to biology, culture, ego-formation experience, or spirit. While many of the feminists in this class claimed to believe in some sort of social constructivism, it was never clear what they meant by this. In any case, women and men and their differences were talked about unproblematically, as if they were clear and distinct kinds.

12. I do not mean to suggest that all these writers have the same positions, only that they are considered more or less advocates of a radical feminism, sometimes also called cultural feminism. As such, they are often differentiated from liberal feminists, socialist feminists, or postmodern feminists. It was also the case that most feminists I had met before, whether liberal NOW-style feminists, postmodern academics, or psychoanalytically oriented feminists considered this sort of cultural feminism passé.

13. It is important to point out here that I do not consider myself to have been "oppressed" in this class. For starters, this one small class was a tiny point on the cultural landscape (if the views expressed in it were the dominant ideology, however, then my reaction might have been different). I should also reiterate that this one class, in this one program, does not represent all feminists—any more than my Christian Family Living class represents the views of all Christians. I make this point because it is not unusual for uncritical readers to take incidents like these and use them as "evidence" that feminism is just as militant and oppressive as patriarchy—or for that matter to claim that all Christianity is oppressive. I would ask then, that the reader not take the views I describe as paradigmatic of all feminists, or of all Christians, and then condemn these movements in a broad sweep—though on the other side, I would also argue that the reader should feel free to criticize and render judgments on these *particular* views without being accused of anti-feminist, or anti-Christian sentiment.

14. For example, in language, students' names that had suffixes of "man" or "son" (such as Loehman or Simpson) were sometimes changed to suffixes like "daughter" or were dropped altogether.

15. It is not at all unusual for some cultural practice to enforce what is supposed to be "natural." The obvious problem is: If something is "natural" why does it have to be enforced? Why does it have to be taught? Often, what is "natural" is what culture teaches us, obscuring its own cultural origins.

16. Let me make it clear that I do not assume here that appealing to personal experience is a particularly or intrinsically valuable way to analyze the larger issues. Nor do I assume that personal experience is an objective guide. In this case I draw on autobiographical experience more as a close and accessible social datum that can inform theoretical critique. It may also be the case that I have a relatively unusual experience that can highlight some theoretical problems. In any event, perhaps a narrative of two very different gendered locations in the world, experienced by the same individual (setting the philosophical problems of "same" aside for the moment) can shed light on the way in which "maleness" and "masculinity" are more ephemeral, contextual, and complicated than sometimes thought, which draws into question the value of including or excluding individuals from the class of "feminists" based on their supposed possession.

17. Of course, when we begin inserting the names of individual, actual women,

problems do arise. Many of us, especially in academe, know women whom we would not consider feminists, whom we would not want to teach feminist courses, who have taken on the mantle of "feminism" opportunistically in order to teach extra classes or make their vita more appealing. But this is rather the point—the category of "women" isn't that effective in relating individual women to feminism.

18. This kind of thing is also often assumed among male faculty and administrators who believe that men can not or should not teach courses in feminist theory or women's studies.

19. The term "masculinity" is necessarily fuzzy here. I will use it as a catch-all term suggesting "characteristics of men" and "characteristic of being male." To define it more than that assumes too much too soon.

20. Judith Butler, *Gender Trouble: Feminism and the Subversion of Identity* (New York: Routledge, 1990), p. 122–23.

21. It might amuse some readers to find that among some feminists, particularly gay male ones, radical feminists such as MacKinnon and Dworkin have been referred to as "typical straight men"—alluding to their essentialist, exclusionary, confrontational, and statist practices which happened to match up nicely with their own characterizations of "masculine" behavior.

22. Rosi Braidotti, *Nomadic Subjects: Embodiment and Sexual Difference in Contemporary Feminist Theory* (New York: Columbia University Press, 1994), pp. 138–139.

23. Ibid., 137.

24. Stephen Heath, "Male Feminism," in Alice Jardine and Paul Smith, ed., *Men in Feminism* (Routledge: New York, 1987), p. 1.

25. Judith Grant has written a tremendously clear, useful, insightful, thought-provoking, and information-packed, though succinct, book on this subject. She explains and investigates three core concepts of feminist thought, including the category of Woman and of experience. I am indebted to her in this section of the paper. I also strongly recommend to anyone interested in feminist theory that they read Grant's *Fundamental Feminism: Contesting the Core Concepts of Feminist Theory* (Routledge: New York, 1993).

26. See Grant, *Fundamental Feminism*, especially ch. 2.

27. This is not to say that class, and especially race, are in fact easily or objectively definable. They are also very complicated terms.

28. Grant, *Fundamental Feminism*, 31.

29. Ibid., 32.

30. Ibid., 160.

31. Joan W. Scott, "Experience" in Judith Butler and Joan W. Scott, ed., *Feminist Theorize the Political* (New York: Routledge, 1992), p. 37.

32. Grant, 156–57.

33. Not, as Braidotti puts it: "Feminism is also the liberation of women's ontological desire to be female subjects . . ." Braidotti, *Nomadic Subjects*, 144.

34. Grant, 181.

35. Even as I write this, a fundamentalist revolution in Afghanistan demonstrates the evil which metastasizes out of the heart of sexism. As theology students and peasants take over the capitol, women are forced to quit their jobs, to swath themselves in heavy clothing from head to toe to avoid "tempting" men, are not allowed to leave their homes without a husband's permission, and are

beaten or killed for violations of these orders. Some widows, who no longer have husbands to give them permission to leave the house, are starving.

36. The issues of exclusion addressed here have been mostly ones of epistemology and conceptual coherence. However, there is another argument for excluding even admittedly feminist men from feminist activities. It is a pragmatic sociological argument which says: Women have been trained to respond in detrimental ways around men—overtrusting, deferential, nurturing, and self-sacrificing. As such, men should not be allowed in some female groups—such as women's studies classes or support groups, because their mere presence by itself will be disruptive. While this argument is an important one, it deserves a lengthy treatment I do not have room for here. So let me just make five preliminary points:

a) If the strong version of these empirical claim are true, then it would no doubt count as a reason for excluding men from certain contexts. If men unavoidably prevent women from learning or some other beneficial activity, they should be excluded.

b) However, this argument would not only apply to women's studies classes or women's support groups. If accurate, it might apply to all settings. If women are damaged by men's sheer presence in a class, for example, they are damaged whether the class is Intro. to Women's Studies, Calculus, or the History of Jazz. This is in fact, an argument now being used for separate girls' math and science classes in public high schools.

c) It is not clear, even if such empirical claims are true (and they may very well be overgeneralizations) that the best course of action is to accede to statistical tendencies. Perhaps having men in classes or other groups who were sensitive to such issues would be more beneficial, because they could help train women out of such deleterious behavioral patterns.

d) Sometimes part of this argument says that women and girls tend to accept claims from men much more readily than from women, having been trained to defer to men. If that is true (though it seems overgeneralized) then it might be a reason for having *more men than women teaching feminist classes* because it would imply that students would take feminist claims from men's mouths more seriously.

e) Arguments about sociological and psychological facts must be taken seriously. However, it should not be assumed that these arguments for exclusion are only those of morally sensitive progressives. The very same arguments used to exclude male feminists from teaching Women's Studies, or white antiracists from teaching African American Studies, or Christians from teaching Jewish Studies, are used to exclude gays and lesbian from the military and women from military colleges—among other cases. In both of these latter cases, the argument is not that gays, lesbians, and women cannot be good soldiers, but only that straight and male soldiers will not function well around them because of negative attitudes. Since the only question is one of efficiency, gays, lesbians, and women must be excluded from military contexts—even though the fault lies entirely with some heterosexual men's dispositions. Now, this comparison proves nothing about the former cases (they all may be good arguments), but it does illustrate that issues of just treatment are often in conflict with issues of efficacy whether decorated lesbian officers are being kicked out of the army or good male feminists are being excluded from teaching.

37. May, Strikwerda and Hopkins, *Rethinking Masculinity*, back cover.

Chapter 3

Who's Afraid of Men Doing Feminism?

Michael S. Kimmel

Can men *do* feminism? Ought men to do it? What happens when they do? These are questions with which I am constantly confronted, in my pedagogy, and in both my public and private lives.

Each year, I'm invited to give about twenty or more lectures at colleges and universities all over the country. Usually, the invitation comes from a coalition of women's studies faculty, sociologists, and the occasional student organization that has actually heard of NOMAS (The National Organization for Men Against Sexism, of which I am National Spokesperson) or my work. (On rare occasions, the funding comes from both the Women's Studies and the Intrafraternity Council—often the first time those organizations have collaborated on anything!) The motives for the invitation are similar. In each case, the Women's Studies faculty tell me that they feel frustrated by the fact that their courses have roughly the same gender composition today as they had twenty years ago. Today, they tell me, they typically have only one or two men in a class, and they spend much of their time cringing defensively in the corner, feeling blamed for the collective sins of two millennia of patriarchal oppression. Colleagues who teach more general courses on gender issues like Sociology of Gender or Psychology of Gender report only slightly less skewed gender composition of their classes. These colleagues believe, as I do, that it is imperative to find ways to bring men into the conversation about gender issues that women have been having for more than two decades.

That, then, is the starting point for my lecture. I try to explain why virtually every month there is a new name added to that growing list of men who have come to symbolize the gender issues currently in play. I began to work on that lecture the day after Clarence Thomas had been confirmed to his appointment to the Supreme Court. I sat down to write a short op-ed piece for a local newspaper about the ways in which Anita Hill's testimony opened up an opportunity for men to rethink the ways we had been taught to treat women in our workplaces. I called the piece "Clarence . . . and Us" to suggest the ways in which what I believe Clarence Thomas did to Anita Hill is not as atypical as it might at first have sounded. In fact, what most middle-aged men probably were taught was "typical office behavior"—explicit requests for dates, implicit sexual innuendos, assumptions that seniority has its privileges of access to women, pornographic pinups or calendars on the walls —might now be called sexual harassment. I argued that it was about time men took on the issue of sexual harassment.

A few months later, I was invited to expand upon that op-ed piece in a lecture. Wave after wave of women had been coming forward in the aftermath of Anita Hill's compelling testimony, describing their experiences in the workplace. Suddenly men seemed so confused, so defensive and resistant to what they were saying. William Kennedy Smith and Mike Tyson were standing trial for date rape. It seemed another opportunity for us addled, middle-aged men to rethink what we had been taught as adolescents, for what I grew up calling "dating etiquette" or even just plain "dating"—to keep trying to get sex, to see sexual conquest as an entitled right, to wear down her resistance, to keep going despite that resistance—is now called date rape. Mike Tyson and William Kennedy Smith were not, it seemed to me, monsters, but men, assuming and doing what regular guys had been doing and assuming for a very long time. Here, again was an opportunity to rethink what we had been taught, and I was determined to raise these issues so that we could rethink our own behaviors and assumptions.

Then Magic Johnson announced that he was HIV positive, and that he had contracted the virus through unprotected heterosexual contact with any one of the more than two thousand five hundred women whom he had "accommodated" sexually—that was his term for it—during his career as a sexual athlete.

Suddenly, it seemed that America was taking a crash course on masculinity, on masculine sexual entitlement, aggression and abuse, and our instructors were Anita Hill, Patricia Bowman, Desiree Washington, and any one of those anonymous two thousand five hundred women whom Magic Johnson had "obliged." Just as suddenly, American corporations, state and local governments, universities and law firms were scrambling to implement procedures to handle sexual harassment. Many seemed motivated more by fear of lawsuits than a general concern for women's welfare, more interested in adjudicating harassment after the fact than in developing mechanisms to prevent it.

Many men reacted defensively. "Men on Trial" was a common headline in newspapers and magazines. And other men seemed interested in more of a defensive retreat, running off to the woods to chant, drum, and *bond* with other men. It hardly seems coincidental that 1991 was the same year that the American media discovered the "men's movement," and in which Robert Bly's *Iron John* and Sam Keen's *Fire in the Belly* soared to the top of the best-seller lists. Just when women had found a voice through which they could finally speak about their experiences, men declared themselves tired of listening, and then trooped off to the woods to be by themselves.

I tried to address these themes in that lecture, paying attention to what I saw as the possibilities for change that these cases presented to us, as men, possibilities to think about our selves, and our relations with women in new ways. I titled that first lecture "Clarence, William, Iron Mike, Magic . . . and Us: Issues for Men in the 1990s."

Since then, I've given that lecture at over one-hundred colleges and universities. And virtually each month I have to revise the title to reflect the steady stream of men's names that capture the issues with which I think we are struggling. Today, I might give it the title "Clarence, William, Iron Mike, Magic, Senator Packwood, Woody, Tailhook, the U.S. Military, Spur Posse, John Wayne Bobbitt, The Citadel, Tupac, O.J. . . . and Us." The students usually get the point.

In the course of the lecture, I point to the ways in which women's lives have changed in the past thirty years, and how these changes have forever transformed the landscape upon which gender relations are carried out. I try and cover a lot of ground: sexuality, date and acquaintance rape, AIDS, the workplace, the balance of work and family life, sexual harassment. In every case, I suggest that men should want to support feminist reforms: not only because of an ethical imperative—of course, it is right and just—but also because men will live happier and healthier lives, with better relations with the women, men, and children in their lives if they do. I take as an epigraph a line from a 1917 essay by the Greenwich Village writer Floyd Dell. "Feminism," he wrote, "will make it possible for the first time for men to be free."

When I'm finished, the reaction is almost always the same: a substantial contingent of feminist women students visibly and vocally appreciate my lecture. A smaller—much smaller—contingent of male students come up afterwards and thank me, usually asking what they can do on their particular campus. The Women's Studies faculty and sociologists are also usually pleased. I feel good, as though I've contributed to an opening of dialogue between women and men on the campus.

Then the criticism comes, and always from two sources. First, there are what I've come to call the angry-white-men-in-training. These young men are defensive, angry, and fully resistant to anything that remotely hints of

feminism. Armed with the latest platitudes from Rush Limbaugh, the
proceed to offer the false stereotypes of feminist women that we've a
come to know and detest. They whoop and holler as if the lecture hac
become a daytime television talk show bashing feminism. (It is significant that a discussion of men is so easily transformed into another opportunity to trash feminist women.) In about one in five lectures, I experience
something like the following, which happened recently.

A burly white male student, sitting in the back row, arms folded across
his chest, the brim of his baseball hat turned around, raised his hand as
the moderator for the evening's lecture announced there was time for one
more question. "What makes you such an expert on men?" he began
with a challenge masquerading as a question. "The way you talk about
listening to women, and supporting feminism, you must be a faggot or
something. You sure aren't a real man."

I shifted to a kind of mental remote control, and tossed his question
back to him. I asked what was it about my support for feminism that
made him think I might be gay. He declined to pick up the question and
disengaged, mumbling inaudibly. The lecture ended.

No matter how many times I've been gay-baited, been rhetorically or
literally called out, my manhood questioned, I'm still somewhat startled
by it. Why would some people believe that supporting feminism is somehow a revelation of sexual orientation? I offer no clues to my sexuality in
my lectures or in my writing, no references to the gender of a "friend,"
"partner," or "lover." All I do is agree with women that inequality based
on gender is wrong, and that women and men should be equal in both the
public and the private spheres.

Does this make me less of a real man? The reviewer of one of my
books, a collection of men's writings examining the feminist debate about
pornography, called me a "traitor." Another wrote that anyone who supports equality for women or for gays must be a wimp.

The second critical reaction is more complex, and somewhat more
troubling. One or two feminist women express their displeasure at my
lecture by poking holes in my argument, revealing what they see as inconsistencies and contradictions. Their followup questions and the ensuing
discussion unravel quickly to what one might call "patriarchy-baiting,"
trying to elicit some reaction, some slip-up, some element of defensiveness, some point of weakness that will reveal my own patriarchal biases.
These are inevitably revealed, to which their response is a loudly triumphant "Aha, we knew it!" and a quieter, but no less pronounced sigh
of relief. All men *are* the same, and that *same* is patriarchal.

What are these two groups so afraid of? Why can't men *do* feminism,
or at least be seen to support feminism? After all, feminism provides both
women *and men* with an extraordinarily powerful analytic prism

through which to understand their lives, and a political and moral imperative to transform the unequal conditions of those relationships. Why should men be afraid of feminism? And why should some feminist women be afraid of profeminist men?

To address these question, two caveats are in order. First, to address the former question, we must make a distinction between feminism as that analytic prism and feminism as a set of policy initiatives designed to remove obstacles to public sphere participation for women. After all, although most American men remain, at best, indifferent, and, at worst openly hostile, to the term feminism, and especially dismissive of the term feminist, it is also the case that most men support every single element in what we might call a feminist political and social policy agenda when its elements are disaggregated and presented as simple policy options. And second, in addressing the latter question, I want to be clear that I do not intend to be a ventriloquist, explaining women's experiences for them. Instead, I speak from my experience as a man whose work is devoted to making feminism, as I understand it, apprehensible and even acceptable to men.

While I will want to address each of these fears of feminism separately, I want to pause to point out one significant similarity. In both cosmologies, profeminist men cannot exist. To the angry white men, profeminist *men* cannot exist, and so their effort is to unmask me as a fraud of a man. Hence the gay baiting and wimp baiting, which often amount to the same thing. To that small group of feminist women, *profeminist* men cannot exist, because such men are potential allies, not enemies. So often these women, like the angry white males, discredit the motives or intentions of the men who support them. To move feminism forward, both as a cluster of theories and as a political project, I believe that we will need to honestly confront both of these fears of feminism.

I begin by speculating about the fear that some feminist women have of profeminist men, based upon my conversations with several of these women who have challenged and pushed these issues. Each of their perspectives is doubtless true, but even taken together, they are not the whole truth.

To some women, fear of profeminist men comes from a fear of men in general. All men are men, monolithically constructed essences, incapable of change. In this model, some things are eternal verities, always signifying the same thing. Erections signify domination and nothing else. Men embody unmediated patriarchal oppression. To be a man means to be an oppressor.

Thus *we*—men who could support feminism—cannot be said to exist if the polar dichotomy by which they see the world is to remain in place. In some cases, of course, this is more complicated than a simple "women good, men bad" world view. Rather, I understand these women to say that since all men benefit from patriarchy in a myriad of ways, seen and unseen, it is not possible for men to renounce patriarchy and come over to the other side. Since privilege is indelibly inscribed onto men, and men embody it whether they choose to or not, then the only possibility for men to be redeemed is for them to renounce masculinity itself. One simply cannot be a man and support feminism. (This position is also echoed by some men, like political activist John Stoltenberg, who encourages men to "refuse to be a man" in his first book, and celebrates the "end" of manhood in his second.) We can always retreat if the going gets tough or dangerous. This would be especially true for heterosexual white men, who can slide seemingly without effort, into the arenas of privilege, which often remain invisible to those who have it.

To others, it's simply too easy for men to declare themselves profeminist. They fear a syndrome among men that a friend of mine has labeled "premature self-congratulation," in which men declare themselves liberated by masculine fiat. Or they observe that cinematic trope in which profeminist men, like the cavalry, come to the rescue of the damsel in distress. "Thanks for bringing this patriarchy stuff to our attention, ladies," they can almost hear us say. "We'll take it from here." What have they given up, what risks do they take, by declaring their support of feminism?

To still others, the expression of a fear of profeminist men is triggered more by what I actually argue in my lecture than by anything I might be seen to embody. Although I suggest that the ethical imperative—that feminist reforms are right and just—should be the basis for men's support for feminism, I also argue that it is in men's interests to support feminism, that men will actually *benefit* from their support of feminism. I argue that men's efforts to end sexual harassment, date and acquaintance rape, to share housework and child care will actually enable men to have more fulfilling lives, more satisfying relationships with women, with children and with other men. "Just what we need," one woman sneered derisively, "a feminism that will benefit men. Count me out."

One expression of this fear of feminism is a particular hostility to men who have embraced feminism in the academy and are using a feminist perspective to understand gender relations. No sooner do women get a foothold on a legitimate domain in the academy than men rush in to a new growth area, displacing women and setting up shop, much the way obstetricians and gynecologists displaced midwives at the turn of the century, or that men are entering nursing as other fields dry up.

There is, perhaps, some truth in this. But for every male academic who uses feminist analysis as the framework for their work, there are hundreds, even thousands, who remain resolutely and defiantly hostile to the idea of feminism as a theory in the first place. I do not purport to do this new academic practice called "Men's Studies," which sounds so defensively reactive, as if it were the academic wing of the men's rights movement. I simply *do* the sociology of gender. I do it from a feminist perspective, which takes as its starting point that gender relations are constructed in a field of power. And the gender that I study is men.

I believe that each of these positions seems partly true. Privilege is invisibly but indelibly conferred upon men, whether we renounce it or not. But there are also costs to men for renouncing it, costs that the antifeminist men recognize more readily, if less enthusiastically, then these few feminist women. The reaction of men to feminism does, I believe contain an angle of vision that needs to be addressed.

That issue concerns power. Feminism requires an analysis of power; indeed, one of feminism's central tenets is that gender relations are constructed in a field of power. At the political level, feminism addressed a symmetry in women's lives. At the aggregate level, women were not *in power*. Just look at those corporate boardrooms, those collegiate boards of trustees, those legislatures and executive mansions, feminist women said. It's evident that women are not in power. And, at the individual level, women did not *feel powerful*. Feminism, then, was a political movement to challenge women's social powerlessness and their individual feelings of powerlessness.

But that tidy symmetry breaks down when applied to men. Sure, men are *in power* at the aggregate level. Again, the gender composition of those legislatures, board rooms and trustees don't lie. But ask individual men to *give up* power and you are more likely to get a blank, defensive stare, as if you were from another planet. "What are you talking about?," the men will respond. "I have no power. My wife bosses me around, my children boss me around, my boss bosses me around. I'm completely powerless!"

Several groups on the political front privilege men's experience of powerlessness and ignore the continued social aggregate power of men over women as groups. Antifeminist purveyors of men's rights, like Warren Farrell, claim that male power is a "myth." "Feel powerless?" he seems to say. "Of course, you do. Women have all the power. Currently, we men are the real victims of reverse discrimination, affirmative action, custody and alimony laws. Let's get some of that power back from those feminists!"

Some of the followers of Robert Bly and other leaders in the mythopoetic men's movement also seem to privilege the personal feeling over the social and political analysis. If you don't feel powerful, then you're not powerful. "Come with us into the woods," they seem to say. "We'll go get some power. Here's the power chant, the power ritual, the power drumming." I remember a few years ago when mainstream American men, who were supposed to feel such renewed power under Reaganism, resorted to wearing power ties and eating power lunches to demonstrate their power—as if power were a fashion accessory. What better expression of political and economic impotence than to be eating and wearing the signs of one's power!

Farrell frequently uses the analogy of the chauffeur to illustrate the illusion of men's power. Think about a chauffeur. He's in the driver's seat. He knows where he's going. He's wearing the uniform. So, you might say, he has the power. But from *his* perspective, someone else is giving the orders. He's not powerful at all. His power is a *myth*.

This analogy has some limited value: individual men are not powerful, at least all but a small handful of individual men. And most American men do not feel powerful. But the analogy is right for the wrong reasons. What if we ask one question of our chauffeur, and try to shift the frame just a little, to reveal what is hidden by the analogy. What is the gender of the person who *is* giving the orders? Who is sitting in the back seat?

When we shift from the analysis of the individual's experience of his position to a different, relational context, the interactions between and among men become clear as relations of power. Of course, men as a group do have power, and that power is organized against women. But some men also have power over other men. Profeminism, a position that acknowledges men's experience without privileging it, possesses the tools to bring those levels together, to both adequately analyse men's aggregate power, and also describe the ways in which individual men are both privileged by that social level of power and feel powerless in the face of it.

It seems to me that men's defensiveness reaches its zenith around the question of power, as if to identify and challenge men's power was to ignore men's pain. Such a trade-off is unacceptable politically, and, frankly a non sequitur. Men's pain is caused by men's power. What else could it be? Would we say that the unhappiness of white people was caused by black people's power? The pains and sexual problems of heterosexuals was caused by gays and lesbians? Profeminism requires that both men's social power and individual powerlessness be understood as mutually reinforcing, linked experiences, both of which derive from men's aggregate social power.

For men to support feminism, it seems to me, means acknowledging men's experience of powerlessness, which often makes feminist women uneasy, while placing it within a context of men's aggregate power—the power of men as a group over women as a group, and the power of some men over other men. Disaggregating the term *masculinity* into its plural masculinities is one way to address that second dimension of power. Some men are disempowered by virtue of class, race, ethnicity, sexuality, age, able-bodiedness. But all men are privileged vis-a-vis women.

There is another dimension that must be addressed with men, and upon

.t pivots our political work as men who seek to support feminism and challenge other men. It requires adding another dimension to the discussion of power and powerlessness—the issue of entitlement. I recently appeared on a television talk show opposite three "angry white males" who felt that they had been the victims of workplace discrimination. The show's title, no doubt to entice a large potential audience, was "A Black Woman Took My Job." In my comments to these angry men, I invited them to consider what the word "my" meant in that title, that they felt that the jobs were originally "theirs," that they were entitled to them, and that when some "other" person—black, female—got the job, that person was really taking "their" job. But by what right is that his job? By convention, by a historical legacy of such profound levels of discrimination that we have needed decades of affirmative action to even begin to make slightly more level a playing field that has tilted so decidedly in one direction.

Men's sense of entitlement is the source of much of men's experience of powerlessness. Consider the work of Robert Bly. The reaction to Bly's *Iron John* was curious in at least one respect. Readers of the book, as well as virtually all the men I've observed at mythopoetic retreats—men who are, themselves, fathers, and, indeed, often even grandfathers—identify with the young boy in the fairy tale. There are three other men in the story with whom one could identify: the boy's father (the king), the father of the woman that the boy eventually marries (another king), and Iron John himself (who turns out to also have been a king). Three kings and one little boy. And all these fifty year old men, fathers themselves, identify as the boy, not as any of the kings. What are we to make of this?

Let us ask who exactly is the little boy. He is a prince—that is, he is a man who is entitled to be in power but who is not yet in power. He will be; he is entitled to it. But not yet. In short, he is entitled to power, but feels powerless.

It is from this place—shall we call it the "Inner Prince"?—that I believe men speak, a place of gnawing, yawning anxiety, a place of entitlement unfulfilled. No wonder men are defensive when we present feminism to them. It feels like they will be forced to give up their sense of entitlement. Feminism, to men, feels like loss—a loss of the possibility to claim their birthright of power.

And when men feel their entitlement being snatched from them, they are likely to lash out. Thus, for example, the media-created mischaracterizations of feminist women as man-hating harpies seeking to dethrone academic standards and demolish democracy and individual freedom. Feminists are, in fact, "reasonable creatures," as feminist essayist Katha Pollitt titles her book, capable of sound judgement, informed opinions, and justifiable outrage at continued injustice. They're feminists because they know that feminism will enlarge the arena of individual freedom for women and ensure their equality and safety under the law. Those ideals seem as American as apple pie and fatherhood. And feminist women do not hate men. Most of the feminist women I've met love us enough to believe in men's ability to change, despite the pain they have endured both institutionally and individually from a world dominated by men.

Much of this vilification of feminists as man haters coincides with men's fear of feminism. The media assassination attempt, after all, reinscribes men as the centerpiece of the feminist project. Feminism is not about empowering or protecting women (or, obviously, both); rather, feminism is about hating men. Men are, after all, still the center of the universe—as they are entitled to be. To characterize feminism as an ideology that is about men is to return the framework of political ideas to the position to which men are entitled. The world revolves around men, either positively or negatively charged. And, according to Harry Brod, much of men's fear of feminism is not that it is about men's loss of power, but that it is not *about* men at all. If men are redundant, irrelevant, or even insignificant to the feminist project, then the world as we men have come to expect it is no longer a familiar one.

Profeminist men become targets for such anger as well as do feminist women. When hegemonic manhood is threatened, it almost always lashes out sexually. Thus do all the *others* become sexualized—black men, Latinos, and Italians become rapacious beasts, and profeminist men become feminism's court eunuchs, emasculated pussy-whipped wimps. Our masculinity is questioned, usually by questioning our heterosexuality. Any man who supports feminism cannot be a real man, hence he must be gay. Thus does internalized homophobia often keep men from supporting feminism.

Contemporary men did not invent this equation. We are in good company. I spent five years researching the history of men who have supported women's equality in the United States. Since 1776, these profeminist men have included a pantheon of respected Americans who supported women's rights to equality in the workplace, the classroom, and the polling place, who believed that women had the right to control their own bodies, their own names, and their own property. Men like Thomas Paine, William Lloyd Garrison, Frederick Douglass, Walt Whitman, Wendell Phillips, Robert Dale Owen, W.E.B. DuBois, John Dewey, Matthew Vassar, and Rabbi Stephen Wise. (The results of this research were published in *Against the Tide: Profeminist Men in the United States, 1776–1990*, a documentary history, published in 1992.)

And ever since the origins of the American women's movement, profeminist men have had their manhood questioned. Profeminist men were consistently vilified by other men, jeered as they marched in demonstrations, mocked in the media, and occasionally, even physically attacked. The day after he gave the rousing speech at the First Woman's Rights

Convention that turned the tide toward the suffrage plank, Frederick Douglass was vilified in the Syracuse newspapers as an "Aunt Nancy Man," an antebellum term for wimp. Another recalled that when he marched in suffrage parades with the Men's League for Woman Suffrage, onlookers shouted "Look at the skirts!"

When he marched in the great parades for Woman Suffrage in the first decades of the century, playwright George Middleton recalled being heckled with such cries as "Take that handkerchief out of your cuff" and "You forgot to shave this morning." And the anonymous author of a profeminist pamphlet called *How it Feels to be the Husband of a Suffragette* noted that he did not wash the dishes in his home (neither did his wife) despite the fact that "something over 11,863 of you requested me to go home and wash them on the occasion of that first suffrage parade." Even the *New York Times* anticipated that male marchers would "be called endearing names by small boys on the sidewalk," but extended to the male suffragists their "sympathy and admiration."

Opponents of feminism always questioned the virility of any man who supported women's rights. In 1913, Senator Heflin of Alabama (grandfather of Senator Howard Heflin) made this charge explicit. "I do not believe that there is a red blooded man in the world who in his heart really believes in woman suffrage. I think every man who favors it ought to be made to wear a dress."

Such sentiments contain two false equations. There's the implicit equation of manhood with oppression and inequality—as if real men support injustice. And there's the equation of supporting gender equality with effeminacy—as if only "failed men" could learn how to listen to women's pain and anger. But feminist women can also take a lesson here. Men do stand to lose something by supporting feminism—our standing in the world of men. There are some costs to our public position as profeminists.

What can we do to challenge these fears of feminism? One thing that seems necessary is to clearly and carefully demarcate men's relationship to feminism, particularly what ways men can support feminism. What is the best way for men to support feminism, and for feminist women to welcome men to the struggle? I believe that we might begin by considering ourselves the Gentleman's Auxiliary of Feminism. This is, to my mind, an honorable position, one that acknowledges that this is a revolution of which we are a part, but not the central part, not its most significant part.

It will be the task of this Gentlemen's Auxiliary to make feminism comprehensible to men, not as a loss of power, which has thus far failed to trickle down to most individual men anyway, but as a challenge to that false sense of entitlement to that power in the first place. Like all auxiliary organizations, I think we need to remain accountable to headquarters.

In the conclusion to a recent article in *The New Republic*, sociologist Orlando Patterson outlined an ineluctable feature of all social change movements. Speaking of the movement for racial justice, he wrote that

> ... the burden of racial and ethnic change always rests on a minority group. Although both whites and blacks have strong mutual interests in solving their racial problem, though the solution must eventually come from both, blacks must play the major role in achieving this objective—not only because they have more to gain from it but also because whites have far less to lose from doing nothing. It is blacks who must take the initiative, suffer the greater pain, define and offer the more creative solutions, persevere in the face of obstacles and paradoxical outcomes, insist that improvements are possible and maintain a climate of optimism concerning the eventual outcome.

So too, I would propose, with feminism. Profeminist men are, as we social scientists like to say, necessary but not sufficient elements in feminism's eventual success. We can be its cheerleaders, its allies, its footsoldiers, and we must be so in front of other men, risking our own fears of rejection, our own membership in the club of masculinity, confronting our own fears of other men. But what choice do we have—we, women and men, who embrace a vision of sexual equality and gender justice?

Acknowledgments

This paper was originally prepared for a session on "Fear of Feminism" at the annual meetings of the American Philosophical Association, New York City, 28 December, 1995. I am grateful to Amy Aronson, Harry Brod, and Tom Digby for their comments on an earlier version.

Chapter 4

On Your Knees:
Carnal Knowledge, Masculine Dissolution,
Doing Feminism

Brian Pronger

When the question arises whether men can do feminism or can even actually *be* feminists, the answer is often constructed as a matter of deciding what it takes, personally, politically, philosophically, or biologically, to fit the category "feminist." I would like to refrain from deciding who can be what and speak instead of states of desire that prevent men from embodying feminist insights, and alternatively, I want to explore forms of desire that could help men become feminist. What sort of desire would make it easier for men to appreciate feminist insights? I am speaking here not of an achievement that once recognized by authorities might qualify one to be a feminist, as passing a set of examinations qualify one to be a doctor, priest, psychotherapist, accountant, or professional hockey coach. I am thinking instead of reflective practices that could help men experience feminist desire.

I am focusing on desire because it seems to me that implicit in the question of men doing feminism is the energy of desire: men desiring not only the status of "feminist" but, more so, the desire to actualize life in more feminist than masculinist forms. This paper, consequently, will be about the nature of masculinity, a socio-cultural discourse that is (re)produced in bodies, actualized by desire. I will begin by briefly outlining what I mean by the body and desire, by sketching a theory of the relationship between desire and discourse and by specifying what I mean by the discourse of masculinity. I will then describe the tension between masculine and feminist forms of desire, and conclude by suggesting some practical bodily moves that men who experience masculine desire can make in order to open their bodies to the possibilities of feminism.

This short essay is certainly not intended to be an exhaustive account of the body, desire and gender, but is guided by the much more modest goal of suggesting some practical strategies for men who desire feminist ways of life. To explore these possibilities I will borrow, liberally but selectively, from the collaborative work of Gilles Deleuze and Félix Guattari (Deleuze and Guattari 1983; Deleuze and Guattari 1987), which analyzes the intersections of desire and discourse as crucial to the organization of (post)modern life and which suggests emancipatory strategies for dealing with that organization. Brian Massumi, in his *User's Guide to Capitalism and Schizophrenia: Deviations from Deleuze and Guattari*, points out that Deleuze imagines philosophical concepts not as components of great philosophical edifices, but as offering tools that help one dismantle various oppressive edifices [such as gender]. Deleuze "calls his kind of philosophy 'pragmatics'; because its goal is the invention of concepts that do not add up to a system of belief or an architecture of propositions that you either enter or you don't, but instead pack a potential in the way a crowbar in a willing hand evokes an energy of prying" (1992, 8). Similarly, I am suggesting tools that could create the energy to pry apart masculine desire.

For Deleuze and Guattari, the body is not fundamentally a biological organism, a physiological form of existence that is in some way subject to socio-cultural discourses. The body is a form of energy that is produced in historical discourses; understanding it as a biological organism is one, particularly modern way of organizing its energies, of setting the course for desire. The body is not an object that experiences desire; it is the power of desire, which Deleuze and Guattari understand not as lack (the desire for that which one does not have), but as the free flow of productive energy, the power of human being/becoming/actuality. Desire, they say, is "a process of production without reference to any exterior agency" (Deleuze and Guattari 1987, 154). Desire is a power in and of itself, ontologically prior to physiological function, morality, or any other cultural reference, although desire is a resource for any of these constructions. Just as the water flowing down a river is ontologically prior to hydroelectric development and tourism, desire can be shaped by cultural imperatives. While desire is operative in sexual reproduction, it is not confined either to reproduction or genital sexuality. For Deleuze and Guattari, desire extends well beyond what is known generically as sex (love-making, casual genital encounters, sado-masochistic scenes, and the like). Desire is the life force by which we move, by which we are engaged in being or becoming at all.

Desire (the body) is produced historically in the tension between two forms of power: *puissance* and *pouvoir*. Massumi defines them succinctly as follows:

Puissance refers to a range of potential. It has been defined by Deleuze as a "capacity for existence," "a capacity to affect or be affected" [which refers not to emotion, but to the augmentation or diminution of the body's capacity to act], a capacity to multiply connections that may be realized by a given "body" to varying degrees in different situations. . . . It is used in French translation of Nietzsche's "will to power.". . . The authors use *pouvoir* in a sense very close to Foucault's, as an instituted and reproducible relation of force, a selective concretization of potential. (Massumi 1992, xvii)

The *puissance* of the body is its power to connect, to be connected, to make connections. *Pouvoir* is a form of power that "territorializes" *puissance,* our capacity for making connections, thus governing the connective potential of human existence. For example, Deleuze and Guattari speak of Oedipalized desire as a particular governance of the body that channels the flow of desire in the basic structure of what they call the "holy family": Mommy, Daddy, and Me. Territorialized by this social structure, desire reproduces the *pouvoir* of the Oedipus complex in an array of human relations. There are many other forms of *pouvoir*. Foucault has explored some of them as "biopower," the active production of life through discourse: (i) the discourse of the body as a machine, i.e., "the anatomo-politics of the human body," and (ii) the discourse that renders the population as a controllable biological set of processes, i.e., "the biopolitics of the population" (Foucault 1980, 140). Similarly, I suggest, desire is produced in the discourse of gender. Our free capacity to exist, to connect, to affect and be affected, which is to say our *puissance* is channelled by the *pouvoir* of the gendered governance of life. Desire is shaped by the discourse of gender. The body is territorialized by gender.

Discourses of gender are actualized in the bodies of both men and women, although it is the latter that have received more attention in feminist theory. A number of feminist authors have described the ways in which patriarchal socio-cultural processes have shaped women's bodies (Bordo 1993; Cole 1993; Cole and Hribar 1995; MacNeill 1994; Markula 1995; Wolf 1990). Susan Bordo (1993), particularly, has shown the way in which many women, subject to misogynist discourses, embody the culturally-based desire for women to disappear—this is the cult of slenderness that finds its ultimate expression in death by anorexia nervosa. Women's desire is territorialized by misogynist discourse, refigured as the desire to take up as little space as possible. As individuals and collectives perform gender (Butler 1990) the *pouvoir* of this governance is given the *puissance* of existence. In a decidedly bleak irony, it can be said that anorexic women perform the disappearing act of femininity, thus giving the *pouvoir* of misogyny the *puissance* of diminishing existence in women's bodies.

Gender, of course, is an immensely rich discourse. I am going to look at only one particular stream of it, one which I believe makes it impossible for men who experience this particular *pouvoir* of desire to enjoy the emancipation of feminist desire. This is the particularly masculine desire for the territorialization of space: it is the desire to conquer and protectively enclose space, the desire to make connections according to the laws of spatial domination. Here the capacity to exist is circumscribed by the will to control space and by the fear of the violability of the same. It is a fetishized neurotic form of desire that appreciates its own existence only in so far as it is in control of its space. Loss of the control of space is the death of masculinity.

For the sake of this argument, I will define men as *bundles-of-desire-with-penises*. My argument is not that masculinity is confined to men, or is somehow essentially related to them. In dominant North American cultures, however, masculinity is very much encouraged in bundles-of-desire-with-penises and discouraged in bundles-of-desire-with-clitorises. I am speaking of discourses of desire, territorializations of the body, that flow unevenly and discontinuously through those cultures. Sometimes these discourses are embodied in men, sometimes in women, sometimes in black people, sometimes in white people, rich, poor and so on. I am speaking not of individual fixed identities, but of an organization of the energy of human desire that is more or less operative at various moments, in various intensities, in various lives. Because this anthology is about *men* doing feminism, I am not considering the implications of my analysis for women who actualize themselves with masculine desire—although that certainly would be very interesting to do at another time.

Masculinity begins with the rather minor fact that there are bundles-of-desire-with-penises and then produces and channels those desires according to territorializing spatial imperatives. Masculinity engorges little penises with the conquering power of the phallus. This is the point of masculinity: to become larger, to take up more space, and yield less of it. It is the opposite of feminine anorexic desire. The transformation of the limp penis into the large, hard phallus is the flowering of masculine desire. The expanding phallus is protected by the other side of this desire: the closed anus. Just as the phallus realizes its masculinity by taking space, so the tight anus protects masculine space by repelling invasion. Masculine desire protects its own phallic production by closing orifices, both anus and mouth, to the phallic expansion of others. Rendered impenetrable, the masculine body differentiates itself, produces itself as distinct and unconnected. It is conquering and inviolable. Masculine desire is expressed both metaphorically and literally in the will to power (*puissance*) of the *pouvoir* of the ever expanding phallus and ever contracting anus. The discourse of gender territorializes men's bodies by constructing this form of desire, simultaneously channelling it and damming it up. That territorializing *pouvoir* is actualized, given *puissance*, where human connections are either made or negated through metaphorically generalized or sexually specific phallic expansions and anal contractions. The more desire is channelled by the *pouvoir* of the masculine production of space the more masculine it is.

While this masculine desire is not restricted to men (bundles-of-desire-with-penises), it is expected of them, and women are largely discouraged from producing their desire so assertively and protectively. *Pouvoir* is always an historical creation—there is no historically transcendent essence to bundles-of-desire-with-penises that makes them masculine in the way I am describing. As Robert Connell (1987) and others have argued, masculinities are produced by complex historical processes of socialization. Indeed, since no penis could ever live up to the phallic hope of its master and patriarchal society, a host of strategies and practices are promoted to encourage men and boys to take and enclose more space, to differentiate themselves from the vortex of free-flowing desire. Not all bundles-of-desire-with-penises are equally territorial, of course. Consequently there are vast systems of indoctrination into masculine desire and many rewards for its success. One of the most influential training grounds for masculine spatialization is sport, at least for middle and upper class Western men for the last one hundred and fifty years. As David Whitson (1990; 1994), Bruce Kidd (1987), Don Sabo (1995; 1980), Brian Messner (1992; 1994), myself (Pronger 1990), and others have argued, sport is masculinizing; which is why women in patriarchal societies have been mostly discouraged from participating. Boys raised on sport learn to desire and to make connections according to the imperative to take space away from others and jealously guard it for themselves. Sport trains desire to conquer and protect space. The most masculine sports are those that are the most explicitly spatially dominating: football, soccer, hockey. In these sports players invade the space of others and vigorously guard against the same happening to themselves. The only honorable form of desire in these sports is domineering and protective; it is anathema to welcome other men into one's space. The team whose desire produces the most invasive phallus and tightest anus wins the game. Boys and men gain more than phallic and anal masculine game skills through their athletic training. They also learn to move and hold their bodies on and off the playing field. They learn the powerful muscular ways that embody masculine desire: the unyielding occupation of space that communicates the latent power to dominate. The masculine desire to conquer and protect is constructed similarly in other domains. The accumulation of capital and property, for example, depends on a similar desire for acquisition and retention. Certainly much of academic debate is phallicly aggressive and anally closed. And anyone who has dealt with masculine bundles-of-desire-with-penises in day-to-day interpersonal affairs has experienced the force of phallic dominance and anal invulnerability that makes these men difficult to deal with.

The problem, of course, with masculine desire, is that it is essentially dominating, seeking to dominate others in ever expanding phallic spaces and to dominate the self by tightening the holes that could be the undoing of masculine selfish spaces. Turned outward in phallic prominence masculine desire dominates surrounding space by appropriating it as its own. Turned inward as anal closure it remains impervious to external probing influences, thus dominating internal space with the insistence of self-centered phallic "integrity." The closed orifices of masculine desire territorialize the freedom of desire by enclosing the masculine differentiated individual. This is desire directed by the imperatives of dominance and control. The more masculine the desire, the more rigorously is the *puissance* of human connection channelled as *pouvoir*. Desire, territorialized by masculine spatialization achieves the power of existence (*puissance*) by this territorial imperative.

Masculine desire is an impediment to feminist desire. At the very least feminist desire is opposed to domination, to the territorial project that seeks to govern desire along phallogocentric lines. I think it is safe to say that all feminisms are fuelled by the energy to produce emancipatory modes of desire. And of course as arguments about prostitution, pornography, Madonna, and other issues attest, there are many visions of what such emancipated desire might look like. In this essay I am not going to suggest any particular vision of feminist desire. What I do want to suggest is that bundles-of-desire-with-penises that manifest desire in the masculine form I have outlined are poorly disposed to experience or promulgate any of the emancipatory potential of feminist visions. As long as desire is produced in the logic of territorial domination and protection it is antifeminist.

As other essays in this volume make abundantly clear there are many issues involved in men becoming feminist. The argument I am about to make does not claim to cover all that needs to be done in order for men to be feminist. What I will suggest here is a necessary, but not sufficient, condition for men to become feminist, for men to enjoy the benefits of feminist desire. I will argue that for men to embark on a feminist course they need to dissolve their masculine desire, by overcoming their homophobia. Masculine desire is essentially homophobic and homophobia I will argue is an obstacle to the embodiment of feminism.

A common definition of homophobia is that it is an ignorant and irrational fear of homosexuality. The idea is that "more accurate" knowledge of homosexuality diffuses irrational fear: Homosexuality is not contagious; one can be in the presence of homosexuals and maintain one's own sexual identity. And a fully knowledgeable appreciation of homosexuality shows that it is not *that* different to heterosexuality; it is simply, and unproblematically a preference for intimate encounters with members of the same sex. What is stressed here is a liberal respect for the humanity of homosexual people and tolerance and acceptance of different ways of life. Because liberalism is a powerful force in Western cultures today, this accepting and tolerant view has become quite influential. It is not at all uncommon for liberal, well-educated people to like homosexual men, to be friends with them, to go to clubs where homosexuals drink and dance, to ensure their representation on committees, to argue for their rights, and so on. For the most part, however, this liberal acceptance stops short of having homosexual sex. This lack of homosexual engagement is often explained in the polite consumer-driven language of "preference"; such men are not "irrationally fearful" of homosexual men, they simply "prefer" sexual relations with women and would simply "rather not" have them with men: "Different strokes for different folks." "The world is an open marketplace."

I suggest that the lack of interest that some men, probably most of them, have in explicit sex with men is still a fear of homosexuality, but not an irrational fear. It is a fear founded in the perfectly rational appreciation of the damage that homosexual sex can inflict on the territorializing construction of masculine desire. For liberal men, homosexuality is acceptable as long as it doesn't penetrate their own desire. Leo Bersani argues, most eloquently, in his book *Homos* (1995) that what is left out of this liberal acceptance of homosexuality is the entirely problematic significance of homosexuality. That significance is the damage that homosexual sex, specifically, the desire to be a "bottom" (to be on the receiving end) does to masculinity. Bersani, in a well-known earlier article (1987), answered the question "Is the rectum a grave?" saying: yes, it is the grave of masculine power. When the rectum receives the thrusts of another man, masculinity is dealt a deathly blow, as it were.

I have argued that masculine desire is the desire to conquer and protect space; it is desire shaped in the *pouvoir* of the expanding phallus and closed anus. Being a homosexual bottom inverts this desire. Space is given away. An enthusiastic bottom opens his anus, welcomes other forces, deterritorializing the claim that masculinity had staked both to that orifice and to *his* penis. Giving oral sex works similarly, perhaps even more effectively. Anally penetrated, a man can maintain at least some semblance of masculine desire in the belief that he is being raped, that his space is being opened *against his will,* that given the chance, it would be *his* masculine force that would be doing the penetrating. This is the honor that remains in defeat in sport: the loser at least tried to preserve his space. In fellatio there can be no such pretence; a mouth, after all, has teeth that can do considerable damage to a phallic "invader." But with fellatio one caresses the insinuating presence of another man, voluptuously welcoming him into one's space, by cushioning one's teeth with one's lips. Rather than repelling the entrance of another man one does everything one can to make him feel welcome. Giving space to another man, particularly the most intimate spaces of anus and mouth is the opposite of masculine desire. When men eroticize the entrance of other men into their space, anally or orally, they are giving *puissance* to the deterritorialization of their masculine desire. The erotic event of being willingly, indeed joyfully, penetrated orally or anally, deterritorializes the bodies of bundles-of-desire-with-penises and literally opens the gates to the freedom of demasculinized desire.

Homophobia is the reluctance to give up masculine space; it is the fear men have of the inversion of the expanding phallus and closed anus into a deferential phallus and open anus. This fear is evident beyond the physical space of the body in the reluctance some men have to give way in sport, commerce, academic debate, or interpersonal relationships. Physically, or more accurately, erotically, homophobia finds its deepest and perhaps most intractable expression in the reluctance of many men to open their mouths and anuses to other men. This is, of course, a deep erotic reluctance to yield their own will to masculine domination of their own bodies. Homophobia is the fear of giving up control, the fear of becoming an open vessel that can be freely filled by the desire of others, especially other men. Reluctance to yield such masculine control is an impediment to the experience of feminist desire, which is at the very least the desire to liberate human beings from the yoke of masculine desire, from the masculinization of space.

Men who desire feminist ways of life might benefit from reflecting on the nature of their desire, from considering the question of their homophobia, the degree to which they are willing or unwilling to invert their masculinity. Certainly, many men who desire feminism have worked very hard at examining the manner in which their masculine desire has shaped them in anti-feminist fashion and have thus worked very hard to reshape their methods of dealing with people and situations in ways that are less domineering, more gentle. And obviously one of the most important methods to do so is to reconstruct traditional patriarchal relationships with women along more feminist lines. Without a doubt men who have thus refigured their desire for women have made important steps toward the transformation of gendered relations. Most of this refiguring of masculine desire has been concerned with diminishing the aggressive and domineering tendencies of the expanding phallus. Such refiguring clearly makes masculinity less violent. And no man, regardless of what he does with his orifices, can experience feminist desire unless he is able and indeed most willing to enter into de-phallusized relations with women.[1] But as long as their orifices remain closed, men will perpetuate the masculine territorialization of space.

I am not suggesting that men need to take on homosexual identities in order to be feminist. Indeed homosexual identity is no guarantor of feminist insight. In fact I would argue that a life of exclusively male homosexual relations, because it excludes women from intimate contact is a profoundly sexist, and thus antifeminist life—it is yet another form of anal closure that channels desire, rather crudely, according to the rubrics of gender difference. What I am suggesting is that men need to be free to experience the erotic intensity of the deterritorialization of their masculine space. Those who are most reluctant to open their mouths and anuses to other men are those who are in most need of doing so.

An important condition needs to be attached to my suggestion that men deterritorialize their masculine desire by engaging in opening erotic acts. Little, if anything, will be gained in the project of men opening themselves to the possibilities of feminist desire if that deterritorialization does not extend beyond the intimacies of particular body parts. It is crucial that these erotic pragmatics be reflective moments that aid in the inversion of masculine desire in other spheres as well. Deleuze and Guattari have helpful advice here. Deterritorialization, they say, occurs where desire is not limited by external forces. They suggest that this can happen in the experience of *puissant* plateaus of intensity, which break through the organizational power of *pouvoir* and leave an after-image of their dynamism (Massumi 1992, 7) that can be reactivated in other activities. This entails men developing erotic intensities in the opening of their mouths and anuses that give them the power to see and reflect upon the dynamics of *puissance* (the power of existence) and *pouvoir* (the power of masculinity) in their own lives, and then do something about their future construction. This of course would be a matter of men refiguring their productions of desire in ways that are inspired by the freedom of *puissance*, rather than controlled by the government of masculine *pouvoir*. We need to extend the joy of the eroticization of opening spaces and deterritorializing masculine desire in the anus and mouth to the joy of erotically opening up such spaces in conversation, in interpersonal relations, in games, in academic discourse, in economics, etc.

It is not necessary in all cases for men to get other bundles-of-desire-with-penises to help them in their deterritorializations. Of course, women can also open up such blocked holes. I would say, however, that men who are willing to let women into these spaces but maintain an inhospitable, indeed masculine reluctance to admit other men, will probably need to ask other men to help them pry open the homophobic territories of their desire. Ideally, since gender is a form of *pouvoir*, a territorialization of the body, the gender of one's helper should not matter. But as long as gender does matter in the form of a preference to open holes with women and reluctance to do the same with other men, men continue to produce the *pouvoir* of gender in the construction of their desire. In which case, the *puissant* transcendence of masculinity will depend upon eradicating the homophobic territorialization of men's bodies by embracing its opposite: homoerotic love. Given sufficient thoughtful, open, erotic practice, the restrictions of gender just might give way to the free-flow of deterritorialized desire, a taste of the freedom of feminism.

Note

1. Which is not to say that relations should never be phallic—there are worthwhile lessons and pleasures to be had in the considered and consensual use of domination—but the context for phallic relations must include the potential for inversion, otherwise, it is simply the reproduction of fixed and thus nonemancipatory relations of dominance.

Bibiliography

Bersani, Leo. 1987. Is the rectum a grave? *October* 43:197–222.

Bersani, Leo. 1995. Homos. Cambridge, Mass.: Harvard University Press.

Bordo, Susan. 1993. *Unbearable Weight: Feminism, Western Culture and the Body.* Berkeley: University of California Press.

Butler, Judith. 1990. *Gender Trouble.* New York: Routledge.

Cole, Cheryl. 1993. Resisting the canon: Feminist cultural studies, sport and technologies of the body. *Journal of Sport and Social Issues* 17 (2):77–97.

Cole, Cheryl, and Amy Hribar. 1995. Celebrity feminism: Nike style. Post-Fordism, transcendence, and consumer power. *Sociology of Sport Journal* 12 (4).

Connell, Robert. 1987. *Gender and Power: Society, the Person and Sexual Politics.* Cambridge: Polity.

Deleuze, Gilles, and Félix Guattari. 1983. *Anti-Oedipus: Capitalism and Schizophrenia.* Translated by Robert Hurley, Mark Seem, Helen R. Lane. Minneapolis: University of Minnesota Press.

Deleuze, Gilles, and Félix Guattari. 1987. *A Thousand Plateaus: Capitalism and Schizophrenia.* Translated by Brian Massumi. Minneapolis: University of Minnesota Press.

Foucault, Michel. 1980. *The History of Sexuality: Volume I: An Introduction.* Translated by Hurley, Robert (1978). Vol. I. New York: Vintage.

Kidd, Bruce. 1987. Sports and masculinity. In *Beyond Patriarchy: Essays by Men on Masculinity*, edited by M. Kaufman. Toronto: Oxford University Press.

MacNeill, Margaret. 1994. Active women, media representations, and ideology. In *Women, Sport and Culture*, edited by S. Birrell and C. Cole. Champaign: Human Kinetics.

Markula, Pirko. 1995. Firm but shapely, fit but sexy, strong but thin: The postmodern aerobicizing female bodies. *Sociology of Sport Journal* 12 (4).

Massumi, Brian. 1992. *A User's Guide to Capitalism and Schizophrenia.* Cambridge, Mass.: MIT Press.

Messner, Mike. 1992. *Power at Play*. Boston: Beacon.

Messner, Michael, and Donald Sabo. 1994. *Sex, Violence and Power in Sports: Rethinking Masculinity*. Freedom, CA: Crossing Press.

Pronger, Brian. 1990. *The Arena of Masculinity: Sports, Homosexuality and the Meaning of Sex*. First ed. New York: St. Martin's Press.

Sabo, Don, and Dave Gordon, eds. 1995. *Men's Health and Illness: Gender, Power and the Body*. London: Sage.

Sabo, Donald, and Ross Runfola. 1980. *Jock: Sports and Male Identity*. Englewood Cliffs: Prentice-Hall.

Whitson, David. 1990. Sport in the social construction of masculinity. In *Sport, Men, and the Gender Order: Critical Feminist Perspectives*, edited by M. Messner and D. Sabo. Champaign: Human Kinetics.

Whitson, David. 1994. The Embodiment of Gender: Discipline, Domination, and Empowerment. In *Women, Sport, and Culture*, edited by S. Birrell and C. L. Cole. Champaign, Ill: Human Kinetics.

Wolf, Naomi. 1990. *The Beauty Myth*. London: Vintage.

Chapter 5

Profeminist Men and Their Friends

Richard Schmitt

I spent the last year in Ecuador. Because mail between the U.S. and Ecuador was rare and precarious, my partner and I kept up relationships with our friends by electronic mail. But while I sent and received a few short messages from my friends, many of them having to do with business of one sort of another, Lucy kept up a large, complex set of correspondences with an extensive network of her male and female friends. Some of my friends did not write at all; others wrote rarely and impersonally. I went about blaming them for their unenlightened stance until it occurred to me one day that I too had missed many opportunities to keep up connections with my friends. I was as lackadaisical and unenlightened as a friend as they.

This disturbed and puzzled me. I asked myself why heterosexual men[1] have the friendships we have and why they tend to play a relatively peripheral role in our lives. Looking for answers to these questions, I began to read some of the voluminous literature about heterosexual men and women and their relationships, about the ways they talk (or don't) to one another. That literature describes heterosexual men as unemotional, as ignorant of their own emotions, and unwilling to examine their feelings or listen to other persons expressing their emotions. The explanations of why these men are that way ranged from psychoanalytic theories about the manner in which little boys grow up to more or less bogus quasi-Darwinist talk about Man the Hunter and Woman the Mother.

But none of that seemed quite to apply to me or to my friends. All of us are profeminist heterosexual men. We do not show affection for each other by punching and calling each other vulgar and insulting names. We are not spending our time with each other bragging about our (usually fictitious) sexual exploits or making jokes at each others' expense. We do not constantly compete with each other. In our relations with women we are open to emotion: we think about our feelings and are prepared to talk about them; we are aware of what others feel and are ready to help, support, encourage, or cheer on. We have learned to listen and to pay careful and concentrated attention. But our friendships with each other remain—with occasional exceptions—distant, emotionally cool, and apparently not essential to our life. It is not clear, however, that the standard explanations of men's friendships apply to us and therefore these explanations do not clarify why our friendships are as they are and why they play a relatively peripheral role in our life. However different our attitudes and behaviors are toward women, in relation to one another we still act very much like the majority of more or less misogynist men. Only the external expressions of heterosexual male friendships have changed, not their substance. As profeminist men we need to ask ourselves whether the character of our friendships with men means that our dedication to the struggle against patriarchy is deficient. Could it be that the friendships between profeminist men betray our reluctance to surrender traditional male ways that are oppressive to women?

In order to understand our distance from our friends (primarily, but not only our male friends) we need to examine the standard account of differences and relations between heterosexual men and women. We will see that this standard account is too simple. I will then outline a more complex understanding of typical men's relations to women and to one another, which will allow us to see that the reluctance even of profeminist men to yield a central role in their lives to friendships serves to maintain patriarchal structures. The conclusion is that profeminist heterosexual men must transform their friendships with other men in order to continue their opposition to patriarchy.

The Standard View

A. The Majority View

In the vast and ever growing literature about heterosexual men and women,[2] their differences and relations, the different role of friendship in the lives of men and women as well as the different character of these friendships is documented at great length. Here is a summary of these often repeated findings:

> The Hite Report (1987) found that, although only roughly one in four of their respondents had had a sexual relationship with another woman, the overwhelming majority of both married and single women had their deepest emotional relationship with a woman (15). "Friendships between women . . . created a universe where woman's personal identities could be validated (21) . . . Mutual helpfulness is most central to female friendships

whereas shared activities and similar interests are most central to males . . . females use more non-verbal expressions of affection (29). Feminine styles . . . are incompatible with control . . . men [are] . . . equally capable of intimate interaction, [but] they prefer to interact intimately less often than women . . . men's definitions of intimacy in terms of proximity and shared activities effectively protect them from situations of emotional vulnerability and potential loss of control. Intimacy for women . . . typically involves admitting dependency, sharing problems and being emotionally vulnerable (30). The maintenance of an intimate style of relating amongst females and a non-intimate one amongst males reflects and ultimately reinforces power relationships between the sexes (33). (O'Connor 1992; Block and Greenberg 1985)

Women's relationships are of central importance in women's lives. With their friends they talk, exchange confidences, share emotions, support each other in word and deed. Heterosexual men, in contrast, work together, play sports, or joke. If they talk, the talk tends to be impersonal. Their friendships are of secondary importance to them.

Explanations for these differences are also endlessly repeated and differ to some extent by the source. Profeminist men give us a somewhat different explanation from men who are not feminists. Women's slant on men's friendships differs from that of men. Profeminist men tend to stress that men are always competing with one another (Gilmore 1990; Kimmel 1994; Stoltenberg 1993). As a result, they tend to be unsure of themselves, their manhood is always in question and must be demonstrated over and over again. Weakness is to be feared because it invites aggression from stronger males. Open shows of emotion are signs of weakness as is dependence on others. Hence, living in a very competitive, male world, men seek independence and shun emotional entanglements; they want to appear strong (Brittan 1989) and thus fear displays of emotions (McGill 1985:18). As a consequence, their relationships to both men and women are distant, impersonal, and unemotional. Emotional ties are avoided or, where not avoided, turned into matters of sexual exclusivity. Profeminist men see the competitive struggle between men—it is not always quite clear over what men struggle—as the source of male distance from emotion and other persons.

Non-feminist heterosexual men give us the same descriptions of men but they find problems in different places. Yes, men value strength and independence. Yes, their friendships with other men are often weak, but what is missing in their lives is not so much open emotionality, ability to be dependent, but on the contrary "forceful actions . . . without cruelty" (Bly 1990:8). While profeminist men deplore the competitiveness of men that compels them into a defensive, self-protective, and emotionally barren stance, men who are not feminists complain that men have in recent years acknowledged the feminine side of their nature to the detriment of their strength and ability to act forcefully. They suffer not from an excess of male competition but, on the contrary, from a deficit of maleness—here understood as being powerful, self-contained, and independent. As a consequence they cannot form strong, typically masculine friendships with other men because "only men can initiate men" (Bly 1990, 16) and we, not being initiated by men, are therefore unable to have genuine friendships with other men.

Women tend to see the condition of men differently again. Whether they stress that "men and women are different" (Tannen 1990) or take a more critical stance that sees male emotional sterility as oppressive to women, they all describe men as more or less defective. The milder version of this description says of men that in their relations to women and to other men, they do not share their feelings or, if they try to share feelings, are not very good at it. A stronger version says that men cannot share their feelings because they are unaware of them (McGill 1985, 13). Another version tells us that men do not share feelings because they are utterly self-absorbed and thus oblivious to others and to the feelings and needs of these others. From a woman's perspective men are either incompetent in a one of the primary skills of human beings or are morally defective. When it comes to being aware of, expressing, and sharing emotions, men are either pathetic bumblers or endlessly needy tyrants.

In these different perspectives, the descriptions overlap: men are inexpressive and unresponsive to the feelings of women. In their relations to other men, the prevailing distance explains the secondary importance of those friendships in men's lives. These facts are explained differently depending on the gender of the author and on the extent to which they see men as victims of social forces, as simply different from women, or as their oppressors.

B. The Minority View.

If the majority view represents heterosexual men as emotionally crippled by the competitive situation in which they find themselves, with few male friends, and often distant also from their spouses, the minority view reminds us that in many cultures, including our own, these men have strong bonds with one another which are for them—as their friendships are for women—among the most powerful connections in their lives (Tiger 1970).[3] One attraction of athletics for boys is that they find connections there. In the team they find the emotional home they do not find with parents or siblings (Messner 1992). Many authors document the close connections men make with each other in war (Gibson 1994; Gray

1992; Theleweit 1988). Equally powerful is shared misogyny: men who may barely know each other have a strong common bond around jokes about women drivers, vulgar sexual comments about women passing in the street, or a familiar litany of complaints about women. It is true that men's friendships are not like women's friendships and that they do not play the role in men's lives that their friendships play in the lives of women. But it is not true that heterosexual men do not have strong connections with one another (Cohen 1992; Wellman 1992).

Nor is it as universally true that men are unemotional, or unaware of their feelings as the majority account tells us. Historians document the intimate, expressive, and heartfelt friendships between men in New England in the nineteenth century (Hansen 1992). Men get intensely emotional about sports; they get very emotional about the good name of "their" women, or their country, about their political candidate or issue. Men also get very emotional about abortion as infanticide and others expend comparable emotion on the glorious future of the working class. Heterosexual men have always been presented to us as impassioned lovers; the poets, the majority of them men, have sung their passion for a woman in many different modes. Romantic love is as much, if not more, the province of men than of women and romantic love is the epitome of passion. It is not true that men are not emotional. The legendary friendships portrayed in literature are also those of men. The Old Testament tells us about King David and his friend Jonathan, Homer about Achilles and Patroclus; our children still thrill to the adventures of the three musketeers. In our mythology, at least, friendship is important and friendship is the friendship of men. What is more, men do confide in friends—more often than not women. McGill found that:

> ... approximately one-third of the men in the research reported that they have revealed things about themselves to other women that they have not revealed to their wives ... these men may be more intimate with other women than they may be with their spouses ... the common male defense of ignorance (of their feelings) or inability to be intimate is groundless ... (78) In the important areas of the private and the personal selves, men disclose a great deal to other women, in many instances as much and more than they reveal to their own spouses. It appears also that in these relationships they really listen to the woman and the exchange of intimacy is mutual. (McGill 1985; Wellman 1992)

The picture painted by the majority account of the lack of emotionality or the isolation of men is contradicted by this minority story. The image of men as lacking in emotion is very one-sided, partial, and, by and large, fictional.

An Alternative Story

There are real contradictions in the sorts of things the literature tells us about heterosexual men and women, their relationships, and their emotionality (Sherrod 1987). One can take these contradictions as indications that there is something the matter with our theories. Men cannot be both unemotional and emotional, unwilling to talk and freely communicative. It can't be true that men have no friends—certainly not among other men—and that their ties to other men are the most important in their lives. If our account of men is full of self-contradiction, we may be tempted to say, it needs to be discarded and replaced by one that is internally coherent.

But, of course, human beings are not all of one piece. While our theories, we hope, are internally consistent, the framers of those theories barely are. As a consequence, these contradictory accounts of the emotional lives of men show that men, much of the time, act in utterly contradictory fashion. It is not our account of men's behavior that is incoherent. The actions of men are often inconsistent with one another. Much of the time, heterosexual men play a double game. They present themselves as independent and strong but are dependent and weak. They make us believe that they are solitary and isolated but their patriarchal power is a power collectively held and defended by men in association with one another.

Virginia Woolf in *To the Lighthouse* documents this duplicity of men exhaustively. The bulk of the novel describes a summer day at the country house of the Ramsays. Mr. Ramsay is an Oxford philosopher for whom his work is the central interest in his life, more than his wife, his four children, or his friends. His relations to other men always have a competitive edge. His conversation with the admiring graduate students with whom he surrounds himself is about:

> ... who had won this, who had won that, who was a "first rate man" at Latin verses, who was "brilliant but I think fundamentally unsound," who was undoubtedly the "ablest fellow at Balliol." ... (Woolf 1927:15)

To his family he shows an abstracted, absent minded face. He does not know what he eats, he does not notice that his daughter is growing up into a beautiful young woman. He does not care about the disappointments of his younger son. He cares about the truth and about his accomplishments as a philosopher. All the while, Mrs. Ramsay has to work to keep the social fabric mended: she sees to the children, to the meals; she makes sure that the various house guests are comfortable and are enjoying themselves. She tries to promote relationships between young men and women. At the meals, while the men spin out abstract conversations that strike her as utterly barren, she makes sure that the conversation includes all. It its her job to make things "merge and flow."

Ramsay is "his own man." Engrossed in his own concerns and interests, he is independent, competitive, unemotional—the paradigm male. But there is another part to that same paradigm male: he depends on Mrs. Ramsay to arrange for house, food, and family. The entire summer day with its, mostly internal, complexities depends on the constant work of Mrs. Ramsay. There is a social world in the Ramsays' summer home only because of Mrs. Ramsay's constant efforts. But, what is more, Mr. Ramsay personally depends on his wife for constant support and ego building. At certain moments, the strong and independent male comes around for support, for nurturance, for reassurance when he fears that his latest book is not a success. But being a typical man, who is committed to being, or at least to pretending to be, strong and independent, he cannot ask her for what he needs and she must guess what it is he wants and when he wants it. If he does want it, she must give and give generously, whether she feels like it or not. He comes up and stands there mutely and miserably and:

> ... Mrs. Ramsay, who had been sitting loosely, folding her son in her arm, braced herself ... to pour erect into the air a rain of energy ... and into this ... fountain and spray of life, the fatal sterility of the male plunged itself like a beak of brass, barren and bare. He wanted sympathy. He was a failure, he said. ... Mr. Ramsay repeated, never taking his eyes off her face, that he was a failure. She blew the words back to him. "Charles Tansley [an admiring graduate student] ... ," She said. But he must have more than that ... But he must have more than that. (Woolf 1927:58)

There are two Ramsays—the rational, intelligent manipulator of abstract concepts, the admired mentor of bright young men, equally abstracted and oblivious to the material and human aspects of their lives; and the fearful, unhappy, inarticulate Ramsay whose wife must not only maintain the setting for him and his friends to impress each other with their cleverness but must also divine when his black moods come upon him when he is helpless in face of his own feelings. Now his dedication to the truth fails him—she must lie to him about his accomplishments and he wants always more. His rationality does not serve him either because he cannot think about the causes of his black moods. Mrs. Ramsay has to help him: he is incompetent, dependent, and weak.

The apparent contradiction between the different descriptions of men—isolated and unemotional or firmly bonded with other men and open about their emotional needs—turn out not to be contradictions at all: men are both in order to maintain their patriarchal power. They get women to meet their emotional needs but without asking: thus they can appear independent and be, in fact, dependent. As Jean Baker Miller put this in describing one particular man:

> Like many people he wanted at least two things. He wanted, first of all, to sail though every situation feeling "like a man," that is strong self-sufficient, and fully competent. . . . At the same time . . . he harbored the seemingly contradictory wish that his wife would somehow solve everything for him. . . . She would do this without being asked; it was essential that he never have to think or talk about his weakness. (Miller 1976:33)

Heterosexual men compete with other men for status in the world of work, but bond with other men in a compact to keep women down: the abstract conversation at the Ramsays' dinner table deliberately excludes the women at the table; it is just one more way in which the male pack reasserts its superiority in another form. It does not need to see that everyone at the table is included in the conversation. Mrs. Ramsay and the other women present will see that things will merge and flow. The men, as lords of creation, need only to please themselves in their competitive games with one another. But this independence and self-reliance of men is in many, if not most cases, a sham. It is a pretense. When the time comes men will be as weak, as dependent as women or children. But the power they have enables them to suppress that information. Privately women complain about the excessive demands made for emotional support (Cohen 1992). These demands are very burdensome, as Virginia Woolf makes amply clear in the passage cited earlier. But no public mention of male weakness is allowed.

It is therefore not true that heterosexual men are independent and self-sufficient. What is true is that men pretend to be independent and self-sufficient. But this does not prevent them from depending a great deal on women to cater to their emotional needs and from complaining vociferously when those needs are not met when and as they desire. Neither it is true that they do not have relationships to other men; that men do not have friends. It often seems that way, even to men (Levinson 1978), but it seems that way only to the extent that the pervasive solidarity of men against women is ignored or suppressed. The oft repeated story of the "difference" between men and women in the way they talk and use talk, and the way in which they fashion their relationships is true but leaves out a great deal, namely that these differences are not all genuine but are put on to maintain male positions of power.

It is clear that this duplicity of heterosexual men is oppressive to women:

> In all significant interpersonal relationships, save those with each other, men get more than they give in love and intimacy (212). By withholding information from our relationship, I not only retain power over my actions, I also gain power over your actions. . . . The mystery presented by men is a path to mastery over others (231/2/3). (McGill 1985)

Here emerges a more complex story than the standard account about men, women, and their relationships to other men or women. The dominant conception of (heterosexual) masculinity demands that men be strong, that they be able to dominate others, that they be able to get from others what they want without reciprocity. The strong take from the weak; they do not exchange goods or services. Heterosexual men prove their strength in contests with any adversary: in sports, in hunting animals, in dominating other men. But as Stoltenberg suggests, contests between men are often put aside so that men can jointly dominate women (Stoltenberg 1993). The favored arena in which men prove their strength is in relation to women. The domination of women is the common project of heterosexual men for which they form strong bonds with one another. Strength requires that one be independent, that one meets one's own needs. Strength in this context means that one not be at the mercy of emotions but be stoical in the face of pain and loss. Hence the appearance of men as unemotional. At the same time, many men use their emotional needs as the arena in which to dominate women. Women are there to serve their emotional and bodily needs. Without needs there cannot be any services. Male neediness, paradoxically, serves their striving for strength and domination. One asserts one's strength precisely by getting services without asking. The weaker is constantly in attendance, eager to guess what the other might want and trying to keep him happy. Here the man remains in charge. Men do not give that kind of unremitting attention to women. The apparent incoherences in male behavior cease to be perplexing if understood in the context of male domination of women.

Since emotional display, having emotional needs, and having those needs met are all in the service of domination—primarily of women—the bonds heterosexual men establish with each other are relatively unemotional and are, in the majority of cases, bonds cemented by joint contests in war, in sports, in the use of women. Male friendships rest on the common effort to win or to survive. Male friendships are shared efforts at being strong and dominating. Friendships between men are therefore relatively unemotional and impersonal—after all emotions are serviced by women and in allowing oneself to be emotional in heterosexual relationships one continues to maintain one's dominant position.

But this story does not seem to apply to profeminist heterosexual men who have forsworn the traditional conception of masculinity. We do not affirm ourselves as men by lording it over women; we do not lord it over each other.[4] As a result, the more complex story that I have been telling about men and why their friendships have this peculiar air of distance to them does not explain why the friendships of heterosexual profeminist men also rarely have the range and intensity and importance possessed by the friendships of women. The questions raised at the beginning of this paper remain: what makes even the friendships of profeminist men so distant, and what does that tell us about our profeminist stance?

In order to answer those questions, we need to consider how women's friendships differ from those common among men.

Separate or In-Relation?

It is a familiar fact that women's relationships are different from those of men. But those differences are not always defined as clearly as they should be. The differences between men and women with respect to relationships has been popularly expressed by saying that "men are separate; women in relation." In the literature this is often repeated by saying that women are "connected" and men are not (Eichenbaum & Orbach 1988; Lyons 1983; Radden 1996). But that is not altogether adequate: men as we saw are connected or have relations too—to other men, to family, to their wives and children, to their friends. In a similar vein, it is often said, following Carol Gilligan, that "caring" plays a more important role in the lives, actions, and thought of women, while men are more swayed by or dedicated to considerations of rules of justice. But the same problem faces us here: surely men also care for their children in a variety of senses of caring. A more detailed account is needed of the different ways in which men are related to other persons and the ways in which women are. Correspondingly a much more detailed discussion of caring is needed to bring out the differences that that word was meant to indicate.

I will use the terms "separate" and "in-relation" to refer to the different types of relationships. In the literature these are used as technical terms; they do not have the same meanings they have in ordinary English (Gilligan 1987). Unless we insist on the technical sense of these terms, the distinction between typical male relations that are very separate and typical women's relations that are not seems open to obvious, common sense objections such as that men also have relations and men also care for their parents, partners, friends, or children. But that objection misses the mark because the difference between relationships that are separate and those that are in-relation has a special sense here that still remains to be defined.

Separateness and being in-relation are attributes of relationships, not

Separateness and being in-relation are attributes of relationships, not of persons. One's *relations* can be separate; one can have friends or be married in a separate manner. What differentiates separate relations from those that are in-relation is that the latter are joint projects and the former are not. In a joint project, the actors constitute a "we"—they become a social subject that is neither all mine or all yours (Gilbert 1989). A joint project is shared. The participants share a certain understanding of what is being done, what is planned, what the purpose and expected outcomes of the project are. As long as we maintain our separate stances, on the other hand, we can engage in projects in common but those simply consists of your doing your part and my doing mine. A public bus has a number of passengers who all are going in the same direction. Some of them may even go to the same final destination. But their going there is a separate project for each even though when they get off at the same bus stop or ring the bell of the same house they may say, in surprise, "We went to the same place." But they went there separately. If a group of friends, on the other hand, go on an outing they all go on the same bus, to the same place, but their's is a joint project. They share an understanding of what is happening and what they are doing. They decided to take this outing jointly.

The passengers who all happen to be going to the same place separately decided separately. They each decided by themselves. Joe decided by himself and Mary decided by herself and both went. The group that goes on an outing together may also decide separately; each decides by his or herself and then they tally up the results. If they agree to go, they say that "we" have decided to go on this outing. Then they apportion the work: you do this part, I do that part, and we go off in our separate ways to do what we each promised to do. A decision made in-relation, on the other hand, emerges from a conversation that we have: at a certain point it is clear what we will do. As we set about doing what we decided, we may divide up the jobs, but that division of labor is fluid and is constantly open to change and discussion. What each of us does is not ours alone but is done under the eyes of and with the knowledge of and often the comments of the other. Neither of us thinks of what we do as our own but rather as putting into action a part of a joint project. In such a joint project no one can say, truthfully, that "I decided." *We* decided; the decision is not owned by any one person by his or herself; it is made jointly. To that extent such a group forms a "we."

Of separate actions we claim that they are all "our own." If the product of your activity is put together, i.e., between the covers of the same book, with the result of my activity, then we can say that we worked on this book together. But we did so separately. Of course, there must be some common project in most of such cases: there must be a shared understanding of what the book will be about, what sort of audience it addresses itself to and other such general characteristics of the project. Before each of us goes off to our separate studies to do our work we must share a minimal under-standing—whether fully explicit or not—of what we are about to work on. Here too there is a tendency toward pretense: complete separateness is difficult to achieve where more than one person works on something. But if one is bound and determined to be as separate as possible one can certainly reduce the element of being in-relation to a minimum and ignore this minimum in order to pretend that one's work is all one's own.[5]

We can now see how the friendships of typical men are different from those of typical women. Heterosexual men remain largely separate in their friendships. When we work together, we work alongside each other. The constant joking maintains distance. Independence is preserved, or at least the pretense of it. On special occasions we will breach this distance and confide in another man; on special occasions we will ask for support from women. But when the conversation is over we become a separate man again. There are emotional episodes where we are open to our own feelings and, at best, also to the emotions of the other, but then we pull down the shutters again over our emotional storehouse and retreat behind a jocular, unemotional front neither displaying emotions of our own nor taking account of the feelings of the other. For the most part, men's friendships are emotionally low-key.[6] We can ignore the other to a considerable extent because we do not have joint projects but do things together, as separate persons where each pays attention to his part of the common undertaking. Male friends are easily replaced—friends are exchangeable.

By contrast, friendships between typical women tend to be in-relation, they form a "we" and that demands that one be attuned to the other person. That requires, to begin with, a lot more conversation than men need to be friends. It also requires that one listen carefully not only to what is said, but also to how it is said and to what is not said. It requires that one be finely attuned to the other's nonverbal communications (Hall 1984). Actions undertaken by one person are completed by the other, as Nel Noddings points out, (Noddings 1984:4) requiring that one pay very close attention to one another. The characteristic of typical women's friendships, that they are pegged at a much higher emotional pitch than the friendships of typical heterosexual men, is one important manifesta-tion that women's friendships tend to be much more in-relation. The friendship itself is a project that is undertaken jointly, carefully explored, developed and maintained by changing it over an extended period of time. As a consequence, women's friends are not replaceable. Each pro-ject is unique; the friendship that women have with each other is differ-ent from friendships the same woman has with others (McGill 1985:21).[7]

especially philosophers, speak volubly and with enthusiasm about how they are autonomous and how everyone ought to be autonomous. By autonomy they mean that they live by a life project chosen by themselves or even that they live by moral rules of their own choosing. Their life, their person, they say, is "all their own." They are exclusive owners of themselves (Dworkin 1988). But Virginia Woolf's portrait of Mr. Ramsay has prepared us for being skeptical of the encomiums of autonomy as separate self-determination. In their abstract, parochial academic banter, the men at Mrs. Ramsay's dinner table are engaged in a common project. They jointly constitute their identities as exceptionally intelligent (and entitled) members of an intellectual elite. Ramsay's role in the family as the distracted and distant scholar is not his alone. If his family refused to accept that identity for him, if they refused to play along, he could not be a husband and father and the abstracted philosophy professor. It is possible to be genuinely separate, that is, separate without pretense and hidden dependencies even though that requires a good deal of effort, but it is not possible to be a husband and father and to be genuinely separate. Husbands and fathers can only *pretend* to be separate if the rest of the family will allow them the pretense.

It is true then that heterosexual men are more separate than women. But it is also true that a good deal of this separateness is pretense. Men, as do women, construct their identities jointly with other persons while they pretend that those identities are "all their own." This imposes complex and onerous burdens on women. They cannot choose whether to be separate or to be in-relation with respect to the man in their life. They must be there to be openly in-relation when that is demanded. Hence there exists for them no choice of autonomy as men define it. What is more, they must pretend that the man is autonomous when they not only know better and he ought to know better too. Added to the injury of being unable to choose whether to be in-relation or separate is the injury of playing a life-long charade. The pretense of male separateness is oppressive to women.

Men's Friendship—A Refuge?

In our relationships to women, heterosexual, profeminist men are not exploitative through pretending to be separate men in the manner of the Mr. Ramsays of this world. We know that our identity is, in part, constructed in that relationship and we know that our partner constructs hers, in part, in-relation to us. Hence we do not demand elaborate pretense in order to salvage our disingenuous claims to autonomy, we do not demand that our needs be met without asking for anything, nor do we expect to receive support and care where we give little. But in relation to other men, not much has changed. Profeminist heterosexual men to other men, not much has changed. Profeminist heterosexual men either have few relations to men because they really do not like men, or their friendships to men are perhaps no longer openly misogynist, but they remain distant, impersonal and low key and unimportant.

There is no question that profeminist men lose out by our limited capacity in this respect. But since we are doing our level best in relation to women friends and lovers and do not try to dominate by controlling the conversation or the level of emotion in relationships, since we are trying hard to be responsive and open to our women friends and partners, since we do not ridicule them for being "emotional" or wanting to talk all the time, have we not earned the right to preserve the oasis of emotional neutrality that our male friendships represent? Departing from traditional male stereotypes is an effort and from time to time one needs a rest to just talk without "communicating" anything more weighty than facts, or a good story. So why can we not rest occasionally by throwing a ball around with our male friends or talking about "the job, the car, the family" as impersonally as we are accustomed to? Men and women are different in this respect. Why can't we leave it at that?

But if the previous account of the differences between relations among typical heterosexual men and relations among typical women is at all correct, our male friendships with their lack of emotionality are not as innocent as I have portrayed them in the preceding paragraph. In the preceding pages I have explained how one form of the oppression of women is the duplicity of men who pretend to be strong and independent and demand from women that they maintain this fiction in order to maintain men in their secret dependence. As long as we profeminist men maintain relations to other men in which the pretense of separateness is maintained, we are not actively struggling against an important aspect of typical masculinity—the pretense of separateness. Instead we are maintaining as legitimate the images and practices of male autonomy. We are as much as saying: for women it is fine to be in-relation and when you are with them you have to try to be like them. But men are different. They are autonomous, self-reliant. We repeat the old mythology of how men and women are different. We still enact that mythology by having important relationships only to women, by being openly in-relation only to them. Thus the women in our lives continue to bear the burden of our well-being, constructing and validating our identity. Only now she gets something in return. That is no doubt worth something, but as long as we have very different sorts of relationships to men, we maintain the prevailing ideology of how men and women are different—an ideology that is oppressive to women.

We cannot be profeminist men and maintain the old misogynist ideology.[8] We confront a choice. We can give up all being in-relation and thus maintain separateness from men and women. But that is an arduous project. If we are not willing to isolate ourselves in that way, if we want to construct and validate our identity in-relation to others, then these others cannot only be women. We must strive to be in-relation to all our friends.

How Can We Change?

It is easy to confuse wishful thinking and the dramatic enactment of our dreams with real change to move in the direction of our ideal. It is easy to spend a weekend with other heterosexual men and to do a lot of hugging, some weeping, and plant a few cautious kisses. It is probably great fun to play with a group of men and beat drums, or demolish cars with sledge hammers. But that does not change anything. Men have not learned how to be openly in-relation. We have not learned that that is what we need to do and how to go about doing that. We have not yet learned that being separate in our relations to other men is humanly unacceptable.

When I was a boy and living in a boarding school I noticed and was surprised at the shifting friendships and enmities among the girls in my age group. Their emotional life was turbulent and active. My friends and I were busy building forts, playing sports, and tormenting new boys in our room. Relationships were not an issue. It never occurred to us that we had relationships. At that time we learned to be men while the girls prepared for being women. Now almost sixty years later, it will not be easy to make up for many years in which my relations to others, especially men, were quite separate. I lack practice in friendships that are in-relation. I need to perfect the fine art of conversation that very many women have practiced from very early on.[9] But that is what we need to learn.

It is not difficult to see how we should go about that. We have begun to be in-relation inasmuch as we have close relations to women who demand that from us. But most of us have not demanded that from one another.[10] After all, even in relations to women we have mostly done what was necessary to "stay out of trouble." But rarely do we take the initiative to take up more of the emotional work in the family, to remember birthdays and organize them, to maintain the networks of friends and family by writing and making phone calls. Even less do we turn to our male friends, instead of women, when we feel the need of talking to someone. We rarely, if ever, challenge our own avoidance of open relationships to men. But our profeminist convictions demand a more active effort to learn to be in complex and rich ways in-relation even where no one demands that of us. We know that that is difficult but we have to do it.

Notes

1. The men I talk about in this paper are heterosexual. I know little about their relations to one another among homosexual men and what I have to say here most likely does not apply to them.

2. It must be clear throughout that we are not talking about all men or all women, but about different relations that, to different extents, and different frequencies are experienced by or observed in men, or in women (Spelman 1991). What is more, the rough and ready generalizations about men and women in this paper do not presuppose or imply the existence of any male or female essences. Claims about male or female essences are claims that anyone who is to be regarded as either male or female *must* have the properties that are said to constitute their essence. I do not know whether there is such a male or female essence. But I do know that the different tendencies to conduct one's human relationships are not parts of such an essence, should it turn out to exist.

3. It is important to remember, though, that in most situations white men do not bond with black men against women, but that more often white men bond with white women against black men.

4. I do not know to what extent profeminist men remain devoted to sports. The relation between profeminism and sports will have to be investigated elsewhere.

5. I have developed these distinctions in much greater detail in my *Beyond Separateness: The Relational Nature of Human Beings—Their Autonomy, Knowledge, and Power* (Boulder: Westview, 1995).

6. And that, to be truthful, makes them so restful and attractive.

7. The differences between men's and women's friendships are even more complex. Men can also be very demonstrative and affectionate; women, on the other hand, may be very reserved when it comes to expressing feelings. But women's friendships are joint projects and thus the friends must be attuned to each other in ways that men with their separate, side-by-side undertakings are not. I have developed some of these complexities in the chapter on "Love and Anger" in *Beyond Separateness*.

8. The case here is analogous to that of the fear of male impotence. Many men are deeply afraid of impotence. The sources of this fear are patriarchal beliefs about sexuality as one means of dominating women. Even men who oppose patriarchy in many ways unwittingly support that form of oppression of women as long as they believe that the functioning penis in vaginal penetration is an important element in their manhood. This is another case where profeminist men find themselves supporting patriarchy by holding certain beliefs and attitudes that are the precondition for certain forms of women's oppression, even though they do not, as profeminist men, practice that oppression (Candib & Schmitt 1996).

9. "Women talk about almost everything . . . but the daily fare is apt to be pretty plain. That is what makes it an art." (Gouldner and Strong 1987).

10. Clearly one reason for not taking on that task is the pervasive fear of homosexuality. But that is a complex and confusing topic. The male fear of homosexuality is flagrantly ambivalent. Male relations in the most masculinist institutions such as the military, sports, or fraternities are often erotically

bonding for the sake of the domination of women. All of that needs to be discussed elsewhere.

Bibliography

Block, Joel, and Diane Greenberg. 1985. *Women and Friendship*. New York: Franklin Watts.

Bly, Robert. 1990. *Iron John: A Book about Men*. New York: Vintage.

Brittan, Arthur. 1989. *Masculinity and Power*. Oxford: Blackwell's.

Candib, Lucy M., and Richard Schmitt 1996. "About Losing It: The Fear of Male Impotence" in Larry May, Robert Strikwerda and Patrick Hopkins, eds. *Rethinking Masculinity*. 2nd edition. Lanham: Rowman and Littlefield.

Cohen, Theodore F. 1992. "Men's Families, Men's Friends: A Structural Analysis of Constraints on Men's Social Ties" in Peter M. Nardi, ed., *Men's Friendships*. Newbury Park: Sage.

Dworkin, Gerald. 1988. *The Theory and Practice of Autonomy*. Cambridge: Cambridge University Press.

Gibson, James Walter. 1994. *Warrior Dreams: Violence and Manhood in Post-Vietnam America*. New York: Hill and Wang.

Gilbert, Margaret. 1989. *On Social Facts*. Princeton: Princeton University Press.

Gilligan, Carol. 1987. "Moral Orientation and Moral Development" in E. F. Kittay and D. T. Meyers eds., *Women and Moral Theory*. Totowa, NJ: Rowman and Littlefield.

Gilmore, David D. 1990. *Manhood in the Making*. New Haven: Yale University Press.

Gouldner, Helen, and Mary Symons Strong. 1987. *Speaking of Friendship: Middle Class Women and their Friends*. New York: Greenwood Press.

Gray, J. Glenn. 1992. "The Enduring Appeals of Battle" in Larry May, Robert Strikwerda, and Patrick Hopkins eds., *Rethinking Masculinity*. 2nd edition. Totowa: Rowman and Allenheld.

Hall, Judith A. 1984. *Non Verbal Sex Differences: Communication, Accuracy and Expressive Style*. Baltimore: Johns Hopkins University Press.

Hansen, Karen V. 1992. "Our Eyes Behold Each Other: Masculinity and Friendship in Ante-Bellum New England." In Peter M. Nardi, ed., *Men's Friendships*. Newbury Park: Sage.

Kimmel, Michael S. 1994. "Masculinity as Homophobia" in Harry Brod and Michael Kaufman eds., *Theorizing Masculinities*. Thousand Oaks: Sage.

Levinson, Daniel J. 1978. *The Season's of a Man's Life*. New York: Alfred A. Knopf.

McGill, Michael E. 1985. *The McGill Report on Male Intimacy*. New York: Holt Rinehart and Winston.

Messner, Michael. 1992. *Power at Play: Sports and the Problem of Masculinity*. Boston: Beacon Press.

Miller, Jean Baker. 1976. *Toward a New Psychology of Women*. Boston: Beacon Press.

Noddings, Nel. 1984. *Caring—A Feminine Approach to Ethics and Moral Education*. Berkeley: University of California Press.

O'Connor, Pat. 1992. *Friendships Between Women: A Critical Review*. New York:

O'Connor, Pat. 1992. *Friendships Between Women: A Critical Review*. New York: The Guilford Press.

Radden, Jennifer. 1996. "Relational Individualism and Feminist Therapy." *Hypatia* 11:71–96.

Schmitt, Richard. 1995. *Beyond Separateness: The Relational Nature of Human Beings—Their Autonomy, Knowledge and Power*. Boulder: Westview.

Sherrod, Drury. 1987. "The Bonds of Men: Problems and Possibilities in Close Male Relationships" in Harry Brod ed., *The Making of Masculinities*. Boston: Allen and Unwin.

Spelman, E. V. 1991. "The Virtue of Feeling and the Feeling of Virtue" In Claudia Card, ed., *Feminist Ethics*. Lawrence: University of Kansas Press.

Stoltenberg, John. 1993. *The End Of Manhood*. New York: Dutton.

Tannen, Deborah. 1990. *You Just Don't Understand: Men and Women in Conversation*. New York: William Morrow.

Theleweit, K. 1988. *Male Fantasies*. 2 vols. Minneapolis: University of Minnesota Press.

Tiger, Lionel. 1970. *Men in Groups*. New York: Vintage Books.

Wellman, Barry. 1992. "Men in Networks: Private Communities, Domestic Friendships" In Peter M. Nardi, ed., *Men's Friendships*. Newbury Park: Sage.

Woolf, Virginia. 1927. *To The Lighthouse*. New York: Harcourt Brace and Co.

Chapter 6

Tracing a Ghostly Memory in My Throat: Reflections on Ftm Feminist Voice and Agency

C. Jacob Hale

It is from all those who have abandoned the traditional conception of sexual morality that the transsexuals differ. Unlike militant homophiles, enlightened therapists and liberated women, transsexuals endorse such traditional values as heterosexuality, domestic roles for women, the double standard of sexual morality, the traditional division of tasks and responsibilities, and the discreditation of deviant sexuality. Unlike various liberated groups, transsexuals are reactionary, moving back toward the core-culture rather than away from it. They are the Uncle Toms of the sexual revolution. With these individuals, the dialectic of social change comes full circle and the position of greatest deviance becomes that of the greatest conformity.

—Thomas Kando (Kando, 145)

Ultimately, female-to-constructed-male transsexuals are the "final solution" of women perpetrated by the transsexual empire. Male-to-constructed-female transsexuals attempt to neutralize women by making the biological woman unnecessary—by invading both the feminine and feminist fronts. Female-to-constructed-male transsexuals neutralize themselves as biological women and also their potentially deviant power. This is merely the most extreme form of neutralization that is taking place also with unnecessary hysterectomies and with the movement toward androgyny. With both, the biological woman is not only neutralized but neuterized.

—Janice G. Raymond (Raymond, xxiv–xxv)

There are also female transsexuals. They have been studied less, since they appear to be less common. They are also less spectacular. Theirs is not the Star System; rather, they ground their beings in the dullness of male attire. As one surgeon has remarked, they want to be like everyone else, that is, men. Women are never like everyone, for they do not make the world. To be a man, in short, is to be part of the common lot. This, it appears, is what female transsexuals aspire to: they want to be fellows, fellows of their fellows.

—Catherine Millot (Millot, 105)

Demanding sex change is therefore part of what constructs the subject as a transsexual: it is the mechanism through which transsexuals come to identify themselves under the sign of transsexualism and construct themselves as its subjects. Because of this, we can trace transsexuals' agency through their doctors' discourses, as the demand for sex change was instantiated as the primary symptom (and sign) of the transsexual.

—Bernice Hausman (Hausman, 110)

and I doubt I should answer
that unspoken question with a scream
for fear of discovering I no longer exist
for perhaps my voice too is no longer alive
except as a memory in my throat—
—Xavier Villaurrutia (Villaurrutia, 33)

The Society for Women in Philosophy (Pacific Division) meeting on May 20, 1995, provided the first occasion upon which I presented an academic paper on an overtly transgender topic from an openly ftm subject position.[1] This was the day after I received my first injection of exogenous testosterone. Despite being beside myself from the profound shifts in consciousness engendered by that first shot of boy-juice, some trepidation about the reactions I would meet slipped through the haze of my excitement. I was fearful that some of the feminist philosophers who had been active in SWIP/Pacific for many years, women whom I deeply respect, would ostracize me for my female-toward-male transition. Sandra Harding was the first to allay that fear; her kindness and sincerity after my somewhat scattered performance clearly conveyed respect and welcome. Later that evening, I asked SWIP members who had stayed to share salad, pizza, wine, and conversation if they thought I should continue teaching "Philosophy and Feminism." I was temporarily reassured to hear the verdict they reached after a long discussion: having seen the world as a woman and as a man, I would have a unique perspective from which to approach the subject.[2]

During the fall of 1995, I asked the same question on SWIP-L, an email list. Although there was much that was useful in the ensuing discussions, I met three distinct types of erasure:

1. Responses in which I was classified as still a woman; this was usually accomplished by use of feminine pronouns, sometimes through use of my former name.
2. Responses that invoked oppressive, totalizing, distorting constructions of transsexuality, abundant in medical, psychotherapeutic, social science, and some feminist and critical studies discourses (a few samples of such are in the quotes with which I begin this essay).

For example, my transition was equated with "sex change surgery" and it was expected that I should welcome discussions of Janice Raymond, whose 1979 book *The Transsexual Empire* is widely regarded in trans-community circles as the paradigm example of transphobic hate literature; among ftms, Raymond's notoriety is surpassed only by Leslie Lothstein's 1983 *Female-to-Male Transsexualism: Historical, Clinical and Theoretical Issues*, the only book-length consideration of ftms in print at the time I wrote this essay.

3. Responses in which my question was figured—reconfigured, that is—as tantamount to asking "Can men be feminists?" Responses to that question I had not asked differed. Some people thought it was a tired old question that feminist philosophers had long since answered or dissolved, others held strong views about how it should be answered, and some proposed conditions under which it would be acceptable for a man to teach a feminism course.

It may seem strange that I took the third as an erasure, especially since I took being classified as a woman as an erasure. Leaving aside for a moment the varieties and complexities of ftm self-identifications, embodiments, and subjectivities, as well the problematic assumption that I am or self-identify as a man, one reason I took this as erasing the specificities of my subject position was that the paradigmatic men about whom these questions have been asked, the paradigmatic men whose participation in feminist politics and theorizing has been the site of contestation, are non-transsexual men. The discussion ensuing from this paradigm elided differences between ftms' and non-transsexual men's relationships to feminist theory and feminist practice, as well as erasing differences between our relationships to other cultural structures of power, oppression, and regulation. This set of erasures came as no surprise, since it results from a familiar coupling: the bipolar assumption that one who is not a woman must, therefore, be a man, conjoined with the normatively paradigmatic status of non-transgendered people, in—and on—whose terms most feminist, queer, anti-racist, post-colonialist, and other resistant discourses are conducted.

Apparently, the obvious points of difference between ftms and non-transsexual men were not obvious, or not obviously relevant, to those who participated in this discussion. Unlike non-transsexual men, ftms have lived parts of our lives as girls and as women with fairly unambiguous female embodiments and all that means in this cultural and historical moment. Thus, we have had years of experiencing the oppressions to which women and girls are subjected, differently depending on our racial, ethnic, class, geographical, and other locations, again differently depending on the extents to which we resisted the attempts at female socialization to which we were, still differently, subjected. Many ftms have long histories of participation as women in women's communities in ways that, generally, men are not allowed to participate, although these experiences may have been fraught with anxiety for us, especially if our gender performativities challenged gender boundaries policed by such communities. We may not have been allowed full participation if our masculinities crossed some imaginary, unspoken yet policed line between allowably masculine and too masculine (cf. Billy quoted in Deva, 155–56). Our participation may also have been hindered if our behaviors and gender presentations unsettled notions of a masculinities-continuum by engaging in feminine, effeminate, or non-masculine behaviors not expected for someone of our apparent gender status: for example, a nellie queen of a butch dyke (cf. Halberstam 1998; Hale 1998; Jones). Some ftms have had years of experience living as lesbians, some as heterosexual women, some as bisexual women, and some have occupied all of these subject positions prior to medical or social transition. Unlike most non-transsexual men, most ftms have had months or years of experience moving about the world—or attempting to—as highly gender ambiguous. Sometimes this occurs prior to medical transition, sometimes it only occurs once medical transition begins. Here, one sees different kinds of oppressions than those seen by people for whom others' gender attributions are fairly univocal and confident. During periods of gender ambiguity, we tend to develop finely-grained observations about how gender attribution works, about our degrees of agency in manipulating the cultural meanings of engendered bodies, and we are subjected to firsthand experiences of the abjection—falling out of realm of social existence, entering a field of deformation/abjection—which accrue, Judith Butler writes, to people who fall outside the established gender boundaries (Butler 1987, 132; Butler 1993, 16). Insofar as gender ambiguous people, and people who claim transsexual subject positions, tend to be assumed to be male-to-female transsexuals, many ftms learn from personal experience about how mtfs are treated in this culture. In my personal experience, being taken to be mtf has led to being loudly verbally abused in public, as well as to attempted rape.

Self-identification provides another nexus of differences between ftms and non-transsexual men. While many ftms self-identify as men simpliciter, not all ftms self-identify as men in any simple, stable, or non-problematic way. Some non-transgendered people with fairly unambiguous male embodiments do not identify as men either, but the range of identificatory alternatives available to ftms is different. Some ftms, such as David Harrison, self-identify as transsexual men, and view that as "a different gender from what people commonly think of as 'man'" (Due, 18; Harrison, 36).[3] Michael Hernandez writes, "My sexual orientation is queer. I consider myself to be a hybrid of woman and man, thus lesbian as well as gay."[4] Just as some mtfs, such as Kate Bornstein, self-identify as neither man nor woman (Bornstein), some ftms discursively position themselves as neither, or both, or "all of both and neither of either," or as members of a third gender, or look "forward eagerly to the day when there [will] be more genders from which to choose" (Devor 1995). Some ftms, such as myself, are profoundly uncomfortable with all of the already given sex/gender categories. However, in some situations we are forced to locate ourselves within these categories, i.e., my United States passport must bear one of two designations: "F" or "M," and which of these two it bears matters for my mobility and my safety. In some situations, we may choose tactically to locate ourselves within already given sex/gender categories to achieve particular ends, i.e., in this paper I claim a right to speak as one, assuredly not representative, ftm transsexual, although in some other situations I resist location of myself within the category *transsexual* as a means of disrupting certain aspects of hegemonic gender taxonomy. Further, we may be located in already given sex/gender categories against our wills in some situations, i.e., sometimes other transsexuals insist on referring to me as a transman, transmale, or MTM despite my objections to being so positioned.[5]

In this essay, I will try to speak from my subject position as it is constituted by those multiple, apparently indiscriminate erasures to which I am subjected and with which I am, to some extent, complicit because of my lack of language with which to move beyond them. From this position, I will chart the contours of an epistemological subject position from which some ftms can engage productively in feminist theorizing and practice. It is important to stress that this is not the only possible nor the only legitimate ftm feminist subject position: differences within the category *ftm* are exemplified in different ftm projects of self-construction, which lead to different types of political projects. My project aims to unsettle the categories *man/men,* whose feminist agency is asserted in the title of this anthology,[6] to trouble totalizing constructions of the category *ftm,* to suggest some particular contributions ftms might have to make to feminist theorizing, and to articulate some particular problems we face in undertaking feminist projects. Thus, my project in this essay is simultaneously political, ontological, and epistemological.

Flesh and Blood, Memory, Narrative, and Consciousness: A Whirlwind Tour of a Contested Colony

> The people who have no voice in this theorizing are the transsexuals themselves.
> —Sandy Stone (Stone 1992, 163)

These are my words to Victor Frankenstein, above the village of Chamounix. Like the monster, I could speak of my earlier memories, and how I became aware of my difference from everyone around me. I can describe how I acquired a monstrous identity by taking on the label "transsexual" to name parts of myself that I could not otherwise explain. I, too, have discovered the journals of the men who made my body, and who have made the bodies of creatures like me since the 1930s. I know in intimate detail the history of this recent medical intervention into the enactment of transgendered subjectivity: science seeks to contain and colonize the radical threat posed by a particular transgender strategy of resistance to the coerciveness of gender: physical alteration of the genitals.

—Susan Stryker (Stryker 1994, 244)[7]

In her landmark essay "The *Empire* Strikes Back: A Posttranssexual Manifesto," first published in 1991 and revised for re-publication in 1992, Allucquère Rosanne (Sandy) Stone began the project of articulating transsexual resistance to our production and containment within binary, phallocentric, misogynistic, medicalized, and pathologizing gender purity genres. Stone's title responds directly to Raymond's *The Transsexual Empire*—aptly, since Raymond singled Stone out to vilify for her participation in the Olivia women's music collective as a recording engineer (Raymond, 101–103; cf. Gabriel; Stone 1992, 154). Stone's essay is the first piece of academic writing in which a transsexual breaks from complicity with/in those discourses she critiques, and I take its publication to be the founding moment in the nascent interdisciplinary field of transgender studies.

In her essay, Stone charts some of the similarities between discourses about transsexuality and other minority discourses that are, perhaps, more familiar to non-transsexuals. She reads the historical movement from the first autobiographical accounts of mtf "sex change" to establishment within psychiatric nosology in 1980 as exhibiting the following broad structure: "The initial fascination with the exotic, extending to professional investigators, denial of subjectivity and lack of access to the dominant discourse; followed by a species of rehabilitation" (163).

This "species of rehabilitation" is deeply pathologized, through a system which requires that we be diagnosed (get ourselves diagnosed) with DSM-IV 302.85 (Gender Identity Disorder in Adolescents and Adults) before obtaining medically regulated embodiment technologies, many of which non-transsexuals obtain without inserting themselves into psychiatric nosology.[8] For transsexuals, inserting ourselves into this nosology is a necessary condition for exercising agency over our own bodies. It is also an act of self-muzzling, of complicity in our own erasure; for, when we speak, when we claim a place for our voices in theorizing about us, no one need listen. As Susan Stryker writes:

I live daily with the consequences of medicine's definition of my identity as a mental disorder. Through the filter of this official pathologization, the sounds that come out of my mouth can be summarily dismissed as the confused ranting of a diseased mind. (Stryker 1994, 144)

Through accepting this "species of rehabilitation," through coerced adoption of the patient role, transsexuals submit to an intricate, tightly woven set of regulatory regimes. If we desire medically regulated technologies, however, we must either insert ourselves into these regimes or forego both adequate medical care and access to juridical mechanisms for changing sex/gender status on legal documents.[9] As Stryker points out, "the current medical system imposes some tough choices on transsexuals about how we exercise power over our own bodies" (Stryker and High, 228). That we confront these "tough choices," that we often experience ourselves—to borrow Marilyn Frye's words out of context—as "caged in: all avenues in every direction, are blocked or booby trapped" (Frye, 4), can best be explained by noticing that the presence of such "double-bind" situations is constitutive of oppression.[10] As Frye argues:

One of the most characteristic and ubiquitous features of the world as experienced by oppressed people is the double bind situations in which options are reduced to a very few and all of them expose one to penalty, censure, or deprivation. For example, it is often a requirement upon oppressed people that we smile and be cheerful. If we comply, we signal our docility and our acquiescence in our situation. We need not, then, be taken note of. We acquiesce in being made invisible, in our occupying no space. We participate in our own erasure. On the other hand, anything but the sunniest countenance exposes us to being perceived as mean, bitter, angry or dangerous. This means, at the least, that we may be found "difficult" or unpleasant to work with, which is enough to cost one's livelihood; at worst, being seen as men, bitter, angry or dangerous has been known to result in rape, arrest, beating and murder. One can only choose to risk one's preferred form and rate of annihilation. (Frye, 2–3)

It is only by ignoring that this is an effect of oppression that Raymond can attempt to impale mtf lesbian-feminists on the horns of the following dilemma:

The question of deception must also be raised in the context of how transsexuals who claim to be lesbian-feminists obtained surgery in the first place. Since all transsexuals have to "pass" as feminine in order to qualify for surgery, so-called lesbian-feminist transsexuals either had to lie to the therapists and doctors, or they had a conversion experience after surgery. I am highly dubious of such conversions, and the other alternative, deception, raises serious problems, of course.[11] (Raymond, 104)

Ignoring Frye's insight and its applicability to transsexuals also enables framing the more recent question of whether transsexuals are duped or duplicitous or both (Hausman; Shapiro, 251; cf. Halberstam 1996).

Stone argues that "the [gender] clinic is a technology of inscription" of a dissolving ontology of gender as essential, natural truth" (Stone 1992, 164). In the wake of the demise of most U.S. gender clinics and programs, technologies of inscription, domination, containment, and colonization of transsexuals' gendered embodiments, identifications, and performativities have become more diffuse. Currently, these technologies circulate through a number of structures, in addition to the remaining gender clinics and privately practicing psychiatrists, psychotherapists, endocrinologists, plastic and reconstructive surgeons, gynecologists, urologists, internists, and general practitioners. The American Psychiatric Association is another such structure, which regulates by means of its *Diagnostic and Statistical Manual* codifications of Gender Identity Disorder (GID) in Children, GID in Adolescents and Adults, GID Not Otherwise Specified, and Transvestic Fetishism. Another regulating structure is the Harry Benjamin International Gender Dysphoria Association, Inc. (HBIGDA), an organization of predominantly non-transsexual medical and psychotherapeutic "professionals" that has appointed itself to set and promulgate so-called "standards of care" for transsexuals. HBIDGA's "standards of care" are misleadingly named: although the phrase "standards of care" is usually used in malpractice, insurance, and managed care contexts to refer to standards of medical quality within particular medical communities (delineated by specialty and by geographical region), HBIGDA's "standards of care" are almost exclusively standards for access to medical technologies.[12] Most U.S. physicians providing hormones or surgical alteration to transsexuals require their transsexual patients to meet to HBIGDA's standards. Those involved in regulating and applying regulations governing change of name and sex/gender designations on legal documents—legislators, judges, and a wide variety of federal, state, county, and municipal employees—constitute another regulatory nexus.

In this arena, colonization has been resituated: rather than imperializing blood, soil, natural resources, national treasures, memory, narrative, and consciousness, it territorializes flesh, blood, memory, narrative, and consciousness. This colonization is effected not by guns and tanks, but instead by scalpels, syringes, pills, and sex/gender markers on those documents that allow one to move about in the world, by means of the conditions under which they are obtained, withdrawn, or denied. These conditions not only regulate culturally meaningful gendered embodiment, they constitute it by establishing, marking, and policing boundaries between those embodiments that have cultural meaning and those that are abjected, cast out of social ontology.

Heterosexism and phallocentricity, as well as the illusion of a natural order of biological sex and biologically-based gender, are inscribed upon our very bodies. By way of illustration of this point, here's a quiz for non-transsexual readers: can you spot what's wrong with these pictures?

1. Prior to performing penile inversion vaginoplasty (in which penile skin forms the inner lining of the neo-vagina), Eugene Schrang (Neenah, Wisconsin) measures the penises of his mtf patients to ensure that they are long enough to provide "adequate vaginal depth." If they are not, he grafts skin from other parts of their bodies to achieve "adequate vaginal depth." Basing their judgments on the appearance and functionality of Schrang's results, many mtfs consider him to be the most skilled surgeon currently performing vaginoplasty in the U.S.

2. Speaking at the First Annual FTM Conference of the Americas, held in 1995 in San Francisco, Michael Brownstein (San Francisco, California) asserts that, although a number of his ftm patients seeking breast reduction/chest reconstruction tell him that they do not wish to have their nipples or aureole reduced, almost all ftm patients need such reduction. He also told his mostly ftm audience that, prior to surgically reconstructing ftm chests, he measures his own chest to ensure proper proportions. Many ftms believe that Brownstein's "top surgery" results are the best currently available in the U.S., at least for those who require double incision.

3. Also speaking at the First Annual FTM Conference of the Americas, Donald Laub's (Palo Alto, California) presentation on phalloplasty includes a slide bearing nothing but black serif upper case type on a white background. This slide reads: "THE PROBLEM: NO PENIS" (cf. Rubin 1996, 174–175).[13] Laub, along with David Gilbert (Norfolk, Virginia), is currently considered to be one of the two best surgeons who perform phalloplasty in North America.[14]

4. Speaking at the 1991 Southern Comfort convention, Gilbert tells his audience that he will not construct a scrotum from labia when performing genital surgery on an ftm patient, since labial tissue is "girlie tissue."[15] In his presentation at the 1993 HBIGDA conference, Gilbert states that he will not allow ftm patients on whom he performs phalloplasty to retain their vaginas, because to do so would be to make "a chick with a dick—and no one would want that!"[16]

These examples foreground medical refusals to grant transsexuals agency over our own embodiments, however, they also point toward ways in which medical power focuses on our tongues: simply by writing this, I risk foregoing any further surgical alterations of my body. That Brownstein, Laub, and Gilbert so clearly have the upper hand in systematic power relations is shown by the fact that they made their remarks from conference podiums to audiences composed primarily of transsexuals. I hope these examples will lead non-transsexual theorists who would critique medical interventions in transsexual embodiment to recognize that, despite that power differential, the critiques of those of us who are directly subjected to the medical regime are launched from epistemologically privileged positions.

As is the case with other colonized peoples, our problems with voice and agency are deeper than those in privileged epistemological positions; we are coerced into silence or are dismissed as mad when we do speak. Silencing techniques exerted upon us often reinscribe our words within non-transsexual discourse when we speak in ways that do not fit within their monolithic constructions of us that accord with their hegemonic beliefs about the proper connections between gender self-identifications, performativities, and embodiments. Sometimes this results from a kind of selective deafness of non-transsexuals. For example, at the First Annual FTM Conference of the Americas, endocrinologist Richard Cherlin stated that ftms do not have pap smears as often as we should because we hate our vaginas. Cherlin's remark was made in answer to a question from an ftm who had asked the medical panel whether he might face any possible medical complications were he to act in accord with his desire to retain his vagina after metaoidioplasty. Clearly, this ftm's relationship to his vagina was not that which Cherlin attributed to ftms: simple hatred.

Sometimes such silencing is performed by non-transsexuals' unwillingness to transfer what they know from other contexts to considerations of transsexuality. For example, at the SWIP/Eastern Division table at the American Philosophical Association/Eastern Division reception in 1994, I found myself arguing with a feminist philosopher, one whose work I admire greatly and whom I had never met before, about her assertion that because feminist philosophers have shown that Cartesian dualism fails and transsexuals are women trapped in men's bodies, transsexuals cannot exist. Would she similarly have used a recent Weight Watcher's commercial in which a woman said that she had known all along that she was a thin woman trapped in a fat woman's body to argue that women who want to lose weight cannot exist? In another context, Carole S. Vance writes: "When we come to sex, our minds grind to a halt: normal distinctions become incomprehensible, and ordinary logic flies out the window" (Vance, 17); this seems especially true of much non-transsexual thinking about transsexuality. When we think about a desire to lose weight, we realize that there are non-dualistic ways to express this desire, that limits of contemporary discourse on a topic are not limits to all pos-sible discourse on that topic, and that difficulties with expressing a desire in extant discourse do not necessarily invalidate that desire but may, instead, point to problems with the discourse. When we think in contexts of non-transsexual feminist, lesbian/gay/bisexual, or queer theorizing and activism, we are familiar with using tactics of inversion to disrupt hege-monic assumptions of male, heterosexual, or normally sexualized cen-trality. Why, then, should non-transsexual feminist or queer theorists profess to be confounded by the phenomenology of transsexual desires, as if their own non-transsexual desires were utterly transparent, and stan-dards of reference for transsexual desires (cf. Scheman)?

Marjorie Garber's *Vested Interests* is a prime example of non-trans-sexual unwillingness to see that epistemological and political tenets obvi-ous in other contexts apply to theorizing about transsexuality. Garber recognizes problems with medicalized discourses when speaking about non-transsexual subjects and succinctly states that "reading *through* . . . puts the interpreter in the position of the subject who knows—knows somehow 'better' than the person whose life is under scrutiny" (Garber, 171), however, she forgets this in her chapter about transsexuality. Garber adopts from Robert Stoller a conception of the demarcation between "male" transvestites and "male" transsexuals that locates cate-gorical differences in their purportedly obsessive relationships to their penises as insignia of maleness. She achieves this by conjoining three rhetorical techniques: quoting uncritically from Stoller, citing his author-ity as "one of the most widely respected interpreters of gender identity today," and lauding his narrative style as "both sympathetic and empa-thetic, adopting the affective subject position of the transvestite" (Garber, 95). On this construction, Stoller knows at least as much about mtfs as they know about themselves and empathetically occupies a sub-ject position that can serve as a stand-in for mtfs themselves, so there is no need to examine what mtfs might have to say about themselves. In fairness, I must note that Garber also cites several mtf autobiographies and some works of transvestite erotica in support of her claims. How-ever, she elides any exploration of the cultural and historical forces that produce these genres, as well as any investigation of their functions or their relationships to community discourses. Thus, Garber has cleared the path for her conclusion that, while transvestism and transsexuality threaten to radically undermine gender identity essentialism (Garber, 102), "male transvestites and transsexuals radically and dramatically essentialize their genitalia" (Garber, 98); in so doing, Garber's use of "*male* transvestites and transsexuals" (italics mine) re-asserts the pro-priety of birth-assigned sex/gender for people assigned male at birth, reinscribing the very phallic essentialism for which she is faulting "male" transsexuals and transvestites.[17]

What, then, does Garber see when she reads through those of us whom she, asymmetrically, terms "female-to-male transsexuals"? She uncritically quotes Leslie Lothstein, and totalizes his transphobic claims even more than he does; for example, after recounting Lothstein's remarks about two ftms who "developed massive castration anxiety" after serious post-phalloplasty difficulties, Garber comments: "*The* female-to-male transsexual . . . gets more than he (or she) bargained for: together with the penis, he/she . . . gets not only castration anxiety but something that sounds very much like castration: his (or her) penis falls off, and has to be replaced (again)" (Garber, 103; italics mine). At Garber's hand, ftms become penis-obsessed, deluded (both because we conflate the penis with the absolute insignia of maleness and because, according to Lothstein, some ftms go bare-chested in public despite poor mastectomy results), and uncritical victims of a misogynist production of the notion that "a 'real one' can't be made, but only born" (Garber 104–105).[18]

Garber proposes a new project for gender studies, one predicated on denying transsexual agency in the discourse about gender: build a discourse about us. ". . . it is to transsexuals and transvestites that we need to look if we want to understand what gender categories mean. For transsexuals and transvestites are *more* concerned with maleness and femaleness than persons who are neither transsexual nor transvestite" (Garber, 110). Who speaks, in Garber's text, for those whose lives are under scrutiny? Non-transsexuals, including two of the most transphobic psychotherapists who have been actively engaged in pathologizing and regulating gender embodiment, identification, and expression—and a feminist literary critic. Are we to presume these theorizing subjects know more or better about our lives than do we, the objects of their scrutiny?

Another silencing technique is deployed when transsexuals are folded into non-transsexual paradigms, and our words, subjectivities, and subject positions are understood in non-transsexual terms; this is the type of silencing to which I was subjected when my question on SWIP-L was answered as if it were a question about the propriety of non-transsexual men teaching feminism courses. Another example of this occurred at the first American Philosophical Association/Pacific Division meeting I attended after beginning medical transition. During the discussion period, I spoke about how all three papers presented on gay and lesbian issues differently elided transgendered phenomena directly relevant to the topics of those papers; since each of these three papers accomplished these elisions differently, it took more than a brief comment to make the elisions visible to a non-transgendered panel and audience. After the session, a feminist philosopher told me that now that I was a man I seemed all too ready to take up too much verbal space. With no more than a modification in tense—"Because you used to be a man . . ."—the same rhetorical device could have been used equally well to erase, by explaining away, the words of an mtf transsexual speaking from her mtf transsexual subject position. In either case, our transsexual subject positions are reduced to non-transsexual manhood in an explanatory and dismissive scheme in which the complex specificities of the transsexual subject positions from which we speak are folded into non-transsexual paradigms. It is not that ftms and mtfs bear no relationships to masculinity, manliness, or manhood; of course we do. Rather, my point is that these relationships are complicatedly different than those had by non-transsexual men, so simple assimilations of our words to paradigms of non-transsexual manhood function to erase the specificities of our subject positions.

> I'm tired of being a scapegoat for the gender trouble of everybody else. Ask yourself—why do you look when we transsexuals make spectacles of ourselves? Is it the curiosity of the freak show, the same voyeuristic desire mixed with dread and titillation that makes you scan the asphalt for gobs of red as you drive slowly past the accident scene? Or is it some fantasy of transcending material limits to behold the sex of angels? And ask yourself, too, what it is that you see. Monsters, mutants, cyborgs, perverts, exotic objects of queer lust? Or just men and women by other means?
>
> —Susan Stryker (Stryker 1995, 40)

Transsexuals are convenient sites for colonization such as Garber's, as well as for struggles between gender colonizers of all kinds and of all political locations. Insofar as there is such a monolithic entity as "the transsexual," this peculiar object is—to borrow Frantz Fanon's psychoanalytic concept from a different context—"a phobogenic object, a stimulus to anxiety" (Fanon, 151). This phobogenic object often bears very little resemblance to transsexual lives as lived, and it is a monolithic fiction constructed stunningly well not only to stimulate anxiety but to function as a depository for the displacement of others' anxieties. Because of our multiply ambiguous relationships to paradigmatic constructions of manhood and womanhood, mtf and ftm transsexuals serve equally well as sites for anyone's—including other transsexuals'—anxieties about their own or another's masculinity or femininity, maleness or femaleness, manhood or womanhood. Thus, as a construct the transsexual is a site for displacement of such anxieties.

Not only does this preposterous construct stimulate and absorb others' displaced anxieties, it is a device of containment; indeed, it must be to structure: compared to transsexual lives as lived, the transsexual is onto-logically stable, for this stability is necessary to the maintenance of the illusion of a relatively sharp boundary between transsexuals and non-transsexuals. Containment and inscription of radical difference between subjects and others who are constructed as markers of their radical dif-ference, encoded in categories of differential diagnosis as well as in wider cultural totalizations, are twin boundary-marking effects that enable dom-ination, colonization, and oppression: individual transsexuals are figured as mere instantiations of the construct the transsexual, our specificities and complexities are policed and erased, our embodiments heavily regu-lated, our voices silenced, our subjectivities restricted and elided, and our radical threats contained and plundered in service of gender hegemonies.

Contemporary categories of sexual desire are inflected through cate-gorical sex/gender placement: a person's placement within sexuality cat-egories is taken to be determined by a relationship between the sex/gender of that person qua desiring subject and sex/gender of that sub-ject's desired objects. Thus, transsexuals are stimulae to anxieties about sexual identity, desire, and practice, as well as containers for such anxi-eties. As Kate Bornstein writes:

> As an exercise, can you recall the last time you saw someone whose gender was ambiguous? Was this person attractive to you? And if you knew they called themselves neither a man nor a woman, what would it make you if you're attracted to that person? And if you were to kiss? Make love? What would you be?
>
> I remember one time at a gay and lesbian writers' conference in San Francisco, I was on a panel and asking these same questions. Because it was a specifically gay and lesbian audience, an audience that defined itself by its sexual orientation, I wanted to tweak them on that identity. I asked, "And what if I strapped on a dildo and made love to you: what would that make me?" Without missing a beat, panelist Carol Queen piped up, "Nostalgic." (Bornstein, 40)

Insofar as our practices of self dislodge familiar, comfortable notions about the naturalness of bodies and the natural foundations of the rela-tionships between bodies, selves, others, and the rest of the world, we are cultural placeholders for anxieties about nature/culture/artifice/perversity, human dominion over nature/natural limitations on human manipula-tion and control, science/culture, normal/pathological, inside/outside, relationships of alterity, spectacle/propriety, display/taboo, agency/domination, self/body, self/culture, and self/other. Because different regimes of power compete to control cultural discourses of the sexed/

gendered/desired/desiring self in relation to these distinctions, we become contested battlezones: psychiatry and other medical specialties, different psychological and psychiatric schools of thought, psychology, sociology, anthropology, feminist theory, and queer theory compete for hegemony over the terrain of transsexual representation and production. Since the structure of the sexed/gendered world rests on foundations which our practices of self belie, we are a system of interlocked faultlines threatening to undermine that world's structure, to shake it off its foundations and bring it crashing to the ground. With so much at stake, is it any wonder that so much meaning, so much tension between so many competing meanings, circulates through transsexual bodies (cf. Halberstam, 1996), that so many people have so much invested in controlling our unruly pluralities by figuring that placeholder for their anxieties, that phobogenic object: the transsexual? With so much invested in and contested on our bodies, on our tongues, how can we speak in and on our own terms?

Moreover, our ability to speak with our own voices is limited by, as Stryker puts it, ". . . the inability of language to represent the transgendered subject's movement over time between stably gendered positions in a linguistic structure" (Stryker 1994, 241). For example, once when my father started telling a story about one of his memories of me as a child, he said: "When Jake was a little boy . . . , I mean a little girl . . . , I mean a little child . . . , he . . . , I mean she . . . , I mean . . . , I don't know what I mean!" There he broke off. My father was right to be frustrated, for there are no grammatical structures he could use to compose one sentence with which to refer to me both as a girl child and as an adult man. Moreover, additional complications come to the fore when we consider attempting to refer to a transsexual in a transitional period. But the linguistic problem is deeper than temporality: representations of me as a *stably* gendered girl child (or boy child) or as a *stably* gendered adult man (or adult woman) would all be false. Structurally, insertion into language—and, therefore, into social ontology—requires greater gendered stability both over time and at any given time than some of us have.

For those of us on whom the limits of already available discourse press the most closely, it would seem that refusing colonizing discourses leaves us in a position of near speechlessness: reverse discourse (cf. Stryker 1994, 240). Yet we know that sounding trumpets of resistance will not, by itself, fall flat upon the arid earth those walls of oppression that shut us out of the city of language, out of social ontology, out of intelligibility. If some queer feminist ftm can speak only reverse discourse, how can he speak with a feminist voice?

Displaced Persons:
Discursive Dislocatedness and Ftm Feminist Agency

And we do have something else to say, if you will but listen to the monsters: the possibility of meaningful agency and action exists, even within fields of domination that bring about the universal cultural rape of all flesh.

—Susan Stryker (Stryker 1994, 250)

I suggest we think carefully, butches and FTM's alike, about the kinds of men or masculine beings that we become and lay claim to: queer masculinities, ultimately, will fail to be queer to the extent to which they fail to be feminist.

—Judith Halberstam (Halberstam 1998)

The core of one's being must love justice more than manhood.

—John Stoltenberg (Stoltenberg, 185)

. . . may we have to be monstrous enough to greet our predicament?

—Nicholas Mosley (Mosley 1990, 3)

On January 17, 1994, the Northridge earthquake left me a "displaced person." This media construction meant that, although I did not have a place to live, I had not joined the ranks of the homeless. I did not have to sleep in a park, at a Red Cross shelter, or on the street. Since I had financial resources, documentation verifying that it is legal for me reside in the U.S., and since I qualified for federal and city assistance, I was able to find another home in four months. About a year later, I entered a period of more enduring displacement, constituted both by my permanently transsexing embodiment and by my discursive dislocatedness.

I want here to map the contours of one possible ftm subject position from which to engage in feminist theorizing and practice. It is crucial for readers to understand that there are many viable ftm subject positions quite different from my own, and to recognize that some of these will lead to very different ftm feminist projects. The subject position to which I lay claim here is one of displacement, dislocation, and erasure, yet it is also a space of creative reconstruction.

My discussion of discursive dislocatedness builds on the view of definitions of gender category terms that I developed with regard to the category *woman* in a recent article (Hale 1996). In this article, I advanced a descriptive reconstruction of the contemporary U.S. dominant cultural definition of "woman," which has thirteen defining characteristics, clustered into several different groups, and weighted differently. None of these thirteen characteristics are necessary or sufficient for membership in the category *woman,* instead, they are best understood as Wittgensteinian family resemblances. On this view of the logical type of gender category term definitions, some members of one category may be more ian family resemblances. On this view of the logical type of gender category term definitions, some members of one category may be more paradigmatically—centrally—located within that category than other members of the same category, in virtue of possessing more or more heavily weighted defining characteristics; further, category boundaries are fuzzy. Borders between gender categories, then, are zones of overlap, not sharp lines.

Those of us who are dislocated from already given gender categories—both normative and non-normative ones—are dislocated in that we cannot fully inhabit any of them. We place ourselves and are placed by others in the margins of any number of gender categories, never close to the paradigmatic core of any but also never falling fully outside all. I am, i.e., not fully man nor woman, nor male nor female, nor medically-induced hermaphrodite nor drag queen nor butch leatherman nor lesbian man nor faggot butch dyke nor transsexual nor ftm nor transgendered nor third gender nor fourth gender nor . . . anything, since I do not fit the paradigms of any of these categories. I flit about the margins of each of these categories; therefore, since some of these categories share unions with one another, I flit through overlapping borderzones constituted by the margins of several gender categories.

Flitting about the margins is not a refusal to own my location, nor is it valorization of genderplay, celebration of gender fluidity, or a pomoplace of gender transcendence. Flitting is movement proper to ghosts, to creatures abjected from full social existence, creatures who have only partial, limited social existence and agency. For reasons as personal, various, and idiosyncratic as the personal, various, and idiosyncratic connections we borderzone inhabitants draw between our embodiments, identifications, social statuses, and subjectivities, we find in already given discourses—transsexual and otherwise—little else than indefinite sequences of indiscriminate erasure. Already given discourses may elide the specificities of those with firm locations within already given categories, but not to the same degree that they elide the specificities of those of us who are dislocated from already given categories. Those of us who live in borderzones constituted by the overlapping margins of categories do so because our embodiments and our subjectivities are abjected from social ontology: we cannot fit ourselves into extant categories without denying, eliding, erasing, or otherwise abjecting personally significant aspects of ourselves. The price of committing such violence against ourselves is too great, though our only other option is also very costly. Those of us who are dislocated have fallen through the cracks that structure the gendered world. Having slipped off all the handholds we have ever tried to grasp, we have fallen between the cracks of language and life. Unintelligible to ourselves and to others, our anguish drives us to search for new category out of the world of social existence already, ghosts never again expect a social world, structured by discourse, to provide homely comforts; we have already learned that home was an illusion, so we forego nostalgia for origins lost (because never properly had). While we try to carve out zones of safety in which to create new discourse—structures and category terms—with which to call ourselves and others into fuller social being, we recognize that this fuller social existence will always be precarious and partial. So we are always cautious, drawing tentatively upon the various discourses of the various locations we only partially inhabit, always ready to shift in resistance to the tactical shifts of hegemonic, normalizing, totalizing, and colonizing forces. Here is queer gender; here is genderqueer. Here is a range of abjected subject positions from which the displaced can speak, a range of dislocated locations. Here is where I stake my place between places.

"Dislocated locations" may sound paradoxical, but it is not, for dislocatedness is not utter absence of location. Rather, our dislocatedness is constituted by our locations in the overlapping margins of multiple gender categories. Different genderqueer borderzone denizens are, of course, differently located: not only do we exist in the areas of overlap of different gender categories but also our placements in those areas of overlap are different. Only by speaking quite specifically about those located elements of our dislocatedness can those who dwell in borderzones speak at all. Such lengthy, detailed specifications do not provide the material for full occupancy of social ontology, which presently requires more central, less multiple instantiation of social categories.[19]

The concept of world-travelling María Lugones develops in "'World'-Travelling, and Loving Perception" provides conceptual tools for understanding the epistemological subject positions of genderqueer borderzone denizens. On Lugones' provocative conception, a "world" is always presently inhabited by some flesh and blood people, need not be a construction of an entire society, and it may be incomplete in that things in it may not be altogether constructed or some things in it may be negatively constructed. Thus, a world may be an incomplete visionary non-utopian construction or it may be a traditional construction of life; some of the inhabitants of a world may not understand or accept their constructions within it (Lugones, 395). Based on this conception, Lugones argues that some of us, especially "those of us who are outside the mainstream U.S. construction or organization of life," travel between worlds and that some of us are in more than one world at once (Lugones, 396). When we travel between worlds, we "have the distinct experience of being different in different worlds and ourselves in them," and we are more at ease in some worlds than in others (Lugones, 396). We may be at ease in a world in any of four ways: (1) by understanding the norms and discourses in that world; (2) by being normatively happy because in agreement with the world's norms; (3) by being humanly bonded with others within that world; and, (4) by sharing a history with others in that world. A person is maximally at ease in a world in which that person is at ease in all four senses (Lugones, 397).

Dislocated genderqueers whose locatedness is constituted both by their dislocatedness and by the specific gender categories, embedded in worlds, in Lugones' sense, which they only marginally inhabit, are creatures who cannot be at ease in Lugones' second sense: since we are only marginally within any gender category, we will not be normatively happy because in agreement with the norms that constitute that gender category's core. Yet we may be at ease in many worlds in each of Lugones' other three senses. We may understand the norms within worlds of the normatively gendered, within transsexual worlds, within ftm-specific worlds, and within other queer worlds. We may have close, loving, human bonds in each of the worlds about whose margins we flit (though we are more likely to form loving bonds with other marginal, flitting creatures in each of our worlds), and we may share histories with others in many worlds. Thus, we may have more plural self-images than those double images of ourselves Lugones locates in our memories of ourselves in different worlds (Lugones, 398); we may travel to indefinitely many worlds and, thus, see indefinitely many images of ourselves, and we may also see ourselves as constructed differently than we construct ourselves in indefinitely many worlds. Some of these constructions of ourselves may be ones in which we cannot recognize ourselves at all; i.e., I cannot recognize myself in Kando's Uncle Tom of the sexual revolution, Raymond's "final solution" of women, Millot's fellow who wants to be a fellow of his fellows making the world, or Hausman's transsexual whose agency is fully contained by a demand for sex change and thus can be read off from medico-legal discourses about transsexuality. Worlds in which we cannot even glimpse ourselves in others' constructions of us may be ones from which we need to emigrate with alacrity and finality, or they may be worlds in which we must try to exercise agency to bring about change. Choosing between these alternatives is always a decision about which resistant, oppositional tactics will produce the most gender liberatory results for all of those who suffer from gender oppression.

World-travelling genderqueers' subject positions lead to particular kinds of gender theory, politics, and practice, forged from the particular zones of overlap that we occupy and through which we travel. In the rest of this paper, I will explore two clusters of such projects of particular ftm feminist concern: (1) problems of manhood, manliness, and masculinity, and (2) creating wider conditions of possibility for genderqueer discursive agency and bodily autonomy.

Problems of manhood, manliness, and masculinity are especially poignant to dislocated genderqueers assigned female at birth who have travelled and still travel in feminist worlds. This poignancy arises from the following concatenation of lived experience and self-identification: our lived histories as girls and women have given us many of the same experiences of oppression as normatively gendered women, for our bodies have carried cultural meanings similarly embedded in misogyny and male dominance, yet we are deeply implicated in masculinities.

Compared to non-transsexual men, we have both advantages and disadvantages with regard to feminist theory, politics, and practice. Our lived experiences tend to give us epistemological advantages of the sort I have already noted. Beyond this, though, we tend to experience much more directly that how we embody masculinity, manliness, and manhood is a matter of existential choice—"masculinity is what we make of it," as Halberstam writes (Halberstam 1988)—to which we bring feminist and other genderqueer political standards. Indeed, for some ftms one of the more disconcerting aspects of social and medical transition is the extent to which we become privy to displays of non-transsexual men's sexism as our gender presentations and embodiments come to elicit attributions as men, fellows of our fellows. Thus, we are in strong positions from which to be reticent to fit ourselves into already given models of masculinity, most of which it must be said have been given by non-transsexual men. As David Harrison notes, "[t]here are not many positive role models out there in the culture" (Harrison, 34). We must be willing to examine our implications in masculinities, and to hold masculinities that attract us—and ourselves—to feminist and other genderqueer political standards of non-oppressiveness. To do this, we must hold onto those human bonds and histories we share with non-transsexual feminist women and to those understandings we have gained from feminism about oppressive structures of masculinity—in short, to continue to move in our feminist worlds.

However, continuing to participate in feminist worlds can be especially difficult for genderqueers assigned female at birth. Non-transsexual men have never been told by feminists that they simply delude themselves into thinking that they exist or that they are the final solution to women. Not having been women, non-transsexual men are not subject to being told they are gender traitors grasping at male privilege when they leave the category *woman*. Nor are non-transsexual men's masculinities subjected to the tightly coercive regulations enacted within those structures that control access to medically regulated technologies for re-embodiment.

Although we face difficulties, we bear moral and political responsibility for that which we make from already given masculinities. Remaining in our feminist worlds, even if only marginally, may require that we exercise great patience with ourselves and with others, and that others exercise similar patience with themselves and with us. In particular, the easiest course, when we are faced with the types of silencing techniques I have outlined earlier in this paper, would be simply to walk away from our feminist worlds. Effort and pain is involved both in self-examination and in the attempts to work through erasure to a point where multiple gender oppressions can be seen, where both men's domination of women and normatively gendered colonization of non-normatively gendered peoples can be seen simultaneously within the same visual field.

It is only when we can hold both simultaneously within our own visual fields that we are in positions from which to engage problems of manhood, manliness, and masculinity—for these constructs have been produced in opposition to normatively gendered womanhood, womanliness, and femininity, and in opposition to abjected gender subjectivities, embodiments, and identifications. To engage these problems productively, we must be cautious of the identifications we make.

Self-identity is always doubly relational (at a minimum). We form and maintain our identities by making continually reiterated identifications *as* members of some category U(s). This is accomplished both positively and negatively by repeated identifications *with* some (not necessarily all) members of U, and by reiterated identifications *as not*-members of some other category T(hem). Identifying *as* and identifying *with,* while closely related, are not identical. Identifying *as* U always involves identifying *with* some members of U, but the converse does not hold; for example, I identify *with* leatherdykes, as a result of historical ties, continuing friendship circles, and some affinities of sensibilities and values, but I no longer identify *as* a leatherdyke. Some members of U serve as positive identificatory referents, whereas some members of T serve as negative identificatory referents.[20]

The borderzone statuses of dislocated genderqueer ftms give us choices of primary positive identificatory referents and our multiple alterities provide many possibilities from which to select primary positive and negative identificatory referents. There are many pressures on us to select dominant men as our primary positive identificatory referents and lesbians, particularly butches, as our primary negative identificatory referents, yet in making our identificatory choices we can exercise moral and political agency rather than succumb to imperialist coercion.[21] In making our identificatory choices wisely, we will gain much from conversations with others who face similar yet different choices, particularly feminist butches and feminist (or anti-sexist or profeminist) non-transsexual men. We must particularly exercise caution when forming identifications with non-transsexual men and in locating non-transsexual men or ftms as our primary positive identificatory referents. Holding those whom we locate as primary positive identificatory referents, as well as those with whom we identify more loosely, to feminist and other gender liberatory principles is, fundamentally, holding ourselves to our own moral and political principles at the level of construction of ourselves.

We may find that self-definitions in which we take our gender identifications—as men, as manly, or as masculine—as core aspects of our beings will obstruct our abilities to construct selves with which we can live morally or politically. As John Stoltenberg writes:

> We must be transformers of selfhood—our own and others'. If we are not, we will have betrayed women's lives utterly, and we will have lost a part of ourselves that is precious and rare on this earth. (Stoltenberg, 198)

My claim is not that we must jettison our gendered subjectivities, embodiments, and self-identifications, that we must live in a fictional space of gender transcendence, but rather that we may need to make our gendered self-identifications secondary to other aspects of those selves we construct: we must care more about our moral and political values than we do about our gendered self-identifications. At the level of self-identification, this would mean that we would self-identify primarily as particular kinds of moral and political beings, and that our primary positive identificatory referents would be other people with similar moral and political self-identifications. If those moral and political self-identifications that we select to constitute central aspects of our selves are based on feminist and other gender liberatory principles, our primary positive identificatory referent class will likely include more non-transsexual women than non-transsexual men, it may include more mtfs than ftms, and it will be heavily populated by other kinds of genderqueers.

For some dislocated ftm genderqueers, locating our moral and political values at the cores of our beings may lead to refusing to be men, as Stoltenberg urges for non-transsexual men (Stoltenberg).[22] While it is difficult to make such refusals legible to others, we can write creatively on context-sensitive paper. Our refusals may be verbal or textual, or they may be more visual public displays. Writing about drag queens, Richard Smith remarks that "homosexual effeminacy is less about wanting to be a woman, and more about wanting to be a man" (Smith, 237). In the right context, such as an ftm gathering, doing drag or even just over-the-top nellie camping is often read as a powerful refusal of manhood.

Whether manhood is a morally and politically viable subject position is an issue that needs further investigation, and this investigation will be most productive if engaged across boundaries of gender identity categories with people who share feminist and other gender liberatory political commitments and if engaged performatively as well as in more traditional prose forms. I have argued elsewhere for a multiple strategies approach to struggling against the oppression of women, an approach that both remakes the category *woman* from the inside, redefining and revaluing womanhood out from under heterosexism and male domination, and encourages gender proliferation (Hale 1996). I believe that a similar approach is necessary with regard to the category *man*. This is not because I take *woman* and *man* to be parallel categories, for surely they are not. Rather, this is because insofar as anyone continues to occupy the category *man* it must be remade lest it continue to be oppressive to all of us who are not within that category, or who are not centrally or solidly within that category, whether we be women, men at the margins, or something other than women or men. This consideration holds independently of whether manhood is a morally and politically viable subject position. Further, some genderqueer feminist ftms may be in better epistemological subject positions than non-transsexual men, for reasons I have cited earlier, to engage this task of re-creating manhood.

Whichever strategy an ftm chooses, he will necessarily be locating himself marginally, as a flittingly disruptive, ghostly borderzone presence. We must be monstrous enough to meet our moral and political predicament, to embrace our agency and to exercise it in accordance with feminist and other gender liberatory principles.

We must also be monstrous enough that we restructure the world, that we create spaces for new cultural formations and new forms of discursive agency, which recognize the fractures that already exist between those aspects of embodiment, subjectivity, performativity, and self-identification taken to constitute unitary sex, gender, and sexuality status—and which broaden the conditions of possibility for new faultlines to appear. In so doing, we may be creating the conditions for our own obsolescence.

Bodily autonomy and freedom of choice provide fairly smooth links between feminist political concerns about reproductive technologies and transsexual political concerns about access to medically regulated technologies. Moreover, the political goals of ending sexist and heterosexist gender role and performativity restrictions provides links between feminist, lesbigay, and transgender political concerns about regulation of gender embodiment, subjectivity, performativity, and self-identification. Insofar as medicine, psychotherapy, and the law are the primary regulatory institutions in this arena, it is on these institutions that our political efforts must focus.

There are powerful alliances to be forged between lesbigay efforts to end the psychiatric abuse of gender lesbigay children enabled by the GID diagnoses, feminists' attempts to ensure women's autonomous access to reproductive technologies and to end coercive abuse of such technologies (i.e., sterilization abuse and female genital mutilation), intersex activists' efforts to stop genital mutilation of intersexed infants and children (cf. Chase), sex radical activists' work to remove adult, consensual sexual activities—"paraphilias"—from the DSM, and transsexual activists' goals of depathologizing transgender identities, practices, and embodiments, and breaking the regulatory medico-therapeutic-juridical stranglehold that allows for our colonization and puts psychotherapists, physicians, lawmakers, judges, and government bureaucrats in positions of power to regulate theoretical and political beliefs about gender, as well as specific gender performativities in anti-feminist and heterosexist ways. Medical nosology, enacted primarily by the American Psychiatric Association at this particular historical juncture, functions to draw and police taxonomic divisions that make these fruitful areas of alliance opaque. Yet if we were to eliminate the strategies of colonization and containment that focus specifically on transsexual bodies, we would thereby create a world in which the technological and performative means for embodiment of sex, gender, and sexuality would be available on the basis of desire alone. Such a world is one in which there would be greater freedom to think and enact gender as existential choice, made in accordance with moral and political principles.

The structures of such a world are not predictable from our vantage point in our heavily regulated world, but we can be sure that it would be a world in which unforeseen categorical, discursive, and cultural formations would appear and in which many of our present formations would become archaic. If we are serious about eradicating those structures that are the architecture of contemporary gender oppressions, we must form stronger alliances based on shared feminist, lesbigay, queer, intersex, transgender, transsexual, and genderqueer moral and political values. Even though some of our short-term goals may be incompatible, even though we may all be undermining the structures that provide the very conditions of our categorical locations, if those of us who are working to end the cultural rape of all flesh do not strengthen such alliances we will either leave in place structures of gender oppression or fail to restructure the world in ways that accord with our moral and political values.

Those of us who are genderqueers must protect our dislocated locations, our borderzones; they may be places from which to launch new discourses and new ways of being, so that, in short, we may participate in restructuring a world in whose social ontology we can come into existence.[23, 24]

Notes

1. Throughout this essay, I use "ftm" as a primitive, not necessarily abbreviatory, broadly ranging term of self-identification; I attempt to signal its non-abbreviatory meaning by disrupting the customary capitalization of "FTM." "Female-to-male," is the most common specification of "FTM," though it sometimes is used as an abbreviation for less standard self-identifications such as "female-toward-male," which I sometimes apply to myself to disrupt the assumption that I am striving for "complete" male embodiment. When used adjectivally, "ftm" can modify either "transgendered" or "transsexual" (or both, when *transsexual* is viewed as a subcategory of *transgendered*). Some people prefer "MTM," an abbreviation for "male-to-male," as a self-identificatory term to indicate that they are acquiring male embodiments in line with their already male self-identifications; on the day that I completed my final version of this essay, I saw an ftm bulletin board post on America Online's Transgender Community Forum (TCF) that shouted (i.e., stated in capital letters) that ftm is a "stupid" term "because we never were female." According to the post's author, the term "should be male to completely male." Others prefer the terms "metamorph" (Morton), "transmale," "transman," or "MBF" (man born female). This is a place, similar to others in this essay, where I cannot supply adequate citations, since much of newly forming, contested ftm community discourse circulates through informal conversations and on-line. Such conversations often carry the presumption of confidentiality, and many are not open to non-ftms. My knowledge comes from my own community participation.

2. At the time, I was so afraid of being called a gender traitor yet again, of facing yet again the presumption that my transition is a grasp for male privilege (cf. Cromwell), that I felt reassured and comforted by their verdict about my epistemological privilege. Once my initial need for their reassurance, I became troubled by the notion that I, as an ftm, have a better epistemological position than non-transsexual women from which to make claims about the oppression of non-transsexual women, because it too easily warrants dismissals of non-transsexual women's claims about their own oppressions. Further, conceiving of me as someone who has traveled through the world as a woman and who now travels through the world as a man is too simple. This conception may fit some ftms and it may have fit the self-construction I presented at SWIP/Pacific in May 1995, but it clearly does not accurately depict the dislocated creature I have been nor that which I have become.

3. Not all ftms and MTMs who self-identify as transsexual men or transgendered men conceive of this as a gender category different from *man*; "transsexual man" may be used to indicate a different route to manhood, or to indicate that one is differently located within the category *man*.

4. Hernandez is not the only ftm who self-identifies as lesbian in one sense or another. Holly Devor reports that one of her ftm informants, "reluctant to leave behind a well-loved place as a member of a lesbian community, called himself a lesbian man" (Devor 1993, 313).

5. Some mtfs take on the identity of a transsexual understood as distinct from *man* or *woman* (County, 139; Harlow and Rheims, 27); this is not to be con-

Perhaps this self-identification is less attractive to ftms than to mtfs because transsexuality unmarked is male-to-female transsexuality. No doubt there are other ftm self-identifications than those I have listed in text.

6. This is the most positive interpretation I can find for this anthology's title. Donald E. Hall comments on this unfortunate phrasing, "suggesting objectification and mastery," "that is as reductive and inflammatory as its even more commonly perceived counterpart: the patriarchal perception that 'Feminism Does Men'" (Hall).

7. Stryker's formulation reflects a confluence of dominant cultural, medical, legal, and mtf transgender community discourses that tend to situate the penis as transsexuality's placeholder. By contrast, I claim that coerced complicity with medico-juridical power-structures functions to contain and colonize the numerous radical threats posed by transsexuals' use of a wide variety of medically regulated technologies to alter physically—surgically and hormonally—a wide range of culturally marked bodily zones, including breasts/chests, internal and external reproductive organs, genitals, voice, hair growth, musculature, and skin texture, many of which non-transsexuals alter by means of the same technologies without similar regulation. This is not the contest the claim that penises bear more cultural meaning than any other pieces of flesh, nor that non-transsexual regulation of transsexual bodies has fastened itself more compulsively on penises than onto any other bodily zone.

8. The most hotly contested political issue among contemporary U.S. transsexuals is whether or not to work toward removing Gender Identity Disorder (GID) from the DSM; many transsexuals fear that without this, or a similar, diagnosis, our abilities to access medically regulated technologies for re-embodiment, and to have use of such technologies covered by private and public medical insurance plans, will be diminished (Stryker 1996). Trans activism aimed at removing GID from the DSM began with a Transgender Nation disruption and protest at the 1993 American Psychiatric Association meeting in San Francisco (Editorial: Transgender Liberation; IFGE Booth; Protest at American Psychiatric Association Convention; Stryker 1994, 237), and has continued through more recent demonstrations (cf. Neff). This issue is a prime example of one around which transsexual, gay/lesbian/bisexual, queer, and feminist solidarity can be built, since GID is used to regulate gendered embodiments, identifications and expressions in children, adolescents and adults, in ways which reproduce heterosexist, sexist, and phallocentric constructs of man and woman (cf. Burke; Hale 1997).

9. To change the sex/gender designation on, i.e., one's U.S. passport, California birth certificate, or California driver's license, one must have certification (of differing sorts) from physicians. In some regions of the U.S. it is possible to obtain exogenous testosterone, estrogen, progesterone, and androgen suppressants without inserting oneself into the psychiatric taxonomy; however, it is difficult to do so without violating the law and while still receiving adequate medical monitoring of, i.e., liver and kidney function, and adequate medical care unrelated to one's desires for re-embodiment.

10. Frantz Fanon's study of the psychology of colonized Martinician black men foregrounds a number of such dilemmas produced by colonization (Fanon).

11. In the years intervening since Raymond's book was published, most psychiatrists, psychotherapists, and surgeons who control access to re-embodi-

ment technologies have ceased imposing a requirement of heterosexuality on transsexuals, although this requirement was dropped for mtfs before ftms. However, insofar as these practitioners regulate transsexuals' gender performativities, they still often impose heterosexist gender norms on transsexuals.

12. HBIGDA's standards of care are written primarily to provide standards for mtf access to medical technologies, yet they are applied to ftms as well (Bergstedt, 4). One goal of some trans activists is to break HBIGDA's hegemony.

13. My memory and notes from this conference do not agree with Rubin with regard to the punctuation on Laub's slide.

14. Phalloplasty and metaoidioplasty are the two main procedures available for surgical construction of a neo-phallus in ftms. Phalloplastic techniques use grafts (from non-erectile tissue) to construct a neo-phallus within the size range typical for non-transsexual males' penises. There is wide disagreement among ftms about the adequacy of phalloplasty, with regard to sensation, appearance and function (eliminatory and sexual). Phalloplastic techniques have been developed primarily for reconstruction of non-transsexual men's penises after damage in combat or in vehicular, industrial, or agricultural accidents. Metaoidioplasty is an ftm-specific procedure in which the erectile tissue an ftm already has, which enlarges with the use of exogenous testosterone, is used to form the neo-phallus. While this technique constructs a neo-phallus with sexual sensation and erectile capabilities, such a neo-phallus is considerably smaller than penises within size range typical for non-transsexual males. With either phalloplasty or metaoidioplasty, urethroplasty can be performed to allow an ftm to urinate through his neo-phallus though there are some medical risks attendant to urethroplasty. Much contemporary ftm community dialogue centers on dissatisfaction with both techniques (cf. Green; Leonard).

15. Jason Cromwell, who was in the audience for Gilbert's presentation, related this remark to me. Southern Comfort is a gender convention held annually by the American Educational Gender Information Service (AEGIS), a nonprofit membership-based clearinghouse for information on transsexual and transgender issues based in Decatur, Georgia.

16. Susan Stryker, who was in the audience for Gilbert's 1993 HBIGDA presentation, told me about Gilbert's statement. This remark, of course, implies that mtfs who have not had penectomy—as well as ftms who have not had vaginectomy—are undesirable, as well as erasing ftm subjectivity with regard to gender identifications.

17. On the paramount role of the penis in the assignment of birth sex/gender, see Kessler, 223–224, 227–228; cf. Chase; Hale 1996, 107–108.

18. Since the primary use for which phalloplastic techniques have been developed is reconstruction of non-transsexual men's penises after damage in combat or in vehicular, industrial, or agricultural accidents, Garber's feminist analysis of the reasons for the inadequacies of these techniques is misguided. If patriarchy wanted anyone to have a fully-functioning penis, would it not want to bestow that honor upon war heroes along with their Purple Heart decorations?

19. I also explore dislocatedness in Hale 1988. My discussions of this topic are deeply indebted to private discussions with Judith Halberstam.

20. Identifications *with,* *as,* and *as-not* may be partial, incomplete, mediated, or crossed. This becomes clear in José Esteban Muñoz's exposition of his different though related notion of disidentification (Muñoz, 145).

21. I examine ftms' motivations for locating butches as primary negative identificatory referents and how this placement of butches functions in ftm self- and
community-construction in Hale 1988.

22. At first glance, this seems much easier for Stoltenberg to say than for an ftm.
As a non-transsexual person assigned male at birth, Stoltenberg faces quite different consequences than does an ftm for opting out of manhood on moral or
political grounds. It is less likely that he will be told that he is a woman, and
even if he is, his history and embodiment give this very different meanings than
it will have for an ftm. Further, a non-transsexual man will not face some of
the particular types of violence used to police gender boundaries and
performativities that an ftm disloyal to men might, especially vaginal rape, and
many ftms tend to be ill-equipped for survival in violent situations. However, if
I am to take seriously my claim that moral and political values provide a better
core for my sense of self than gendered subjectivity, then I must also take seriously its implication that it should be less damaging to be discursively located
by others within a gender category with which I disidentify—woman—than to
lose a more central aspect of my subjectivity.

23. I investigate borderzone defense more thoroughly in Hale 1988.

24. For productive conversations on topics I discuss in this essay or for help with
sources, I thank Talia Bettcher, Cheryl Chase, Jason Cromwell, Ann Garry,
Judith Halberstam, Sandra Harding, Michael M. Hernandez, JordyJones, C.
Julian Leonard, Jay Prosser, Naomi Scheman, Ben Singer, Gail Sondegaard,
and Susan Stryker.

Bibliography

Bergstedt, Spencer. 1996. Conference Report: Fifth International Law Conference—
FTM Panel. *FTM Newsletter* n.n. (Autumn): 4, 6.

Bornstein, Kate. 1994. *Gender Outlaw: On Men, Women, and the Rest of Us.* New
York: Vintage Books/Random House.

Burke, Phyllis. 1996. *Gender Shock: Exploding the Myths of Male and Female.*
New York: Anchor Books/Doubleday.

Butler, Judith. 1987. "Variations on Sex and Gender: Beauvoir, Wittig and
Foucault." In *Feminism as Critique: On the Politics of Gender,* eds. Seyla
Benhabib and Drucilla Cornell, 128–142. Minneapolis: University of Minnesota
Press.

———. 1993. *Bodies That Matter: On the Limits of Discursive "Sex."* New York:
Routledge.

Chase, Cheryl. 1988. Hermaphrodites with Attitude: Mapping the Emergence of
Intersex Political Activism. *GLQ: A Journal of Lesbian and Gay Studies,* forthcoming.

County, Jayne, with Rupert Smith. 1996. *Man Enough to Be a Woman.* New York:
Serpent's Tail.

Cromwell, Jason. 1994. Default Assumptions, or the Billy Tipton Phenomenon.
FTM Newsletter 28 (July): 4–5.

Deva. 1994. FTM/Female-to-Male: An Interview with Mike, Eric, Billy, Sky and
Shadow. In *Dagger: On Butch Women,* eds. Lily Burana, Roxxie, and Linnea
Due, 154–167. Pittsburgh: Cleis Press.

Devor, Holly. 1993. Sexual Orientation Identitites, Attractions, and Practices of

Female-to-Male Transsexuals. *The Journal of Sex Research* 30:4 (November): 303–315.

———. 1995. The Fallacy of Duality in Conceptualizations of Sex, Gender and Sexuality. Plenary speech presented at the 38th annual meeting of the Society for the Scientific Study of Sexuality (November).

Due, Linnea. 1995. Genderation X. *SF Weekly* 14:37 (October 25–31): 12–14, 16–17, 18–19.

Editorial: Transgender Liberation. 1993. *T.N.T.: Transsexual News Telegraph* 1 (Summer): 3.

Fanon, Frantz. 1967. *Black Skins, White Masks*. Translated by Charles Lam Markmann. New York: Grove Press.

Frye, Marilyn. 1983. Oppression. In *The Politics of Reality: Essays in Feminist Theory*, by Marilyn Frye, 1–16. Freedom, California: The Crossing Press.

Gabriel, Davina Anne. 1995. Interview with the Transsexual Vampire: Sandy Stone's Dark Gift. *TransSisters: The Journal of Transsexual Feminism* 8 (Spring): 14–27.

Garber, Marjorie. 1992. *Vested Interests: Cross-Dressing and Cultural Anxiety*. New York: HarperPerennial.

Green, James. 1995. Getting Real about FTM Surgery. *Chrysalis: The Journal of Transgressive Gender Identities* 2:2, 27–32.

Halberstam, Judith. 1996. Right Bodies, Wrong Bodies, Border Bodies: Transsexualism and the Rhetoric of Migration. Unpublished paper presented at the American Studies Association conference (October).

———. 1998. "Female-to-Butch: Butch/FTM Border Wars and the Masculine Continuum." *GLQ: A Journal of Lesbian and Gay Studies* 4:2, forthcoming.

Hale, C. Jacob. 1996. Are Lesbians Women? *Hypatia* 11:2 (Spring): 94–121.

———. 1997. Review of *Gender Shock*. *T.N.T: Transsexual News Telegraph* 7, forthcoming.

———. 1998. Consuming the Living, Dis(re)membering the Dead in the Butch/FTM Borderlands. *GLQ: A Journal of Lesbian and Gay Studies*, forthcoming.

Hall, Donald E. 1996. Reflections of a Male "Femi-Nazi." Unpublished paper presented at Society for Women in Philosophy/Pacific Division (May).

Harlow, Kim, and Bettina Rheims. 1994. *Kim*. Translated by Paul Gould. Munich: Gina Kehayoff.

Harrison, David. 1996. Becoming a Man: The Transition from Female to Male. In *Assaults on Convention: Essays on Lesbian Transgressors*, eds. Niocola Godwin, Belinda Hollows, and Sheridan Nye, 24–37. New York: Cassell.

Hernandez, Michael M. n.d. Author's statement. In *Looking Queer*, ed., n.p., forthcoming.

IFGE Booth; Protest at American Psychiatric Association Convention. 1993. *T.N.T.: Transsexual News Telegraph* 1 (Summer): 4.

Jones, Jordy. 1995. Another View of F2M. *FTM Newsletter* 29 (January): 14–15.

Kando, Thomas. 1973. *Sex Change: The Achievement of Gender Identity Among Feminized Transsexuals*. Springfield, Illinois: Charles C. Thomas.

Kessler, Suzanne J. 1994. The Medical Construction of Gender: Case Management of Intersexed Infants. In *Theorizing Feminism: Parallel Trends in the Humanities and Social Sciences*, eds. Anne C. Herrmann and Abigail J. Stewart, 218–237. Boulder: Westview Press.

Leonard, C. Julian. 1996. Phallusies: Exploding the Myth of 'Penis Formation'. *TransFagRag* 1 (Fall): 8–9.

Lothstein, Leslie. 1983. *Female-to-Male Transsexualism: Historical, Clinical and Theoretical Issues*. Boston: Routledge and Kegan Paul.

Lugones, María. 1990. Playfulness, "World"-Travelling, and Loving Perception. In *Making Face, Making Soul/Haciendo Caras: Creative and Critical Perspectives by Feminists of Color*, ed. Gloria Anzaldúa, 390–402. San Francisco: Aunt Lute Books.

Millot, Catherine. 1990. *Horsexe: Essay on Transsexuality*. Translated by Kenneth Hylton. New York: Autonomedia.

Morton, Shadow. 1994. A Man By Any Other Name. *FTM Newsletter* 27 (April): 11.

Mosley, Nicholas. 1990. *Hopeful Monsters*. New York: Vintage International/Random House.

Muñoz, José Esteban. 1996. Famous and Dandy Like B. 'n' Andy: Race, Pop, and Basquiat. In *Pop Out: Queer Warhol*, eds. Jennifer Doyle, Jonathan Flatley, and José Esteban Muñoz, 144–179. Durham, North Carolina: Duke University Press.

Namaste, Ki. 1996. "Tragic Misreadings": Queer Theory's Erasure of Transgender Subjectivity. In *Queer Studies: A Lesbian, Gay, Bisexual, and Transgender Anthology*, eds. Brett Beemyn and Mickey Eliason, 183–203. New York: New York University Press.

Neff, Lisa. 1996. Fighting Transphobia: Transgender Activists Challenge Psychiatrists' Definion of Mental Disorder. *Windy City Times* 12:8 (October 31): 4.

Raymond, Janice G. 1979. *The Transsexual Empire*. London: The Women's Press.

Rubin, Henry S. 1996. Report on the First FTM Conference of the Americas: A Vision of Community. *Journal of Gay, Lesbian, and Bisexual Identity* 1:2 (April): 171–177.

Scheman, Naomi. 1996. Queering the Center by Centering the Queer: Reflections on Transsexuals and Secular Jews. In *Feminists Rethink the Self*, ed. Diane Tietjens Meyers. Boulder: Westview Press.

Shapiro, Judith. 1991. Transsexualism: Reflections on the Persistence of Gender and the Mutability of Sex. In *Body Guards: The Cultural Politics of Gender Ambiguity*, eds. Julia Epstein and Kristina Straub, 248–279. New York: Routledge.

Smith, Richard. 1994. Frock Tactics. In *Drag: A History of Female Impersonation in the Performing Arts*, by Roger Baker with contributions by Peter Burton and Richard Smith, 236–262. New York: New York University Press.

Stoltenberg, John. 1989. *Refusing to Be a Man: Essays on Sex and Justice*. New York: Meridian.

Stone, Sandy. 1991. The *Empire* Strikes Back: A Posttranssexual Manifesto. In *Body Guards: The Cultural Politics of Gender Ambiguity*, eds. Julia Epstein and Kristina Straub, 280–304. New York: Routledge.

———. 1992. The *Empire* Strikes Back: A Posttranssexual Manifesto. *Camera Obscura* 29 (May): 151–176.

Stryker, Susan. 1994. My Words to Victor Frankenstein above the Village of Chamounix: Performing Transgender Rage. *GLQ: A Journal of Lesbian and Gay Studies* 1:3, 237–254.

———. 1995. Looking at You Looking at Me. *On Our Backs* 11:1 (January/February): 21, 40.

———. 1996. Delusions of Gender. *Out* No. 37 (October): 34.

———, and Kathy High. 1995. Across the Border: A Discussion between Susan Stryker and Kathy High on the Anarchorporeality Project. *Felix: A Journal of Media Arts and Communication* 2:1, 228–236.

Vance, Carole S. 1989. Social Construction Theory: Problems in the History of Sexuality. In *Homosexuality, Which Homosexuality?*, by Dennis Altman, Carole Vance, Martha Vicinus, Jeffrey Weeks, and others, 13–34. London: GMP Publishers.

Villaurrutia, Xavier. 1993. Translated by Eliot Weinberger. *Nostalgia for Death*. Port Townsend, Washington: Copper Canyon Press.

Chapter 7

Teaching Women Philosophy (as a Feminist Man)

Thomas E. Wartenberg

The title of this paper is meant to be provocative. By it, I want to high-light my claim that there is something special about teaching philosophy to women, that there is something that differentiates this activity from that of teaching philosophy to an audience of students that is primarily male. The question that I shall address in this paper is precisely what it is that makes the teaching of philosophy to women an especially prob-lematic task in our culture.

Lest I be misunderstood, let me immediately state that I am not claim-ing that there is something about women themselves, about their capac-ities or abilities, in virtue of which it is difficult to teach them philosophy. Unlike philosophers of earlier ages, I am not saying that women are unable to participate as fully as men in the "life of reason" and hence are more difficult to teach philosophy to.[1] Rather, I want to call attention to the problematic nature of the practice of teaching philosophy to women in a male-dominated society. Because our society and those from which it developed are characterized by patterns of male domination, teaching philosophical texts that originated in those societies has a problematic character.

Although the question "What constitutes male domination?" requires a good deal of analysis, for the purposes of this paper, I shall simply assume the fact of male domination as a general background for my discussion.[2] It is the presence of such male domination that makes the difference I am talking about significant. This also means that the topic of this paper is paralleled by questions of what difference it makes when those to whom one is teaching philosophy are members of other minor-ity or dominated groups. For the purposes of this essay, I will nonetheless limit myself to the question of teaching philosophy to women.

I shall not approach this issue as a theoretical issue alone, but as an issue of which I have been made aware as a result of my experience teaching at Mount Holyoke College, an all-women's institution. Because of this experience I have come to believe that the teaching of the central texts of the philosophical tradition has a problematic character that is not generally sufficiently recognized. It is this issue that I wish to discuss in this paper.

Let me begin with a few autobiographical remarks. When I began to teach at Mount Holyoke College, I already considered myself to be a feminist. In fact, through the influence of a number of my friends and colleagues, I had been reading feminist literature of various sorts since the early 1970s. (I think that the first feminist text of any significance that I read was Doris Lessing's *The Golden Notebook*.) I thought that feminism had important things to tell us all, both in personal and intellectual terms. I had even written an essay about the film *With Babies and Banners* in which I explored various issues in feminist theory concerning the ideas of a "feminist consciousness."[3] I mention these facts in order to say that I did not consider myself a neophyte in regard to feminism.

In fact, my feminist convictions made me look forward to teaching at an all women's school because it created a context in which I felt I could both teach philosophy and also help empower women. I saw a real benefit in the fact that by teaching philosophy to women I would not simply be educating them in the tradition of Western philosophic thought, but I would also be equipping them with the sort of skills necessary to compete equally with men in certain contexts. Thus, for example, by teaching women certain skills necessary to carry on a philosophical discussion, I thought I would be serving feminism while at the same time doing what I liked to do, namely teach philosophy. I also looked forward to being in an environment in which I thought that feminism would be a natural starting point for the examination of society in general. I thought that, because virtually every woman would have an experience of living in the midst of social relations in which they were in some sense being exploited, I would be able to draw on this type of experience in discussing various theories of society and that this could be helpful to my teaching.

So I arrived at Mount Holyoke with a very optimistic sense of what I would be doing when I taught women philosophy and a pretty clear sense of what I wanted to do when I taught it. Feminism was much on my mind and I had a notion of how to go about teaching in a feminist manner.

One of the courses I had agreed to teach was entitled "The History of Ancient Philosophy." It was in my preparation for this course that I developed a new level in my awareness of sexism and, as a result, came to a new insight into the importance of teaching feminism as an issue that needs to be taken seriously in our culture. I'll concentrate on that course because it did have deep significance for me, although many of the conclusions that I reached in regard to that course were similar to my experiences in thinking about and teaching other courses as well.

"The History of Ancient Philosophy" was a new course for me. My own research has, for the most part, focused on Kant and nineteenth century German philosophy as well as certain issues in contemporary social theory. "Going back to the Greeks" was a switch for me, although I had regularly used Plato and Aristotle in my introductory courses. It meant that I had to consider the entire world view of these two philosophers and not just use them to illustrate a point that I wanted to make. I mention this because it meant that I approached teaching this course in a different manner than I approached teaching my other courses. For example, I had taught the History of Modern Philosophy a number of times in a co-educational environment and it concerned philosophers whose ideas had played a large role in my own research on Kant and his followers. That course was one that I therefore did not approach with as great a sense of its being a new undertaking. The project of developing a course on the History of Ancient Philosophy, however, was a new one for me and one that I began, in a certain sense, from scratch.

So teaching Ancient Philosophy meant that I had a lot of work to do over the summer before I came to Mount Holyoke and a lot more work to do during the year as I prepared my lectures on the texts I had chosen to read in the course. When I sat down to read the ancient texts in order to decide how and what I would teach, I saw something that I knew was there, but whose significance I had not realized: that there was a systematic denigration of the nature of women in these texts. For example, I began reading Hesiod. I wanted to begin my course with a consideration of Greek mythology as a means of setting up the context within which the pre-Socratics emerged with a genuinely new form of understanding. What I found, upon so doing, was a text that included an incredible myth concerning the origin of women. In the *Theogony*, Hesiod tells us that, when Zeus found himself unable to torment men by keeping fire out of their hands—as a result of the intervention of Prometheus to whom we all owe a debt of thanks—he decided to create women in order to make male life miserable. I'll just quote a little of the story here:

> From her [Pandora, the first woman] comes all the race of womankind,
> The deadly female race and tribe of wives
> Who live with mortal men and bring them harm,
> No help to them in dreadful poverty
> But ready enough to share with them in wealth.

After a catalogue of the ills that women bring to men, Hesiod concludes:

> Women are bad for men, and they conspire
> In wrong, and Zeus the Thunderer made it so.[4]

This is quite a startling myth about the origin of women, one that calls out for some sort of interpretation. So you can imagine my surprise when I turned to the textbook that I chose in order to present the pre-Socratics. Although the text included selections from Hesiod, it did not include this particular myth.[5] So I asked myself, "Should I follow the example of the textbook and just ignore this? Or do I have a responsibility to introduce it to the class as a significant omission that deserves discussion?"

This is one example, the first I actually encountered as I reread the texts of classical literature and philosophy. As I continued on through the texts, I found numerous examples, with Plato's justification of the role of women among the guardians as one striking counter-example. Whether it was one of the characters in a Socratic dialogue saying that he did not want to act "like a woman" or Aristotle treating "women, slaves, barbarians, and children" as belonging to categories of human beings inferior to the full-bodied humanness of male citizens, I began increasingly to note a sexist strain in the texts that I would be teaching. Consider, for example, Aristotle's discussion of the nature of society in his *Politics*:

> In the first place there must be a union of those who cannot exist without each other; namely, of male and female, that the race may continue ... and of natural ruler and subject, that both may be preserved. For that which can foresee by the exercise of mind is by nature intended to be lord and master, and that which can with its body give effect to such foresight is a subject and by nature a slave; hence master and slave have the same interest. Now nature has distinguished between the female and the slave. For she is not niggardly ... she makes each thing for a single use, and every instrument is best made when intended for one and not many uses. But among the barbarians no distinction is made between women and slaves, because there is no natural ruler [i.e., aristocratic male citizen] among them: they are a community of slaves, male and female.[6]

Aristotle is here comparing the distinction between male citizens and their wives to that between the citizen and his slave. Although he does not want to assimilate the status of women to that of slaves, Aristotle clearly sees both of these types of beings as created by nature to work in the service of the male citizen of Greece.

Now we could spend a long time analyzing this passage from Aristotle for the various forms of sexism and ethnocentrism it contains and try to see how he could view the world this way. It would be instructive to think about the use of a teleological world view to justify male dominance, and even to think about links between a technical conception of Being and such forms of domination. But for my purposes here, the important thing to notice is how his treatment of women is linked to his claims about men—and he is thinking here, of course, only of his own social equals, Greek citizens—having greater insight and thus being destined by nature to rule.

So I increasingly began to see a pattern of sexism in Greek Philosophy. Now, as I've said, this perception of a sexist tradition in philosophy was not new to me. After all, I had been made aware of the sexism in the philosophic tradition over the previous fifteen years or so. But what was new to me was the context in which I was reading about this sexism: that I was supposed to be teaching these texts to women and women alone. I began to ask myself what it would be like for them to read texts like this one.

At first this occasioned a sort of crisis of conscience: How could I teach these texts in a positive way when there was so much sexism in them? My initial solution was to think of such sexism as itself a part of what I would make the subject matter of the course. Not just metaphysics, epistemology, and ethics, but also an inquiry into the nature and roots of sexism in Greek society. The presence of sexism in Greek philosophy could then itself be interrogated in a philosophic manner, especially using some of the ideas—such as a critique of binary oppositions—that the tradition of deconstruction had made available for use in reading texts.

But the more I thought about this, the more unsatisfied I became with just taking a day or two to think about sexism in Greek philosophy and then returning to the philosophic texts themselves. For I began to see such a solution as too *ad hoc* and not really addressing the issue at the level I believed it had to be addressed. I will get at this by relating something that I discovered about myself and my own assumptions while reading, for I think that these discoveries convey something important and can serve as a justification for the sort of treatment of sexism that I have begun to elaborate in my courses and, in particular, in the one on Greek philosophy.

What struck me most about this situation was not so much the presence of such sexist remarks in these classical texts, but my previous failure to accord them the sort of centrality that I now did. It is true that I noticed some of them before. I had even said to myself, "This is really bad. Aristotle is such a racist and sexist. How could he really have thought that they—women and slaves—were not people? How could he be so ethnocentric to call all non-Greek people 'barbarians' and to equate them with those he held in total contempt, the slaves?" But what I did not notice, before I began to teach philosophy to women, was that I had myself been complicit in this sexism because of my strategy as a reader. Let me attempt to explain what I mean by this.

In order to get at the point I am trying to convey, I need to make a quick detour into a bit of literary theory. I want to begin by saying that texts are always addressed to an audience, that they are written to a particular type of reader who I shall call the implied reader of the text. Such a reader, we can say, is hailed or addressed by the text. The group of readers who are thus included within the set of people who are intended as the addressees of the text I will call the "textual community." In making these assertions, I am relying on claims by a number of people, but putting them together in a very different context. The concept of "implied reader" was introduced into literary theory by Wolfgang Iser, though for purposes very different than those for which I am using it here; it has become the basis for a school of literary theory known as "reader-response criticism."[7] The notion of a text addressing its audience is based both on Louis Althusser's idea of "hailing" or "interpellation" as central to understanding the nature of ideology and also on Jean-François Lyotard's notion of culture being narratively and discursively constituted.[8] Finally, the notion of a textual community is one that Richard Rorty uses, although once again in a very different sense than I would like to.[9] What I want to do here is to put these various ideas together and claim that *a text is implicitly addressed to certain individuals as members of a certain group.*

The idea that a text is implicitly addressed to a certain specific type of audience is certainly something that is true of various specific types of texts. For example, there are political texts where such implicit assumptions are made explicit. One need only think of Karl Marx and Frederick Engels' famous slogan at the end of *The Communist Manifesto*, "Workers of the World Unite!" in order to see that some texts are addressed to a particular audience and not to others. I am claiming that this situation is true generally: that literary texts address us as members of a specific audience that the text intends to address. The scope of the "we" that an author uses is a way of thinking about who might be included in this notion of an implied reader. For there is an implicit sense of community established by this implicit sense of a "we" in a text and it is this sense of community that I am claiming is essential to understanding how a text functions. What I am saying is that there is in a text just such a specific sense of whom that text is addressing, of who the possible readers of a text are, and of what sorts of values they ought to hold.

We can see what I am driving at if we consider the passages I have previously quoted. Hesiod's myth about the nature of women is certainly something addressed to males. The fact about women that needs to be explained by the myth is why they are such a torment to males. This very fact is, obviously, something that a female audience would dispute and criticize. Hesiod's text is certainly addressed to males, perhaps even to males in the context of a banquet, seeking a certain sort of entertainment.

A similar point can be made about the passage from Aristotle's *Politics*, which I quoted. Clearly, in that text, Aristotle is addressing his social equals, the aristocratic male citizens of Greece, and not the so-called "barbarians." We can see this, because Aristotle's text assumes a consensus of values that his addressees, the all-male citizens of Greece, can be expected to share. If he were interested in addressing some "barbarians," he would not be able to write in the same way. He would have to think about addressing them through his words and that would have an effect on the structure of any text he so addressed.[10]

As a result of thinking about texts in this manner I began to see that when I read the great works of Western philosophy prior to coming to Mount Holyoke I did so *as a white male citizen.* That is, being a white male, I was able to feel a certain solidarity with the author of these texts because I could feel myself to be, in a certain sense, a member of his implied audience in virtue of the fact that I was not being explicitly excluded from it. This was a fact that I had not been aware of previously, but one which, nevertheless, affected how I had read these texts. Even when I saw Aristotle or Plato's sexism, for example, my response to that sexism was mediated by the fact that I thought of myself as one of the implied readers of the text—to a certain degree, of course, since I was not a citizen of Ancient Greece. The interesting thing to me was that I never noticed this fact. That is, I simply saw myself as a reader of a text and never acknowledged the fact that my being addressed by the text, or my taking the text as one to which I could respond, meant that I was a person in a certain social group. Prior to this realization, the act of reading had been transparent to me. I had not seen it as itself contributing to the establishment of the meaning of the text. In a sense, what I began to see was the need to problematize the act of reading itself, to render it non-transparent.

What teaching Ancient Philosophy to a class composed entirely of women did, then, was to cause me to change how I read the central texts of the Western philosophic tradition: I now began to read them in the role of a person teaching them to women. And this caused me to take a different stance in regard to them as a reader of these texts. I now began to ask a new question, one that I must honestly say I had never asked myself before: What would it feel like to be asked to take seriously the ideas in a text that also argued that I, in virtue of my gender, was inherently inferior to other human beings?

What I began to see was that it would be very hard for me—now the imagined female student to whom I would be teaching these texts—to accord them the sort of canonical status they had had for me as a student, when the issues of class, race, and gender were not as central as the "important questions" about the nature of human existence that the texts themselves put forward. I saw that a female student would be placed in a schizophrenic relationship to the text in virtue of its assumed audience. On the one hand, she would feel a part of the implied audience of the text insofar as the author was talking about being human and having to struggle with human questions of value and existence.[11] On the other hand, she would feel put down when the author dismissed women as less than human or as created in order to torment men, when, that is, she was explicitly being ruled out of the author's intended audience.

This raised for me the increasingly difficult question of what I would be doing when I taught philosophy to women. I mean, of course, when I taught women those great philosophic texts that I considered to be the basis of the philosophic tradition and which, I now realized, were penetrated through and through with sexist ideas and assumptions. Insofar as I believed that there was really something worthwhile in the tradition of philosophic thought that I was teaching, I had to ask myself how I could teach it to women in a way that did not demean their sense of themselves rather than elevate it as I hoped to do? That is, I began to see a fundamental contradiction between my assessment of philosophy as an important intellectual activity that could help people come to terms with the nature of their lives and the specific effect these texts would have on women reading them.

Let me just note in passing that these questions were ones that I might have stumbled on in thinking about these texts if I were teaching them in a co-educational environment. I believe that there is a need to think them through independently of the context in which they occurred to me and that they have validity that transcends the context of their occurrence. But what I want to also suggest is that the context is an important one, for it made me—in many ways a member of the implicit audience of the texts—see myself as really being a member of such an audience for the first time and to take more seriously than I ever had what it would be like to be "the Other," the one left out of such an audience.[12]

The result, then, of my being faced with the fact of teaching philosophy to women is that I have come to see that the act of reading such texts is much more problematic than I previously had acknowledged. In particular, I have come to realize that a text is structured in such a way as to address an audience and that to accept that address is to accept many of the values that the text endorses or assumes.

As a result of this, I want to acknowledge the fact that there is a new sort of textual ethics that I am aware of as a result of my increasingly critical attitude toward reading itself. But this means that being a feminist is harder than I had thought, for I not only have to worry about what it is that Aristotle says about women and why it is unreasonable, I also need to worry about the whole question of whom he is addressing when he says "We." And this means that the whole question of Aristotle's community and its racist, sexist, and exploitative practices has a bearing on the meaning of the text, for the reader is being addressed by the text as a member of these groups, as a participant in these practices.

This means that teaching philosophy to women is a complicated thing to do, perhaps especially for a man, though I think that that idea needs to be thought about more deeply than it has been. It means that one has to do a sort of balancing act. On the one hand, as a philosopher, that is, as someone who finds enough worthwhile in the tradition of Western philosophy to spend his life thinking about it and the various problems it puts forward, I want to teach my students to appreciate what is worthwhile in that tradition. For example, to stick to the example of my course on the History of Ancient Philosophy, I find the idea of *phronesis* or practical wisdom one from which we can learn a great deal and that we, as a culture, would do well to re-appropriate. On the other hand, as a feminist (and anti-racist, among other things), there is much that I find objectionable in that tradition. In particular, its degradation of women, non-Greek peoples, and non-aristocrats. The question is how does one manage to teach both of these things at the same time?

The solution that I am advocating is one that introduces a view of reading that places the problematic of reading and textuality at the center of my agenda in a course like the History of Ancient Philosophy. Reading itself has to be seen as an activity that takes place in a society and that, as such, is implicated in all the problematic aspects of such a society. I am suggesting that it is no longer possible to treat reading as simply coming to see the meaning that is present in a text, for the act of reading is, at the most fundamental level, an ethical and political act, one through which our sense of who "We" are is constituted.

I have been arguing that, as a result of this new conception of reading, we—as teachers and readers of philosophical texts—need to conceive of a text in a different manner than we might previously have done. Instead of seeing a text as a unity, we need to acknowledge two conflicting moments in it. The first is governed by a logic of inclusion. It is a discourse in which there is an implied audience and the text establishes a textual community around this audience. In this discourse, a great deal is said or implied about who "We" are and how "We" ought to go about our business. But equally present in the text is a logic of exclusion, a discourse about an "Other" or "Others" from whom "We" distance

"Ourselves" in various ways. The meaning of the text must then be conceived of as a dynamic result of the tension between these two logics, one of self-affirmation and creation and one of negation and denial.

I have tried to demonstrate how such a logic would work in the reading of two passages, one from Hesiod and one from Aristotle. In each case, I have claimed that the passage demonstrates the creation of a certain community and the exclusion of specific groups from that community. This is the sort of political and ethical act that the text seeks to constitute and that I have been arguing needs to be made into a theme for our explicit reflection as readers of a text.

In teaching philosophy to women, it will be particularly important to show how the tradition of Western philosophy operates with this dual logic in order to enable our students to decide how, as feminists, they ought to regard the tradition and make sense of its positive as well as negative moments. It means that feminism is not some marginal presence whose intrusion onto the field of "serious philosophic concerns" can be regarded as an intrusion of the political into the domain of the true concerns of the serious student, but rather it forces one to acknowledge the political nature of reading itself and of being confronted with the task of understanding oneself within the context of an ambiguous tradition.

I am not here making a claim about texts in general, some sort of metaphysics of textuality. I am claiming that the Western tradition of philosophy, and more specifically that of Greek philosophy, is constituted in this way. I put it forward as a sort of empirical hypothesis about the nature of this textual tradition in opposition to the idea of a monological tradition, be it one of progress or decline.

The point that I offer is that the act of teaching philosophy to women is an especially complex act because of its relation to the male-dominated society in which we all live. The sexist nature of the texts we teach as part of our "tradition" requires that we think deeply and carefully about what it means to teach them to our students. For we cannot simply teach them to our students without an awareness of the effects that such teaching can have upon them. As well as showing our students that these texts have messages that are addressed to them if they can only hear them, we need to make them aware that certain of these messages need to be heard with a critical ear.

My suggestion has been that we teachers of philosophy need to do more in dealing with this problem than simply make sexism one of the themes of our course, while also trying to convey the positive aspects of the tradition we are seeking to bring alive to our students. What needs to be done, from my point of view, is to introduce this very tension in the tradition into our courses at a foundational level. This should be done by making the act of reading non-transparent and problematic, by showing our students that reading is one of the central means by which we are constituted and constitute ourselves as human beings. For we come to think of ourselves, at least in part, as the creatures that we are addressed as being by others. What I have been trying to show is that one of the most central and problematic forms of address in this culture is that of a reader of philosophical texts.

Epilogue: Further Thoughts, 1997

The above is a paper written over ten years ago as an invited talk before the Mount Holyoke College Philosophy Club. What seemed unusual to me back then is by now second nature to me. That the primary audience for my teaching is female is something that no longer seems odd to me, though that does not mean that it has not fundamentally altered my sense of what it is to be a teacher, especially one who teaches texts from the Western philosophic tradition.

In rereading the original paper, I find myself still agreeing with its central claims: that the philosophic texts of the Western tradition are constituted by competing logics of inclusion and exclusion and that it is important for those who teach that tradition to make their students aware of this often unnoticed fact. However, I now would place those claims in a broader theoretical perspective that sees texts as immersed in relationships of power. For me, the goal of teaching a text now includes the explication of how those relationships of power govern the production of textual meaning, both for its author and its readers.

The texts that I chose to use in the paper as examples of how I made students aware of the opposed logics of inclusion and exclusion were relatively easy ones for my purposes since they involved explicit sexist remarks. This left open the more difficult question of showing how power relationships affect the structure of texts that are not explicitly sexist (or racist or classist). I shall now give an example of how I have sought to uncover these power relationships in texts whose relationships to structures of power and domination are less straightforward.

Near the beginning of that Plato's *Republic*, Socrates attempts to construct an ideal community in order to provide some guidance as to how to conceptualize justice. The procedure that Socrates and his interlocutors adopt is simply asking who they would want to include in their ideal society. In exploring this text, I have asked my students to examine carefully the assumptions about human sociality that structure the construction of this society. In particular, I have argued that this construction imposes a social bond on men whose positions as the heads of households are already in place. As a result, this supposed construction of human sociality takes place on the already constituted set of social relationships making up a household, a unit whose sociality is thereby passed over and obscured. Exposing this "pre-social sociality" to the view of my students allows them to see how power relationships within the household—which includes husband-wife, parent-child, and owner-slave relationships—are occluded from the argument about the nature of justice.[13]

This example illustrates that even texts that seem free of sexism need to be interrogated carefully in order to see how sexist assumptions function in their construction and reception. My claim is that Plato as well as readers of his text simply assume that the only significant social relationships that need to be discussed as such are those between male citizens. The relationships that those male citizens have to their wives, children, and slaves are left out of Socrates' consideration of the rationale for creating a social bond. Only by interrogating this text for the ways in which it conceives of human sociality do we arrive at this critical reading.

Another important aspect of teaching philosophy to women that I did not mention in the original paper is the inclusion of texts written by women philosophers. In attempting to get female students to see that, despite the fact that they are sometimes explicitly excluded from the intended audience of philosophic texts in the Western tradition, philosophy can be an important tool for their self-definition, it is crucial to give them some examples of women who have used philosophy in this manner. In teaching a course in Existentialism, for example, I make sure to include Simone de Beauvoir's *The Second Sex* as one of the central texts studied. While this may seem an obvious thing to do, I am still struck by how many courses on Existentialism treat de Beauvoir as a minor figure, thus failing to see the radical implications of her great work for the tradition of existential philosophy as well as for female students. Seeing that a woman can use philosophic discourse as a means of addressing her situation has had an important effect on my students.

The inclusion of works by women philosophers in my courses also provides an opportunity to explore how our understanding of these texts reflects the power relationships that structure them. This comes out clearly when I discuss Princess Elisabeth's letters to René Descartes, letters in which she asks him to clarify his account of the mind-body connection, a connection she claims she cannot conceive clearly and distinctly. Rather than accepting the terms within which the letters are written, where Elisabeth adopts the pose of a dutiful student asking for clarification, I ask my students to consider whether the traditional conventions of epistolary exchange might not have obscured the more radical intent of Elisabeth's queries of Descartes. Can we be sure that, in asking Descartes for clarification, Elisabeth was really only doing that and not criticizing his theory as inadequate to her understanding of what it is to be a human being? In particular, do Elisabeth's observations about her own life as a noblewoman challenge the possibility of giving the sort of non-contextualized account of human nature that Descartes proposes? By raising questions such as these, I have attempted to get my students to think about how the power relationships within which Elisabeth and Descartes lived and wrote affected the character of their philosophic interaction, and how important it is for us to make those power relationships the object of our critical attention rather than allowing them to assume their customary transparency.[14]

These examples—by demonstrating how our habits of reading those texts reflect our lack of attention to issues of power and gender—illustrate how it is possible to go beyond simply calling attention to the sexist claims made by philosophers in the Western tradition.[15] The interpretations that I ask my students to consider are meant to show that issues of power structure the texts of the Western tradition in ways that have not yet been fully analyzed or understood. The goal of my teaching, now as then, is to make visible a set of assumptions that structure the texts of the Western philosophic tradition, assumptions that are usually allowed to remain invisible and thus elude our critical attention.

In the original paper, I centered on my situation as a male teacher whose task it was to teach philosophy to women. I shall conclude by considering both my role as a man teaching philosophy to women and the question of whether the model of teaching philosophical texts I have articulated as one appropriate for teaching women is valid beyond that specific audience.

To tackle the second issue first, I believe that the model I have developed for teaching the texts of the Western philosophic tradition is one that ought to be employed whenever and wherever those texts are taught. While it was in the context of teaching those texts to women students that I first came to see the importance of laying bare how power relationships structured both philosophic texts and our reception of them, the validity of this approach transcends its context of discovery. For one thing, the Western tradition has not only excluded women; there are excluded Others besides women who benefit from seeing how they are asked both to participate in Western philosophic discourse at the same time that they are denied full participation in it. But even more generally, I believe that an adequate understanding of these texts *requires* that they be seen as conditioned by power relationships. While this angle of vision is particularly important for those who traditionally have been excluded by these texts, it is potentially useful for anyone. A white heterosexual male student, for example, may benefit enormously by coming to see that he is unproblematically included in a text's community, for he can come to understand the enormous privilege that his race and gender bestows upon him, a privilege of which it may otherwise be difficult for him to become aware.[16]

But what about my role as a man teaching these texts? I have been asked by readers of my original paper whether my awareness of the sexist nature of the Western philosophic tradition doesn't make me uncomfortable with my position as a male teacher of these texts to women.

My response is that precisely because I have struggled, and continue to struggle, to become aware of the sexist nature of that tradition—and my own participation in it—it is especially important that I as a man continue to teach the great works of that tradition to women. When my women students see a male teacher thematizing how their situation as women makes their relationship to the Western philosophical tradition complex, it helps them not only in articulating their own feminist perspectives, but in understanding that the struggle against sexism (and other forms of oppression) is not simply the work of the oppressed themselves, for others can and will join in their struggle as their allies. As a male teacher of philosophy to women, my gender thus functions as a resource as well as a problem for my feminist teaching practice. So despite the difficulties that I have faced in my ongoing struggle to become aware of my own complicity in a sexist (and racist, classist, heterosexist) tradition, I see that struggle not just as an important one for myself and my own self-awareness as a teacher and a philosopher, but also as a significant one for my students to witness as they attempt to understand how living in a sexist society affects their lives and the lives of us all.

Notes

This paper began as a talk to the Philosophy Club at Mount Holyoke College. I want to thank my audience on that occasion for encouraging me to develop that presentation into the present paper. I would also like to thank the referees for *Teaching Philosophy* for their helpful advice and criticism of the original essay.

1. Georg Wilhelm Friedrich Hegel's relegation of women to the sphere of the family while men attend to the business of the state is but one example of this general view. See his *Philosophy of Right* ¶ 158–180.

2. For an interesting discussion of what male domination is, see Iris Marion Young, "Is Male Gender Identity the Cause of Male Domination?" in Joyce Trebilcot, *Mothering: Essays in Feminist Theory* (Totowa: Rowman & Allenheld, 1984), pp. 129–146.

3. This essay is published as "Beyond Babies and Banners: Towards an Understanding of the Dynamics of Social Movements," *new political science*, Number 14, Winter 1985–6, pp. 157–171.

4. Hesiod, *Theogony*, translated by Dorothea Wender (Harmondsworth: Penguin, 1973) ll. 588–592, 600–1.

5. The text was John Manley Robinson, *An Introduction to Early Greek Philosophy* (Boston: Houghton Mifflin Company, 1968).

6. Introduction to Aristotle, edited by Richard McKeon (New York: Random House, 1947) 1152a25-b8. As one of the referees for *Teaching Philosophy*

called to my attention, Aristotle does refer to nature as female in gender. This raises the issue of a dualistic conception of women in Greek thought, an issue that goes beyond the scope of this paper.

7. Wolfgang Iser, *The Implied Reader: Patterns of Communication in Prose Fiction from Bunyan to Beckett* (Baltimore: John Hopkins University Press, 1974).

8. Louis Althusser, "Ideology and Ideological State Apparatuses," in *Lenin and Philosophy* (London: NLB, 1971). The idea of interpellation is amplified in Göran Therborn, *The Ideology of Power and the Power of Ideology* (London: Verso and NLB, 1980). For Jean-François Lyotard's view, see his *The Postmodern Condition: A Report on Knowledge* (Minneapolis: University of Minnesota Press, 1984).

9. Richard Rorty, *Philosophy and the Mirror of Nature* (Princeton: Princeton University Press, 1979).

10. There are clearly many ramifications of this idea of an implied reader that need to be developed and clarified. In the present context, let me just say that the notion of an implied reader goes much farther than that of an intended audience. I do not mean to suggest that the implied textual community is one that the author establishes. It is rather something that is constituted by the text and its relation to communities that read it.

11. It goes without saying that establishing this sense of textual community with these ancient texts is no easy task. Indeed, we can think of the establishment of this sense of community as one goal of teaching these texts at all. One way of looking at the problem I am posing is how to recapture our sense of being in the community with these texts once we notice their deeply sexist and racist assumptions.

12. I do not mean to suggest that I never have felt myself left out of the implied audience of a philosophic text. As a Jew, much of the writings of Christian philosophers has had that affect on me. I have, needless to say, been able to feel myself part of the implied audience of these texts in other respects.

13. I discuss this interpretation in detail in an unpublished manuscript, "Power and Sociality in Plato's *Republic.*"

14. I elaborate my reading of Elisabeth's correspondence with René Descartes in "Descartes' Mood: The Question of Feminism in the Correspondence with Elisabeth," in *Feminist Approaches to Descartes*, edited by Susan Bordo (University Park, PA: University of Pennsylvania Press, forthcoming).

15. My emphasis on the *Western* tradition of philosophy is not meant to restrict my claims about the nature of textuality to that tradition, but only to reflect the character of my own teaching.

16. Whether heterosexuality includes or excludes one from the textual community of the texts of Western philosophy is an interesting question, given the sexual practices of Plato among others. I do not even broach that issue in this text.

Chapter 8

A Black Man's Place
in Black Feminist Criticism

Michael Awkward

The main theoretical task for male feminists, then, is to develop an analysis of their own position, and a strategy for how their awareness of their difficult and contradictory position in relation to feminism can be made explicit in discourse and practice.[1]

—Toril Moi

She had been looking all along for a friend, and it took her a while to discover that a [male] lover was not a comrade and could never be—for a woman.[2]

—Toni Morrison

Critics eternally become and embody the generative myths of their culture by half-perceiving and half-inventing their culture, their myths, and themselves.[3]

—Houston A. Baker, Jr.

Nor is any theorizing of feminism adequate without some positioning of the person who is doing the theorizing.[4]

—Cary Nelson

I

Many essays by male and female scholars devoted to exploring the subject of male critics' place(s) in feminism generally agree on the uses and usefulness of the autobiographical male "I." Such essays suggest that citing the male critical self reflects a response to (apparent) self-difference, an exploration of the disparities between the masculine's antagonistic position in feminist discourse, on the one hand, and, on the other, the desire of the individual male critic to represent his difference with and from the traditional androcentric perspectives of his gender and culture. Put another way, in male feminist acts, to identify the writing self as biologically male is to emphasize the desire not to be ideologically male, and to explore the process of rejecting the phallocentric perspectives by which men traditionally have justified the subjugation of women.[5]

In what strikes me as a particularly suggestive theoretical formulation, Joseph Boone articulates his sense of the goals of such male feminist autobiographical acts:

> In exposing the latent multiplicity and difference in the word "me(n)" we can perhaps open up a space within the discourse of feminism where a male feminist voice *can* have something to say beyond impossibilities and apologies and unresolved ire. Indeed, if the male feminist can discover a position *from which* to speak that neither elides the importance of feminism to his work nor ignores the specificity of his gender, his voice may also find that it no longer exists as an abstraction . . . but that it in fact inhabits a body: its own sexual/textual body.[6]

Because of an awareness that androcentric perspectives are learned, are transmitted by means of specific (and, at this point, well-identified) sociocultural practices in such effective ways that they come to appear natural, male feminists such as Boone believe that, through an informed investigation of androcentric and feminist ideologies, individual men can work to resist the lure of the normatively masculine. That resistance for the aspiring male feminist requires, in Boone's phrase, the exposure of "the latent multiplicity and difference in the word 'me(n),'" in other words, the (dis)rupturing of both ideologies' unproblematized perceptions of monolithic and/or normative maleness (as villainous, antagonistic "other" for feminism, and, for androcentricism, as powerful, domineering patriarch). At this early stage of male feminism's development, to speak self-consciously—autobiographically—is necessarily to explore, implicitly and/or explicitly, why and how the individual male experience (the "me" in men) has diverged from, has created possibilities for a rejection of, the androcentric norm.

While there is not yet agreement as to what constitutes an identifiably male feminist act of criticism or about the usefulness of such acts for the general advancement of the feminist project, at least one possible explanation for a male critic's self-referential discourse is that it is a response to palpable mistrust—emanating from some female participants in feminism, and perhaps from the writing male subject himself—about his motives. A skeptical strand of opinion with regard to male feminism is represented by Alice Jardine's "Men in Feminism: Odor di Uomo Or Campagnons de Route?"[7] Having determined that the most useful measure of an adequately feminist text is its *"inscription of struggle,* even of *pain"* (58)—an inscription of a struggle against patriarchy that Jardine finds absent from most male feminist acts, perhaps because "the historical fact that is the oppression of women [is] . . . one of their favorite blind spots," (58)—she admits to some confusion as to the motivations for males' willing participation: "Why . . . would men want to be in feminism if it's about struggle? What do men want to be in—in pain?"

In addition to seeking to cure its blindness (if such blindness still generally exists) where the history of female oppression is concerned, a male feminism must explore the motivations for its participation in what we might call, in keeping with Jardine's formulations, a discourse of (en)gendered pain. If one of the goals of male feminist self-referentiality is to demonstrate to females that individual males can indeed serve as allies in efforts to undermine androcentric power—and it seems invariably that this is the case—the necessary trust cannot be gained (if this type of trust is at all possible) by insisting that motivation as such does not represent a crucial area that must be carefully negotiated. For example, I accept as generally accurate and, indeed, reflective of my own situation Andrew Ross's assertion that "there are those [men] for whom the facticity of feminism, for the most part, goes without saying. . . who are young enough for feminism to have been a primary component of their intellectual formation."[8] However, in discussions whose apparent function is a foregrounding of both obstacles to and possibilities of a male feminism, men's relation(s) to the discourse can never go "without saying"; for the foreseeable future at least, this relation needs necessarily to be rigorously and judiciously theorized, and grounded explicitly in, among other places, the experiential realm of the writing male subject.

Yet no matter how illuminating and exemplary one finds self-referential inscriptions of a male feminist critical self, if current views of the impossibility of a consistently truthful autobiographical act are correct, there are difficulties implicit in any such attempt to situate or inscribe that male self. Because, as recent theorizing of the subject of autobiography has demonstrated, acts of discursive self-rendering unavoidably involve the creation, for the duration of the writing process at least, of what is in some ways an idealized version of a unified or unifiable self, we can be certain only of the fact that the autobiographical impulse yields but part of the truth(s) of the male feminist critic's experiences. As is also the case for female participants, a male cannot—can never—always tell the whole truth and nothing but the truth about his relationship to feminist discourse and praxis.

But while autobiographical criticism, like the genre of autobiography itself, is poised tenuously between the poles of closure and disclosure, between one representation and another, between a lived life and an invented one, I believe that even in the recoverable half-truths of my life are some of the materials that have shaped my perceptions, my beliefs, the self and/or selves that I bring to the interpretive act. By examining discussions of the phenomenon of the male feminist—that is to say, by reading male and female explorations of men's place(s) in feminist criticism—and exploring responses of others to my own professional and personal relationships to feminism, I will identify autobiographically and textually grounded sources for my belief that while gendered difference might be said to complicate the prospect of a non-phallocentric black male feminism, it does not render such a project impossible.

At the outset, I acknowledge my own full awareness of the fact that, in this elaboration, mine is a necessary participation with regard to black feminist criticism in the half-invention, half-perception which, in Houston Baker's compelling formulation, represents every scholar's relationship to cultural criticism.[9] Such an acknowledgment is not intended to indicate that my (male) relationship to feminism is naturally that of an illegitimate child, as it were. Rather, it is meant to suggest, like Elizabeth Weed's insistence on "the impossibility" of both men's and women's "relationship to feminism," my belief that while feminism represents a complex, sometimes self-contradictory, "utopian vision" that no one can fully possess, a biological male can "develop political, theoretical [and, more generally, interpretive] strategies,"[10] which, though at most perhaps half-true to all that feminist ideologies are, nevertheless can assist—in unison both with more voluminous and productive female myths and with other emerging antipatriarchal male acts—in a movement toward the actualization of the goals of feminism.

II

I have been forced to think in especially serious ways about my own relationship to feminist criticism since I completed the first drafts of *Inspiriting Influences*, my study of Afro-American women novelists.[11] I have questioned neither the explanatory power of feminism nor the essential importance of developing models adequate to the analysis of black female-authored texts, as my book attempts to provide on a limited scale in harmony, I believe, with the black feminist project concerned with recovering and uncovering an Afro-American female literary tradition. Yet, I have been confronted with suspicion about my gendered suitability for the task of explicating Afro-American women's texts, suspicion that has been manifested in the forms of both specific responses to my project and general inquiries within literary studies into the phenomenon of the male feminist.

For example, a white female reader of the manuscript's first drafts asserted—with undisguised surprise—that my work was "so feminist," and asked how I'd managed to offer such ideologically informed readings. Another scholar, a black feminist literary critic, recorded with no discernible hesitation her unease with my "male readings" of the texts of Zora Neale Hurston, Toni Morrison, Gloria Naylor, and Alice Walker. I wondered about the possibility of my being simultaneously "so feminist" and not-so-feminist (i.e., so "male"), about the meanings of these terms both for these scholars and for the larger interpretive communities in which they participate. Consequently, in what was perhaps initially an act of psychic self-protection, I began to formulate questions for which I still have found no consistently satisfactory answers: Were the differences in the readers' perceptions of the ideological adequacy of my study a function of their own racially influenced views of feminist criticism, a product, in other words, of the differences not simply *within me* that could lead to the production of a discourse characterizable as both feminist and androcentric, but *within feminism itself?* And if the differences within feminism are so significant, could I possibly satisfy everybody with "legitimate" interests in the texts of Hurston, et al. by means of my own appropriated version(s) of black feminist discourse, my unavoidably half-true myth of what that discourse is, means, and does? Should my myth of feminism and its mobilization in critical texts be considered naturally less analytically compelling than that of a female scholar simply as a function of my biological maleness? And how could what I took to be a useful self-reflexivity avoid becoming a debilitating inquiry into a process that has come to seem for me, if not "natural," as Cary Nelson views his relationship to feminism,[12] then at least *necessary?*

Compelled and, to be frank, disturbed by such questions, I searched for answers in others' words, others' work. I purchased a copy of the then just-published *Men in Feminism*, a collection that examines the possibility of men's participation as "comrades" (to use Toni Morrison's term, which I will return to below) in feminist criticism and theory. Gratified by the appearance of such a volume, I became dismayed immediately upon reading the editors' introductory remarks that noted their difficulty in "locating intellectuals, who, having shown interest in the question, would offer, for instance, a gay or a black perspective on the problem."[13] While a self-consciously "gay ... perspective" does find its way into the collection, the insights of nonwhite males and females are conspicuously absent.[14]

Even more troubling for me than the absence of black voices or, for that matter, general inquiries into the effects of racial, cultural, and class differences on males' relationships to feminism, is the sense shared by many contributors to *Men in Feminism* of male feminism's insurmountable obstacles. In fact, the collection's initiatory essay, Stephen Heath's "Male Feminism," begins by insisting that "[m]en's relation to feminism is an impossible one."[15] Heath's formulations are insightful and provocative, if not always, for me, persuasive, such as when he claims:

> This is, I believe, the most any man can do today: to learn and so to try to write or talk or act in response to feminism, and so to try not in any way

to be anti-feminist, supportive of the old oppressive structures. Any more, any notion of writing a feminist book or being a feminist, is a myth, a male imaginary with the reality of appropriation and domination right behind.[16]

Is male participation in feminism restricted to being either appropriative and domineering or not "anti-feminist"? Must we necessarily agree with Heath and Robert Scholes, another contributor to *Men in Feminism*, that "a male critic . . . may work within the feminist paradigm but never be a full-fledged member of the class of feminists"?[17] To put the matter differently, is gender really an adequate determinant of "class" position?

Despite the poststructuralist tenor of Heath's work generally and of many of his perspectives here, his is an easily problematized essentialist claim—that, in effect, biology determines destiny and, therefore, one's relationship to feminist ideology; that womanhood allows one to become feminist at the same time that manhood necessarily denies that status to men. And while Heath embraces feminist notions of history as a narrative of male "appropriation and domination" of gendered Others, he appears resistant at this point in his discourse to evidence of a powerful feminist institutional *present* and *presence*. I believe that we must acknowledge that feminism represents, at least in areas of the American academy, an incomparably productive, influential, and resilient ideology and institution that men, no matter how cunning, duplicitous, or culturally powerful, will neither control nor overthrow in the foreseeable future; one whose perspectives have proven and might continue to prove convincing even to biological males. In other words, in surveying the potential implications of the participation of men in feminism, we must be honest about feminism's current persuasiveness and indomitability, about its clarifying, transformative potential, and about the fact that the corruptive possibility of both the purposefully treacherous and the only half-convinced male is, for today at least, slight indeed. Surely it is neither naive, presumptuous, nor premature to suggest that feminism as ideology and reading strategy has assumed a position of exegetical and institutional strength capable of withstanding even the most energetically masculinist acts of subversion.

Below, I want to focus specifically on the question—on the "problem," as the editors of *Men in Feminism*, among others, might put it—of a black male feminism. Rather than seeing black male feminism necessarily as an impossibility or as a subtle new manifestation of and attempt at androcentric domination, I want to show that certain instances of afrocentric feminism provide Afro-American men with an invaluable means of rewriting—of *re-vis(ion)ing*—our selves, our historical and literary traditions, and our future.

III

Few would deny that black feminist literary criticism is an oppositional discourse constituted in large part as a response against black male participation in the subjugation of Afro-American women. Treatments range from Barbara Smith's castigation of black male critics for their "virulently sexist ... treatment"[18] of black women writers, and her insistence that they "are, of course, hampered by an inability to comprehend Black women's experience in sexual as well as racial terms"[19] to, more recently, Michele Wallace's characterization of the "black male Afro-Americanists who make pivotal use of Hurston's work in their most recent critical speculations" as "a gang"—in such texts Afro-American men are generally perceived as nonallied Others of black feminist discourse.[20] Not only are Afro-American males often so regarded but, as is evident in Wallace's figuration of male Hurston scholars as intraracial street warriors, they are also viewed at times as always already damned and unredeemable, even when they appear to take black women's writing seriously. We—I— must accept the fact that black male investigations informed by feminist principles—including this one—may never be good enough or ideologically correct enough for some black women who are feminists.

This sense of an unredeemable black male critic/reader is in stark contrast to perspectives offered in such texts as Sherley Anne Williams's "Some Implications of Womanist Theory." In her essay, she embraces Alice Walker's term "womanist"—which, according to Williams, connotes a "commit[ment] to the survival and wholeness of an entire people, female and male, as well as a valorization of women's works in all their varieties and multitudes"—because she considers the black feminist project to be separatist in "its tendency to see not only a distinct black female culture but to see that culture as a separate cultural form" from "the facticity of Afro-American life."[21]

I believe that a black male feminism, whatever its connections to critical theory or its specific areas of concern, can profit immensely from what female feminists have to say about male participation. For example, Valerie Smith's suggestion in "Gender and Afro-Americanist Literary Theory and Criticism" that "Black male critics and theorists might explore the nature of the contradictions that arise when they undertake black feminist projects"[22] seems to me quite useful, as does Alice Jardine's advice to male feminists. Speaking for white female feminists and to white males who consider themselves to be feminists, Jardine urges:

> ... we do not want you to *mimic* us, to become the same as us; we don't want your pathos or your guilt; and we don't even want your admiration (even if it's nice to get it once in a while). What we want, I would even say

what we need, is your *work*. We need you to get down to serious work. And like all serious work, that involves struggle and pain.[23]

The womanist theoretical project that has been adopted by Williams, Smith, and others provides aspiring Afro-American male feminists with a useful model for the type of self-exploration that Smith and Jardine advocate. What Williams terms "womanist theory" is especially suggestive for Afro-American men because, while it calls for feminist discussions of black women's texts and for critiques of black androcentrism, womanism foregrounds a general black psychic health as a primary objective. For instance, Williams also argues that "what is needed is a thoroughgoing examination of male images in the works of black male writers." Her womanism, then, aims at "ending the separatist tendency in Afro-American criticism," at leading black feminism away from "the same hole The Brother has dug for himself—narcissism, isolation, inarticulation, obscurity," at the creation and/or continuation of black "community and dialogue."[24]

If a black man is to become a useful contributor to black feminism, he must, as Boone argues, "discover a position *from which* to speak that neither elides the importance of feminism to his work nor ignores the specificity of his gender."[25] However multiply split we perceive the subject to be, or deeply felt our sense of "maleness" and "femaleness" as social constructions, however heightened our sense of the historical consequences and current dangers of black androcentrism, a black male feminism cannot contribute to the continuation and expansion of the black feminist project by being so identified against or out of touch with itself as to fail to be both self-reflective and at least minimally self-interested. A black male feminist self-reflectivity of the type I have in mind necessarily would involve, among other things, examination of both the benefits and the dangers of a situatedness in feminist discourse. The self-interestedness of a black male feminist would be manifested in part by his concern with exploring "a man's place." Clearly if, as several feminists insist, convincing mimicry of female-authored concerns and interpretive strategies—or, in the words of a long-standing debate, speaking *like* a female feminist—is not in and of itself an appropriate goal for aspiring male participants (and I am not fully convinced that such mimicry is avoidable at present, at least as an initiatory moment of a male feminist's development), then a male feminism necessarily must explore, among other matters, males' various situations—in the (con)texts of history and the present—as one of its central concerns.

Perhaps the most difficult task for a black male feminism is striking a workable balance between male self-inquiry/interest and adequately feminist critiques of patriarchy. To this point, especially in response to the commercial and critical success of contemporary Afro-American women's literature, scores of black men have proven unsuccessful in this regard. As black feminist critics such as Valerie Smith and Deborah McDowell have argued, the contemporary moment of black feminist literature has been greeted by many Afro-American males with hostility, self-interested misrepresentation, and an apparent lack of honest intellectual introspection. McDowell's "Reading Family Matters" is a useful discussion for black male feminism, primarily as an exploration of what such a discourse ought not to do and be. She writes about widely circulated androcentric male analyses of Afro-American feminist texts by writers such as Toni Morrison and Alice Walker:

> [C]ritics leading the debate [about the representation of black men in black women's texts] have lumped all black women writers together and have focused on one tiny aspect of their immensely complex and diverse project—the image of black men—despite the fact that, if we can claim a center for these texts, it is located in the complexities of black female subjectivity and experience. In other words, though black women writers have made black women the subjects of their own family stories, these male readers/critics are attempting to usurp that place for themselves and place it at the center of critical inquiry.[26]

Although I do not believe that "the image of black men" is as microscopic an element in Afro-American women's texts as McDowell claims, I agree with her generally about the reprehensible nature of unabashed androcentricism found in formulations she cites by such figures as Robert Staples, Mel Watkins, and Darryl Pinckney. Nevertheless, where the potential development of a black male feminism is concerned, I am troubled by what appears to be a surprisingly explicit element of turf protection manifest in her perspectives. McDowell's formulations echo in unfortunate ways those of antifeminist male critics of the last two decades, white and black, who consider feminism to be an unredeemably myopic and unsupple interpretive strategy, incapable of offering subtle readings of canonical (largely male-authored) texts. Despite the existence and circulation of reprehensibly masculinist responses to Afro-American women's literature, black feminist literary critics do not best serve the discourses with which they are concerned by setting into motion homeostatic maneuvers intended to devalue all forms of inquiry except for that which they hold to be most valuable (in this particular case, a female-authored scholarship that emphasizes Afro-American women's writings of black female subjectivity). If the Afro-American women's literary project is indeed as "immensely complex and diverse" as McDowell claims, bringing to bear other angles of vision, including antipatriarchal male ones, can assist in, among other things, the analysis of aspects of that complexity.

While the views of Staples, et al. are clearly problematic, those problems do not arise specifically from their efforts to place males "at the center of critical inquiry," any more than feminism is implicitly flawed because it insists, in some of its manifestations, on a gynocritical foregrounding of representations of women. Rather, these problems appear to result from the fact that the particular readers who produce these perspectives do not seem sufficiently to be, in Toril Moi's titular phrase, "men against patriarchy."[27] Certainly, in an age when both gender studies and Afro-American women's literature have achieved a degree of legitimacy within and outside of the academy it is unreasonable for black women either to demand that black men not be concerned at all—or even centrally, if this is their wish—with the ways in which they are depicted by Afro-American women writers or necessarily to see that concern as intrinsically troubling in feminist terms. If female feminist calls for a nonmimicking male feminism are indeed persuasive, then black men will have very little of substance to say about contemporary Afro-American women's literature if we are also to consider as transgressive any attention to figurations of black manhood. It seems to me that the most black females in feminism can insist upon in this regard is that examinations that focus on male characters treat the "complexity" of contemporary Afro-American women novelists' delineations of black manhood with an antipatriarchal seriousness, something the essays McDowell cites clearly lack.

From my perspective, what is potentially most valuable about the development of a black male feminism is not its capacity to reproduce black feminism as it has been established and is being practiced by black females who focus primarily on "the complexities of black female subjectivity and experience."[28] Rather, its potential value lies in the possibility that, in being antipatriarchal and as self-inquiring about their relationship(s) to feminism as Afro-American women have been, black men can expand feminist inquiry's range and utilization, that they will be able to explore other fruitful applications for feminist perspectives, including such topics as obstacles to a black male feminist project itself and new figurations of "family matters" and black male sexuality.

For my purposes here—for the purpose of theorizing about a black male feminism—perhaps the most provocative, enlightening, and inviting moment in womanist scholarship occurs in Hortense Spillers's "Mama's Baby, Papa's Maybe: An American Grammar Book." Indeed, Spillers's essay represents a fruitful starting point for new, potentially nonpatriarchal figurations of family and of the black male's relationship to the female. Toward the end of this illuminating theoretical text, which concerns itself with, among other matters, slavery's debilitating effects on the Afro-American family's constitution, Spillers envisions black male identity formation as a process whose movement toward successful resolution seems necessarily to require a serious engagement of black feminist principles and perspectives. Spillers asserts that as a result of the specific familial patterns that functioned during American slavery and beyond, which "removed the African-American male not so much from sight as from *mimetic* view as a partner in the prevailing social fiction of the Father's name, the Father's law," "[t]he African-American male has been touched by the *mother, handed* by her in ways that he cannot escape."[29] Because of separation from traditional American paternal name and law,

> the black American male embodies the *only* American community of males which has had the specific occasion to learn *who* the female is within itself. . . . It is the heritage of the *mother* that the African-American male must regain as an aspect of his own personhood— the power of "yes" to the "female" within.[30]

Rather than seeing the "female strictly as Other for the Afro-American male, Spillers's afrocentric re-visioning of psychoanalytic theory insists that we consider the "female" as an important aspect of the repressed in the black male self.[31] Employing Spillers's analyses as a starting point, we might regard Afro-American males' potential "in-ness" vis-à-vis feminism not, as Paul Smith insists in *Men in Feminism*, as a representation of male heterosexual desires to penetrate and violate female spaces,[32] rather, as an acknowledgement of what Spillers considers the distinctive nature of the Afro-American male's connection to the "female." If Afro-American males are ever to have anything to say about or to black feminism beyond the types of reflex-action devaluations and diatribes about divisiveness that critics such as McDowell and Valerie Smith rightly decry—diatribes that have too often marked our discourse and patently ignore the extent to which the practice of patriarchy has already divided us—the investigative process of which womanist acts by Spillers and Williams speak is indispensible. Such a process, if pursued in an intellectually rigorous manner, offers a means by which black men can participate usefully in and contribute productively to the black feminist project.

Black womanism demands neither the erasure of the black gendered other's subjectivity (as have male movements to reacquire a putatively lost Afro-American manhood) nor the relegation of males to prone, domestic, or other limiting or objectifiable positions. What it does require if it is indeed to become an ideology—a world view—with widespread cultural impact, is a recognition on the part of both black females and males of the nature of the gendered inequities that have marked our past and present and a commitment to working for change. In that sense, black feminist criticism has not only created a space for an informed Afro-American male participation, but it also heartily welcomes—in fact, it insists upon—the joint participation of black males and females as *comrades*, to invoke, with a difference, this paper's epigraphic reference to *Sula*.

IV

Reading "Mama's Baby, Papas Maybe" was of special importance to me, in part because, as nothing I had read previously or since, it helped me to clarify and articulate my belief that my relationship to feminism need not mark me necessarily as a debilitatingly split subject.[33] The source of that relationship can only be traced autobiographically, if at all. Having been raised by a mother who, like too many women of too many generations, was the victim of male physical and psychological brutality—a brutality that, according to my mother, resulted in large part from my father's frustrations about his inability to partake in what Spillers calls masculinity's "prevailing social fiction"—my earliest stories, my familial narratives, as it were, figured "maleness" in quite troubling terms. My mother told me horrific stories, one of which I was, in a sense, immediately involved in: my father, who left us before I was one year old and whom I never knew, kicked her in the stomach when my fetal presence swelled her body because he believed she'd been unfaithful to him and that I was only "maybe" his baby.

As a youth, I pondered this and other such stories often and deeply, in part because of the pain I knew these incidents caused my mother, in part because, as someone largely without a consistent male familial role model, I sought actively a means by which to achieve a gendered self-definition. As one for whom maleness as manifested in the surrounding inner city culture seemed to be represented only by violence, familial abandonment, and the certainty of imprisonment, I found that I was able to define myself with regard to my gender primarily in oppositional ways. I had internalized the cautionary intent of my mother's narratives, which also served as her dearest wish for me: that I not grow up to be like my father, that I not adopt the definitions of maleness represented by his example and in the culture generally. Because the scars of male brutality were visibly etched—literally marked, as it were—on my mother's flesh and on her psyche, maleness, as figured both in my mother's stories and in my environment, seemed to me not to be a viable "mimetic" option. I grew up, then, not always sure of what—or who—I was with respect to prevailing social definitions of gender, but generally quite painfully aware of what I could not become.

In order to begin to understand who my mother was, perhaps also who my father was, what "maleness" was, and what extrabiological relationship I could hope to have to it, I needed answers that, for a variety of reasons, my mother was unable to provide. I found little of value in the black masculinist discourse of the time, which spoke ceaselessly of Afro-American male dehumanization and castration by white men and black women (our central social narrative for too long). This rhetoric seemed, perhaps because of my particular familial context and maturational dilemma, simplistic and unself-consciously concerned with justifying domestic violence and other forms of black male brutality.

Afro-American women's literature, to which I was introduced in 1977 as a sophomore at Brandeis University, along with black feminism, helped me to move toward a comprehension of the world, of aspects of my mother's life, and of what a man against patriarchy could be and do. These discourses provided me with answers nowhere else available to what had been largely unresolvable mysteries. I work within the paradigm of black feminist literary criticism because it explains elements of the world about which—for strictly autobiographical reasons—I care most deeply. I write and read what and as I do because I am incapable of escaping the meanings of my mother's narratives for my own life; in their enunciation to the next generation, the pain and the sense of hope for better days that characterize these familial texts are illuminatingly explored in many narratives by black women. Afro-American women's literature has given me parts of myself that, incapable of a (biological) "fatherly reprieve," I would not otherwise have had.

I have decided that it is ultimately irrelevant whether these autobiographical facts—facts that, of course, are not, and can never be, the whole story—are deemed by others sufficient to permit me to call myself "feminist." Like Toril Moi, I have come to believe that "the important thing for men is not to spend their time worrying about definitions and essences ('am I *really* a feminist?'), but to take up a recognizable anti-patriarchal position."[34] What is most important to me is that my work contribute, in however small a way, to the project whose goal is the dismantling of phallocentric rule by which black females—and, I am sure, countless other Afro-American sons—have been injuriously "touched."

V

My indebtedness to Spillers's and other womanist perspectives is, then, great indeed, as is my sense of their potential as illuminating, originary moments for a newborn—or not-yet-born—black male feminist discourse. However, utilizing these perspectives requires that we be more inquiring than Spillers is in her formulations: not in envisioning liberating possibilities of an acknowledgment of "the 'female' within" the black community and the male subject, but in noting potential dangers inherent in such an attempted embrasure by traditional and/or historically brutalized Afro-American men whose relationship to a repressed "female" is not painstakingly (re)defined.

Clearly, more thinking is necessary not only about what "the 'female' within" is, but also about what it can be said to represent for black males; there also needs to be serious analysis of useful means and methods of interacting with a repressed female interiority and subject. Spillers's theorizing does not perform this task, in part because it has other, more compelling interests and emphases—among them the righting/(re)writing of definitions of "woman" so that they will reflect Afro-American women's particular, historically conditioned "female social subject" status. But a black male feminism must be especially focused on exploring such issues if it is to mobilize Spillers's suggestive remarks as a means of developing a fuller understanding of the complex formulations of black manhood found in many (con)texts, including Afro-American women's narratives.

Below, I want to discuss these matters a bit more fully, to build on Spillers's provocative theorizing about the Afro-American male's maturational process and situation on American shores. To this end, I will briefly look at an illuminating moment in Toni Morrison's *Sula*, a text that is, to my mind, not only an unparalleled Afro-American woman's writing of what McDowell calls "the complexities of black female subjectivity and experience," but also of black males' relationship to "the 'female' within" as a consequence of their limited access to "the prevailing social fiction" of masculinity. In this novel, the difficulty—the near impossibility—of negotiating the spaces between black male lack and black female presence is plainly manifested in such figures as the undifferentiable deweys; BoyBoy, whose name, in contrast to most of the authorial designations in *Sula*, speaks unambiguously for him; and Jude, whose difficulty in assuming the mantle of male provider leads him to view his union with Nel as that which "would make one Jude."[35]

The response of Plum, the most tragic of *Sula*'s unsuccessful negotiators of the so-called white man's world, vividly represents for me some of the contemporary dangers of black male "in-ness" vis-à-vis the "female." Despite (because of?) a childhood characterized by "float [ing] in a constant swaddle of love and affection" (unlike Hannah, who is uncertain whether her mother ever loved her, Eva's son did experience traditional manifestations of maternal love, reflecting a gender-determined disparity in treatment) and his mother's intention to follow the Father's law by "bequeath[ing] everything" (38) to him, Plum appears incapable of embracing hegemonic notions of masculinity. Instead, he returns from World War I spiritually fractured, but, unlike a similarly devastated Shadrack, lacks the imaginative wherewithal to begin to theorize or ritualize a new relationship to his world. Consequently, he turns to drugs as a method of anesthetizing himself from the horrors of his devastation and, in his mother's view, seeks to compel her resumption of familiar/familial patterns of caretaking. In the following passage, Eva explains to Hannah her perception of Plum's desires as well as the motivation for her participation in what amounts to an act of infanticide:

> When he came back from that war he wanted to git back in. After all that carryin' on, just gettin' him out and keepin' him alive, he wanted to crawl back in my womb and well . . . I ain't got the room no more even if he could do it. There wasn't space for him in my womb. And he was crawlin' back. Being helpless and thinking baby thoughts and dreaming baby dreams and messing up his pants again and smiling all the time. I had room enough in my heart, but not in my womb, got no more. I birthed him once. I couldn't do it again. He was growed, a big old thing. Godhavemercy, I couldn't birth him twice. . . . [A] big man can't be a baby all wrapped up inside his mamma no more; he suffocate. I done everything I could to make him leave me and go on and live and be a man but he wouldn't and I had to keep him out so I just thought of a way he could die like a man not all scrunched up inside my womb, but like a man. (62)[36]

What is significant about this passage for a theorizing of the possibilities of a nonoppressive black male's relationship to feminism—to female experience characterized by a refusal to be subjugated to androcentric desire(s)—is its suggestiveness for our understanding the obstacles to a revised male view of the repressed "female" that result in large part from black males' relative social powerlessness. If black feminism is persuasive in its analysis of the limitations of Afro-American masculinist ideology, which has emphasized the achievement of black manhood at the expense of black female subjectivity, if, as a growing body of social analyses indicates, we can best describe an overwhelming number of Africa's American male descendants as males-in-crisis, then the question a black male feminism must ask itself is: On what basis, according to what ideological perspective, can an Afro-American heterosexual male ground his notions of the female? Beyond its (hetero)sexual dimension, can the "female" truly come to represent for a traditional black male-in-crisis more than a protective maternal womb from which he seeks to be "birthed" again and a site upon which to find relief from or, as in the case of Jude's relationship to Nel, locate frustrations caused by an inability to achieve putatively normative American male socioeconomic status? If embracing normative masculinity requires a movement beyond, indeed an escape from, the protection and life-sustaining aspects symbolized by maternal umbilical cords and apron strings, and an achievement of an economic

situation wherein the male provides domestic space and material suste-
nance for his dependents (including "his woman"), black manhood generally is, like Plum, in desperate trouble. And if, as has often been the
case, a black female can be seen by an Afro-American male-in-crisis only
if she has been emptied of subjectivity and selfhood, if she becomes visible for the male only when she is subsumed by male desire(s), then the
types of refiguration and redefinition of black male subjectivity and
embrasure of the "female" central to Spillers's formulations are highly
unlikely.

This question of seeing and not seeing, of the male gaze's erasure and
re-creation of the female, is central to *Sula*'s general thematics. It seems
to me that Morrison's figuration of black female subjectivity in all of her
novels is largely incomprehensible without some serious attention both to
her representation of black manhood and to her exploration of the relationships between socially constructed gendered (and racial) positions.
To return explicitly to the case of Eva: what Eva fears, what appears to
be a self-interested motivation for her killing of her intended male heir, is
that Plum's pitiful, infantile state has the potential to reduce *her* to a static
female function of self-sacrificing mother that, according to Bottom
legend, had already provoked her decision to lose a leg in order to collect
insurance money with which to provide for her children. Having
sacrificed so much of herself already, Eva chooses instead to take the life
of her self-described male heir. And if Plum dies "like a man," in Eva's
estimation, his achievement of manhood has nothing to do with an
assumption of traditional masculine traits, nothing to do with strength,
courage, and a refusal to cry in the face of death. Instead, that achievement results from Eva's creation of conditions that have become essential
components of her definition of manhood: death forces him to "leave"
her and to "keep . . . out" of her womb. It would appear that manhood
is defined here not as presence, as it is represented typically in Western
thought, but rather—by and for Eva at least—as liberating (domestic and
uterine) absence.

VI

One of the intentions of this essay is to suggest that feminism represents
a fruitful, potentially nonoppressive means of reconceptualizing, of figu-
ratively birthing twice the black male subject. But, as a close reading of
the above passage from *Sula* suggests, interactions between men and
women motivated by male self-interest (such as necessarily characterizes
an aspect of male participation in feminism) are fraught with possible
dangers of an enactment of or a capitulation to hegemonic male power
for the biological/ideological female body. Indeed if it is the case that, as
Spillers has argued in another context, "the woman who stays in man's

company keeps alive the possibility of having, one day, an unwanted guest, or the guest, deciding to 'hump the hostess,' whose intentions turn homicidal"[37] then male proximity to feminism generally creates the threat of a specifically masculinist violation. If, as I noted earlier, the dangers of a hegemonic, heterosexual, Euro-American male's "in-ness" vis-à-vis feminism include (sexualized) penetration and domination, then those associated with a heterosexual black male's interactions with the ideological female body are at least doubled, and potentially involve an envisioning of the black female body as self-sacrificingly maternal and/or self-sacrificingly sexual. Because of a general lack of access to the full force of hegemonic male power, Afro-American men could see in increasingly influential black female texts not only serious challenges to black male fictions of the self, but also an appropriate location for masculine desires for control of the types of valuable resources that the discourse(s) of black womanhood currently represents.

But a rigorous, conscientious black male feminism need not give in to traditional patriarchal desires for control and erasure of the "female." To be of any sustained value to the feminist project, what such a discourse must provide are illuminating and persuasive readings of gender as it is constituted for blacks in America—sophisticated, informed, and contentious critiques of phallocentric practice—in an effort to redefine our notions of black male (and female) textuality and subjectivity. And in its differences with black feminist texts that are produced by individual Afro-American women—and surely there will be differences, for such is the nature of intellectual and political life—black male feminism must be both rigorous in its engagement of these texts and self-reflective enough to avoid, at all costs, the types of patronizing, marginalizing gestures that have traditionally characterized Afro-American male intellectuals' response to black womanhood. What a black male feminism must strive for, above all else, is the envisioning and enactment of the possibilities signaled by the difference feminism has exposed and created. Being an Afro-American male in black feminist criticism does not mean attempting to invade an/other political body like a lascivious soul snatcher or striving to erase its essence in order to replace it with one's own myth of what the discourse should be. Such a position for black men means, above all else, an acknowledgment and celebration of the incontrovertible fact that "the Father's law" is no longer the only law of the land.

Notes

1. Toril Moi, "Men Against Patriarchy," in *Gender and Theory: Dialogues on Feminist Criticism*, ed. Linda Kauffman (New York: Basil Blackwell, 1989), 184.

2. Toni Morrison, *Sula* (New York: Plume, 1973), 71.

3. Houston A. Baker, Jr., *Afro-American Poetics: Revisions of Harlem and the Black Aesthetic* (Madison: University of Wisconsin Press, 1988), 8.

4. Cary Nelson, "Men, Feminism: The Materiality of Discourse," in *Men in Feminism*, eds. Alice Jardine and Paul Smith (New York: Methuen, 1987), 156.

5. For example, Joseph Boone's and Gerald MacLean's essays "Of Me(n) and Feminism: Who(se) Is the Sex That Writes" and "Citing the Subject," in *Gender and Theory: Dialogues on Feminist Criticism*, ed. Linda Kauffman (New York: Basil Blackwell, 1989), assume that the foregrounding of gendered subjectivity is essential to the production of a male feminist critical practice. Consequently, in an effort to articulate his perspectives on the possibilities of a male feminist discourse, Boone shares with us professional secrets: he writes of his disagreement with the male-authored essays that begin Alice Jardine's and Paul Smith's *Men and Feminism* (New York: Methuen, 1987), and of being excluded, because of his gender, from a Harvard feminist group discussion of Elaine Showalter's "Critical Cross-Dressing: Male Feminists and the Woman of the Year." And MacLean's essay (composed in the form of letters to Jane Tompkins that, as a response to Tompkins's response to Ellen Messer-Davidow's "The Philosophical Bases of Feminist Literary Criticisms," assumes an at least doubly supplemental position vis-à-vis female-authored feminist discourse) discloses painfully personal information about his difficult relationship with his mother, his unsatisfying experience with psychoanalysis, and an incident of marital violence.

6. Joseph Boone, "Of Me(n) and Feminism: Who(se) is the Sex that Writes," in *Gender and Theory*, 159. For my purposes here, Boone's remarks are suggestive despite their employment of language that might seem to mark them as a (hetero)sexualization of men's participation in feminism ("open up a space," "discover a position"). I believe that Boone's passage implies less about any desire for domination on his part than it does about the pervasiveness in our language of terms that have acquired sexual connotations and, consequently, demonstrate the virtual unavoidability—the seeming naturalness, if you will— of the employment of a discourse of penetration to describe interactions between males and females. But it also appears to reflect a sense of frustration motivated by Boone's knowledge that while feminism has had a tremendous impact on his thinking about the world he inhabits, many of the discourse's practitioners do not see a place in it for him or other like-minded males. In order to make a place for himself in the face of female opposition to his involvement in feminism, violation and transgression seem to Boone to be unavoidable. Also, Boone's self-consciousness about the implications of using a discourse of penetration to describe male participation in feminism is further evidence that we should not read his statement as possessing a (hetero)sexualized subtext. For example, toward the end of his essay, he argues that "a recognition of the presence and influence of gay men working in and around feminism has the potential of rewriting feminist fears about 'men in feminism' as a strictly heterosexual gesture of appropriation." (174).

7. Alice Jardine, "Men in Feminism: Odor di Uomo or Compagnons de Route," in *Men in Feminism*, eds. Alice Jardine and Paul Smith (New York: Methuen, 1987), 58. Subsequent page references are included parenthetically in the text.

8. Andrew Ross, "No Question of Silence," in *Men and Feminism*, 86.

9. Houston A. Baker, Jr., *Afro-American Poetics: Revisions of Harlem and the Black Aesthetic* (Madison: University of Wisconsin Press, 1988), 8.

10. Elizabeth Weed, "A Man's Place," in *Men in Feminism*, 75.

11. Michael Awkward, *Inspiriting Influences: Tradition, Revision, and Afro-American Women's Novels* (New York: Columbia University Press, 1989).

12. About his own relationship to feminism, Cary Nelson writes: "Feminism is part of my social and intellectual life, has been so for many years, and so, to the extent that writing is ever 'natural,' it is natural that I write about feminism" (153). Nelson's "Men, Feminism: The Materiality of Discourse" (*Men in Feminism*, 153–72) is, in my estimation, a model for self-referential male feminist inquiries that assume—or, at the very least, seek to demonstrate—a useful place for males in the discourse of feminism.

13. Jardine and Smith, "Introduction," *Men in Feminism*, vii–viii.

14. See Craig Owens, "Outlaws: Gay Men in Feminism," in *Men in Feminism*, 219–32. It is hard for me to believe that Jardine's and Smith's difficulty reflected a lack of interest among Afro-Americans in exploring the relationship(s) of men to black feminism. Texts such as the 1979 *Black Scholar* March/April special issue devoted to investigating black feminism as manifested primarily in Ntozake Shange's *for colored girls who have considered suicide when the rainbow is enuf* and Michele Wallace's *Black Macho and the Myth of the Superwoman* (see Robert Staples, The Myth of Black Macho: A Response to Angry Black Feminists," *Black Scholar* March/April 1979); the Mel Watkins and Darryl Pinckney essays published in the *New York Times Book Review* and the *New York Review of Books* respectively (Watkins, "Sexism and Black Women Writers," *New York Times Book Review,* June 15, 1986, 1, 35–36; and Pinckney, "Black Victims, Black Villains," *New York Review of Books* 34 [January 29, 1987]: 17–20) that critique such black male investigations of feminism offer clear evidence of Afro-American interest in "the problem." Jardine and Smith's difficulties, it would appear, at least where inclusion of Afro-American male perspectives was concerned, might have stemmed from the fact that (1) most of the men who had spoken publicly on the subject were open about their hostility to black feminism and (2) they generally did not speak the language of contemporary theory, a high academic idiom that demonstrates that the contributors to *Men in Feminism* are, despite significant differences between them, members of the same speech community.

15. Stephen Heath, "Male Feminism," in *Men in Feminism*, 1.

16. Ibid., 9.

17. Robert Scholes, "Reading as a Man," in *Men in Feminism*, 207.

18. Barbara Smith, "Toward a Black Feminist Criticism," *Village Voice Literary Supplement*, April 1988, 173.

19. Ibid., 172.

20. Michele Wallace, "Who Dat Say Dat when I Say Dat?: Zora Neale Hurston Then and Now," *Village Voice Literary Supplement*, April 1988, 18.

21. Sherley Anne Williams, "Some Implications of Womanist Theory," *Callaloo* 9 (1986): 304.

22. Valerie Smith, "Gender and Afro-Americanist Literary Theory and Criticism," in *Speaking of Gender*, ed. Elaine Showalter (New York: Routledge, 1989), 68.

23. Jardine, "Men in Feminism," 60

166 / Michael Awkward

24. Williams, "Some Implications," 307.

25. Boone, "Of Me(n) and Feminism," 159.

26. Deborah McDowell, "Reading Family Matters," in *Changing Our Own Words: Essays on Criticism, Theory, and the Writing by Black Women*, ed. Cheryl Wall (New Brunswick: Rutgers University Press, 1989), 84.

27. Toril Moi, "Men Against Patriarchy," in *Gender and Theory*, 181–88.

28. It seems to me that a full reading of the figurations of gender in the writings of Hurston, Marshall, Morrison, Walker, et al. is impossible without some attention to these novelists' diverse and complex figurations of black male subjectivity. McDowell's views notwithstanding, constructions of black male and black female subjectivity are too obviously interrelated in black women's narratives for feminist criticism to profit in the long run from ignoring—or urging that others ignore—the important function delineations of black male subjectivity possess for these narratives' thematics. Certainly the threat of antifeminist male critical bias—especially when that bias is as transparent and easily deconstructed as in the examples that McDowell cites—is not cause to erase or minimize the significance of black male characters' in these writers' work.

29. Hortense J. Spillers, "Mama's Baby, Papa's Maybe" An American Grammer Book, *Diacritics* (1987): 80.

30. Ibid.

31. In this sense, Spillers's perspectives complement those of Sherley Anne Williams. Williams demands, in effect, that we consider the extent to which male black repression of the "female" results from an attempt to follow the letter of the white Father's law.

32. Paul Smith, "Men in Feminism: Men and Feminist Theory" in *Men in Feminism* 33.

33. Henry Louis Gates, Jr. "Whose Canon Is It, Anyway?" *New York Times Book Review*, February 26, 1989, 1, 44–45. Because it introduced me to Spillers's formulations and because of its (apparently controversial) discussion of connections between black mothers and sons, expressed by a self-consciously male critical voice employing elements of black feminist methodology. Gates's essay served as an enabling pretext to this essay. Gates states that his initial encounter with Spillers's essay was a crucial, illuminating moment—the point at which he began to understand that "much of my scholarly and critical work has been an attempt to learn how to speak in the strong, compelling cadences of my mother's voice" (45). However, the autobiographical elements of my essay were inspired not only by what Gates might call his own "autocritographical" moment, but as importantly by the recent call for an Afro-American autobiographical criticism by Houston Baker and by the self-referential dimension in much feminist criticism and theory (especially, because of my own positionality, that which appears in the work of male feminists). These acts convinced me of the crucial nature of self-referentiality in this initial effort on my part to theorize about a black man's place(s)—or perhaps more accurately, *my* place—in black feminist criticism.

34. Moi, "Men Against Patriarchy," 184.

35. Toni Morrison, *Sula* (New York: Plume, 1973), 71. Subsequent references to this novel appear in the text in parentheses.

36. At least one other reading of Eva's murder of her son is possible: as protection against the threat of incest. In a section of her explanation to Hannah—very

little of which is contained in my textual citation of *Sula*—Eva discusses a dream she has had concerning Plum:

> I'd be laying here at night and he be downstairs in that room,—but when I closed my eyes I'd see him . . . six feet tall smilin' and crawlin' up the stairs quietlike so I wouldn't hear and opening the door soft so I wouldn't hear and he'd be creepin' to the bed trying to spread my legs trying to get back up in my womb. He was a man, girl, a big old growd-up man. I didn't have that much room. I kept on dreaming it. Dreaming it and I knowed it was true. One night it wouldn't be no dream. It'd be true and I wouldn't have done it, would have let him if I'd've had the room but a big man can't be a baby all wrapped up inside his mamma no more; he suffocate. (72-73)

In this construction, Morrison reverses to some extent the traditional dynamics of the most prevalent form of intergenerational incest. Instead of the physically and psychologically irresistible male parent creeping to the bed and spreading the legs of his defenseless female child, in Eva's dream, her large man-child Plum is the active agent of violation. Eva's emphasis on Plum's physical immensity and her own uterus's size—and, clearly, the obvious intent of this is to suggest the impossibility of a literal return of even the regressive male body to the womb—makes connections to incestuous creeping and spreading possible. It is not difficult to imagine, given Plum's constantly drugged state, that frustrations caused by an inability to reinsert his whole body into his mother's womb during what Eva views as an inevitable encounter might lead to a forced insertion of a part that "naturally" fits, his penis. At any rate, a reading of this scene that notes its use of language consistent with parent-child incest serves to ground what appear to be otherwise (at least in literal terms) baseless fears on Eva's part concerning both the possible effects of Plum's desire for reentry into her uterine space and her own inability to deny her son access to that space ("I would have done it, would have let him").

37. Hortense Spillers, "Black, White, and in Color, or Learning How to Paint: Toward an Intramural Protocol of Reading." Paper presented at the "Sites of Colonialism" retreat, Center for the Study of Black Literature and Culture, University of Pennsylvania, March 15, 1990.

Part II

Feminist Theory
in Men's Lives

Chapter 9

Can Men Be Subjects of Feminist Thought?

Sandra Harding

1. Hesitations and Possibilities

Can men be not just objects but also subjects of feminist thought? Can men create feminist insights for themselves and the rest of us, too? This question has vexed feminists, women and men (or "profeminist men," as the latter are sometimes called). Here I intend to show the diversity in possibilities for men's distinctive feminist subject positions that have been provided by the main "public agenda" feminist theories—those such as liberal, Marxist, radical, socialist, and others that guide attempts to change public policies.

Let me make clear what is not the issue here. Of course there have been men feminist activists. Obviously many men have played important roles in improving the conditions of women's lives through designing, advocating, and maintaining changes in social policies and practices. They have worked to advance women's control over their lives in local, national, and international government agencies, labor halls, educational institutions, and publishing houses. They have done so also as lawyers, women's employers, community activists, family members, and in all the other contexts where social policies and practices can limit or expand women's resources.

Moreover, it is clear that in the past men have made significant contributions not only to women's conditions, but also to feminist philosophy and theories in other fields. Many of us teach the insights of John Stuart Mill, Karl Marx, and Friedrick Engels as central parts of the legacy of earlier eras of feminist philosophy, political theory, and social theory. Some even teach Plato's *Republic* as a more progressive representation of women's abilities and recommendation of state policy than those one finds in much contemporary thought. Moreover, men researchers and scholars have made contributions to contemporary feminist thinking in philosophy, history, sociology, literature, and most other disciplines. If we did not already know that the authors of some such studies were men, we would not hesitate to refer to these authors as feminists.

But we do so hesitate—or, at least, most men and women do. As I have argued elsewhere (1987, 1991, 1995), this hesitation contributes to problematic gaps and inconsistencies in feminist thinking and practice. Are we really supposed to assume that our enthusiastic men students and colleagues are unable to think for themselves and come up with original feminist understandings, just as our women students and colleagues learn to do? Are men only supposed to parrot what women feminists say? Not only is such an assumption unreasonable in itself; it is also paradoxical since many of us assume that European American feminists are perfectly capable of using the insights of women from other parts of the world to generate important anti-racist and anti-imperialist insights of our own. So how could it be that no men can create anti-sexist, anti-androcentric, feminist thought? Such assumptions seem to ask us to believe that in the case of sex/gender differences, biology and/or history determine our thought, even though there are no other cases where such an assumption should be made (Cf. Collins 1991, Ch. 1 and 2). Of course there are men's movements and men's studies, some parts of which have closer and others more distant or even oppositional relations to the history of women's feminist movements and thought (Cf. i.e., Clatterbaugh 1990; Brod 1987; Brod and Kimmel 1995). Such reflections lead to the realization that issues about men feminists are part of the larger discussion of the strengths and limitations of "identity politics"—here, "identity thought" or "identity philosophies."

Perhaps it will appear to some readers that it is too formulaic to explore the possibilities for men's feminist subjectivities within the conventional way of dividing up the last two centuries of Western feminist philosophy into liberal, Marxist, radical, socialist, and the more recent public agenda feminist theoretical approaches. However, I think it is worth doing because, for one thing, this conceptual scheme locates differences in feminist thinking about male feminists in the context of the history of modern Western political philosophy. These theories are the main ones that have guided feminist demands on the state and other public institutions. The possibilities for men's feminist subjectivities have only been explored in fragmented ways within this framework. Furthermore, some of these philosophical frameworks increasingly are adopted in other parts of the world as Western-style economic and political relations continue to spread to other cultures. It is valuable explicitly to focus on the diverse options these theories make available to men so that men and women around the world can envision better how men can contribute to, or resist on progressive grounds, the ways such feminisms are being integrated into governmental and cultural policies at local, national, and international levels. Finally, this framework is familiar to hundreds or perhaps even thousands of faculty who teach feminist social and political theory. It is illuminating for our students to be able to see what these diverse legacies also offer to men in their capacities as feminist thinkers.

Let us set aside at the start several other issues that may be on readers' minds. First, nothing said below undermines the necessity of hiring women faculty. Women should be hired for many reasons regardless of whether men can also generate feminist thought—for example, accurate and fair assessments of women's research and scholarship, and the need for women and men students to be able to see women legitimated as college teachers, researchers, and scholars. Additionally, there are certain important topics for classroom discussions—especially those having to do with violence against women, sexuality, standards of beauty, and other issues about women's bodies—where women hesitate to engage in frank and illuminating discussions unless these are led by women.

Next, there seems to be a significant difference between a woman referring to a man's thinking as feminist and a man making such an attribution to his own or another man's thought. In both cases, one certainly can argue whether or not the piece of work or the individual is feminist. But the male-to-male attribution is suspicious for reasons that the female-to-male attribution may not be. Namely, men would be the least likely group to be able to detect whether their own or anyone else's (men's or women's) beliefs and actions do actually meet some set or other of feminist standards. Because the prevailing social institutions and discourses have been designed largely to match the understandings of men in the social groups that design and maintain such institutions and discourses, professional and administrative men would be least likely to be able to detect how those institutions and discourses do not serve women, or do not serve them as well as they do men. The deepest, most widespread, and most influential forms of sexism and androcentrism are neither overt nor intentional, but, rather, institutional, social, and "civilizational" or philosophic (See Scheurich and Young 1997). Some such influential assumptions are so camouflaged precisely by their pervasiveness in modern Western thought that it is a feat for any feminists to detect them. For such reasons, and others that will be identified in the analyses below, it can seem less contentious for women to attribute feminist standards to a man's thought or actions than it will for a man to do so.

Finally, "feminist" is not just a term that locates thoughts or actions within a set of familiar categories; it also attributes a certain political position to the thoughts or individuals it is said to describe. It "names" persons in ways they may not, or may not wish to, name themselves. Is it appropriate to call someone a feminist who does not claim such a label for himself? And what if he denies that he is a feminist, while continuing to advance claims that look to others like feminist claims? I do not intend to settle this issue, but simply to note that this kind of question has arisen about women also. Historians have puzzled about whether, for example, certain nineteenth century women who did not claim feminism for themselves and in some cases explicitly denied that they were feminists could or should still be discussed as advancing ideas and programs that look feminist to us today, and perhaps even did so to some of their nineteenth century peers.

Here I shall set these questions aside. Instead, I want to examine the different possibilities for men developing feminist subjectivities and thus making contributions to feminist thinking that are encouraged or permitted by major contemporary Western public agenda feminist theories. Such a project can have a number of benefits. As indicated earlier, it can show that the major public agenda feminist movements and their associated theoretical frameworks each do make available arguments about what can be men's distinctive contributions to feminist theory. Therefore, one would have to argue against these theories in order to deny that men can be subjects of feminist thought. Second, we shall see that the kinds of subject positions offered to men differ greatly in these theories. Such a project can enable us to identify the strengths and limitations of each such form of men's feminism, and to grasp how both strengths and limitations are outcomes of the feminist political philosophy on which each draws. We can better evaluate each proposal for men's feminist subjectivity by a comparison with the diverse possibilities envisioned by the other feminist theories.

Moreover, this project can enable us to appreciate that some of these theories (such as socialist feminism) at least imply that there are contributions to feminist thought that are more easily (in some cases uniquely) made by men—there can be distinctive feminist men's standpoints on nature and social relations that are different from those initially available to most women. For such theories, feminist thought is disadvantaged by a lack of contributions from men's feminist subjectivities.

Finally, in enabling us to see more clearly just what is problematic about the concept of feminist *men,* some of these theories enable us also to see more clearly what is problematic about the concept of feminist *women.* This particular project can contribute to ongoing feminist discussions of essentialist accounts of gender relations.

In examining the kinds of feminist subjectivity that these public agenda feminist theories offer men, I shall be focusing on each theory's epistemology. Political philosophies always have epistemological implications; they contain or assume specific theories of knowledge. This is so since political power is always distributed in part through policies and practices that determine which social groups get to produce, to legitimate, to maintain, and to use which kinds of knowledge about natural and social worlds. (And so, in turn, different epistemologies offer possibilities for different distributions of political power.) The question of this paper is what kinds of knowledge men can produce as contributions to feminist knowledge, so it is each feminist political philosophy's theory of knowledge that will be of special interest to us. Of course this is much too big and complex a project to be completed in a single paper. But hopefully even this brief outline of main parts of such a project can indicate the diverse and rich options existing public agenda feminist theories already offer for men's feminist theorizing.

Let us first turn to liberal feminism and its empiricist epistemology.[1] What opportunities does this offer men?

2. Becoming Truly Rational Men: Feminist Empiricism

Liberal feminism and its associated empiricist epistemologies retain the focus of seventeenth and eighteenth century social contract theory on the role of individuals' reason and will power, on how laws and institutional policies tend to codify custom and tradition, and on the importance of empirical tests of belief by "experience" in order to produce objective facts. They also stress the importance of professional communities of inquiry and their standards for the advance of knowledge.[2] Even when feminist philosophers creatively and usefully revise and stretch such concerns and principles to what one might think would be the limits of an empiricist terrain in order to accommodate contemporary feminist projects, clear traces of such empiricist themes still remain centered in their accounts (Cf, i.e., Antony and Witt 1992; Code 1991; Lennon and Whitford 1994; Longino 1990; Nelson 1990).

From this perspective, both women and men can gain feminist subjectivities, and there is little or no difference in the thought that can emerge from women's and men's feminist thinking. In both cases the point is to achieve just practices and bias-free beliefs by eliminating sexist and androcentric assumptions. In knowledge-seeking, there is only "bad science" and "good science" (or knowledge); feminist communities—ones that adopt the more rigorous standards for "bias-free" that feminists have produced—turn the former into the latter. In philosophy, feminist analyses eliminate the false and inadequate elements of existing philosophic arguments to create empirically and theoretically more reasonable and useful philosophies. Some feminist empiricists have pointed to how women's movements provide important resources for such processes since they enable everyone, women and men alike, to detect phenomena that were otherwise invisible, such as the social construction of gender, and gendered cultures and practices, including sexist and androcentric beliefs that have had extensive influence in the disciplines and in public life. Men, no less than women, can learn to identify and eliminate sexist and androcentric biases (Cf. Millman and Kanter 1987).

Just as Thomas Kuhn pointed to the importance of scientific communities in producing the most fruitful context for the growth of scientific knowledge, so, too, some feminist empiricists have seen membership in feminist communities, such as women's studies programs and the readerships of feminist journals, with their combination of support for and also rigorous criticism of new ideas, as providing valuable climates for the growth of knowledge. Clearly feminist empiricists hold that neither men nor women are doing the best philosophy of which they are capable if they do not engage appreciatively yet critically with feminist thought.

This position has great strengths. One of its greatest is that of all the feminist epistemologies developed recently, it can be inserted into the prevailing epistemologies with the least difficulty—even though it is far too radical for many conventional epistemologists. Moreover, feminist empiricists have importantly claimed that when the subject is women, sex, gender, or feminism, the ordinary clear thinking, resistance to superstitions, and critical attitude that people exhibit on other topics seems to weaken or disappear. Men, like women, can learn to exercise their critical thinking more rigorously in these areas. They can become more alert to the need to pursue vigorously ideals of rationality and objectivity on such topics. Moreover, the new facts that feminist research produces are not the products of female biology or of gendered histories that determine the emergence or acceptance of ideas. Though other theorists will see the situation as more complex than feminist empiricists imagine, there is something extremely valuable about the latters' assumption that whatever their origins, evidence of the empirical and theoretical adequacy of feminist claims must be available for anyone to inspect.

Limitations. Yet there are a number of weaknesses with the way feminist empiricism supports men's engagement in contributing to feminist thought. These appear to be characteristic of liberal feminism more generally. Such limitations will appear most sharply when this epistemology is contrasted to others below, but we can here at least mention some of the most obvious of them.

For one thing, feminist empiricism conceptualizes thought, reason, and the emotions as fundamentally properties of individual persons. Yet other epistemologies have identified patterns of these that appear to be characteristic of cultures rather than in any interesting way of the individuals in them. The kinds of thought, reason, and emotions that advance the growth of knowledge and the kinds that retard it differ from culture to culture, not just from individual to individual; and they vary in different historical periods within "the same culture" (See, i.e., Galison and Stump 1996). It is a limitation of liberalism and its empiricist epistemologies that cultures or societies are conceptualized as fundamentally merely collections of individuals. Thus only the psychology of error—not the sociology, social history, or politics of knowledge—is imagined as relevant to epistemological concerns.

Second and relatedly, the liberal/empiricist self or person who knows is conceptualized as pre-socially constituted and essentially disembodied. The self is thus imagined to be free to choose its own beliefs and actions. Yet other approaches point to the ways cultures, political relations, and psychic genealogies make likely some and unlikely other beliefs and actions; our powers to choose rationally are far weaker than liberalism assumes. Third, empiricism tends to adopt a narrow conception of rationality that ignores the positive roles that emotions can play in the advance of knowledge, and which is itself symbolically at least associated with manliness (Cf. Bordo 1987; Jaggar 1989; Lloyd 1984).

Fourth, feminist empiricism's conception of objectivity as requiring value-neutrality ignores the positive role that historically local interests, discursive resources, values and ways of organizing the production of knowledge can play in producing knowledge, not just in producing superstition or error. There are two issues here—one about men and women as feminists, and the other about men and women as gendered humans. Liberalism/empiricism must present the feminism of feminist discourses either as value-neutral (i.e., feminist science is simply "good science"), or else as not central to the production of knowledge. This strange choice points toward something contradictory in liberal feminism. Moreover, the conceptual resources that feminist empiricism has available to draw upon do not permit understanding how women's or men's distinctively different activities and the different meanings of masculinity and femininity in any particular culture provide men and women with specific resources that can make positive contributions to the growth of knowledge. Feminist empiricism's disregard of these empirical realities leaves it less empirically adequate than some of the other theories. Fifth and relatedly, such epistemologies stop short of the radical transformations of the conceptual frameworks and methods of the disciplines to which other epistemologies are led. Since such frameworks and methods are themselves constructed from male-supremacist subject-positions, feminist empiricisms leave disciplines' and cultures' deepest and most influential androcentric assumptions unchallenged. They protect from more critical feminist inspection fundamental features of social institutions, their cultures, and practices that most disadvantage women.

These problems conjoin to imply that, from a liberal/empiricist view-point, while men may contribute to the "good thought" that feminists can produce, they have nothing distinctive to contribute "as feminist men." Of course feminist empiricism asserts the same for women philosophers: women feminists have nothing distinctive to offer to philosophy that men could not supply. The liberal feminist goal for each of us should be to become that truly "rational man" envisioned in the Enlightenment's liberal philosophies.

3. Criticizing Bourgeois, Sexist Ideology: Marxist Feminism

Where liberal feminism was originally conceptualized to confront the conditions of women in the educated classes in the eighteenth century, Marxist feminism was formulated to deal with the conditions of working class women during the heyday of European and U.S. industrialization in the late nineteenth and early twentieth centuries.[3] Karl Marx, Friedrick Engels and much later the Hungarian theorist Georg Lukács developed the original standpoint epistemology in their thinking about the "standpoint of the proletariat," from which social position political economy could be grasped for the first time. The conceptual framework of this epistemology was borrowed and transformed for specifically feminist purposes by socialist feminists of the 1970s. So the discussion of this distinctive feminist epistemology and the opportunities it offers for men's subjectivities will be saved for the section on socialist feminism.

Here we can reflect on the obvious fact that the routine inclusion in introductory feminist theory courses and texts of Marx's and Engels' powerful critiques of women's exploitation under class systems clearly indicates that these men are recognized to be speaking from and occupying an important feminist subject position, though their gender presumably contributes nothing to such analyses. *Of course* men can produce feminist thought, such a positioning of these writings would seem to say. Men and women can join together to criticize the hegemonic bourgeois ideology, along with its institutions and practices, that distort human social relations, including those between the sexes, as well as the social theories, disciplines, and institutions that naturalize or idealize these kinds of gender relations. Moreover, if men, too, do not focus on such ways that false beliefs and exploitative practices are produced, they will fail to produce maximally adequate accounts of nature and social relations. Marxian analyses and politics will suffer, Marxist feminism seems to say, from inattention to feminist issues. It should not be surprising to see that this traditional Marxist feminism shares with the liberal thought it criticizes fundamental Enlightenment assumptions about the irrelevance of the gender of the authors of feminist thought to either the fact of its production or to its character.

Limitations. The limitations of this position for developing men's feminist subjectivities are largely those of its historical era. On the one hand, it is Marxism that first begins to see family relations and social relations between the sexes as distinctive social phenomena not controlled by biology. And Marxism sees knowledge systems as products of historically specific economic and political activities. So it almost can see what—more than a century later—would be perceived as gendered thought patterns. Yet it does not do so. Thus while it offers men the possibility of powerful feminist subjectivities of the sort Marx and Engels themselves possessed, it can not yet offer them the possibility of gender-distinctive feminist subjectivities, as later feminist theories will. Nor can it offer men (or women) the kinds of insights about oneself and social relations that become available for all post-Freudian thinkers.

4. Refusing to Be Men: Radical Feminism

Radical feminism emerges in the 1960s and early 1970s as a response to a very different world than the ones liberal and Marxist feminisms initially encountered. These earlier feminisms have lacked the conceptual resources to grasp the oppression of women by men that became fully visible only after World War II, not just the ignorance about and bad attitudes toward women entrenched in law and custom, or the exploitation of women's labor by capitalism that could be seen by the older theories.

Often radical feminist writings seem to imply that "feminist men" is a contradiction in terms. Here all men appear deeply and firmly implicated in women's oppression because they receive the benefits of male supremacist culture, its institutions and practices, whether or not they actively or consciously engage in sexist acts or the construction of androcentric conceptual frameworks. All men benefit from some men's control of women's bodies through the state's toleration of rape, wife abuse, incest, and other forms of violence against women. And many men benefit from the control of women's reproduction by the state, medical, and health care institutions, and from culturally-sanctioned ideals of women's beauty. Moreover, because men cannot have women's experiences, they "can never really know" what it is that women can know that enables the latter to produce feminist thought. Finally, radical feminists (like socialist feminists) point out that the very standards of what passes for objectivity, rationality, fairness, and justice—standards that shape the law, public policy, and the sciences—are deeply linked to ideals of manliness and are, thus, far from maximally objective, rational, fair, or just. Radical feminism would seem to regard the idea of men feminist philosophers or theorists as a contradiction in terms.

Yet there is another way to read radical feminism's positions that offers men the possibility of developing important feminist subject positions.

Moreover, such a reading of radical feminism opens into, or prefigures, some of the most important revaluations of sex and gender in poststructuralist and queer thinking, thereby highlighting this often undervalued potential in radical feminism more generally. In spite of its limitations, radical feminism remains far more radical than most of it critics have been able to detect.

For one thing, can't men use in innovative ways the kinds of insights that women gain in the kinds of cases on which radical feminism focuses? Does all radical feminist thought really issue directly from the individual experiences of its authors? Is radical feminist thought biologically or historically determined? After all, presumably not every radical feminist who offers illuminating insights about women's experiences of, and how the dominant institutions "think about," rape, incest, or battery has in fact experienced such acts. Catharine MacKinnon and others have taught me to think from the perspective of women's experiences of rape (and I do not mean to imply that she speaks from the experience of rape; she never says so), just as Patricia Hill Collins and others have taught me to think from black women's mothering experiences—experiences that I also have not had (MacKinnon 1982; Collins 1990). Shouldn't I, too, be expected to be able to teach and write in ways that are informed by, "in dialogue with" such writings (to borrow a phrase from Collins' somewhat differently focused analysis)? We all learn from, empathize with, the reports of friends' and loved ones' experiences, not to mention from such reports on television, in the newspapers, and in Plato's dialogues or William Shakespeare's plays. None of us except philosophy's imaginary solipsists are in fact isolated in our own experiences in the ways radical feminism is often presumed to hold. Cannot men, too, learn to listen in these ways and go on to use what they learn critically to rethink the institutions of society, their cultures, and practices? And will not such teaching and writing combine in novel ways insights emerging from experiences that they (and, perhaps, I) have never had?

Obviously women's reports of their experiences must remain central resources for feminist accounts, but it is hard to see why men cannot also make important contributions to radical feminist thinking. In her illuminating consideration of who can be a black feminist and therefore produce black feminist thought Patricia Hill Collins usefully situates her account as rejecting both the Enlightenment's idealist position that anyone can in principle know anything and everything anyone else can know, and also the excessively materialist position that only persons with certain kinds of biology or social histories can make contributions to the production of black feminist thought. Black feminism is for her a political/theoretical category, a discourse one might say. Let us leave this issue here simply by noting that the most defensible account of who can author feminist thought will have to avoid both the excessive idealism and the excessive materialism of conventional epistemologies while retaining the strengths of these two positions. We need a better epistemology than those two choices offer (See Collins 1991 Ch. 1 and 2; Roof and Weigand 1995).

Perhaps the most important resource for men to which radical feminism has drawn attention, however, is precisely the problems with manliness and womanliness per se—with these gender categories.[4] Where liberal and Marxist feminisms do not question the desirability or inevitability of gender categories, one stream of radical feminism locates the most fundamental causes of women's oppression precisely in these categories. It is not just that masculinity has been overvalued and femininity undervalued, or that each has been valued for the wrong reasons. Rather, the categories themselves serve primarily male supremacist interests. That is, it has been primarily in men's interests to distinguish their gender from femininity in order to link manliness to the distinctively human and to ideals of nationalism, race, "the worker," reason, militarism, the heroic, the ethical, etc. It is not just that such a practice overvalues masculinity and undervalues femininity, but also that the preoccupation with trying to fit so much of nature and social relations into gender categories obscures aspects of ourselves and our surroundings that do not easily fit into such categories no matter how they are evaluated.

Thus radical feminism challenges men to transform themselves at the most fundamental levels of their identity—to refuse to be "men," as the title of John Stoltenberg's book proposes.[5] Men can refuse to respect the masculinity ideals that structure the cultures, policies, and practices of so many social institutions. When women refuse feminine ideals, public institutions can no longer function in their usual, male supremacist ways, as political scientist Cynthia Enloe has pointed out in her analyses of women's positions in international relations (Cf. Enloe 1990). Harry Brod (1987) has pointed out that ideals of masculine identity are highly dependent on public discourses. Consequently, disruption of public discourse regularly troubles men's senses of their masculine identity. For example, when the U.S. economy weakens, misogynist discourses about the excessive costs of social programs for children, women, and the poor (all coded feminine) reach a higher volume. Or when the end of the Cold War results in decreased funding for scientific and technological research tied to military priorities, in the aerospace industry for example, feminist science critics are blamed for the incipient national "flight from reason" and its purportedly accompanying decreased science funding. However, one can ask if the causal relation might not go the other way, too. Could men's refusals of masculinity ideals have powerful effects on public discourses about international relations, economic strategies, national welfare systems, the research priorities of modern sciences, and so on? If men refused to regard as ideal such familiar masculinity figures as the warrior, the "worker," the "head of household," or the "rational man" of philosophy, economic theory, and jurisprudence, how would public discourses about militarism, the family, the economy, philosophy, and the law change?

One might be tempted to think that a man who refuses to become a man thereby becomes queer or even becomes a woman. Even this latter possibility now appears imaginable in the sense that trans-gendering, or gender-changing, has become more widespread. Some men have been able to become a "different kind of woman." Such alternatives to becoming a man conventionally have been the threats that have kept many men firmly focused on becoming as manly as possible every day in every way. But there certainly are other possibilities. A man could become "a different kind of man," or perhaps even better, a human, a person, in a truly gender-neutral sense. The very difficulty of imagining such possibilities indicates that radical feminism invites men to work out for themselves, in dialogue with women feminists, a creative transformation that could have widespread consequences for social relations. Thus, in contrast to liberal and Marxist feminisms, it can be argued that radical feminism assigns to men an innovative feminist theoretical and practical project that is both for themselves and for feminist thinking.

Limitations. The limitations of radical men's feminisms are the familiar ones of radical feminisms more generally. For one thing, radical feminist theories do not conceptualize the importance of differences among women or among men created by ethnicity, racism, imperialism, heterosexism, and other cultural forces. Such a conceptual silence marks these theories as thinking from the perspective of those privileged groups that can afford the luxury of such disconcern for the intersectional character of gender's mutually supportive relations with these other social structures and kinds of meanings. One has to suspect that radical feminist approaches also ensure essentialist assumptions about men, too, recuperating a Manichean dualism in which all women are in the same way victims, and all men to the same degree perpetrators of the oppression of women. In daily social relations, the issues are much more complex, and women often are complicitous in and sometimes initiators of the exploitation and domination of other women and of men. Moreover, class, race, ethnicity, sexuality, and other aspects of culture and history create important differences between the ways that different groups of men think about and participate in gender relations. For example, dominant and marginalized forms of masculinity (i.e., European American vs. African American and Latino, or Christian vs. Jewish and Muslim) play off each other in ways radical feminism does not have the resources to grasp (Cf. Brod 1987). Of course many individual thinkers who use radical feminist insights vigorously try to correct for such limitations of these theories. However, it is the conceptual frameworks of radical feminist theories rather than the claims of any individual thinkers that are being discussed here.

Often radical feminisms' reification of oppositional relations between men and women appears to imply the obviously false claim that men are doomed to be unable to resist acting out their oppressive positions in social relations. "Refusing to be men" is one approach to this problem. However, it is worth noting that history reveals many men vigorously helping to organize suffrage or labor union campaigns, trying to institute institutional policies beneficial to women, and in other ways working to diminish the authority over women that the state or other institutions and cultural traditions offer men (Kimmel and Mosmiller 1992). This fact offers a starting point for men's feminist "resistance studies": men have a distinctive interest in asking what leads men to resist thinking and acting in the sexist and androcentric ways to which they are so entitled by the dominant institutions. Much of the field of men's studies, including its research and scholarly analyses in the disciplines, provides evidence of the important contributions that such resistances can provide to everyone's feminist understandings.

In spite of its limitations—after all, no theory is perfect for every explanatory purpose we might have—we can nevertheless conclude that radical feminism's central contention that men *as men* oppress women, not just as imperfectly rational, or as members of a bourgeoisie, draws attention to a possibility not envisioned by liberal or Marxist feminism. Namely, in refusing to be men, paradoxically men can create new kinds of post-patriarchal subjectivities of their own that promise powerful public effects.

5. Becoming Historically Situated Feminist Men: Socialist Feminism

Socialist feminism emerged alongside radical feminism, but encountered women's conditions in the late twentieth century through the lens provided by the older Marxian accounts. It has been able to build on the concerns of these two powerful analyses in innovative ways. Its "standpoint epistemology" enabled these analyses to "start off from women's lives" to examine how women fared in the historically supportive relations between men's roles in patriarchy and capitalism, and their roles in family relations and public life. It is in the continuing historical negotiations within each set of relations that women's destiny is kept out of women's own control as patriarchy and capitalism negotiate over who shall control and benefit from women's labor, and as women's subjection in private life is used to maintain their inferior options in public life, and vice versa. How do the politics of these two dimensions of contemporary social relations enable the production of some kinds of knowledge and limit the possibilities of other kinds?[6]

Thus feminist standpoint epistemologists have argued that the prevailing conceptual frameworks in the disciplines and in public life have represented only the issues that interested—and were in the interests of—men in the dominant social groups. The kinds of knowledge that could advance women's interests were distorted by their representation within such conceptual frameworks, when they were represented at all. What people do and the cultural meanings that their activities have both enable and limit what they can know about natural and social worlds. Thus, for example, it has been the assignment of women to the maintenance of daily life both through their wage labor and in the domestic world that has permitted men professionals, administrators, and managers (these are the forms that "ruling" takes these days, as Dorothy Smith points out) to take as real only their abstract conceptual work. Such work hides and distorts its material preconditions, many of which are to be found in women's physical, intellectual, and emotional labors as mothers, wives, daughters, secretaries, nurses, domestic workers, service workers, etc. It takes both scientific and political struggle to bring such a fact to life, standpoint theorists have argued, since dominant ideologies are hegemonic; they structure the institutions, their cultures and practices through which everyone's daily lives are organized and understood. Thus women's interests could not simply be added to the dominant conceptual frameworks of social life or of research disciplines since such frameworks gained legitimacy only insofar as they could obscure both their material bases in women's activities, and their consequences for the gendered distribution of social benefits.

Feminist standpoint epistemologies have offered men the same resources for producing knowledge that they offer to women. Just as Marx and Engels were not proletarians, and yet could "think from proletarian lives" to produce their powerful analyses of how the class system worked, so, too, men can begin their thought in women's lives, with the assistance that feminist theories have provided, to produce equally powerful analyses of how the gender system works. How they can go about doing so in some respects is perfectly unproblematic. Marx and Engels produced a class analysis and laid the groundwork for standpoint epistemologies; whites have produced powerful analyses of racist systems that started off by thinking from the lives of those who suffer from such systems; therefore men can provide feminist gender analyses with thought that starts off from women's lives. Yet, as discussions of standpoint epistemologies have explored what it means to "start thought from women's lives", for knowledge to be "socially situated" in productive as well as limiting ways, and to use women's experiences in the production of knowledge, standpoint issues here have become both troubling and illuminating. Both such consequences are created by standpoint epistemology's problematization of the idealized positionlessness of liberal epistemologies. At least some of these issues can begin to be sorted out by looking at the strengths and limitations of standpoint epistemologies for creating men's feminist subject positions.

One such strength is to be found in the emphasis in standpoint epistemologies on the political struggle it takes to gain a feminist (or, in some formulations, women's) standpoint. A standpoint is not a perspective; it does not just flow spontaneously from the conditions of women's existence. It has to be wrestled out against the hegemonic dominant ideologies that structure the practices of daily life as well as dominant forms of belief, and that thus hide the very possibility of the kind of understanding that thinking from women's lives can generate. Similarly, men's political struggles against androcentrism and male supremacy in family life, in emotional relations, at work, in public agenda politics, and in the disciplines where dominant conceptual frameworks are organized and packaged all offer men possibilities for learning from the kinds of resistance that their struggles encounter. Some of these sites are completely or virtually woman-free. Such struggles can reveal to them sources and patterns of androcentrism and of resistances to feminisms that are not visible, or not so visible, to women. Thus men can be both sources of kinds of information of interest to feminisms and also producers of analyses of this and other information.

Two other strengths of standpoint epistemologies point to two kinds of "locations" where men can develop feminist subjectivities and have access to distinctive forms of knowledge. Such locations are highlighted by the two kinds of "difference" that standpoint theories have exploited in order to mine their epistemological resources. One kind of difference is created by power relations between the genders: patriarchy assigns men power over women. The other is the "mere difference" in the activities to which men and women characteristically are assigned in each culture (class, ethnicity, etc.). Of course, in everyday life, power relations permeate all aspects of social relations, giving different value and meaning to women's and men's activities; the two kinds of difference are only analytically separable. Let us look at these two kinds of difference in turn.

Any power relations—of class, race, religion, ethnicity, sexuality, as well as gender—give standpoint advantages to the lives of the oppressed. From the standpoint of such lives (and, often, for those who live these lives) there can more easily appear a gap between their interests and how the social institutions, from the design of which women have been excluded, perceive their lives. For example, women's interests and the perceptions of women's lives by the law, managers of the economy, health care professionals, and educational systems can widely diverge when examined from the standpoint of women's lives. But such political relations can also give scientific and epistemic advantages to men who set out to resist male supremacy and its androcentrism. Can there not also be a gap opened up between such men's experiences—men's interests—in their struggles against androcentrism and the way the dominant conceptual schemes characterize men's lives in terms of, for example, ideals of manliness and men's entitlements? Men are socially situated in different places in male-supremacist social relations than are women. They have different relations to their fathers, mothers, sons and daughters, to the "Great Men" of their disciplines, to the meanings of manliness expressed through ideals of patriotism, heroism, physical fitness, professionalism, spirituality, sexual desire and sexual skill, moral behavior, objective and rational thought, etc. Standpoint epistemologies offer opportunities for men to develop distinctive subject positions as socially situated men who have learned to think through feminist theories, descriptions, and practices that themselves started from women's lives. They, too, can come to think about their lives and about the rest of natural and social relations from a gap between how their lives are shaped by their concerns as feminists and how the dominant conceptual frameworks perceive and shape men's lives.

A second set of resources are offered by standpoint epistemologies' recognition of the opportunities for systematic knowledge created by "mere difference" in the activities in which individuals or groups characteristically engage (Cf. Harding 1997 and forthcoming). Women feminists have focused here primarily on the distinctive kinds of knowledge for which women's activities create opportunities, but we can think in parallel ways about the distinctive kinds of knowledge for which feminist men's activities create opportunities. Women and men will tend to be developers of and repositories for distinctive kinds of knowledge insofar as they have different interactions with nature and social relations. There are at least four respects in which such distinctive opportunities can occur. First, women and men have different interactions with nature and social relations insofar as their bodies differ, and insofar as their activities bring them into interactions with distinctively different parts of the natural and social worlds—with babies, the bodies of sick relatives, or with motorcycles and locker rooms (to stick with stereotypes). Moreover, even when women and men interact with the "same environment", their socially assigned activities can give them different interests in it and, consequently, different patterns of systematic knowledge and systematic ignorance. For example, clothing can be manufactured to produce warmth, durability, and/or social status; children can be parented to max-imize their health, their ongoing or potential income production or their marriageability; land can be farmed for subsistence or for cash produc-tion. These different opportunities can represent culturally-local gender-differing interests and, consequently, patterns of systematic knowledge and ignorance.

Third, women's and men's socially assigned activities and the symbolic meanings of masculinity and femininity give women and men different relations to their cultures' discursive resources. For example, in modern Western cultures, women tend to identify less with the "we" of author-ity, some observers report, more often perceiving authority to be "they" (Belenky, et al., 1986). Masculinity discourses are highly dependent on public discourses, as noted earlier—for example, about nation formation and national destiny, the advance of science, the achievements of adven-ture, of "civilization," and of "humanity," the fate of colonial empire, or the lot of "the worker." A men's feminist subjectivity could make impor-tant contributions to our understanding of the models of gender linked to such public discourses.

Finally, women and men can tend to organize the production of knowledge differently in some respects. Evidently they sometimes orga-nize differently the laboratories that they direct, and their publication strategies can tend to be distinctive (Cf. Barinaga 1993). Insofar as there are "women's styles" of doing science or gaining knowledge more gener-ally, then at least some of the alternatives to them, which were formerly conceptualized as the right styles or the only styles, now emerge into clar-ity as distinctively "men's styles." How does this fact create opportunities for men to develop feminist subjectivities?

Thus socialist feminist theory offers men opportunities to produce distinctive feminist subject positions of their own that find resources in men's feminist opposition to patriarchal politics and thought, and in the gendered character (not the generically human character) of their distinctive interactions with nature, their interests, their relations to dominant patriarchal discourses, and their distinctive ways of organizing the production of knowledge. Some of these insights can provide valuable correctives to women's feminisms. For example, one commentator has pointed out that women's feminisms tend to over-valorize femininity, using feminine norms to evaluate men's beliefs and behaviors in spite of feminist theorists' otherwise critical assessment of the restrictiveness of feminine norms (Brod 1987, 6). Another observer points out that women feminists tend to equate masculinity with patriarchy, obliterating any possible space for a men's feminist subjectivity as a third term in the dis-course otherwise restricted to women and patriarchy (Boone 1990, 21). Yet others point to the "phobic space" to which straight men are restricted in the absence of an articulated men's feminist subjectivity. Some feminist as well as male-supremacist cultures restrict straight men to the choice between participating in historical discourses of "normal manly" misogynistic representations of women, on the one hand, or the threat of homophobic accusations on the other. That is, in the absence of men's feminist subjectivities, straight men are offered the options only of "hating women" or becoming socially hated "lovers of men" (i.e. Forrester 1993). Thus there is a need to create space for men's active thinking on feminist topics that can function as something other than confessions or alibis (Forrester 1993, 185).

How shall we conceptualize what happens here? Starting off thought from progressive men's lives, with lenses provided by feminist analyses? Using feminist discourses to think from the lives of men resistant to male-supremacy? Such formulations seem convoluted, but perhaps also illuminating of issues about standpoint theory that need further exploration.

Limitations. Many of the problems plaguing radical feminism, on the one hand, and the older Marxian accounts, on the other hand, appear as problems for the early formulations of standpoint epistemologies. It would take us too far afield to do more here than merely recognize that history. Yet in its poststructuralist formulations, where "women's situation" is understood to be discursively established, not given "by nature" to our "glassy mirror minds," most of these problems recede (i.e., Henessey 1993; Harding, Ch. 7 in 1991, 1992). Indeed, it is the need for understanding feminisms as discursive formations—material institutions, their practices, and cultures within which language plays a central role—that confronted the attempt above to formulate the possibility of men's distinctive feminist standpoints on nature and social relations.

However, other limitations to the usefulness of standpoint approaches arise from *their own* distinctive political social locations, and the interests, discursive resources, and ways of organizing the production of knowledge characteristic of such determinate sites in history. For one thing, standpoint epistemologies are committed to producing "scientific" accounts that more accurately and comprehensively describe and explain the worlds around (and within) us. Yet they thereby relegitimate discourses of scientificity. Moreover, they draw on distinctively European and European-American discursive resources and ways of organizing the production of knowledge—Marxian accounts of the political economy and Marxian epistemology, distinctive modern Western problems in gender relations, current forms of feminism in Europe and North America. They draw on struggles over the role that the Enlightenment and "modernity" do and should play in the production of knowledge, and on many other local intellectual and political discussions. That is, standpoint epistemologies are historically located no less than are the standards for producing knowledge—past, present, and future—that are the objects of their study. Feminist thinkers from outside these cultures, women or men, might well prefer to use discursive resources available within their own cultural legacies for developing men's feminist subjectivities. Indeed, in some cases they might not even find the term "feminist" a resource for describing such a project, since the term has been associated primarily with bourgeois "women's rights" movements that cared little for the miserable conditions of poor women, peasant women, or women of dominated races, ethnicities, religions, or castes. Their "men's feminisms" might well best be developed in some other terms. No doubt there are other historical limitations of the standpoint epistemologies that others will be able to identify.

6. More Recent Feminist Directions; More Opportunities for Men

In recent decades a number of other distinctive public agenda feminist approaches to politics and theory in the disciplines have begun to flourish, and each of these also offers distinctive opportunities for men's feminisms. Multicultural and global feminisms and lesbian, gay, and queer theories are perhaps the most influential of these. They deserve extended analyses, but I must settle here for only indicating some of the most interesting opportunities for men's feminist subjectivities that these newer approaches make available.

Multicultural and global feminists share with socialist feminists interest in both the commonalities and the differences between women. In this respect, these "discourses", their institutions and practices contrast with the three discussed earlier, for each of those could only illuminate commonalities or differences between women, not both. Liberal and radical feminisms could each, in different ways, focus only on the commonalities among women; they did not provide resources for analyzing differences between women. In contrast, Marxist feminism was interested primarily in the differences between women in different classes; proletarian and bourgeois women shared little, according to Marxian theories, and it was only with improving the conditions of proletarian women (and men) that feminists should be concerned.

Multiculturalism has been interested in the similarities and differences in women's (and men's) situations in different cultures—their situations as Chicanas, African Americans, or Jews. Global feminists have been interested in the similarities, differences, and relationships between different groups of women's (and men's) situations at different locations within global political economies. For example, they are interested in the similar and different ways that femininity is constructed for women who work in the textile industries of Taiwan or Costa Rica and the ways it is constructed for us who buy the products of their labor. Again, they are interested in the commonality that violence against women is "managed" by the dominant institutions in their respective cultures in order to keep both groups of women acting "feminine," yet it is used in very different ways against each group.

These related yet differently-focused feminisms also offer distinctive resources for men's feminist subjectivities. They offer men opportunities to think critically about the commonalities, differences, and relations between, for example, the ways that dominant and subordinated masculinities are "managed" in each culture. What is shared and what is different about working class African American, Chicano, and white ideals of masculinity? About the ways each group is expected to think about the sexuality of women of their own ethnicity and of other races/ethnicities? About what they are culturally expected to do with whatever economic resources they can access? About expected attitudes toward nationalism, or "race pride"? Multicultural and global feminisms expand the terrain of commonalities and differences between cultural groups that can offer distinctive resources for developing men's feminist subjectivities. In doing so they also reveal limitations in the ways earlier feminist theories posed their concerns. They open up new horizons for political action and social thought for men as well as women feminists.

Another group of recently-developed political and theoretical approaches also opens up possibilities for men's feminist subjectivities. "Queer theories" develop further some of the themes of the older lesbian and gay approaches, and they introduce new ones of their own. Of course these are not always feminist approaches to issues. Some of the older lesbian and gay issues were overtly feminist or, in other cases, overlapped with feminist concerns; others did not. The same is true for the newer queer politics and theory.

We can briefly note just a couple of the implications for men developing distinctive feminist subjectivities to be found in some of the lesbian, gay, and queer theory concerns. For one thing, older writings made clear how cultural sanctions for misogynous attitudes in both men and women have been ideologically linked to homophobic ones. That is, dominant group models of masculinity have required "real men" to fear "femininity" in themselves, in women, and in men who refuse heterosexual masculinity. Each of these threatens to invoke the others. This is what Joseph A. Boone (1990) and Forrester (1993) were referring to when they wrote about the "phobic space" to which straight men are restricted in the absence of an articulated men's feminist subjectivity. Men are offered the choice of participating in the "normal manly" misogynistic representations of women or of suffering the threat of homophobic accusations. Such discussions point the way to the creation of distinctively masculine feminist subjectivities that refuse the absurdity of having to "hate women," having to fear "loving men," and to fear loving the "feminine" in themselves.

Queer theorists have produced accounts of the historical emergence of sexual identities per se—heterosexual as well as homosexual—as part of the emergence of bourgeois individualism and its "personal life" in Europe and the U.S. in the late eighteenth and early nineteenth centuries (Cf. D'Emilio 1993; Halperin 1993; Katz 1995). It took thought originating from somewhere other than in the dominant conceptual frameworks to be able to see heterosexual no less than homosexual identity as historical emergents. The social sciences have barely begun to contemplate what a disruption of social theory traditions such a realization can create (Cf., i.e., *Sociological Theory* 1994). Queer theory, too, thus uses a kind of standpoint epistemology, since it starts its thought from sex/gender-marginalized lives to look freshly at the different forms of gender and sexual relations created in different cultural contexts, and at how "heteronormativity" (a form of ethnocentrism) has structured dominant social institutions and the conceptual frameworks of public life and of research disciplines (Cf. essays in Abelove, et al. 1993 and Duberman, et al. 1993).

There are many possibilities such queer theory opens up for men to develop distinctively feminist subjectivities. Gay men are, of course, "different kinds of men." So too are female-to-male transgendered and transsexed men, just as male-to-female women are a "different kind of woman."[7] Such subject positions might be thought of as "*nouveau* gendered" ones.[8] When gender comes unfixed for individuals in such ways, new insights are possible not only about gender relations, but also about all of the social institutions and their conceptual frameworks that assume fixed gender identities. However, the distinctive social situations on which queer theorists draw also offer men (and women) opportunities to abandon gender categories entirely, or at least in new ways. This was the possibility that was pre-figured in that strain of radical feminism considered above that insisted on the oppressiveness of gender categories per se, not just of any particular historical ideals of manliness and womanliness. Here men can develop subject positions not as "different kinds of men" or "different kinds of women" (as "*nouveau* gendered"), but as what we might think of as ex-gendered persons. Such positions are so new that we can only begin to glimpse the philosophic issues that can arise from them. In an ironic way, such queer theories return full circle to transform for a later era's feminist (and other) projects the insistence of liberal feminist empiricism that gender should not be a relevant factor in shaping philosophy and social theory. It won't be when "ex-gender" comes into widespread social existence and designs philosophy and social theory, one might respond.

7. Conclusion

I have been exploring the many diverse kinds of subject positions envisioned in existing feminist (and queer) public agenda theories and their epistemologies from which men can make important contributions to feminist philosophy and social theory. One would have to argue against each of these theories—or the reading here of their assumptions and implications—to deny that men can be subjects of feminist thought. Of course each has its strengths and limitations. Some envision distinctive contributions that men can make specifically as feminist men; our feminisms are impoverished by the lack of such analyses. Others insist that gender is, should be, or could become irrelevant to the production of knowledge. Some are firmly socially located within dominant modern Western interests and discursive resources; others take advantage of the interests and resources that are available from other historical, social, and cultural locations.

Perhaps there should be a discussion here of the real concerns both women and many men have about co-optation, paternalism, appropriation, infiltration and the like that provoke such skepticism toward putative feminist men. However, this important theme all too often blocks everyone's ability (and desire!) to reflect on the possibilities sketched out above. Rather, we could begin to think further about how to create environments nourishing the kind of respectful reflections and dialogues evident in the project of this volume itself. As some feminists of color have argued, one will want to appreciate the importance of solidarity, not unity, among groups with different but partially overlapping interests.[9]

Notes

1. "Liberal," "radical," and the other labels here designate proper names of particular historical social movements and their characteristic theories, not merely (or perhaps in some cases, at all) everyday descriptions of individuals, groups, or ideas as liberal, radical, etc.

2. Of course this position is much richer and more heterogeneous than this brief account can indicate. There are many different ways in which feminists in different disciplines and in different projects have tried to make empiricism work for feminist projects. However, the "ideal type" of this position on which I focus here contains central elements of all feminist empiricist epistemologies.

3. The movements of women factory workers and the working class feminist movements in late nineteenth and early twentieth century U.S., Germany, England, and other European countries were often called "socialist feminist" movements. However, today this term is often reserved for the movements and theories that emerged side-by-side with radical feminism after World War II, and "Marxist feminism" then used to designate the earlier movement and its theories. (See, i.e., Jaggar 1983; Jaggar and Rothenberg 1993). This later

socialist feminism, like radical feminism, had to confront forms of women's oppression that became visible only after Sigmund Freud, after the massive entrance of women into higher education, after the increased percentages of working- and middle-class women with children under the age of six had entered wage-labor, etc.

4. Radical feminism is sometimes read only as valorizing the category of the feminine, which some radical feminists do. However, Alison Jaggar and Paula Rothenberg 1993, one of the most widely-used women's studies texts for almost two decades, has consistently included problematization of gender categories as a radical feminist project.

5. John Stoltenberg 1990. It would take this essay on a tangent to go into Stoltenberg's actual analysis, so I am not aligning myself with everything it means to him to "refuse to be a man", but only with this interesting idea that he pursues in the book.

6. The initial feminist standpoint writings can be found in Sandra Harding 1983, 1986; Nancy Hartsock 1983; Alison Jaggar 1983; Dorothy Smith 1987, 1990 and, I would argue, Jane Flax 1983, though Flax herself might disagree. (Some of Smith's essays in these collections originally appeared in the mid-1970s.) See also the development and uses of this epistemology in Patricia Hill Collins 1991, Donna Haraway 1991, Sandra Harding 1993, and Rosemary Hennessey 1993. Significant parts of standpoint epistemology can be found in such otherwise clearly radical feminist writings as Catharine MacKinnon 1982. Moreover, this approach has a social history as well as an intellectual history. The former insures that something like it will emerge when the "view from nowhere", or, in Haraway's phrase (Cf. above), "God-trick" epistemologies are being challenged. The original standpoint arguments were class based; race/ethnicity-based and postcolonial ones are widespread today. We will see in later sections appeals to kinds of standpoint arguments in multicultural and global feminisms, and in lesbian, gay, and queer theories.

7. My thinking here has been improved by conversations with Talia Bettcher, Holly DeVor, and Jacob Hale.

8. The phrase is Tom Digby's (personal communication).

9. I thank Harry Brod, Tom Digby, and David Kahane for their helpful comments on an earlier draft of this paper.

Bibliography

Antony, Louise and Charlotte Witt. 1993. *A Mind of One's Own: Feminist Essays on Reason and Objectivity*. Boulder: Westview Press.

Barinaga, Marcia. 1993. "Is there a 'female style' in science?" *Science* 260, 384–91.

Belenky, Mary et al. 1986. *Women's Ways of Knowing*. New York: Basic Books.

Boone, Joseph A. 1990. "Of Me(n) and Feminism: Who(se) Is the Sex That Writes?" in *Engendering Men: The Question of Male Feminist Criticism*, ed. Joseph A. Boone and Michael Cadden. New York: Routledge.

Bordo, Susan. 1987. *The Flight to Objectivity: Reflections on Cartesianism and Culture*. Albany, N.Y.: State University of New York Press.

Brod, Harry, ed. 1987. *The Making of Masculinities: The New Men's Studies*. New York: Allen & Unwin.

————and Michael Kaufman, eds. 1994. *Theorizing Masculinities*. Thousand Oaks: Sage Publications.

Clatterbaugh, Kenneth. 1990. *Contemporary Perspectives on Masculinity*. Boulder: Westview Press.

Code, Lorraine. 1991. *What Can She Know?* Ithaca: Cornell University Press.

Collins, Patricia Hill. 1991. *Black Feminist Thought: Knowledge, Consciousness, and the Politics of Empowerment*. New York: Routledge.

D'Emilio, John. 1993. "Capitalism and Gay Identity" In Henry Abelove Henry, Mechele Aina Barale and David M. Halperin, eds. *The Lesbian and Gay Studies Reader*. New York: Routledge.

Duberman, Martin, Martha Vicinus and George Chauncey, Jr., eds. 1989. *Hidden from History: Reclaiming the Gay and Lesbian Past*. New York: Penguin.

Enloe, Cynthia. 1990. *Bananas, Beaches and Bases: Making Feminist Sense of International Politics*. Berkeley: University of California Press.

Flax, Jane. 1983. "Political Philosophy and the Patriarchal Unconscious." In *Discovering Reality*, ed. Sandra Harding and Merrill Hintikka. Dordrecht: Reidel/Kluwer.

Forrester. 1993. "What Do Men Want?" In *Between Men and Feminism*, ed. David Porter. London: Routledge.

Galison, Peter and David Stump, eds. 1996. *The Disunity of Science*. Stanford: Stanford University Press.

Halperin, David. 1993. "Is There a History of Sexuality?" In Henry Abelove Henry, Mechele Aina Barale and David M. Halperin, eds. *The Lesbian and Gay Studies Reader*. New York: Routledge.

Haraway, Donna. 1991. "Situated Knowledges," In her *Simians, Cyborgs, and Women: The Reinvention of Nature*. New York: Routledge.

Harding, Sandra. 1986. *The Science Question in Feminism*. Ithaca: Cornell University Press.

————. 1987. "Is There a Feminist Method?" the introductory essay to *Feminism and Methodology: Social Science Issues*, ed. S. Harding. Bloomington: Indiana University Press.

————. 1991. *Whose Science? Whose Knowledge? Thinking From Women's Lives*. Ithaca: Cornell University Press.

————. 1992. "Rethinking Standpoint Epistemology: What is Strong Objectivity?" in *Feminist Epistemologies*, ed. Linda Alcoff and Elizabeth Potter. New York: Routledge. pp. 49–82.

————. 1995. "Subjectivity, Experience and Knowledge: An Epistemology from/for Rainbow Coalition Politics," in *Who Can Speak? Authority and Critical Identity*, ed. Judith Roof and Robyn Weigman. Urbana: University of Illinois Press.

————. 1997. "Women's Standpoints on Nature: What Makes Them Possible?" *Osiris* 12 (forthcoming).

————. forthcoming. *Is Science Multicultural? Postcolonialism, Feminism and Epistemology*. Bloomington: Indiana University Press.

————and Merrill Hintikka, eds. 1983. *Discovering Reality: Feminist Perspectives on Epistemology, Metaphysics, Methodology and Philosophy of Science*. Dordrecht: Reidel/Kluwer.

Hartsock, Nancy. 1983. "The Feminist Standpoint: Developing the Ground for a Specifically Feminist Historical Materialism," in S. Harding and M. Hintikka, eds., *Discovering Reality*. Dordrecht: Reidel/Kluwer.

Hennessey, Rosemary. 1993. *Feminist Materialism and the Politics of Discourse.* New York: Routledge.

Jaggar, Alison. 1983. Chapter 11 of *Feminist Politics and Human Nature.* Totowa, NJ: Rowman and Allenheld.

———1989. "Love and Knowledge in Feminist Epistemology." In *Gender/Body/Knowledge*, ed. Alison Jaggar and Susan Bordo. New Brunswick: Rutgers University Press.

———and Paula Rothenberg, eds. 1993. *Feminist Frameworks*, 3rd ed. New York: McGraw Hill.

Katz, Jonathan Ned. 1995. *The Invention of Heterosexuality.* New York: Dutton.

Lennon, Kathleen and Margaret Whitford, eds. 1994. *Knowing the Difference: Feminist Perspectives in Epistemology.* London: Routledge.

Lloyd, Genevieve. 1984. The Man of Reason: "Male" and "Female" in *Western Philosophy.* Minneapolis: University of Minnesota Press.

Longino, Helen. 1990. *Science as Social Knowledge.* Princeton: Princeton University Press.

MacKinnon, Catherine. 1982. "Feminism, Marxism, Method, and the State: An Agenda for Theory." *Signs* 7:3.

Millman, Marcia and Rosabeth Moss Kanter. 1987. "Introduction to Another Voice: Feminist Perspectives on Social Life and Social Science." In *Feminism and Methodology: Social Science Issues*, ed. S. Harding. Bloomington: Indiana University Press.

Nelson, Lynn Hankinson. 1990. *Who Knows.* Philadelphia: Temple University Press.

Roof, Judith and Robyn Weigand, eds. 1995. *Who Can Speak? Authority and Critical Identity.* Urbana: University of Illinois Press.

Scheurich, James Joseph and Michelle D. Young. 1997. "Coloring Epistemologies: Are Our Research Epistemologies Racially Biased?" *Educational Researcher* 26:3, 4–16.

Smith, Dorothy. 1987. *The Everyday World as Problematic: A Sociology for Women.* Boston: Northeastern University Press.

———. 1990. *The Conceptual Practices of Power: A Feminist Sociology of Knowledge.* Boston: Northeastern University Press.

Sociological Theory, Vol. 12, No. 2. 1994. Special cluster of papers on "Queer Theory/Sociology: A Dialogue," ed. Steven Seidman, p. 166–248.

Stoltenberg, John. 1990. *Refusing to Be a Man.* New York: Meridian.

Chapter 10

To Be a Man, or Not to Be a Man—
That Is the Feminist Question

Harry Brod

Introduction

In this essay I wish to move away from the deficit model of men and masculinities that underlies most discussions of men and feminism. I wish to present a view in which men bring valuable resources to their feminism in so far as they *are* men. In so doing, I simultaneously argue against two opposing views. One such view is that men simply cannot (or perhaps should not) do feminism or be feminists. The other view I shall need to argue against is that in so far as men can do feminism or be feminists, they must leave their masculinity behind, that they cannot do feminism or be feminists and at the same time be men or retain male identities. Rather, on this view, when men act as feminists they do *not* do so *as men,* but as some other kind of being, perhaps as non-gendered moral agents, or perhaps as beings who have somehow managed, at least temporarily, to adopt the standpoint of women.

There is in the United States a context that, though not very well known, has nonetheless been an important forum in which these issues have been discussed, and in which some of the practical implications of various theoretical positions have come to be visible. I have in mind what is called the pro-feminist (or profeminist, an issue to which I shall return) men's movement, represented nationally primarily by the National Organization for Men Against Sexism (NOMAS), formerly the National Organization for Changing Men (NOCM). The organization grew out of a series of annual national "Men and Masculinity" Conferences (the twenty-second held in the summer of 1997). In its earlier incarnation, the organization proclaimed its affirmation of three basic founding principles—it said it was: pro-feminist, gay affirmative, and male positive.

The 1990 name change was in large part a dispute over the third of these principles, a dispute that ultimately created a deep and abiding rift in the organization.

In 1991 at the Sixteenth National Conference on Men and Masculinities, I delivered an opening keynote address in which I attempted to articulate what it meant to be male positive, or what had by then come to be called pro-male or male affirmative, in a way that was not only consistent with but also required by the organization's other principles (i.e., pro-feminist and gay affirmative), and to argue for the centrality of this conceptualization to the organization's mission. The following section is drawn from that address.[1] In it I argue that what enables men to do feminism effectively is a vision of men and of feminism in which their feminism is inseparably linked to their positive vision of themselves as men, which I take to be the basis of what is meant by the ideal of being "male affirmative." It had always been clear that whatever being "male affirmative" meant, it decidedly did not mean affirming traditional male authority or behaviors, and that it meant affirming in some sense the actual or potential humanity and humaneness of persons of the male sex. Despite this having been one of the movement's core principles, however, what it really meant beyond that minimum remained open to question.

Profeminist and Male Affirmative

I begin by drawing on two stories told of Hillel, one of the great teachers in the Jewish tradition. One story has it that the great teacher was once confronted by a skeptic, who promised to devote his life to the study of Torah, the Jewish law, if Hillel would teach him the whole of the meaning of the Torah while he balanced himself on one foot. And he then raised one leg, and stood there, waiting. Hillel replied thusly: "The whole of the Torah is 'Do not do to others what you would not have them do to you.' All the rest is commentary. Now go study." And the man did.

The second story is simply a set of three statements, or rather questions, of Hillel's, often quoted as a guide to life. They are:

> If I am not for me, who will be for me?
> If I am only for me, what am I?
> If not now, when?

So here then, adapted from Hillel, is my summary statement of the meaning for profeminist men of being male affirmative. It is this: "If I am not for me, who else can I be for? All the rest is commentary. Now let us begin the conversation."

As Hillel knew and all of us know, this needs a great deal of commentary, only some of which I shall now be able to give.

First principle: if I am not for me, that is, if I do not have a positive attitude toward myself and others in the group through which I define my identity, I will not be able to sustain effective action in favor of anyone else. I make this my first principle, and the focus of much of what follows, because the challenge to the principle of being male affirmative, what has made it so problematic for so many, is a criticism made on behalf of profeminism, a criticism to the effect that being male affirmative somehow interferes with or is in opposition to being profeminist. On the contrary, I believe being male affirmative is an essential component of profeminism. Without it, no matter how noble one's intentions, profeminist men will simply not be able to sustain their energies over the necessary long haul. Robin Morgan once spoke of a male "ejaculatory" style of politics: periodic brief spurts of great energy, accompanied by long periods of withdrawal. If we think of the human energy required for effective politics, we can say that no one is served by a nonsustainable energy policy. All of us—men, women, children, the planet—need a sustainable supply of positive energy.

For profeminist men to sustain ourselves, we need to see our stake in the feminist future. We need a vision of how feminist transformation will enhance our lives. The male role restrictions from which men suffer in forms such as emotional alienation are best understood as the prices we pay for male power. Healing this damage to our psyches, then, requires the dismantling of male power. And feminism is precisely the movement that does that.

I wish to be clear about what I am and what I am not saying here. I am most definitely *not* arguing that the basis of profeminist men's politics should be to see what's in it for us, to identify our interests as men, and only act where we see such interests. Quite the opposite. I think the reasons for one's activism are the clear moral imperatives behind feminist demands for justice, the demands that we give up our unjust share of power, whether or not we want to, whether or not we think we have things to gain. But, and this is crucial, my study of history and politics leads me to believe that self-sacrificing altruism is insufficient as the basis for a political movement. Energy simply fails. My sense of the requirements of sustained, effective political action leads me to say that while principles of gender justice are the basis of our actions, the moral demand that we act effectively and politically to implement these values creates, if one wishes to put it this way, a moral imperative to go beyond mere moral imperatives, a moral imperative to find a political basis upon which to motivate significant numbers of men to profeminist action. This requires one to articulate how feminism, which requires men to give up power, can in some other sense be seen to be in men's long-term enlightened self-interest, even when it opposes men's immediate interests.

Again, all of this is put forth not in the name of the "what's in it for me" kind of attitude our society encourages toward politics, but in the name of being able to sustain our commitments as men to working toward gender justice, to working against our own power. It seems to me that the challenge is not to posit an opposition between being profeminist and being male affirmative, but rather at each and every step to show their conjunction. The necessity of showing this correspondence means that the rationales behind some standard liberal feminist appeals for men to embrace feminism are radically insufficient.[2] Liberal feminism asks men to surrender the material rewards awarded them by a sexist society, but it does not ask for a fundamental restructuring of that society. On the standard liberal interest group zero-sum redistributive calculus, as one group (i.e. women) gains, another group (i.e. men) correspondingly loses. Here one should recall Barbara Deckard's characterizing the fundamental difference between liberal and radical feminisms in her book *The Women's Movement* by contrasting the slogans "let us in" *vs.* "set us free."[3] Since men are already "in," they can gain only from a program that promises to set all free, rather than one that aims to let some in by kicking others out. Hence, despite the common view that liberal feminism, with its demands for simple equality, is the form of feminism to which men should most reasonably subscribe, the greater emphasis on the personal dimensions of political transformations found in more radical feminisms, epitomized by the slogan that "the personal is political," means they are actually better suited to fulfill men's needs. Liberal feminism's demands for a more equitable slicing up of the social pie actually have less to offer men than more radical feminisms' demands to bake a whole new pie.

We must understand and communicate how feminism is in men's interests, interests now understood in this deeper sense, as interests in transcending gender hierarchy, rather than as interests in grabbing the biggest piece of the pie. In saying this, I am aware that I position myself against a dominant conception that feminism is anti-male. This misconception of feminism as anti-male seems to have taken hold, even among some men who view themselves as most militantly in support of feminism. I think this misconception fuels the resistance to naming oneself as male affirmative, or pro-male. To overcome what I view as this misguided resistance one should recognize that the most deeply anti-male imagery and arguments come not from feminism, but from the antifeminist right. The right, which presents itself as the righteous defender of masculinity against feminist onslaughts, is really the source of our culture's deepest anti-male biases. Its ideology depicts men as raging, lustful beasts, who must be kept leashed and muzzled, lest the damage they can do be unleashed on an unsuspecting population. Hence society requires men to be captivated and captured by the pure souls that reside only in women's bodies. This is why the right believes the nuclear family is so essential to civilization. It keeps men at home and off the streets, it tames these beasts and protects us all. In contrast to this negative attitude toward men, much of feminism has always shown a greater faith in man's nature, in his (our) ability to change and act morally, a faith often held in spite of much more than sufficient experience to warrant anti-male feelings by women.

For this reason, I do not think that any progressive organization or movement can present a negative image of men, picturing men as inherently rapists or perpetrators of violence. Even when it comes packaged in radical rhetoric, or when biological determinism is replaced by social determinism (as in "Oh, of course I don't think this is biological, it's socially conditioned") such images are inherently conservative—they paint a bleak picture of male beings incapable of change, beings who must be simply opposed or written off, rather than beings who must be challenged to change and whose change must be facilitated. Anti-male images must be resisted, precisely in the name of feminism. Such images, no matter the intentions of those who present them, ultimately situate themselves on deeply conservative terrain, and I do not believe any progressive movement can successfully move on this terrain.

To mention some men's names often in the air in progressive political circles, advocates of nonviolence such as Martin Luther King, Gandhi and others understood this perfectly well. Gandhi said his campaign of nonviolence would never have worked without the English sense of fair play, and King knew he had to appeal to the better instincts of white Americans against their worse. Just as this did not require either of them to minimize the crimes against their people, neither does a positive vision of men's morals and potentials require or even permit us to minimize men's crimes.

Nonetheless, I often encounter among men the fixed idea that feminism is anti-male.[4] I have had essentially the same conversation over and over again with many men throughout the years. He will say something about feminism being anti-male, and I will reply that I actually think feminism is pro-female, and it's a little egocentric, isn't it, to think that someone is against you just because they are for themselves. Since this conversation usually fails to make any headway, I have come to the hypothesis that something is missing in the exchange, something essential is not being said. I have come to the hypothesis that the fixed idea that feminism is anti-male is really a defense mechanism. It is a defense mechanism against a deeper fear, namely the fear that feminism is not about men at all. It is in a way more comforting to believe that women are deeply involved with us, even if as enemies, than to believe that we are simply not that relevant to them. The fear is that feminism is about women going off to take care of themselves, leaving us men to take care of ourselves. And *that* is a terrifying thought to men, particularly those of us who are heterosexual, who have learned to depend on women for all sorts of emotional and physical nurturing and support. The fear of abandonment (by mother?) runs deep. After all, we know how to deal with someone who's treating us as the enemy—the usual response is to fight, in good male combative fashion. But among some radical profeminist men this response becomes inverted, and one ends up combating the fear of abandonment by running to obtain feminist women's kiss of approval at all costs, performing backward somersaults way beyond the requirements of essential principles of accountability, which must indeed be maintained. Sometimes anything seems better to men than having to turn to each other in positive ways.

If this analysis is correct, then by bringing men on to the terrain on which feminism stands, while one certainly will encounter resistance, one is then alleviating men's anxieties by disconfirming their great unspoken fear about feminism, offering men a greater involvement with the rest of humanity rather than the threatening specter of abandonment. Granted, men will find that on this new terrain they (we) will have to relate to women on new terms, unable to depend on the nurturing formerly extracted from women. They (we) will have to turn to ourselves and other men for this nurturance. Experiencing and developing new skills for this turn to each other is one of the crucial elements a men's movement has to offer to men and feminism. Here straight men have much to learn from gay men. This issue of men's friendships is but one among many examples of the absolute inseparability of the principles of being male affirmative, gay affirmative, and profeminist. I see real male friendships, that is, not the normal rules of verbal and physical fencing whereby we trade jabs but never really let down our guard, but really shared intimacy and connection, as a fundamental feminist issue. For while women's abilities to be nurturing and supportive are to my mind clearly admirable, the demand that they be so for men is to my mind equally clearly oppressive, for it keeps their energies from themselves and other women.

Being male affirmative has other important meanings. It means that the starting point of our conversations about men and masculinities must be the validation of men's experiences as they experience them. Again, I want to be clear about what I am and what I am not claiming here. I do not think men's accounts of their experiences provide the last word. Power does function to narrow and constrict vision, so that, for example, insights about race will more reliably, though not exclusively, come from people of color than from whites, and insights about gender more reliably from women than from men.

One can think of the different kinds of enlightenment that typically come from subordinated *vs.* dominant groups through a metaphor of different kinds of light beams. The light from above is like that from a laser: powerful and penetrating, it is capable of piercing through anything before it. Yet it illuminates only a tiny area at a time, and indeed it hardly illuminates that before it destroys it by the sheer power of its focused beam. In contrast, the view from below is like that generated by a searchlight aimed into the sky. One can get a sense of the whole, of the grand sweep of things, including the nature and structure of one's environment. But any particular part of what it lights up is only dimly illuminated. By analogy, men can very accurately describe men's experience in a way that women cannot; but to truly understand that experience by seeing it in the context of the whole, our vision must be put into the context of women's vision from below. Analogously, we men need to listen to women's experiences of us to fully understand ourselves. So I do not believe men have the last word on masculinities. But I do believe that to understand men, and promote change, men may need to have the first word. My experience is that before people can listen to whatever new words or ideas one may have to tell them, they must first feel that they themselves have been listened to.

This became particularly clear to me in the following incident. I once did a series of Date Rape Prevention Education workshops organized through the fraternity system at a college. I began the evening's gathering by saying that it occurred to me that if I knew I were coming to such an event, I might well have various thoughts and feelings about it during the day. I invited the young men to share these. What emerged was a sense of themselves as victimized. *They* knew they were nice, caring men, yet women in dating situations seemed afraid of them, blaming *all* of them for what only a very few men did. They described the discomfort of feeling that they had to tiptoe on eggshells around women, regretting the loss of earlier, more carefree times. I let this conversation go on for a while. I expressed understanding of their anger at the injustice done to them by being "stereotyped," as they put it, in these terrible ways. And then I started to raise some questions. Wasn't it egocentric, I asked, to take what was happening in these situations as an unfair judgment these women were making about them personally? After all, as they had just said, these women often didn't know them very well. Wouldn't it make more sense to try to understand the women's experiences that led them to these judgments? And then I started to tell them much of what I've learned from women about the fears they live with, the constrictions on their lives that come from living in a rape culture.[5] I went on at some length in this vein, and then asked for their responses. "I never knew," said one. "I feel like I've been hit in the face with a brick," said another. I think positive changes happened that night. They began to learn a new kind of account-ability and sensitivity. I think positive things happened because these men got a sympathetic hearing of their stories before they were asked to listen to someone else's.

However, at this point one begins to come up against a real problem. It is necessary to listen to men, to allow and encourage men to tell their stories, both to heal their own pain and as part of the process of stopping the pain men inflict on others. But such listening takes time, money, resources. These are in short supply. By what right do we allocate resources to men and their stories, when the victims of patriarchal mas-culinity, of male violence, lack resources to tell their stories, to heal their pain? In its most pointed form, this question sometimes boils down to money for the battered women's shelter *vs.* money for a counseling pro-gram for men who batter. The question often arises when support is being solicited from the state, or from other institutions. This seems to me pre-cisely the point at which being male supportive and being profeminist have seemed most clearly on a collision course. So I feel the need to address this question head on, and to weigh my words particularly care-fully here. There are lives at stake.

I find it necessary to say the following. I think profeminist men must say clearly, loudly, and unambiguously that when faced with a choice between supporting the victims and supporting the perpetrators, we side with the victims. We insist that the violence stop now, even before the men's pain that underlies it can be fully healed. We understand that the violence stems not only from men's pain, but also from their quest for power, and so we challenge that power, and attempt to undermine it. But then we proclaim something else too, with equal vigor. We say that this choice is not of our making. This choice is forced on us by a society that all too often squanders its resources on death, destruction, and pollution, rather than on life, creation, and healing. The denial of desperately needed healing resources to men is not one of our principles, but one of theirs. Our principles would be to fully support allocating all the resources needed to heal both women and men. The patriarchically cre-ated scarcity of resources means that we must make decisions about allo-cating scarce resources in principled ways. And we must, regretfully, advocate that in many cases men will not have their needs met, because women have more pressing claims on those resources. Fortunately, in many cases using resources to support men is not a case of taking resources from women. In many cases, it is perfectly clear that if these resources are not used in profeminist ways, they will in the alternative go not to women, but to the service of antifeminist causes. In such cases, profeminist men should use all available resources, and struggle for a world beyond scarcity.

I have elaborated this point at some length because I really do think it makes a great difference how one says this. I think profeminist men must maintain a supportive stance toward men, even in the very act of having to advocate that some men be denied the support they need. Any hint or suggestion that men are in any way not deserving of our full compassion and attention betrays our moral integrity, and denies our fundamental humanity.

The most militant profeminism is not only compatible with, but requires, the firmest male affirmative stance. There is no question here of compromise, of needing to strike some tenuous balance between competing ideals. Indeed, compromise of this sort is the greatest danger. If the meaning and necessity of sustaining a male affirmative stance is not steadfastly maintained in one's consciousness, one may come to feel that one is at constant risk of having one's profeminism undermined because one may come to believe that profeminism somehow demands that one must harden one's heart and shut one's ears against men's pain, apparently out of fear that emotional appeals may sway one to have pity on men and therefore decrease one's devotion to feminism. I fear that for some profeminist men it may have come to this, a situation in which one has desensitized and dehumanized oneself in the name, irony of ironies, of feminism. In my view, it is rather the ability to take in and honor the pain men suffer that provides the surest foundation for the ability to oppose the pain men inflict.

Having thus argued for the need for men acting in support of feminism to be pro-male I now turn to a more extended discussion of what it really means for men to be profeminist, and especially what it means for men to attempt to create some sort of social and political identity, organization, or movement on this basis.

To Hyphenate Or Not To Hyphenate—That Is the Pro(-)feminist Question

Philosophers are often taken to be people who address the "big" questions. In this section I shall, however, begin with a very small question, indeed one of the smallest questions I can imagine addressing. While philosophers often address the meanings of words, it is relatively rare to address the meanings of *parts* of words. But I shall do so here. I shall address the significance of the hyphen, or the lack thereof, in the terms "pro-feminism" and "profeminism." Though indeed relatively rare, there is nonetheless some precedent for such a discussion in similar political contexts. During the 1970s, for example, there was an extended discussion of the meaning and ostensible need for the hyphen in the then emerging theory and practice of socialist-feminism, and in the late 1980s Marshall Grossman published an article on "The Violence of the Hyphen in Judeo-Christian," in which he related this hyphen to "the Post-Colonial Hyphen."[6]

In my view there is an important but unrecognized ideological difference between being "pro-feminist" and being "profeminist" within the pro-feminist/profeminist men's movement. I shall not be arguing that everyone, or even anyone, who opts for either the hyphenated or non-hyphenated version is making a conscious philosophical statement, but I do nonetheless believe that the differences in meaning between the two versions can be discerned in their common usage. I shall further make an argument advocating "profeminism."

I suspect that until now most of those who have even noticed the difference have attributed it to mere orthographic convention. Any such persons knowledgeable about the publishing industry would probably have attributed the increasing frequency of the dehyphenated version to the recent trend among language specialists away from hyphenation. I believe, however, that much more is at stake.

It seems to me that the place to start such a discussion is not with the distinction between being a "pro-feminist" and a "profeminist" but rather with the earlier distinction between being a "pro-feminist" and a "feminist." "Pro-feminist" came into use among men supportive of feminism who believed that the term "feminist" should be reserved exclusively for women, that for men to call themselves feminists was another act of male appropriation of women's work and identities. Some preferred "pro-feminist" to the at least equally prevalent alternative used to designate the same thing, "anti-sexist," because they wished to affirm a positive identity of what they were for, not wishing to define themselves exclusively or even primarily by what they were *against*. An early formulation of the rationale behind identifying oneself as an "anti-sexist," a rationale also used for "pro-feminist," appeared in Jon Snodgrass's introduction to his edited collection *For Men Against Sexism: A Book of Readings*, in which Snodgrass describes his intellectual development:

> I was attempting to build unity by integrating socialism and feminism, the two movements with which I most closely identify. However, because I believe that men cannot be feminists, I do not call myself a socialist-feminist. Instead, I refer to myself as an anti-sexist socialist, admittedly an awkward term. I feel that for men to refer to themselves as feminists is equivalent to whites calling themselves black militants; I attempt to respect autonomy by thinking of feminism as a women's movement.[7]

I should say here that I think not only that men *may* call themselves feminists, but further that there are good reasons for doing so. To many, if not most, people a man calling himself a feminist is the strongest identity he can take on in support of women. Anything else, such as "profeminist," therefore sounds to them like he is distancing himself from the strongest possible support for feminism. I believe this would be a loss in advancing the cause of feminism, for support breeds support, and men proclaiming themselves as strongly in favor of feminism as possible can go a long way in generating further support for feminism.

However, there are also good reasons for men *not* calling themselves feminists, such as the concern noted above about men co-opting women's identities and struggles. Thus, while I will continue to claim a feminist identity for myself because in my view the benefits to feminism of doing so outweigh the drawbacks, in deference to the latter concerns I do not urge that the profeminist men's movement adopt such an identity.

I take pro-feminism, then, to be the position of men who believe feminism to be essentially of, by, and for women, and who take their position to mean that men should support this feminism. Those who wish to ridicule this position have referred to it as the view that men should form a "men's auxiliary" to the women's movement.[8]

The problem as I see it, however, is not that "pro-feminism" brings men too close to the women's movement, but rather the opposite, that the hyphen leaves too much space between the "pro" and the "feminism," leaving men's politics too detached from women's. It establishes feminism as a pre-existing entity, needing only the support of men. *Certainly* men must support and respect the autonomy and leadership of the women's movement, but "pro-feminism" retains too many of the problems generated by the "men can't be feminists" position that, while put forward by its adherents as radically activist in its denial of the legitimacy of male participation in feminism, ends up leaving men without a *position from which* to be either radical or activist. As Tim Carrigan, Bob Connell, and John Lee trenchantly observe in their important article "Hard and Heavy: Toward a New Sociology of Masculinity":

> The most striking thing about *For Men Against Sexism* [quoted above] is the massive guilt that runs through its major pieces. . . . The book insists that men must accept radical feminism as the basis for their CR groups and have them started and supervised by women. . . . One gets the impression that being subject to constant criticism by feminists is the emotional center of this book, and that the response is to bend over backwards, and backwards again. A relationship with feminism is indeed crucial to any counter-sexist politics among heterosexual men; but a series of back somersaults is not a strong position from which to confront the patriarchal power structure.[9]

There is an essential difference between men accepting women's right of leadership versus men imposing the burden of leadership on women by

denigrating themselves. It is essential that the men's movement be dominated by the former and not contaminated by the latter.

The danger in mistaking one for the other became clear during recent
debates within the National Organization for Men Against Sexism concerning NOMAS's sexual politics. Dissatisfied with the position the organization took on a particular issue as not being feminist enough, a
significant number of those who identify as members of NOMAS's
"Activist Men's Caucus," its ostensibly radical wing, argued that
NOMAS needed to establish a board of feminist women to whom the
organization would be accountable. One can envision the results: each
ideological faction within NOMAS would elect its brand of feminists to
this board, resulting in women fighting men's battles by proxy whenever
disputes arose. Promoted as empowering women, this proposal in reality
therefore exploits women.

In contrast to all this, profeminism is the developing feminist politics
of, by, and for men. Profeminism of course includes pro-feminism as its
primary principle, but it also includes much more. It is a call from and to
men to develop feminist and pro-feminist personal and political principles and actions. It insists that men must recognize their own stake in the
transformations advanced by feminism, *not* because men should put their
own needs ahead of others, but because this recognition is part and parcel
of being able to fully commit oneself to the liberation of others. Thus,
along with its pro-feminism, profeminism articulates men's contributions
to and benefits from feminism. It is *not* an attempt to develop a new
pseudo-generic term that re-subordinates women under the dominance of
men now included within feminism. By naming profeminism as a specifically male development of feminism, profeminism preserves pro-feminism's respect for women's autonomy, but without turning that respect
into a counter-productive and disabling dependency. Profeminism incor-
porates into its fundamental principles its continuing indebtedness to
feminism. But it also insists that it is men's task, both as obligation and
as right, to develop their own brand of feminist politics, albeit in coop-
eration with others.

Profeminist men must take this stand *not* as an assertion of independence for the sake of male pride, but in response to feminist demands
that we *fully* commit ourselves to eliminating patriarchy, for anything
less than this is an abnegation of our moral responsibilities in this regard.
Any ethical stance, including profeminism, presupposes the autonomy of
the moral agent. Men acting on any principle that does not fully embrace
this autonomy is an abnegation of feminist morality. Turning the task of
developing men's profeminist ethics and politics over to women would be
a classic example of the kind of moral failure and inauthenticity that
Jean-Paul Sartre called "bad faith." Men must of course respect the

empirical knowledge and moral imperatives that derive from women's privileged epistemological standpoint that I discussed above, but this does not in any way minimize their full moral autonomy and accountability.

In further consideration of the need for profeminism, who but men have the requisite knowledge to undermine the foundations of patriarchy from within (again, not because this will be the basis for eliminating patriarchy, for it won't—the basic strength of this struggle will come from those oppressed by patriarchy—but simply because this is the task allotted to *us* by our position within the system)? And how can the men's movement do the requisite work on developing men's positive relationships with each other, a necessary part of struggles not only against patriarchy but also against heterosexism, racism, anti-Semitism, and other forms of domination, if men continue to depend on women to develop men's personal and social politics for them? If men cannot work and be with each other in positive and effective ways, they will not be able to work in anyone's interests as effectively as they otherwise would. For example, one of the profeminist men's movement's greatest successes has been in the area of gay-straight alliance work against heterosexism. In this context gay men have pointed out to straight men that a prerequisite for this success has been straight men learning to end their reliance on approval from women and learning to turn to other men for positive support (I am referring here to the debilitating neediness that drives men to women, not the principled and essential accountability of profeminist men to feminist women).

Further, greater profeminism is an essential part of the political response profeminism needs to make the challenge posed to it by the success of the mythopoetic men's movement, usually associated in the public mind principally with the work of Robert Bly. That movement has addressed men's felt need to experience and articulate their own distinctive viewpoint as men with greater success than has profeminism, at least as measured by the number of adherents subscribing to a movement's basic tenets and participating in its activities. Profeminism presents an opportunity for a greater public presence and impact than does mere profeminism, by allowing for the development of a viewpoint stemming from both men and feminism, thereby responding to men's desires for a "men's voice" in our culture's conversation about gender.

I shall cite some examples of what I consider the appropriate uses of "pro-feminist" and "profeminist." Michael Kimmel writes:

Profeminist men believe that their ability to transform masculinity is inspired by and made possible by the women's movement and that the social changes precipitated by the modern feminist movement contain, in

210 / Harry Brod

both theory and practice, significant and desirable changes for men as well, including a vehicle for the resolution of the contemporary crisis of masculinity.[10]

Kimmel here names as profeminist the stance by men that recognizes the connection between the women's movement and the solution of men's problems. But when he co-edited, with Thomas Mosmiller, a book on men who supported women's equal rights, whether or not they saw this connection to their own lives, the book was titled *Against the Tide: Pro-Feminist Men in the United States 1776–1990, A Documentary History*. In these two works the distinction between pro-feminism and profeminism is made precisely as I have argued it should be.

To give another example, on the jacket of John Stoltenberg's *The End of Manhood: a Book for Men of Conscience* (a book Stoltenberg elsewhere describes as "the practical sequel" to his earlier book *Refusing to Be a Man: Essays on Sex and Justice*) he is described as a "radical profeminist author," in contrast to the earlier book's jacket copy, which merely uses the term "antisexist" to describe his activities.[11] Here is evidence of the very recent emergence of the term "profeminist" as well as a demonstration that the term does not imply any kind of backing away from feminist principles.

Stoltenberg's theoretical stance is an instructive one to briefly consider in order to highlight the implications of the quite different thesis of this paper. Stoltenberg offers a powerful radical critique of what he sees as the artificiality and danger of the notion that there is in reality any such thing as masculinity. For Stoltenberg, strongly influenced by Andrea Dworkin, masculinity simply *is* patriarchy, which is itself an artificial and in some basic sense false construct. Therefore for him the idea of any kind of feminist theory or practice that men could undertake *as men* is necessarily an oxymoron, a contradiction in terms. Men must totally refuse to be men, and call for an end to manhood per se. But in Stoltenberg's call to refuse to be a man (often, it seems, by sheer act of will) in order to bring about the end of manhood, what is lacking is precisely the standpoint *from which* to practice a transformative politics that being profeminist *as men* provides. One is left with only an ungendered individual moral identity, rather than a gendered collective political identity that I believe is essential for sustained, effective political action.

I would note that this tendency is not restricted to the question of gender. I would make the analogous argument regarding the recently articulated "new abolitionist" position regarding race. This view, principally articulated by Noel Ignatiev, calls on whites to become "race traitors" in order to eliminate white supremacy.[12] While indisputably morally inspiring and empowering to some individuals, as is Stoltenberg's view, I believe this stance will prove to be similarly ineffective in mobilizing significant numbers of whites to anti-racist action. A sounder theory and practice would stem from whites developing an anti-racist white identity, rather than attempting to refuse any racial identification.

When the left was more influenced by Marxism than it is today there was a phenomenon some called bourgeois individualism. Today, it would more likely be called white Western male individualism. Same thing, different analysis. At the core of this ideology is the belief that individualist ethics are more important that collective politics. Despite its radical self-image, I find a deeply individualist and voluntarist, and consequently apolitical, stance at the core of what styles itself the radical profeminist approach that takes much of its theoretical orientation from Stoltenberg.

It seems to me contradictory to attempt to bring men together against patriarchy while at the same time declaring the very concept of having an identity *as men* illegitimate. I simply do not see how a profeminist men's politics can be coherently derived from this individualist ethics. Indeed, this seems to me to be so much of a contradiction that I would attribute to this faction's Pyrrhic victory within NOMAS the organization's current state of near collapse, and its demise as a presence with significant potential contributions to make to feminist transformations.

Perhaps the simplest way to encapsulate the point of view I wish to put forward is simply to say that positive transformation requires a positive vision, and therefore for men to do feminism requires positive visions of both men and feminism.

Notes

1. "Enhancing Men's Lives: Directions for the Profeminist Men's Movement, with a Critique of Mythopoetic and Ultraradical Politics," *Working Papers on Women and Men*, Institute for the Study of Women and Men, University of Southern California, 1993.
2. The following argument draws on my "Feminism For Men: Beyond Liberalism," in *brother: The Newsletter of the National Organization for Changing Men* 3:3, June 1985, pp. 2 & 5.
3. Barbara Deckard, *The Women's Movement* (New York: Harper & Row, 1975).
4. The following argument draws from my "Why is This 'Men's Studies' Different From All Other 'Men's Studies'?," *Journal of the National Association for Women Deans, Administrators, and Counselors* 49:4, Summer 1986, 44–49.
5. See e.g. Diana E. H. Russell, *The Politics of Rape: The Victim's Perspective* (New York: Stein and Day, 1975); Susan Griffin, *Rape: The Power of Consciousness* (New York: Harper and Row, 1979); Elizabeth Stanko, *Intimate Intrusions: Women's Experience of Male Violence* (London: Routledge and Kegan Paul, 1985); Emilie Buchwald, Pamela R. Fletcher, and Martha Roth, eds. *Transforming A Rape Culture* (Minneapolis: Milkweed Editions, 1993); Timothy Beneke, *Men On Rape* (New York: St. Martin's Press, 1982).

6. The point was of course disputed and trivialized by some—Marshall Grossman's article prompted a response by Yerach Gover titled "Why Be A Nebbish? Response to Grossman." Both are in *Social Text* 22, Spring 1989—Grossman: 115–122; Gover: 123–129.

7. Jon Snodgrass, *For Men Against Sexism: A Book of Readings* (Albion, CA: Times Change Press, 1977), p. 9.

8. See R. W. Connell, "Men and the Women's Movement," *Social Policy*, Summer 1993, pp. 72–78.

9. Tim Carrigan, Bob Connell, and John Lee, "Hard and Heavy: Toward a New Sociology of Masculinity," in Michael Kaufman, ed., *Beyond Patriarchy: Essays by Men on Pleasure, Power, and Change* (Toronto: Oxford University Press, 1987), pp. 162–63.

10. Michael S. Kimmel, "Men's Responses to Feminism at the Turn of the Century," *Gender & Society* 1:3, September 1987, p. 280.

11. The "practical sequel" term is from Stoltenberg's letter to friends of May 1994. John Stoltenberg, *The End of Manhood: a Book for Men of Conscience* (New York: Dutton, 1993) and *Refusing to Be a Man: Essays on Sex and Justice* (Portland, Oregon: Breitenbush Books, 1989).

12. Noel Ignatiev and John Garvey, eds., *Race Traitor* (New York: Routledge, 1996). The book is primarily a collection of essays from the journal *Race Traitor*, edited by Garvey and Ignatiev, the motto of which is "Treason to whiteness is loyalty to humanity."

Chapter 11

Male Feminism as Oxymoron[1]

David J. Kahane

This essay considers possible forms of male feminist knowledge and their implications for male feminist theory and practice. It seems to me that feminist insights into the standpoint-specificity of knowledges, the formation of identities within patriarchy, and the contradictory character of feminist consciousness together should provoke some wariness toward men claiming a feminist commitment. While it is important for men to take feminism seriously, recognize their own roles in sexist privilege and oppression, and work for change, men have to face the extent to which fighting patriarchy means fighting themselves. They can chip away at their sexist inclinations, temper egregious habits, and make sacrifices born of a commitment to ending patriarchal oppression. But even if men become part of the solution and find rewards in this role, we shouldn't deceive ourselves that we can cease being part of the problem. This is a deeply upsetting situation for those of us who wish to live decent lives, and nobody likes continually to be upset; such aversion helps to explain various forms of bad faith and self-deception that beset putatively feminist men.

Several concerns motivate this essay. First, like many men who call themselves "feminist," "profeminist," or "anti-sexist," I feel considerable uncertainty about what living up to this commitment would mean, and doubt that I live up to it very adequately. I wish to address this uncertainty, and to reflect more broadly upon how people on the advantaged end of a social hierarchy—a system of exploitation or oppression—can get a grip on what this position demands of them and negotiate these demands (which can at times seem so far-reaching as to leave one at a political and motivational impasse). So there are analogies between this discussion of male feminism and quandaries around being white in a society of racial privilege, well-fed, clothed, and housed in a world where this is exceptional, and so on.

A second motivation to write about male feminism as oxymoron comes from observing putatively feminist men—as a putatively feminist man myself—in an academic context. At institutions where I've studied and worked, men have on the whole been welcomed as teachers, students, and scholars of feminism. Female undergraduates in feminism classes seem to devote considerable energy, for example, to making sure that their comments don't threaten or reflect badly on those male peers who are not overtly sexist. And the feminist engagement of male academics usually is welcomed by their female colleagues. Yet it has been my observation that men in the academy who call themselves feminists, teach feminist work, and write on feminist themes very often stray from these commitments in interactions with female students and colleagues, and in their decisions as privileged members of institutional hierarchies. In what follows I try to understand the pervasiveness of this slippage between male academics' professed feminist commitments and their everyday personal, pedagogical, and political behaviors.[2]

A third motivation for writing about male feminism is to explore the possibility of strong but non-essentialist generalizations about gender. There is an increasing tendency among philosophers and political theorists to be skeptical toward claims about identities or understandings shared by members of any given group, for such claims always mask a great deal of complexity and contradiction. Yet there are real tensions between this critical disposition, with its postmodern inflections, and the demands of a transformative politics. Now the theoretical escape from this dilemma is to defend generalizations about social groups pragmatically, as claims for particular purposes. But it's one thing to do this in the abstract, another actually to work through the appropriateness of generalizations in particular contexts. In what follows I seek to defend generalizations about men and feminism, notwithstanding my acute awareness of the contingency and limitations of generalizations about gender identities. I am well aware that gender is a construct, that masculinity and femininity do not reliably line up with sexed bodies, that there are subject positions that complicate sexual as well as gender dimorphism, and that identities cannot in fact be segmented into their constituent parts.[3] But it is my contention that notwithstanding their imperfect fit with real-world complexity, my generalizations about men and women do useful work in the contexts I specify. Those who would challenge such generalizations must do more than point to exceptions, or to complexities of identity that I concede from the start; they need to engage with the practical intent of the generalizations, showing how they fail to give us a useful grip on the issues at hand. All of that to say that a further reason for writing about the politics and ethics of men's feminism is to defend the usefulness of a set of generalizations about gender, and so demonstrate a pragmatic response to methodological questions about essential-ism, anti-essentialism, postmodernism, and political practice.

This essay is meant to be a skeptical intervention on the issue of men doing feminism, but not a pessimistic one. Men are capable of deepening their understandings of feminism and making this knowledge operative in their personal, social, and political lives. Many men struggle with the personal and political challenges described in the essay, with important and worthwhile results. My point is that a particular kind of awareness of contradiction is necessary for male feminists adequately to grasp the transformations to which they might aspire, and the sorts of complacency and bad faith they should resist.

The argument proceeds as follows. I begin by stipulating definitions of patriarchy and feminism, then review ways in which women develop and appropriate feminist knowledge given experiences of patriarchal oppres-sion. Against this background, I turn to the central questions of the essay: In what ways can men understand feminist analyses, and what kinds of transformation of consciousness and action are likely to attach to this knowledge? I draw critically upon Sandra Harding's work to consider the very possibility of male feminist knowledge. I then discuss what a man with a thorough understanding of feminism would know about him-self, and the discomforts and obligations that would attach to this knowl-edge. This brings us to a discussion not of possibility but probability: what forms and degrees of feminist engagement are typical of academic men who would claim this label, given the rewards and punishments attached to various paths? I describe the motivations underlying four ideal-typical male feminist stances, those of the poseur, the insider, the humanist, and the self-flagellator. I conclude with some thoughts on how tolerance for complexity, mutual criticism, and activist community together help academic men get past these four detours, toward a more adequate though still oxymoronic male feminism.

Patriarchy and Feminism

For the purposes of this essay, I will stipulate definitions of patriarchy and feminism: these will not be uncontroversial, but should be recogniz-able as lying on the radical/socialist end of a spectrum of feminisms. I would argue—but here simply assert—that we (North Americans, say) live in societies defined by structured inequalities of group-based power, with privilege and oppression defined along lines that include race, class, ethnicity, gender, and sexual orientation. These oppressions intersect and interlock in complex ways, and one must be cautious in segmenting them for analytical or political purposes.[4] Yet in spite of the tendentiousness of generalizations about particular social groups—such generalizations never capture complex intersections, nor the nuanced differences among sub-groups and individuals—these generalizations are politically indispensable.[5] *Patriarchy* names one such generalization, describing structured inequalities of power between men and women, wherein men are oppressors and women oppressed.

For the purposes at hand, we need to notice three aspects of patriarchal power. (i) Patriarchal power structures the interactions of men and women in virtually every sphere of life; it affects prospects and treatment in public life, in civil society, in the workplace, the street, the home, the bedroom. (ii) Patriarchal power not only defines a set of external forces that privilege or constrain us as men and women, but also conditions our deepest understandings, affects, and habits.[6] Every person's story is different, but structures of gender and gendered power produce patterns of identity and behavior that make gender dualism useful as a term of social and political analysis. (iii) Patriarchal power benefits men and harms women—not without important variations and interesting wrinkles, but on the whole. Among patriarchal harms are those of sexual harassment, abuse, and violence; differences in wages and career prospects; the devaluation of women's ideas and speech in a wide variety of institutional settings, including the workplace and the political sphere; and family structures and laws that rely upon women's unpaid domestic labour while offering them less protection when marriages end. This list could go on and on. And for most if not all of these harms there are corresponding privileges for men—access to women's sex-affective production, privileges granted in the workplace, disproportionate credibility attached to one's statements in a number of domains; this list, too, can be extended a very long way.

Now the benefits of patriarchy are not evenly distributed among men, nor its harms among women: here, intersections with other forms of oppression and social stratification are key.[7] But I would defend the generalization that patriarchy does more harm than good to individual women, and more good than harm to individual men. The generalization holds particularly well when it comes to the group that I have most directly in view in this essay: men in the academy, who are mainly white, mainly middle class, and mainly straight.

Where patriarchy denotes a system of gendered power, feminism describes a structured analysis of this system, and a commitment to anti-patriarchal resistance and transformation. Feminism is among other things a form of knowledge, with three domains that correspond to the dimensions of patriarchal power described above. That is, feminism describes a structured understanding of (i) power relations that lie outside oneself, (ii) how patriarchy also shapes one's own identity, and (iii) harms and privileges that correlate with patriarchal power, in one's own life and in society at large. Feminist knowledge is transformative: "getting it" means no longer being able to see or live your life in the same manner. It is to reinterpret your history and identity in ways that can be profoundly uncomfortable, and also to reinterpret your place in the world in ways that permit and demand new forms of action.

There are, of course, ways of engaging with feminist theory and ideology that don't amount to "getting it" in this transformative sense. I'll refer to this variation as concerning the *depth* of feminist knowledge. Those of us who have taught feminism will be especially aware of shallow ways of engaging with the theory. I have had students, for example, who show adeptness at rehearsing the propositional content of Catharine MacKinnon's account of eroticized domination, yet without appearing to have turned her critique upon their own gendered selves; or who talk about their own gendered socialization in radical terms, but without appearing to sense how much of their lives this analysis might throw into question. I don't want to say that such students haven't *understood* MacKinnon, for they seem to have understood her as well as they might Mill or Rawls. But they seem to have engaged with MacKinnon's work as propositional knowledge only, without taking her views as possibly speaking profoundly to themselves, to privileges and harms in their own lives and the lives of those around them, and to changes the analysis enables or requires. Now the "they" I have in mind in this vignette are, much more often than not, men. Is this surprising? Or is something more than chance reflected in the gender of those whose knowledge of feminism fails to extend to careful and prolonged reflection on themselves, and to corollary changes in behavior?

Something more than chance is involved; to see why, we need to look at the experiences that men and women bring to their engagements with feminist theories and ideologies. I will contend that the distinctive standpoint and experiences of men militate against their knowing feminism in a deep way: at best, men can strain to keep feminist insights in view and to act on these—straining against deeply internalized propensities that are non-feminist, and against the temptation to treat gendered privileges as just deserts. Often, putatively feminist academic men find these sorts of strains unpalatable, or even unbearable: at this point, they can travel a number of well-trodden paths, ones that allow them to label themselves feminist while not knowing, or ceasing really to know, those aspects of feminism that are most discomforting and demanding. They thus can avail themselves of a key privilege of the powerful, notwithstanding their affirmation of feminist analyses: that of obliviousness to the practical and ethical implications of their own power. In order to recognize the distinctive obstacles to certain kinds of male feminist knowledge, it will be useful to consider, at least ideal-typically, ways in which women come to feminist knowledge and integrate it into their lives.

Women and Feminist Knowledge

Life within patriarchy gives women a vivid knowledge of patriarchal harms—of sexual abuse, violence, discrimination, condescension, and so on. Absent a feminist analysis, however, these experiences can seem anomalous, inarticulable, or merely private. By describing how these phenomena form parts of patterns of male domination, feminist analyses can meet with a shock of recognition: they offer women a coherent story about intense, if previously inchoate, dissatisfactions and sources of pain.

Feminism thus generalizes from women's experiences under patriarchy; as Marilyn Frye writes:

> Feminism (the worldview, the philosophy) rests on a most empirical base: staking your life on the trustworthiness of your own body as a source of knowledge. It rests equally fundamentally on intersubjective agreement since some kind of agreement in perceptions and experience among women is what gives our sense data, our body data, the compelling cogency which made it possible to trust them.[8]

"Women's experience" isn't a stable or unproblematic category, but nonetheless provides a subject matter that is articulated, reconceptualized, and imbued with meaning by feminist analyses. And to understand such analyses in a deep sense is to transform the way one experiences one's own life, conceptualizes possibilities for personal and social change, and acts in the world.

This is a painful transformation, and the pain derives in part from a recognition of ways in which patriarchy is present in one's own identity; in Sandra Bartky's words, "feminist consciousness, in large measure, is an anguished consciousness."[9] This anguish is due to the incomplete nature of patriarchal socialization: feminist women recognize patriarchal elements in their self-understandings while also becoming aware that these are inadequate to their material experiences, and that change is possible.[10]

Feminist consciousness entails a difficulty in categorizing things; Bartky offers the example of timid behavior in a departmental meeting: is it a personal idiosyncrasy? or:

> a typically female trait, a shared inability to display aggression, even verbal aggression?. . . Uncertainties such as these make it difficult to decide how to struggle and whom to struggle against, but the very possibility of understanding one's own motivations, character traits, and impulses is also at stake.[11]

Painful uncertainty is a commonplace for feminist women: "Whether she lives a fairly conventional life or an unconventional one, ordinary social life presents to the feminist an unending sequence of such occasions and each occasion is a test. It is not easy to live under the strain of constant testing. . . ."[12] Yet women have strong incentives for holding onto feminist knowledge and negotiating its demands, however haltingly. The patriarchal patterns brought into view by feminist analyses work to subvert, manipulate, exploit, and harm women. Letting such harms to self and others slide from view makes them no less harmful; indeed, not knowing these things requires forms of dissociation that are themselves destructive of women's selves and relationships.[13] Feminism not only describes harms but indicates avenues of resistance and visions of social change; these provide motivations for ongoing engagement and struggle. The trajectories that follow are diverse and complex, but even this simple sketch of how women come to feminist knowledge and find ways of negotiating it as a part of everyday life is enough to set up a contrast with male feminist knowledge.

Male Feminist Knowledge

We now can turn to the central questions of this essay: How deeply are men likely to know feminism, and what kinds of transformation of consciousness and action are likely to attach to their knowledge? Let me discuss this question in terms of possibilities for men in general before moving on to the particular case of feminist men in the academy.

On the Very Possibility of Male Feminist Knowledge

Sandra Harding's work is useful in getting a grip on the possibility of men gaining feminist knowledge.[14] Harding's work emphasizes the social situatedness of all knowledges, and argues that once we appreciate the standpoint specificity of knowledge, we see that marginalized and oppressed groups often have a more objective grasp of social relations than the privileged. As Harding writes:

> The logic of the standpoint epistemologies depends on the understanding that the "master's position" in any set of dominating social relations tends to produce distorted visions of the real regularities and underlying causal tendencies in social relations. . . . The feminist standpoint epistemologies argue that because men are in the master's position vis-a-vis women, women's social experience—conceptualized through the lens of feminist theory—can provide the grounds for a less distorted understanding of the world around us.[15]

The distortion of male perspectives on social relations results from men's failure, as a dominant group, critically and systematically to interrogate their advantaged social situation and the power relations that perpetuate it.

There are a number of reasons why women might be better positioned than men to come to understand gendered power relations. First, women do not have the same interest as men in ignorance, but rather have much to gain from understanding and resisting operations of gendered power. Second, women's material existences expose them to aspects of life that men use their power to avoid and ignore: housework, child-rearing, and affective labour, for example. Women therefore are better positioned to appreciate the variety of roles and activities that figure in patriarchal arrangements. Third, women have strong incentives to try to understand the world through men's eyes as well; as María Lugones and Elizabeth Spelman write, oppressed groups learn the perspective of the powerful "through the sharp observation stark exigency demands."[16] Fourth, struggling against social arrangements reveals something of their structure: one discovers where they resist, and how they fight back. Feminist activism therefore brings its own epistemological gains.

For all of these reasons, the standpoints of women provide key starting points for understanding patriarchy (which is not to say that women spontaneously develop such understandings). As an oppressed group, women are in a position to see gaps between their experiences and interests on the one hand, and how their lives are conceptualized and organized by dominant ideologies on the other. Harding sees standpoint epistemology, though, as a route to strongly *objective* knowledge: by combining the perspectives of different social groups, we assemble a body of knowledge more trustworthy than that available from any single perspective, and this body of knowledge, once assembled, can itself be understood by those with various standpoints. This suggests that men *can* gain feminist knowledge: they can understand structures of gendered power by taking on board the aggregated perspectives of those oppressed by these structures, and by using the perspectives of women's lives to reinterpret their own.

Now I agree with Harding that men can draw upon feminist insights to reinterpret their lives and the structures of power undergirding their privilege; indeed, men have a responsibility to do so. Only through this kind of reinterpretation can men integrate knowledge of patriarchal privileges and harms into a minimally decent social and political engagement. Harding's argument staves off an essentialist pessimism that would treat men as patriarchal drones, and gendered standpoints as hermetically sealed.

Yet I find myself more pessimistic than Harding about the likelihood of male feminist knowledge, for at least two reasons. The first concerns the very possibility of men knowing feminism—of our understanding the perspectives of women and generating knowledge on this basis. For it's not clear that empathetic listening can give men an adequate grasp of some of the experiences most central to feminist analyses—the ever-present possibility of sexual assault, for example, or pervasive objectification and sexual harassment, or condescension based on gender. This is not to excuse men from the responsibility of trying to understand, but it is to mistrust any sense they may develop of actually having understood.

A case in point: more than one straight male friend has declared, after unwelcome cruising by another man, that he now understands just what women go through. This seems a paradigm of *not* getting it. To assimilate men's and women's experiences of unsolicited male sexual attention is to ignore the power structures and cultural presumptions that surround these acts. A man being cruised likely experiences this as anomalous, not as a reminder of the pervasiveness of his objectification and of sexualized threats. He has the support of cultural stereotypes wherein gay men prey on straights, and likely can avail himself of the anti-gay revulsion if not violence of many other straight men. So while this man's empathy with sexually harassed women is valuable and may provide an opening to consciousness raising around sexism (not to mention homophobia), his empathy ought not to erase the gulf between experiences typical of men and women, nor the ways in which men's power both isolates them from certain gendered experiences and tempts them to believe that they fully understand.[17]

A second reason I find myself more pessimistic than Harding on the prospects for male feminist knowledge concerns not its possibility but its likelihood. Here we return to the question of how men's concrete situations and experiences inflect and influence their coming to feminist knowledge, and their acting on the basis of this knowledge. I want to consider, in particular, incentives and disincentives that may shape men's movement from shallow to deeper knowledge of feminism. We can begin by assessing what deep feminist knowledge would tell a man about himself.

An Ideal of Male Feminist Knowledge

In coming to recognize the operations of patriarchy, a man would learn some troubling things not only about his society, but about his own life. He would learn that he has internalized patriarchal affects, habits, and desires, in more ways than can be traced or changed; that he has benefited and continues to benefit from male privilege (though this will be differently inflected depending on his situation with respect to other axes of oppression and identity); that he has oppressed and continues to be complicit in the oppression of women in general and of particular women in his own life; and that his every gaze and sentence and interaction is inflected, in large or small ways, by sexism and patriarchal privilege.

Feminist analyses show women how experiences of pain and harm are in fact patterned effects of oppression. For men, however, many of the corollaries of women's oppression have likely been experienced as positive and deserved, since from the standpoint of the powerful and absent a structured critical analysis, the status quo tends to appear natural and just. Absent a feminist analysis, a man easily can regard his accomplishments as proportionate to his abilities; his relationships as emotionally rich; his sexual experiences with women as mutually consensual and pleasurable; and the space allowed him in conversations as commensurate with his knowledge and wit. A feminist analysis retells these stories in unflattering ways, showing a man harms in which he has participated and will continue to participate. For men cannot purge themselves of the power and inclinations that cause and abet patriarchal harms. A man can reshape himself and his actions—he can make political choices informed by feminist commitments, take women's perspectives seriously, alter his desires and propensities (within limits), and change how he acts on these. But it is important to take seriously the depth of male socialization—the micro-behaviors, desires, and beliefs that are constructed and reinforced by patriarchy.[18]

Many profeminist men will be aware of this anguished consciousness of the progressive yet privileged: there is a surplus of areas for reflection and change, and in each of these areas it is hard to grant oneself the luxury of just taking it easy. One example, instructive in its relative triviality, is that of exchanges of looks in the street. I cope with the alienation of life in a largish city by being vaguely friendly with strangers; one way to express this is by meeting a passerby's eyes and smiling. Yet it makes sense for women to feel less than thrilled when beamed at by a strange man; it leaves them to judge whether the attention is benign or a prelude to harassment. So there's a micro-politics around this casual practice: I exercise male privilege, and probably leave some women feeling harassed or put out, by my ostensibly friendly smile. And there's a meta-politics around deciding how much thought or effort to devote to this issue, sitting as it does alongside a wealth of others.

The shock awaiting a man with thorough knowledge of feminism would be acute: he'd lose his sense of secure grounding in the world—his faith in his own judgments, emotions, and desires. Every aspect of his self would become suspect, and also potentially impositional or harmful. Did he just make a sexist comment? Should he hold this door? Was that a pornographic gaze?

There is a further sense in which men are unable to purge themselves of their roles in patriarchal harms. It is not only socialization that is relatively immovable in any given man's case, but also the structures of power that endow him with privilege. Privilege can be given up in particular contexts—bowing out of competitions in areas where women have been especially disadvantaged, for example, or letting a woman decide in a context where masculinity gives one the power to prevail. But men will be treated as men, in an inexhaustible array of contexts. However much men work on themselves, they remain relatively safe from sexual assault, relatively credible in conversations, and so forth. It is for this reason that discussions of male feminism have to deal not only with the extent of men's commitment to giving up privilege, but the ways in which male privilege surpasses the agency of individuals, structuring the situation of every man, no matter how good-willed. Because male privilege derives from female subordination, feminist men face a painful uncertainty about how to deal with the surplus of instances of this privilege in their own lives.

Probable Forms of Male Feminist Knowledge

If these kinds of anguished consciousness are part of a man's knowing feminism, what is the *likelihood* of men actually achieving and living this demanding knowledge? What incentives lie along men's paths to such feminist knowledge, and how do these affect men's propensities to stop in particular places, or carry on in particular ways? In looking at probable forms of male feminist knowledge, I will describe four "types": the poseur, the insider, the humanist, and the self-flagellator. These are *ideal* types, tendencies that rarely are so clear or unmixed in particular lives. Ideal types provide objects of comparison, tools for sorting through the complexities of individual cases and showing politically important commonalities between cases. Most male feminists will in fact exhibit qualities and moments from each of the types, alongside more creditable understandings and behaviors.

Shifting from issues of possibility to probability requires that we be more specific about context and constituency; in what follows I refer most directly to the feminist engagement of that mainly white, mainly middle class, mainly straight constituency of men involved in higher education. I leave open the question of how the probability of transformative feminist engagement differs for other groups of men. Note that my focus is not on academic men in general, but on those men in the academy who profess an interest in feminism; I want to consider whether and how this engagement might become transformative. One can distinguish this issue from the important question of how best to spur a sympathetic interest in feminism among that majority of academic men who are indifferent or hostile.

So let's look at the rewards and punishments that come into play given various levels of feminist engagement on the part of academic men. A first set of rewards and punishments attaches to men being perceived as feminist within the academy. At this historical moment, feminist research comprises some of the most interesting, creative, and influential work in the humanities. In at least some institutions, there is cachet and benefit to men who profess interest and competence in feminism as theory. One's non-feminist research, popularity with students, and curriculum vitae can all be enriched by a pinch of feminist spice.[19] These rewards are not available in the same way for women in the academy, who are at disproportionate risk of being pigeon-holed as feminists, treated as marginal, seen as doing work that is unphilosophical or not genuinely in their discipline, and so on. Feminist academic women are well-justified in their resentment of this gendered dynamic.[20]

How do these rewards vary with the actual depth of a man's feminist engagement? My suspicion is that the most tangible *practical* rewards tend to be allotted by men and women with limited understandings of, or sympathy with, feminism; as such, it may not matter whether a man is serious in his feminism, so long as he can go through certain motions. Indeed, a shallow engagement with feminism gives one scope to tailor one's apparent commitment in relation to circumstances. One can be radical in the approving atmosphere of a feminist conference, yet safe within one's more conservative department.

The rewards and punishments for being perceived as feminist tend also to line up with a theory/practice divide. Men may have a lot to gain (and not much to lose) by dabbling in feminist theory, whereas they have little practically to gain from feminist practice, especially when this practice directly challenges patriarchal structures and behaviors. There are immediate costs to challenging the sexism of friends, colleagues, and superiors: to staking one's authority on unpopular feminist principles and policies, to giving up material entitlements that reflect one's privilege.

This is to say that the practical rewards that accompany being *perceived* as feminist seem to support a shallow engagement with feminism, but do not in themselves provide a very compelling counterweight to the costs and pain involved in deeper feminist knowledge or a more concerted feminist engagement. This gives us one male feminist type: the *poseur*. The poseur is interested in feminist theory, and tends to have a lot to say about it (though he's often read the theory pretty instrumentally, as it serves his non-feminist projects). The poseur is unlikely to have turned feminist critiques upon his own theoretical and practical tendencies—to have extended his feminist analysis from a concern with structures to a consideration of how these structures have informed his own identity, in ways that correlate with patriarchal harms. The poseur is comfortable in his gendered skin, and doesn't experience his putatively feminist commitments as particularly demanding, or painful.

Yet few men's interest in feminism is motivated by external incentives alone; there often is a desire to restore a sense of one's own worth or virtue given a recognition of one's implication in patriarchy. The stance of the poseur is unlikely to meet this need, which draws men to feminist articulations of how patriarchy shapes identities and correlates with gendered harms. There is an inevitable paradox, however, in a man's turning to feminism to feel better about himself, since feminist analyses don't tend to cast men in a particularly flattering light.

If a man's engagement is sufficiently shallow, though, he may be able to experience his feminism as a relatively painless sign of virtue: this gives us a second male feminist type, the *insider*. The insider feels an ethical or political commitment to feminism, and believes that he's doing well at it. He is involved in the right kind of volunteer work, vocal in his support of feminist projects and his revulsion at patriarchal harms, reads the right books, and is feminist from the lectern. Where the poseur has limited interest in feminist activities or in what female feminists actually make of him, the insider premises his comfortable self-image on doing well in the eyes of feminist women, even while his comfort militates against his addressing his own sexist tendencies. The self-perception of insiders doesn't, however, tend to collapse under the weight of this contradiction between self-image and behavior, for a number of reasons.

First, the insider is not likely to be sensitive to cues concerning his gendered behavior; like many non-feminist men, he can remain happily oblivious to the fact that he's boring people, or causing discomfort, or wasting an organization's time. He hasn't learned how gendered privilege encourages such blindness. Second, the insider possesses power over those feminists with whom he interacts—gendered power at least, and often the additional power of academic hierarchy (of a professor with his students, or a tenured man with untenured women). This power increases the likelihood that an insider will be humored or tolerated. Third, the insider's participation in feminist activities may in some ways be useful, notwithstanding the relative shallowness of his own feminist analysis; this is the more likely if he has power within an institutional hierarchy, and if the feminists with whom he is involved are under-resourced or relatively powerless. Fourth, women often can't be bothered to challenge men on their every act of sexism—who has that kind of time? And who wants to have to deal with men's reactions to such challenges, be they angry, defensive, or contrite? Fifth, there are strong psychological incentives for women (and men) to interpret male feminism charitably, be it that of male partners, friends, or colleagues. We want to be able to love and respect those close to us, and to live in a world where change is possible; the oxymoronic quality of male feminism is disconcerting from this point of view, and so there is a temptation to give feminist men the benefit of the doubt. For all of these reasons, the comfortable perspective of an insider is remarkably resilient, and the ideal type finds reflections in the behaviors and attitudes of many putatively feminist men.

Because insiders are prone to involvement in feminist projects, not particularly reflective about their own sexism and gendered propensities, and unsophisticated in their feminist analyses, they can be destructive influences on feminist projects, notwithstanding their good intentions. As Harding notes, "Men love appropriating, directing, judging, and managing everything they can get their hands on—especially the white, Western, heterosexual, and economically over-privileged men with whom most feminist scholars and researchers most often find themselves interacting."[21] Insiders remain unreflective about this gendered tendency, and oblivious to its disrespectful and disruptive consequences within feminist organizations. These consequences are exacerbated because in order to take feminist analyses seriously while continuing to feel good about himself, the insider has to locate the agents of patriarchy elsewhere. Sexism is projected onto other men, who then are figured as problems and targets for activism. This is, of course, a common trope, but represents a deep misunderstanding of patriarchy: in exempting the insider from self-criticism, it also leads to impoverished feminist analyses and strategies.

Insiders take feminism seriously enough to recognize certain patriarchal harms, yet conceive of these harms so as to allow their feminism to be a source of pride without being much of a source of pain. This complacency removes the incentive for a deeper engagement with feminism. Yet there are men who come to feminism with questions and qualms about themselves that push them beyond such complacency. These men wish to address a painful sense of distortion or responsibility, given an awareness of patriarchal aspects of their own identities. I want to discuss two ways in which such men can shy away from the complex implications of feminist analyses for their own situations, before characterizing more successful paths of male feminist engagement.

A first wrong turning awaits men who emphasize ways in which patriarchy has distorted their own sense of self—I'll call this *humanism*. While the humanist sees that patriarchy has benefited him in certain ways, he also feels its constraints. Patriarchal socialization constructs men as competitive; it erects standards of masculinity that leave men feeling inadequate, particularly where class and race place certain masculine roles (such as that of provider) at the very horizon of possibility; it makes men less able to experience and express emotions, or to form intimate relationships with women and other men; it deprives men of the fulfillment of nurturing children; it leaves them exposed to the power and violence of other men. The humanist wants to address these ways in which patriarchy hurts men as well as women.[22]

Humanist men differ from those in the mythopoetic men's movement, refusing nostalgia for a time when men were men and women knew their place. Humanists want to become different kinds of men, more in touch with feminine qualities and less constrained by patriarchal social structures. A lot can be said about this variety of humanism, but the main point is that while it draws upon feminist analyses and is characterized by its own form of anguished consciousness, it is not particularly feminist, focusing as it does on the well-being of men. bell hooks puts the point succinctly: male pain "does not erase or lessen male responsibility for supporting and perpetuating their power under patriarchy to exploit and oppress women in a manner far more grievous than the psychological stress or emotional pain caused by male conformity to rigid sex role patterns."[23]

Nor is it evident that transforming male gender roles to permit men a more nurturing and embodied way of life would itself improve the lot of women: these two agendas are not necessarily at odds, but the complementarities are complex and irregular. So while there may be room for strategic alliances between those interested in liberating men from masculinity and those interested in liberating women from patriarchal oppression, this needs to be established in particular cases. It is sufficient, for our purposes, to notice that humanism can give short shrift to the third domain of feminism—the ways in which patriarchy, as external structure and part of identity, benefits men and harms women.[24]

There is another variety of qualm about the self, one that can draw men to a deeper engagement with feminism than that typified by either the insider or the humanist. There are men who look to feminism to help them address a painful sense of responsibility for patriarchal harms, given their gendered privilege and socialization. This seems a promising route to a transformative male feminism. But before turning to this positive horizon, let me point to one more wrong turning, exemplified by a fourth feminist type: the *self-flagellator.*

Self-flagellators combine a relatively deep knowledge of feminism with an intolerance for ambiguity; their analyses tend to focus on their guilt in relation to patriarchal harms, and on the need to struggle relentlessly against their own sexist impulses and understandings. In the intensity of their self-scrutiny, self-flagellators have a lot right. The problem is that insofar as men focus on their guilt in being tools of patriarchy, they risk self-indulgence in both their theory and their activism. What's more, a preoccupation with one's own abasement sets up no viable alternatives—one strives for a point where one will have purged oneself of sexism, and thus finally have been adequate to the feminist challenge.[25] Because male feminism as self-flagellation is not sustainable as an ethical or political identity, it tends to lead to retreat to the stances of humanist or insider, or from feminism altogether.

Negotiating Male Feminist Knowledge

With the male feminist types enumerated above, we see a number of ways in which men's engagement with feminism can stop short of transformative knowledge. My description of the "types" is not meant to be exhaustive, nor as an exercise in ridicule or castigation: few men express these types completely, and most of us who call ourselves anti-sexist, pro-feminist, or feminist embody aspects or moments of all four. The "types" are meant as critical devices, aids to recognizing common pitfalls as these manifest themselves amidst the nuance and complexity of individual men's lives. Recognizing these pitfalls, we can explore ways of moving beyond them, to more creditable and sustainable forms of male feminist engagement.[26]

A man with deep knowledge of feminism faces a sometimes unflattering re-telling of his life story; he has to reinterpret merit as privilege, and to recognize an inexhaustibility of patriarchal imprints in his habits and understandings. It's not clear how one acts responsibly on this kind of knowledge. Furthermore, in defining sustainable forms of male feminist knowledge, we have to recognize that bad faith is more difficult to resist when comfort and privilege are always on offer. This is particularly true insofar as many of the practical and emotional rewards for male feminism are there given a shallow engagement, whereas much of the anguish and external punishment is reserved for forms of consciousness and action premised on deeper knowledge.

Men do find ways past the various wrong turnings enumerated above—ways to negotiate the mistrust and dislike of self that can be provoked by feminist knowledge, while also creating ethical and political practices that meet some of its demands, and bring their own rewards. The key is to find ways to live responsibly with the contradictions described by male feminism and even to flourish in their presence, rather than trying to flee them, or giving in to those parts of ourselves that crave a greater simplicity, or a less equivocal congratulation for our anti-sexist accomplishments. Necessary conditions for more sustainable forms of male feminism include (i) a willingness to conceive of oneself as ethically complex and incomplete; (ii) an openness to criticism and a propensity to self-criticism; and (iii) engagement in activist friendships and community.

Complex Ethical Implication in Patriarchy

One of the most difficult aspects of male feminist consciousness is awareness of the extent to which one's life story and current identity are defined by patriarchal privilege. It is dizzying and deeply upsetting to recognize one's sense of entitlement as a power-laden fiction, given that the fiction structures so many of one's practices and understandings. Nor can one ever bring the whole of one's patriarchal tendencies into relief. For one thing, patriarchy structures identity in more ways than can be traced: privilege settles deep. And for another, the implications of our privilege in others' pain is not a truth that we can hold in view for long. For example, my experience in the classroom is deeply influenced by gender—by the privileges my gender has secured for me; by the complex play of entitlement and deference between men and women in the room; by the ways our gendered experiences have been shaped by sexual violence and its threat, by the production and consumption of pornography, and so on. Knowledge of these facts should inform my teaching, yet this need not mean—cannot mean—having this knowledge present, in its profusion and its horror, from moment to moment.

Male feminists face the challenge of finding ways to negotiate an awareness of their privilege, while also struggling to change a world that sets up this privilege as part of interlocking inequalities and oppressions. Living with integrity as a feminist man requires both a sensitivity to the small and large harms one inflicts as a bearer of this gender, and a commitment to transforming this state of affairs in oneself and the world. Yet one simultaneously must accept that one will never act with a pure will, nor in ways that are entirely laudable. Ignoring such failings invites a slide into complacency, while fixating on them is a route to burnout or self-indulgent immobilization.

A life of relative privilege is not particularly good preparation for brooking ambiguous pictures of oneself. Most of the men I know have pretty brittle personality structures, which have us feeling either fabulous or in danger of disappearing altogether. But a need for simplicity—in which one is either very good or very bad—lies behind the behavior of the insider and the self-flagellator. A sustainable yet transformative male feminism finds ways beyond this: decent and sustainable ways for men to cycle between forgiveness and anger, seriousness and irony toward self and other, self-scrutiny and self-acceptance.

Criticism and Self-Criticism

For male feminism to be sustainable as a self-transformative and politically engaged way of life, feminist men must find constructive ways to act skeptically toward themselves and each other. If the project of negotiating feminist knowledge is left for each man to work out for himself, the prospects for widespread and transformative consciousness seem pretty bleak. It thus is important for men to address each other's bad faith in connection with gendered privilege and feminist engagements, while supporting one another as feminists.[27] Feminist women clearly should not be expected to play these critical or constructive roles, especially given the meager returns they have come to expect on such investments of time and energy. Feminist men have to find ways of acting that neither assume an inappropriate authority in defining feminist goals and strategies, nor seek ongoing reassurance, praise, discipline, or thanks from women.

The need for feminist men to exercise skepticism toward themselves and each other defines a project in itself: that of developing detailed descriptions of common male feminist pitfalls, and thresholds of decent behavior, in specific contexts. I've done that in a loose way here with respect to the academy. But there's room for more precise and pointed work along these lines; I wish, only half-facetiously, for a flyer headed "So You're a Male Feminist Professor?" followed by a checklist. Male academics might be invited to evaluate their feminist credentials, placing checks beside items like:

- ☐ I do not let sexist language or comments go unchallenged, whether they be from students or colleagues.
- ☐ I am attentive to gendered aspects of my conversational styles, and am careful to give women equal time.
- ☐ I have devoted serious effort to studying feminist work in my field, and integrate it into my courses in a non-tokenistic way.
- ☐ I know the anti-discrimination and sexual harassment policies of my university, do my best to see them honored in my department, and work to improve the policies themselves.
- ☐ I am reflective about my interactions with female students, and am careful about condescension, harassment, and providing adequate support. I mentor female students.
- ☐ I am aware of issues of women's safety on campus, and use my influence to support feminist initiatives.

This checklist could of course be extended a very long way. My point is that men often need clear and specific reminders that a feminist analysis of male privilege brings with it demands that are not to be confronted only in one's spare time, or when the fancy strikes one. Such lists are no substitute for integrated feminist analyses and commitments, but rather are meant to remind men of these in the face of deeply entrenched habits, familiar comforts, and the lure of indifference. Specific reminders and challenges express not piousness, but a clear-headed recognition of the difficulty of sustaining understandings and behaviors that are at odds with deep features of one's self and one's surroundings.

Engagement in Activist Friendships and Communities

To the extent that a man understands feminism in more than a shallow way, he faces epistemological uncertainty, ethical discomfort, emotional turmoil, and extensive political demands. It can be difficult to figure out where to start, how to proceed, or when to allow oneself to rest. One can't solve these dilemmas through mere reflection, and especially not through solitary reflection.

Rather, it is through action that one finds ways to negotiate these dilemmas. How you act and how your actions affect those around you are more adequate indicators of your feminist commitment and consciousness than how you imagine yourself. What's more, men gain a clearer understanding of gendered power, in its complexity and intractability, by actively struggling against it.

Action also provides a way of negotiating uncertainty—about whether you have the right analysis, how you can effect change, how much you need to do in a given context, and how to balance personal with political endeavours. As intellectuals, there is a temptation to work on developing the right analysis before we act. In the case of male feminism, this emphasis on prior understanding is immobilizing, and conveniently so: "I'm doing nothing because I haven't figured out what a man legitimately may do." Feminist knowledge should itself be a goad to action, and is enriched by activist experience.

Action also brings one into community with others, who can provide resources important in negotiating a feminist commitment. This action can be within existing feminist organizations where these make space for men's participation and where men do the work required to curb some of their more disruptive tendencies. Perhaps more appropriately, men can support one another in the anti-sexist education of boys and men, and in campaigns directed at patriarchal aspects of institutions and practices, in the academy and elsewhere. And feminist activism also includes struggles closer to home, to transform relationships with colleagues, students, lovers, family, and friends.

Because feminist action takes place in relationship with others, it is the source of the richest rewards of male feminist engagement. Making feminist understandings operative in one's social and political life opens up possibilities of honest connection, community with others, and participation in valuable personal and social changes. Such rewards do not have to await the resolution of ambiguities within the self, and indeed offer compensations for the dislocations and struggles emphasized in this essay. So activist community offers an important way of living with, though never resolving, the tensions and paradoxes of male feminist consciousness.

Conclusion

Male feminism is an identity rife with contradictions: it requires that one maintain an awareness of the extent to which one acts, feels, and theorizes with a power-laden gender; this means constantly reminding oneself,

232 / David J. Kahane

and being reminded, of specifics of one's patriarchal tendencies and their pernicious consequences for women, while also struggling to change these. As beneficiaries of oppression, men cannot escape the ethical imperative of facing this discomfort and this struggle. And to the extent that men adequately understand feminism, the struggle—in its difficult and rewarding moments—does not have an end. Decent men must try to act as feminists, but only in a profoundly transformed world will male feminism be something other than an oxymoron.

Notes

1. This essay has been helped along by discussions with Judith Asher, Sarah Begus, Monique Deveaux, Tom Digby, Jeremy Goldman, Sandra Harding, Cressida Heyes, Sue James, Michael Kimmel, Linda Nicholson, Rebecca Pates, Henry Rubin, and James Tully. I am grateful to the Women's Studies Graduate Colloquium Series at Brandeis University and to the members of SOFPHIA for opportunities to present the work in progress. I also wish to acknowledge the support of the Social Sciences and Humanities Research Council of Canada and the Minda de Gunzburg Center for European Studies at Harvard University.

2. There is a considerable amount of work on tensions between male privilege and male feminism. See, for example, bell hooks, 'Men: Comrades in Struggle," in *Feminist Theory: From Margin to Center* (Boston: South End Press, 1984): 67–81; Renate D. Klein, "The 'Men-Problem' in Women's Studies: The Expert, the Ignoramus and the Poor Dear," in *Radical Voices: A Decade of Feminist Resistance from Women's Studies International Forum*, Renate D. Klein and Deborah Lynn Steinberg, (eds.) (Oxford: Pergamon, 1989): 106–120; Linda R. Williams, "Men in Feminism," *Women: A Cultural Review* 1,1 (1990): 63–65; and the articles collected in Alice Jardine and Paul Smith, eds., *Men in Feminism* (New York: Methuen, 1988).

3. For a provocative discussion of disjunctures between genders and bodies, and ways in which masculinity and femininity vary independently as attributes of particular persons, see Eve Kosofsky Sedgwick, "Gosh, Boy George, You Must Be Awfully Secure in Your Masculinity," in Maurice Berger, Brian Wallis, and Simon Watson (eds.) *Constructing Masculinity* (London: Routledge, 1995). The collection as a whole demonstrates some of the challenges as well as the limitations of postmodern skepticism about categories of gender.

4. Elizabeth Spelman's *Inessential Woman: Problems of Exclusion in Feminist Thought* (Boston: Beacon Press, 1989) is particularly useful on this point; see also Susan Bordo, *Unbearable Weight: Feminism, Western Culture, and the Body* (Berkeley: University of California Press, 1993).

5. See Judith Butler, "Contingent Foundations" and "For a Careful Reading" in *Feminist Contentions: A Philosophical Exchange*, Linda Nicholson, ed. (New York: Routledge, 1995); and Cressida Heyes, "Back to the Rough Ground: Wittgenstein, Essentialism, and Feminist Methods," in *Rereading the Canon: Feminist Interpretations of Ludwig Wittgenstein*, Naomi Scheman, ed. (Philadelphia: Pennsylvania State University Press, forthcoming 1998).

6. My perspective on patriarchy and feminism differs from more liberal

approaches on this ground (among others). Whereas liberals tend to put a lot of stock in individual volition and reflexivity as means to changing both self and society, I see our selves as socially constituted with inexhaustible depth. This is not to say that we cannot meaningfully change ourselves, but it does disallow a certain naivetè about the extent to which a cognitive appreciation of feminist arguments can, by itself, fundamentally change how we see, feel, desire, or act.

7. The situation of out gay men, for example, differs importantly when it comes to patriarchal harms and benefits: they are subject to harassment, rape, and violence from straight men; are discriminated against and oppressed in many domains; and do not avail themselves of the same patriarchal advantages as other men. So the analysis that follows would be differently inflected given a focus on gay masculinities and the material situation of gay men under patriarchy. Yet other forms of harm and privilege do not vary so sharply between out gay men and straight men (and the variations are even less pronounced for closeted gay men): there are importantly shared features of socialization, types of material privilege in relation to women, and forms of denial concerning patriarchal privileges and harms.

8. Marilyn Frye, "The Possibility of Feminist Theory," in *Feminist Frameworks: Alternative Accounts of the Relations Between Women and Men*, Alison M. Jaggar and Paula S. Rothenberg, eds. (New York: McGraw Hill, 1993): 105–106.

9. Bartky, *Femininity and Domination*, 14.

10. A further component of this anguished consciousness, though one left aside in this essay, relates to ways in which awareness of gendered structures of domination gives rise, at least potentially, to a recognition of other forms of domination, along lines of race, class, language, sexual orientation, disability, and so on. Most women find themselves on the privileged side of certain of these lines, and the pain of recognizing this fact is different than that of seeing oneself as a member of an oppressed group. Which points to an analogy between my discussion of male feminism as oxymoron, and the oxymoronic quality of these other privileged subject positions. See Bartky, 16.

11. Bartky, *Femininity and Domination*, 18.

12. Ibid., 19.

13. Carol Gilligan's work is powerful on this latter point; see *Meeting at the Crossroads: Women's Psychology and Girls' Development* (Cambridge, Mass.: Harvard University Press, 1992); and Carol Gilligan, Jill McLean Taylor, and Amy M. Sullivan, *Between Voice and Silence: Women and Girls, Race and Relationship* (Cambridge, Mass.: Harvard University Press, 1996).

14. See Sandra Harding, *The Science Question in Feminism* (Ithaca: Cornell University Press, 1986); "Rethinking Standpoint Epistemology: 'What is Strong Objectivity?,' in *Feminist Epistemologies*, Linda Alcoff and Elizabeth Potter, eds. (New York: Routledge, 1993); *Whose Science? Whose Knowledge? Thinking from Women's Lives* (Ithaca, N.Y.: Cornell University Press, 1991); and her contribution to this volume. In "Reinventing Ourselves as Other: More New Agents of History and Knowledge," in *American Feminist Thought at Century's End: A Reader*, Linda S. Kauffman, ed. (Cambridge, MA: Blackwell, 1993): 140–164, Harding deals explicitly with the "monstrous possibility" of male feminist knowledge.

15. Harding, *The Science Question in Feminism*, 191.

16. María C. Lugones and Elizabeth V. Spelman, "Have We Got a Theory for You! Feminist Theory, Cultural Imperialism and the Demand for 'The Woman's Voice'," in *Hypatia Reborn: Essays in Feminist Philosophy*, Azizah Y. Al-Hibri and Margaret A. Simons, eds. (Bloomington: Indiana University Press, 1990), 21.

17. On the relevance of structures of power to the possibility of understanding between groups see Iris Young, "Asymmetrical Reciprocity: On Moral Respect, Wonder, and Enlarged Thought," *Constellations: An International Journal of Critical and Democratic Theory* 3, 3 (January 1997).

18. The internalization of patriarchal dispositions and understandings does not in itself differentiate men from women—it is this very quality that defines feminist women's "anguished consciousness." An important difference, though, is that a feminist woman who notices an echo of patriarchy in her behavior—say, a moment of feminine deference—has the shock of abetting her own disadvantage or oppression. A profeminist man who sees sexist echoes in his behavior—acting dismissively toward a woman in conversation, for example—finds himself harming another. Which is to suggest that while both men and women carry an inexhaustible store of habits and understandings formed by patriarchy, the manifestation of these patriarchal imprints makes different ethical demands on men and women.

19. The situation is different for men whose research programs and teaching priorities center on a feminist agenda: this more serious variety of male feminist engagement may meet with suspicion from colleagues and feminist women, doubts about one's intellectual seriousness, and backlash from conservative students. These costs surely vary with the consistency and seriousness of a man's commitment to feminism, as well as from institution to institution, and perhaps among generations of male scholars.

20. See Rosi Braidotti, "Envy; or, with Your Brains and My Looks," in *Nomadic Subjects: Embodiment and Sexual Difference in Contemporary Feminist Theory* (New York: Columbia University Press, 1994); and the articles collected in Alice Jardine and Paul Smith, eds., *Men in Feminism* (New York: Methuen, 1988).

21. Harding, "Reinventing Ourselves as Other," 149.

22. For a valuable and politically perceptive review of theoretical work on masculinity—much of which falls (deliberately or unwittingly) into the humanist mold—see Tim Carrigan, Bob Connell, and John Lee, "Toward a New Sociology of Masculinity," *Theory and Society* 14, 5 (1985): 551–605.

23. bell hooks, "Men: Comrades in Struggle," 73.

24. Note that I am addressing humanism as an ideal type—an approach that uses feminist analyses only insofar as these show how patriarchy constrains and harms *men*. I wish simply to make the point that many of these harms can be mitigated in ways consistent with the continued oppression and exploitation of women—that there are non-feminist ways for men to express their emotions, nurture children, get closer to other men, and so forth.

    Moreover, my questions about the feminist implications of "humanism" reflect this essay's focus on the question of academic men's propensities to move from an initial engagement with feminism to a more transformative knowledge. We can distinguish this from the issue of how men might be brought to engage with feminism in the first place. Humanism may in fact have considerable value as a strategy for getting men interested in feminist analyses of masculinity; Michael Kimmel, for example, seeks to motivate men to be profeminist by drawing attention to how feminist reforms would improve their own lives and relationships. I'm pointing to the need (acknowledged by Kimmel) for strategies capable of moving men on from humanism to less comfortable and less male-centered analyses—that is, to profeminism (Kimmel's preferred term) or feminism.

For an approach to male profeminist activism that focuses both on men's power and men's pain, see Michael Kaufman, "Men, Feminism, and Men's Contradictory Experiences of Power," in Harry Brod and Michael Kaufman, eds. *Theorizing Masculinity*, (Thousand Oaks: Sage, 1994). For a sociological examination of factors that motivate men to engage with feminism and develop an anti-sexist commitment, see Harry Christian, *The Making of Anti-Sexist Men* (London: Routledge, 1994): his findings center on the influence of childhood experiences that depart from conventional gender expectations, and of close relationships with feminist women.

25. I find strong elements of male feminist self-flagellation in John Stoltenberg's work, and in profeminist men who take their inspiration from him. See Stoltenberg, *Refusing to Be a Man* (Portland, Oregon: Breitenbush Books, 1989).

26. I also want explicitly to recognize the value of men's anti-sexism even when it exhibits the pitfalls enumerated above: while these wrong turnings can have pernicious effects, they do not necessarily negate positive contributions, and certainly don't erase the good will of the men involved. The alignment between adequate understanding, admirable character, and good actions in the world is far from seamless. My emphasis on the need for self-scrutiny and on incentives to shallow feminist knowledge is meant not as a call for perfection, but as a strong reminder of concrete difficulties involved in responsibly negotiating a political commitment as fraught as that of male feminism.

27. This defines an important role for the sorts of anti-sexist men's groups that have provided the focus of much writing on male anti-sexism and pro-feminism. See, for example, Michael Kaufman, "The Construction of Masculinity and the Triad of Men's Violence" in Kaufman, ed. *Beyond Patriarchy: Essays by Men on Pleasure, Power, and Change* (Toronto: Oxford University Press, 1987).

Chapter 12

Antiracist (Pro)Feminisms
and Coalition Politics:
"No Justice, No Peace"

Joy James

Progressive Men and Supportive Women

When Dave Dellinger, promoting his autobiography *From Yale to Jail*,[1]
spoke at a Boulder middle school in a benefit for the Pacifica radio
station, KGNU, one of my girlfriends and I decided to check him out.
Finding the parking lot packed, we thought the auditorium would be
likewise; however, the cars outside were for the girls' basketball practice.
Not that many Boulderites heard the radical octogenarian, white activist
speak that night. He described travels to the former Soviet Union, labor
organizing during the depression, strikes and incarceration; but it was
his discussion of the civil rights movement that most moved me. A commitment to anti-racist organizing drew me into Dellinger's recollections
of combatting racism; his descriptions of sexism within the movement,
though, provided the most memorable story.

In the southern movement, civil rights organizers risked personal
injury, if not their lives, in attempting to desegregate and democratize the
U.S. Male and female activists were peers, at least in confronting and
being targeted by racist violence. Dellinger recounted how, anticipating
the brutality of racist sheriffs, Klansmen, or freelance terrorists, nonviolent men argued that if they risked their lives in morning demonstrations,
women co-activists should provide sexual favors that night. Some of their
female comrades complied. Dellinger added that as a married, older
male, he had not participated in this comfort station approach to civil
rights radicalism. His race politics reflected a feminism that years later
refracted his anti-racist narrative into a profeminist testimonial.

Speaking about gender politics the following day at the university, I related Dellinger's story to a multiracial class of student-activists, asking for their perspectives on sexism and the left. Noting that although the role of females in social movements is no longer mythologized as prone and passive before dynamic progressive males, I argued that decades after the civil rights and women's liberation movements, women are encouraged to assume caretaker roles in relationship to progressive males. Today, this nurturing is recycled more often through supportive speech rather than domesticity (crassly reduced in Dellinger's activist era to the kitchen/bedroom). In fact, the class instructor had invited me to address this group of progressives and feminists in order to confront its internal politics: throughout the semester a few articulate men had dominated class discussions despite the fact that the instructors were three women and the majority of students were female. When the issue of sexism in their class was raised, the two dismissed the possibility, pointing out their numerical inferiority as males and their lack of institutional voice as students. Female students met male dismissals with silence.

Raised by parents who had witnessed or worked in the liberation movements, these students understood the need to transgress racism and sexism; that internalized belief and the external leadership of their female instructors suggested to some that sexism could not exist in their group. Encouraging them to analyze this assumption and their avowed feminism, I used Dellinger's story to examine how the expectations placed on women to assist progressive males might reinscribe male dominance. The male students responded that the women they knew were strong (one cited independent, single black mothers). However, without referring to their own classroom dynamics, several women students began to share stories about betrayals and silencing. For instance, a Native American woman recounted being criticized as "divisive" or "whiny"—even by other indigenous women—when she spoke against sexism within a local Native American organization. A Jewish woman described how the image of the strong Jewish mother—as domineering matriarch against whom progressive males must assert and construct themselves—mirrored the stereotype of the black mother as overbearing.

The questions I posed to students are ones with which I struggle: What are the support roles of women to antiracist male feminists? When men (or women) "do feminism," why do we so infrequently ask what type—conservative, liberal, radical? With what critiques of racism, capitalism, heterosexism? The progressivism of both feminists and profeminists may contain contradictions and elements of betrayal. Will emerging heterofeminism partner males and females by asking that they dance with unspoken expectations and that feminists uncritically support their male counterparts? Perhaps in an antifeminist society, women coalesce partly in solidarity and partly from feeling "rescued" by male allies from being ideological wallflowers. Missteps occur in uncritical partnerships where collective movements—two steps forward, one back or one forward, two back—sometimes spare the agile the frustration of tripping over their counterpart. In an uneasy dance, the mere ability to not stumble rarely constitutes progress.

Progress proceeds in the quantitative increase of profeminists or male feminists, but what about the quality of their political ideologies? No doubt, we need more feminist men like we need more antiracist whites, or, greater numbers of the materially privileged to struggle for communalism and socialism, and hegemonic sexuals to battle homophobia. The need for feminist men stems from a larger need to grow community where one can shed a thick skin of indifference and isolation for a translucent one of connection and consciousness for social justice. This shared membrane, woven in writings responsive to subaltern peoples, is found in black male feminists' critical contributions to the genre of antiracist, feminist progressive thought.

Black male feminists appear (and likely are) inherently more progressive than mainstream (a.k.a. white) male feminists by virtue of their social status and familial influence. While dominant society constructs black men or "men of color" as less civilized, as hypermasculinized—and counterfeminist—black male feminists understand themselves to be "feminized" because they have neither the institutional power of white men under white supremacy, nor the familial conditioning of the mythic nuclear Euro-family ruled by a (allegedly benign) patriarch. Not only do black profeminists not share the same structural, patriarchal authority and dominance of white males—the supreme fathers—they simultaneously struggle against racism and feminism (although their progressive positions on class and sexuality are less clearly demonstrated). Most mainstream feminists of either gender rarely prioritize or even acknowledge beyond rhetorical references antiracism in their feminism, which is why black male feminism is so appealing. Logically, black women, collectively, have more commonality with black male feminists than they do with white feminists who are not radical antiracists (for years some African-American women have argued that black women have more in common with black masculinists than they do with white feminists, who in a society shaped by white supremacy are in the absence of a praxis of antiracism by default racist).

Male feminists' antiracist endeavors benefit black women as *women* in a patriarchal society, while their profeminist endeavors assist black women as *blacks* in a white supremacist state. (If it seems that I have erred in reversing the emphasis here, that is only because most do not seriously reflect on how antiracism benefits women and how (pro)feminism uplifts a race.) Given the progressive nature of their politics, it is difficult to argue against naturalizing coalitions between feminists and black male (pro)feminists. Still, questions about coalitions between black profeminists and feminists, and a healthy suspicion toward even the most progressive manifestations of male feminism, remain. Recalling the gender contradictions of progressive males inhibits any uncritical embrace of male feminist works. Interrogating the anti-racist feminisms in Michael Awkward's literary criticism, Lewis Gordon's philosophy, and Devon Carbado's and Richard Delgado's[2] critical race theory, I find models for male feminism that posit and problematize a mutual alliance between black men and women and offer insights into gender progressive politics at the same time that they raise questions about the same.

A Black Male Feminist Manifesto and the Femininity of Blackness

In "A Black Man's Place in Black Feminist Criticism," Michael Awkward presents a black male feminist or womanist manifesto:

> Black womanism demands neither the erasure of the black gendered other's subjectivity, as have male movements to regain a putatively lost Afro-American manhood, nor the relegation of males to prone, domestic, or other limiting positions. What it does require, if it is indeed to become an ideology with widespread cultural impact, is a recognition on the part of both black females and males of the nature of the gendered inequities that have marked our past and present, and a resolute commitment to work for change. In that sense, black feminist criticism has not only created a space for an informed Afro-American male participation, but it heartily welcomes—in fact, insists upon—the joint participation of black males and females as *comrades* (52).[3]

Awkward argues that the value of male black feminism lies in its antipatriarchal stance and self-reflexivity in its relations to, rather than reproduction of, a feminism that focuses on "the complexities of black female subjectivity and experience" (52). For Awkward, male feminists' abilities to expand the range and use of feminist critiques and perspectives include a critical discourse on obstacles to a black profeminist project and new constructions of "family" and black male sexuality (51). (Preferring the terms *feminism* or *feminist* for female and *profeminism* or *profeminist* for male advocates of gender equality, I am reluctant to concede Awkward the use of the label "feminism" given that it now requires the qualifiers *male* and *female* to distinguish advocates for an ideology associated with females; perhaps my uneasiness with male feminists is tied to my desire to biologize this ideology.)

Awkward reassures that male feminists are trustworthy. His manifesto issues a code of conduct or rules for ethical behavior to ensure that they become or remain so. Noting Alice Jardine's concern that male feminists not imitate feminists—"We do not want you to mimic us, to become the same as us; we don't want your pathos or your guilt; and we don't even want your admiration (even if it's nice to get it once in a while)"[4]—he advocates a form of male feminism that neither appropriates nor dominates feminism. His construction of black male feminism seeks to reassure female feminists that they need not fear the increasing entry of profeminist male voices as authoritative in feminist discourse. Aware that our hierarchical society translates biology into social dominance or subordination, Awkward comforts the uneasy by dismissing the political clout wielded by an ascending profeminism: "Surely it is neither naive, presumptuous, nor premature to suggest that feminism as ideology and reading strategy has assumed a position of exegetical and institutional strength capable of withstanding even the most energetically masculinist acts of subversion" (47). I am not completely comforted by Awkward's pronouncements. "Gender Studies," with its increasing presence of male faculty, has begun to replace "Women's Studies" in academe. This in itself is not necessarily a sign of counter-progressive politics. But I wonder if the "institutional strength" Awkward heralds for feminism is a bit overstated and used as a defensive maneuver to preempt critiques of male feminists. Historically, marginalized and oppressed groups such as African Americans, Native Americans, Latinos, and women struggled in social movements that had an impact on academic sites. Today, in the post-mass movement era, such studies have become institutionalized and mainstreamed to a certain degree. What were considered to be marginalized, but thoroughly politicized, studies became legitimized by the inclusion and leadership of populations previously considered dominant elites.

Although I welcome the departure of exclusionary disciplines and Manichean depictions of the oppressed and their oppressor(s), I am still left with the uncomfortable perception that if the validity of an area of knowledge, for instance, women's studies or ethnic studies, garners legitimacy only to the extent that privileged intellectuals, for example, men or whites, shape the discourse, then the exegetical and institutional strengths that allegedly safeguard against subversion or mutation are not as powerfully entrenched as Awkward would like us to believe. Rather than follow Awkward's injunction "not to worry," perhaps the issue is what to worry about in the ascendance of male feminism or profeminist men who make their mark in feminist literature.

Michele Wallace expresses reservations about black male feminists in "Negative Images: Towards a Black Feminist Cultural Criticism."[5] According to Wallace, Henry Louis Gates, Jr., coeditor of *The Norton Anthology of Afro-American Literature* and editor of the Oxford series on black women writers, is "single-handedly reshaping, codifying and consolidating the entire field of Afro-American Studies, including black feminist studies" (251). Given his influential position in academe (as the director of Harvard University's W.E.B. DuBois Institute of African-American studies) and the literary world of upscale lit magazines, Gates wields considerable clout. This institutional power, writes Wallace, means that "he demonstrates an ability to define black feminist inquiry for the dominant discourse in a manner yet unavailable to black female critics. The results so far are inevitably patriarchal. Having established himself as the father of Afro-American Literary Studies, with the help of the *New York Times Book Review*, he now proposes to become the phallic mother of a newly depoliticized, mainstreamed, and commodified black feminist literary criticism" (251).

Wallace references Gates's statement that "learning to speak in the voice of the black mother" is the objective of the discourse of the Other. In literary production, men still have greater access and authority as intellectuals and thinkers. This is also true for black literature, as Wallace notes. Despite or because of the fact that (black) women's greatest recognized achievements in feminism are in fiction, males—whether masculinist, feminist, or hybrid—continue to define the parameters of social and literary nonfiction concerning (black) gender politics. One can hardly ignore the reality of pro forma feminism and opportunism even among those males who highlight the significance of women's contributions. (Paradoxically, male feminists may acknowledge the "exceptional" woman/women as their intellectual equals—just as some whites embrace the exceptional or aberrational black/blacks—while most women function in their lives as supporting helpmates or the disenfranchised to be succored.)

Sensitive to black feminist criticisms, as expressed by Wallace and others, Awkward cautions black men who desire to be productive feminists not to reproduce dominance or erasure in their discourse about black feminism/women. Instead, he argues that they should deal with the specificity of their gender as males. The self-interest at work here, according to Awkward, is not selfish or narrow but self-enlightened and enlightening. What is furthered in profeminism is the ability to explore male identity and gender construction (similar to the opportunity to explore white identity and racial construction in critical white studies or antiracist discourse). To illustrate his point, Awkward offers an insightful reading of Toni Morrison's *Sula*, making connections between "Eva's" infanticide against her only son, an adult male drug addict, whom she feared was attempting to climb back into her womb, and sexism among black males. Awkward writes, "Beyond its heterosexual dimension, can the 'female' truly come to represent for a traditional black male-in-crisis more than a protective maternal womb from which he seeks to be 'birthed' again?" (56) Redefining manhood here, he notes, centers more on not recreating the domestic and uterine enclosure of black women than emulating the acquisitiveness and power of dominant norms.

This profeminism posits the black male as inextricably linked to women by virtue of race-ethnicity. In fact, Awkward's black male is a gender-hybrid. Using Alice Walker's term *womanist* as explored in the work of Sherley Anne William's[6] and other black feminist writers, he contends that for the womanist or black feminist—as opposed to white/mainstream feminist—the discourse centers around women in relationship to the development of a people: "'Womanist theory' is especially suggestive for Afro-American men because, while it calls for feminist discussions of black women's texts and for critiques of black androcentricism, womanism foregrounds a general black psychic health as a primary objective" (49). Although he writes that likely the "most difficult task for a black male feminist is striking a workable balance between male self-inquiry/interest and an adequately feminist critique of patriarchy" (49), framing womanism rather than nonblack feminism as his model, Awkward is able to argue for the place of the black male feminist as noninterloper. This is not because he unilaterally pictures himself with such "insider" status but because womanism constructs him as such: it is a people not just a gender that preoccupies womanist discourse.

Offering the progressive intellectual stance of black male feminism, against an undifferentiated patriarchy, he presents patriarchy monolithically while variegating male identity. Awkward uses Hortense Spillers's "Mama's Baby, Papa's Maybe: An American Grammar Book"[7] to discuss how black male identity evolves in a feminine matrix. In Awkward's case, we may also add "identification." His autobiographical narrative informs that as a consequence of having been raised by a mother who was brutalized by his father, he attempted early in his life to construct an identity not based on male privilege and violence.[8] As Awkward reconstructs Spillers's argument, we see the familiar premise that black males are denied full patriarchal privileges tied to racism, the same racism that engendered the much maligned "female-headed household." Awkward concurs with Spillers whom he quotes: "It is the heritage of the *mother* that the African-American male must regain as an aspect of his own personhood" (52). This heritage constitutes a form of "power" that Spillers describes as "the female within." The "female within" is not defined, as Awkward himself notes, writing that the concept needs more exploration in terms of what it signifies in the lives of black men concerning their "repressed female interiority" (54). The "female within" appears strongly tied to a black identity. Although Awkward rejects the Moynihan thesis of the black matriarch, single black women seem to possess a special essence in his writing. If they are the source of this hybrid-male cognizant of the mother's strong character and will, then what can be said of black men raised by nonblack women? How do they obtain this cultural strength typical of Awkward's matriarchal black communities? In *Get on the Bus* (1996), Spike Lee's film on black males' 1995 pilgrimage to the Million Man March, the fictional character "Gary," the son of a black father and a white mother, embodies both a strong black identity and a feminist consciousness. Art imitates life: African-American males raised by white females display a "black identity" (as nebulous and contested as that may be), and, exhibit the feminization of blackness both in its positive dimensions celebrated by Awkward and its negativity critiqued by Lewis Gordon.

Awkward concludes his argument by asserting that for black male feminists the "Father's law [is] no longer the law of the land" (57). We must ask: Who replaced the father and the father's law? Surely not the mother (and anarchy does not rule). Is it the emergent son, the hybrid with the interiority of the female, who supplants the patriarch? If the new son, or the son for the new age, is ascendant, then how? In a transgender Oedipal drive, can the feminist male supplant not only the father but also the mother (and the sister), proving himself superior to the patriarch because his claims to having transcended the female/male dichotomy of mother/father are buttressed by the authority of his *masculine* feminist speech?

Given that Awkward has stated that black female subjective experience is not the focus of black male feminism, he need not address the mother's law or the liberation of the male interiority of the female/sister. *Sans* patriarch and matriarch, foregoing anarchy, will leadership and the law spring from the progeny's transgender consciousness? And if the "law" or ideology of the hybrid-male, the feminized man, differs from that of the hybrid-female, the masculinized woman, the sistah, will there be contestation or coalition? In disagreements and conflicts among heterogeneous feminists, the hybrid-male retains some unspoken advantage. While the beloved of the interiorized mother (or as black gay-feminist Hilton Als eloquently relates, the "anti-man" or the "negress"), he seems to possess the latent, institutional power of the patriarch, remaining the he(she) who is heir apparent to the father. That not every male feminist de facto relinquishes this latent power suggests that Awkward might wish to explore the degree to which male feminists transcend rather than feminize patriarchal privileges.

While Michael Awkward illuminates the black man who is not really a "man" because of his interiority, Lewis Gordon reflects on the black man who is not truly a "man" because of his exteriority. In the essay "Effeminacy: The Quality of Black Beings," the profeminist chapter in

Gordon's *Bad Faith and Antiblack Racism*, which explores sexism within Jean-Paul Sartre's *Being and Nothingness*, Gordon notes the nuances "of antiblack and misogynous worlds" and their coextensive appearances (124). In his discussions of blackness as femininity, this black profeminist writes: "Our descriptions of sexuality in an antiblack world pose a gender problem. From the standpoint of an antiblack world, black men are nonmen-nonwomen, and black women are nonwomen-nonmen. This conclusion is based on our premise of whites—white men and white women—being both human, being both Presence, and our premise of blacks, both black men and women, being situated in the condition of the 'hole,' being both Absence" (124).[9] Gordon notes that this dichotomy raises "a gender question concerning black men and a metaphysical one concerning black women. Blackness is regarded as a hole in being. Black men are hence penises that are holes; and black women are vaginas that are holes—holes that are holes. If blackness is a hole, and women are holes, what are white women, and what are black men in an antiblack world?" (124)

This exploration of the nature of black males and white females in an antiblack world offers a number of insights. For instance, Gordon argues that white women as "indeterminate" face the choice of choosing between their Presence biologically embodied in their whiteness and their Absence determined, again in biology, by their femaleness. Gordon notes that the choice that white women have for Absence is doubly reified by their racial transgressions, viscerally marked for the racist by white women's ability to bear "black" children. Where biology connotes Presence or Absence, race and gender become determining markers. Gordon contends that for the antiblack racist, the "'essence' of blackness . . . is, if you will, the hole, and the hole is the institutional bad-faith mode of the feminine"; antiblack racism is therefore "intimately connected to misogyny" (125). According to Gordon, "As pure Presence, masculinity is an ideal form of whiteness with its own gradations; the less of a hole one is, the more masculine one is; the less dark, the more white" (127). Therefore, the less dark, or more white, the less feminine. This equation allows Gordon to maintain that the black man "embodies femininity even more than the white woman" (what the black woman embodies as doubly feminized by race and gender is unclear here). A "black man in the presence of whiteness stands as a hole to be filled; he stands to the white man in a homoerotic situation and to the white woman in a heterosexual erotic situation with a homoerotic twist; she becomes the white/male that fills his blackness/femininity" (127). Gordon's feminism depicts with evocative imagery the suspect-status of white women in a racist world: "[T]he white woman should not be regarded as the jewel of the antiblack racist. For hidden in her whiteness—like the secret blackness of milk, the secret abundance of blackness, the fertility that so outrages Manicheanism with its propensity to split apart and weaken the Light—is the antiblack racist's suspicion of her blackness. She stands as a white blackness, as a living contradiction of white supremacy. Out of her comes every white, placing a question mark on the notion of the purity of whiteness in the flesh. Unlike the black woman, out of whom only black children can be born, she can bear both white and black children. Because of this, the white woman ultimately stands on the same ontological level as slime in an antiblack world. She is regarded as a frightening substance that simultaneously attracts and repels" (126).

Despite its incisive analysis of white patriarchy and supremacy, reading *Bad Faith*, I wonder "what are black women in an antiblack world?" Its discussion of black male and female relationships never fully transpires, the focus remaining on black men and white women. Because Gordon does not comprehensively grapple with the issue of where the black man stands in relationship to the black female in his essay on effeminacy as an attribute of blackness, he can argue that whiteness can be worn as a phallus—"The 'phallus,' against which and upon which gender analyses often focus, needn't be and possibly no longer is a penis. In an antiblack world, the phallus is white skin" (128). This assertion is clearly an apt description of an antiblack or "white" world, but what is the phallus in a "black" world? In their relationships with black women and girls, are black men and boys feminized in the same manner in which they appear to be in the nonblack world? Gordon argues that the black man "cannot reject his femininity without simultaneously rejecting his blackness, for his femininity stands as a consequence of his blackness and vice versa" (128). Black men disavow their connection to black women by asserting their "maleness." For him, the black male "has a connection to the black woman in virtue of his blackness, but he can deny who he is by asserting what limited connection to maleness he may have" (128). Interestingly, black men betray their femininity, which is based in blackness, a femininity in a way that is purely negative in its construct, as is this form of blackness, one externally defined and delimited as the antithesis of whiteness/maleness. To go beyond gender, or the male/female dichotomy of dominance, one must go beyond race, or the white/black binary of dominance.

"The black woman stands as the reality of sweet, seductive, open femininity" in an antiblack/misogynist world (128). By the sweet and seductive, Gordon refers to, in the dominant culture's sensibilities toward black females, the putrefying rancidity of rotting fruit. Referencing Hazel Carby, he notes that the black woman appears as "an exotic figure of solution" (129). Her reconstruction as the sugar tit of consolation masks the abhorrence one feels toward her as a source of fecundating decay. But not only blackness constitutes femininity as debased phenomenon. Femininity is more than blackness just as masculinity is more than whiteness. Given that Gordon's work is on antiblack racism, his black male feminism need not explore the ways in which patriarchy reasserts itself in black forms against black females. That racism contributes to sexism, that white women have patriarchal power invested in their wearing of skins/phalluses, are important points to be made. And Gordon does so with turns of language and ideas that illuminate while they unsettle. Still, the defensive murderous rages and desperate protective measures—ranging from "Eva's" immolation of her son to restraining orders—that black females take against black males suggests that what transpires as black men disavow their connectedness to black women to assert "maleness" can often be deadly and misogynist.

The view that black men are suspect masculine beings, not truly male in an antiblack or racist world, is one shared by both Gordon and Awkward. This view speaks in part to a sense of severance from traditional and historical constructs of a masculinity, for one that is humanized rather than animalized, one connected to femininity embodied in the black not the white female. This suggests that, in part, the black male femininity, influenced by the interiority in Awkward's writing and the Absence or "hole" in Gordon's, is a racialized gender construct (or perhaps a sexualized racial construct). Both writers evoke shared skin, Spillers's "captive community" in which at some level, blacks seem to occupy the same skin, uncut by gender and blood. Spillers's "Mamma's Baby, Papa's Maybe" maintains that an enslaved African-American female "shares the conditions of all captive flesh," as the "entire captive community becomes a living laboratory." For such women the theft and mutilation of the body create a special condition in which "we lose at least gender difference in the outcome, and the female body and the male body become a territory of cultural and political maneuver, not at all gender-related or gender-specific."[10] These shared conditions of racial oppression do not erase the female body as a site for sexual violence. Neither Spillers, Awkward, or Gordon argue for black gender essentialism. But their works, referenced here, do not focus on differences separating black males and females. Instead, the writers emphasize commonalties between black men and women. In times where tensions and strife between black women and men seem to garner the attention of spectacle in the larger society, Awkward discusses ties through shared femininity based on familial conditioning that produces male feminine interiority; and Gordon analyzes a shared femininity based on the racialized epidermal in a racist society. We see male feminists respond to the need to stress what black men share with black women. However, those contributions need not efface the battles that cut through the ties that bind, despite the despite the realities of the female within or blackness as Absence. Nowhere are the differences and the battles between black women and men more stark than in the area of domestic violence.

The Pitfalls of Gender Coalition Politics

Legal scholar Devon Carbado explores the issues of coalition politics and anti-essentialism from a black male feminist perspective. In "Race, Domestic Abuse, and the O. J. Simpson Case: When All Victims are Black Men and White Women," he notes that to "the extent that black men ignore the particularities of black women's racial experiences or exclude themselves from discussions about gender dynamics in the black community, they are unlikely to come to terms with . . . the patriarchal privilege they wield. Nor are they likely to challenge the notion that black men, and not black women, represent the paradigm of black being."[11]

Carbado is clearly writing about black masculinists or sexists; but to some degree his critique can be applied to black profeminists whose progressive gender politics or feminization via racism may shield them from their own participation in patriarchal privilege. Carbado's black feminism emphasizes or elevates the status of black women. Hopefully, most black profeminists (and feminists) are unlikely to agree that black women should "represent the paradigm of black being" even if they agree that black men should not be constructed as such under patriarchy. Patriarchy makes men representative of humanity; must a profeminist response make women representative, and must an antiracist profeminist response make black women representative? Surely, even the feminized paradigm remains some form of carceral waiting to be exploded or traded in for some newer, more expansive paradigm.

"Race, Domestic Abuse, and the O. J. Simpson Case" in its concerns about the status of black women focuses on two events in 1995, the O. J. Simpson case and the Million Man March, that generated, and continue to engender, heated debates about black gender politics. Using the Simpson case to raise questions about civil rights advocacy and how the black male "subordinating experience is perceived to have enough cultural currency to represent victimhood for a specific political or legal battlecry" (16), Carbado notes what is generally acknowledged among progressives, that the "racial battlecry" in black antiracist struggles has been gendered male. His essay identifies "unmodified antiracism" as a form of black male essentialism that "derives from intentional sexism and/or functional sexism in antiracist discourse" (3). Functional sexism for Carbado is a strategy or instrumental politics that confronts racism by privileging the male (for example arguments concerning black males as an "endangered *species*"). He argues that "there is no justifiable basis for treating the subordinated status of young men as more deserving of black political solicitude than the subordinated status of young black women" (7). Unmodified antiracism reduces discussions of "black community" or "black people" to references to black males, the struggle against racism to essentially a struggle against black male subordination, while it presents explications of antiblack racism against males as competent to address antiblack racism against females. Carbado provides an example of unmodified antiracism in the Million Man March injunction for women to financially support the March, yet stay at home and take care of children in order to facilitate males' experiences to assert themselves as the head of households. An example of unmodified antiracism stemming from black women is given, as he describes the July 1995 African American Women in the Law Conference's domestic violence workshop. Carbado discusses the dynamics of a workshop in which black women argued against the incarceration of black male batterers for domestic abuse "because such abuse stemmed from black men's collective and individual sense of racial disempowerment" (9). Using his experiences in the domestic violence workshop, he reflects on the ways in which black women, those who do not option "Eva's" homicidal remedy, render their own experiences secondary, and in service to, or protection of, black males. This self-sacrifice, or Catch-22, faced by some black females, mirrors social expectations on their performance in relationship to black males. Women survivors weighed the need not only to protect themselves from brutalization but also to protect the (black) men who brutalized them.

For Carbado, dominant historical narratives on the unfair treatment of black males in the criminal justice system "contain political and legal symbols of race and gender that function to construct O. J. Simpson as a victim of racism in a way that obscures that he was a perpetrator of domestic violence" (18). The dominant narrative of the domestic abuse workshop, that of protecting violent black males, on one level shows how much women have in common given the hegemonic social narrative: "Blackness (which Simpson represents) and not Nicole Brown is the victim" (47). Carbado notes with irony the reductionist stance many took in response to the (racialized and feminized) jury's acquittal in the criminal trial: "While we, and not the jury, were exposed to the most emotional and sensational aspects of the trial, it is the jury that is being accused of rendering a decision based on emotion" (40).

Examining how black communities view racial subordination in a gendered fashion, Carbado's narratives are nonfiction, unlike the fictive feminist tales of fellow profeminist legal theorists Derrick Bell and Richard Delgado. Rather, he uses communal narratives, journalistic accounts, and, in the story of the domestic violence workshop, autobiographical accounts. The use of the latter is very much in keeping with Awkward's consciously—autobiographically—is to explore, implicitly or explicitly, why and how the individual male experience (the 'me' in men) has diverged from, has created possibilities for a rejection of, the androcentric norm" (44). The male-centered paradigm obviously shifts in Carbado's feminism to privilege (black) women. What this paradigm shift represents for coalitions with black women is unclear given that his work does not theorize gender politics in a larger context connected to privileging black women and denouncing of their brutalization by black males.

Richard Delgado's "Rodrigo's Sixth Chronicle: Intersections, Essences, and the Dilemma of Social Reform" discusses coalition politics in ways that both highlight and minimize the presence of black women. Delgado's narrative presents protagonists "Rodrigo," a black male law student whose father is African American and whose mother is Italian, and "the professor," a progressive male legal scholar, a "man of color" who serves as Rodrigo's intellectual mentor and foil. After being ousted from a women's law caucus meeting (and criticized by his female partner "Giannina") because of an uninvited lecture he makes assessing the antagonistic relations between women of color and white women, Rodrigo seeks out the professor for counselling. Discussing the limitations of coalition politics or "the perils of making common cause," the two debate the role of profeminist men in women's liberation struggles.

"Rodrigo" first notes that essentialism appears to be "the usual response of a beleaguered group" seeking "solidarity in a struggle against a more powerful one" (648). For "Rodrigo," essentialism appears in "three guises"—the meaning of words, theory of coalitions, canon of knowledge—which all "share the search for narrative coherence" (649). Identifying relational essentialism, the law student cites the example of black women joining white women because "they stand on the same footing with respect to patriarchy" (649) and share the need to be freed from it. Through "Rodrigo's" pronouncement Delgado paints a rather one-dimensional view of patriarchy. Contrary to "Rodrigo's" assertion, black women do not stand on the same footing with white women in relationship to patriarchy.

Rodrigo discusses intersectionality in order to examine the nexus that black women occupy as women and members of an oppressed ethnic group, blacks. As the editors Gloria Hull, Patricia Bell Scott, Barbara Smith, and contributors note in their pathbreaking work on black women studies, *All the Women are White, All the Blacks are Men, But Some of Us are Brave*,[12] blackness has been masculinized and femaleness racialized white. Because "Rodrigo" acknowledges only two intersections, race and gender, the place of class and sexual identity in this intersectionality remains obscured. He does remark, quoting "Giannina," that a relatively disempowered person, such as "a lesbian single mother" jeopardizes her powerbase by engaging in strategic essentializing coalitions with a more privileged group (652). Paradoxically, the "Sixth Chronicle" notes the importance of alliances in a passage that represents black women as an afterthought, depicting them as the additive rank-and-file to coalitions rather than the impetus behind feminist and antiracist social movements and coalition politics: "Change comes from a small, dissatisfied group for whom canonical knowledge and the standard social arrangements don't work. Such a group needs allies. Thus, white women in the feminist movement reach out to women of color; Black men in the civil rights movement try to include Black women, and so on" (669). Although the historical record reveals that black women such as Ella Baker, Fannie Lou Hamer, and Rosa Parks pioneered the civil rights and feminist movements, their agency disappears in this profeminist essay.

"Rodrigo" critiques the assumed progressivism of coalitions between white women and women of color: "Gains are ephemeral if one wins them by forming coalitions with individuals who really do not have your interest at heart. It's not just that the larger, more diverse group will forget you and your special needs. It's worse than that. You'll forget who you are. And if you don't, you may still end up demonized, blamed for sabotaging the revolution when it inevitably and ineluctably fails" (655).[13] He cites two reasons against coalition politics. First, often in coalitions strategic essentialism leads to a Gramscian "false consciousness" in which "the oppressed come to identify with their oppressors" (653). Second, the pitfalls of "interest-convergence" are a constant liability; for instance, in *Brown v. Board of Education* black civil rights gains progressed only to the extent that they coincided with the interests of dominant whites who mitigated these rights. "Rodrigo" surmises that under interest convergence between subaltern and dominant groups: "Rights won are generally constrained and those with the least power are scapegoated."[14] A certain realism or pessimism informs the essay's observations concerning interest-convergence and coalition politics for disenfranchised groups: "Rights, once won, tend to be cut back. And even when part of them remains, the price of the newly won right is exacted from the most marginal of its beneficiaries" (656). For Rodrigo, one must remain oppositional (despite socialization towards collegiality and civility); he reasons that a "nationalist, counter-essentialist course" benefits both more privileged groups and the outsider group. "Justice first, then peace" becomes "Rodrigo's" epigraph and motto[15] (in radical demonstrations, one often heard the chant "No justice . . . no peace!").

Regarding profeminist males and sexual liberation projects, one wonders what are the interest convergence politics of male and female feminists. With the growing appearance of the articulate male feminist, what sustains coalitions between male and female feminists? Do profeminists, who are more institutionally empowered than their female counterparts, align themselves with feminists only to the extent that the interests of both groups converge? Equally as important, when do coalition politics become caretaking politics for subaltern women aided by the patronage of feminist men (analogies to people of color and liberal whites abound).

Conclusion

There is no way of measuring peerage between male and female feminists. Yet, surely reading and critiquing the works of Awkward, Gordon, Delgado, and Carbado foster gender egalitarianism among antiracists (and hopefully racial equality among feminists). The proliferation of new profeminist writings, and their promising intellectual and political currency shaping the academic market, allow those appreciative of profeminist contributions to recognize ignore potential deradicalizing tendencies within feminist discourse. For instance, the exploration of "self" or male identity in profeminism creates tangible contributions to feminist struggles; it may also paradoxically lead to narcissistic solipsism for an expanding consciousness (this tendency also appears in critical white studies' ambivalent relationship toward antiracist radicalism). The femininity of the black male in a state where "whiteness" is worn as "phallus" adds a critical dimension to feminist analyses addressing the intersections of sexism and racism; yet the disappearance of the black female in such discourse is a possible byproduct of such a profeminist, antiracist paradigm. Focusing on the conditions of black women, particularly those confronted by domestic violence, elevates the status of black females; elevating the black female above the black male in an analytical framework constructs a paradigmatic pedestal that, even as it addresses domestic violence, inadequately addresses institutional violence and/or the selective manner in which dominant society and state apparatus demarcate the "legitimate" spheres in which black males may exercise and abuse masculine power and patriarchal coercion. Finally, if coalitions are inevitably and inherently flawed—as is apparent in the pitfalls of multiracial coalitions that, dominated by the interests of whites, supplant political parity for inclusivity—then where do male feminists of color stand in relation to feminist women of color, and the distance that must logically span between the two groups in the paradigm shaped by the interest convergence argument?

These are questions I hope that male antiracist feminists will find useful. But whatever value they attribute to these inquiries, these questions like those posed to the student-activists reflect both an appreciation for the work of profeminists and a cautious concern that a growing feminist discourse need not always signal a shift in power relations. Men who do feminism will be ostracized and marginalized in some sectors (as are antiracist whites), and validated in others. But increasingly their authoritative voices as male (particularly if they filter their feminism through the hegemony of conservative/liberal ideologies) will allow them to be constructed as the site of the most rational, informed speech. At its best, the feminization of male discourse confronts gender hierarchy, inextricably linked to heterosexism, racism, and classism; it also challenges the privilege of the feminized male voice. At its worst, in the absence of a radical praxis, male feminism will foster a coalition politics that brakes before full justice, and consequently, its politics will downplay disputes among feminists, adding to the restive uneasiness of some of its most natural allies.

Notes

I am grateful to Tom Digby, David Kahane, and Lewis Gordon for their comments on this essay.

1. Dave Dellinger, *From Yale to Jail* (Marion, South Dakota: Rose Hill Books, 1993).

2. All male feminist writers cited here are African American, except Latino legal theorist Richard Delgado whose narratives revolve around the persona of a fictional black man, "Rodrigo," whom Delgado identifies as a relative of "Geneva Crenshaw," the black female (super)protagonist of Derrick Bell's "Chronicles."

3. Michael Awkward, *Negotiating Difference: Race, Gender, and the Politics of Positionality* (Chicago: University of Chicago Press, 1995).

4. Alice Jardine, "Men in Feminism: Odor di Uomo or Compagnons de Route?" in *Men in Feminism*, ed. Alice Jardine and Paul Smith (New York: Methuen, 1987) 60.

5. Michele Wallace, "Negative Images: Towards a Black Feminist Cultural Criticism," *Invisibility Blues: From Pop to Theory* (New York: Verso, 1990).

6. Sherley Anne Williams, "Some Implications of Womanist Theory," *Callaloo 9* (1986): 304.

   Varied definitions of black feminism are not explored by Awkward. For instance, Patricia Hill Collins defines black feminism as "a process of self-conscious struggle that empowers women and men to actualize a humanist vision" and "develop a theory that is emancipatory and reflective" for black women struggles (Patricia Hill Collins, *Black Feminist Thought*. Boston, Unwin, 1990: 139-161, 32). Alice Walker contrasts black feminism with white or Eurocentric feminism, coining the term "womanist"; for Walker, womanist renders the adjective "black" superfluous for women of African descent: "just as for white women there is apparently no felt need to preface 'feminist' with the word 'white,' since the word 'feminist' is accepted as coming out of white women culture." bell hooks, rejecting the term womanist, expands upon Collins's humanist vision and Walker's cultural critique to define feminism as "a commitment to eradicating the ideology of domination that permeates western culture on various levels—sex, race, and class ... and a commitment to reorganizing society so that the self-development of people can take precedence over imperialism, economic expansion, and material desires." (bell hooks, *Ain't I a Woman: Black Women and Feminism*. Boston: South End Press, 1983). Class politics have not always been consistently raised in discussions of (black) feminism.

7. Hortense J. Spillers, "Mama's Baby, Papa's Maybe: An American Grammar Book," *diacritics* (summer 1987).

8. Awkward quotes from Spillers: "the black American male embodies the *only* American community of males which has had the specific occasion to learn *who* the female is within itself"; presumably, a number of communities would disagree.

9. Lewis Gordon, *Bad Faith and Antiblack Racism* (Highlands, N.J.: Humanities Press, 1995).

10. Spillers, ibid.

11. Devon Carbado, "Race, Domestic Abuse, and the O.J. Simpson Case: When All Victims are Black Men and White Women" (forthcoming *Harvard Civil-Rights Civil-Liberties Law Review*).

12. Gloria Hull, Patricia Scott, Barbara Smith *All the Women Are White, All the Blacks are Men, But Some of Us Are Brave* (New York: The Feminist Press, 1982).

13. Richard Delgado, "Rodrigo's Sixth Chronicle: Intersections, Essences, and the Dilemma of Social Reform," *New York University Law Review*, Vol. 68: 639, June 1993.

14. Delgado's Rodrigo argues the case against interest convergence: "Normativity or prescriptive discourse speech constrained by paradigms which infected with racism and sexism interpret events in conformity with paradigmatic bias (for example, that 'minority' students do better in placement after law school does not reflect their superior qualities but an antiwhite bias shaped by affirmative action)."

15. As the professor observes: "'Justice first, then peace'—a motto that others have employed in different versions to highlight the incompatibility between an oppressive regime that contains structures of unfairness, and social stability. Such a regime is inherently unstable because of the everpresent possibility of revolt" (672).

Chapter 13

Feminism and the Future of Fathering

Judith Kegan Gardiner

"For the first six months after they left, I was too depressed to phone," said my friend W, "though I sent a lot of cards and presents and stuff in the mail." W was recalling a difficult period ten years ago when their mother took his children to live a thousand miles away. Well, not exactly his children. W and the children's mother are New Leftists and feminists who had lived in a commune with several other adults from the early 1970s until the mid-1980s. Although he was present at both their home births, lived in the same house with them for years, and took them to school every morning, W is not their biological father, nor did he ever marry his former lover, who is the children's mother, since they both considered marriage a bourgeois institution that is especially oppressive to women. "I thought living communally was the answer, breaking up the nuclear family, smashing monogamy, yet providing children with love and support," said W, "but then it all fell apart." Now W talks to these children on the phone every week, but he can only afford to visit them a few times a year, and his sense of loss is unassuaged.

Another profeminist male friend of mine recently remarried. Estranged from his own son, who lives with his mother in another state, he was eager to try fatherhood again with his new wife's much younger son. Since his new wife must commute a long distance to work, much of the primary care for his stepson falls to him. Both ex and current wives are strong feminists, though my friend nevertheless blames his ex for turning his son against him.

After their politically-correct father left our family to remarry and start a new career on the West Coast, my two teenaged daughters heard many "impossible father" stories from their friends, all of whom lived with their mothers. There was the father who invited one sister to Thanksgiving but cut the other, the millionaire realtor who refused to pay for his son's college tuition when the boy got one C grade—in tennis, the father who doted on his new baby but no longer spoke to his firstborn daughter, who was older than his bride. I encouraged my daughters to see their father, certainly never prohibited them, or stood in the way, but I was relieved when he moved because I wouldn't have to deal with him as much, and I let my daughters negotiate on their own for occasional visits with him in California. Mostly as I shared such stories with my friends, I portrayed the mothers, including myself, as reasonable people with their children's best interests at heart; the children as innocent victims of adult fecklessness; and the fathers as hypocritical or irresponsible or confused men who failed to live up to their feminist principles and either broke apart their families or handled separation badly when they didn't cause it themselves. Now I'm rethinking my views about families and especially about fathering, not blaming feminism for dissolving families as many members of the new men's movements do, but trying to see how we can move forward, not from where we were decades ago but from where we are now.

As a mother of daughters and a Women's Studies teacher, I was attracted to Nancy Chodorow's emphasis on mother-daughter bonding in her enormously influential book, *The Reproduction of Mothering*, when it appeared in 1978. Like feminist psychologist Dorothy Dinnerstein, Chodorow hypothesized that the cross-cultural fact of mother-dominated childrearing accounted for the unpleasant, apparently universal fact of male social dominance. Her solution was to get men involved far more intimately in childrearing. If men did fifty percent of childcare, furthermore, women would be free to do much more of everything else, but the root of her theory was psychoanalytic, not simply pragmatic. This view was widely accepted among profeminist men, many of whom pledged to implement shared parenting with their own children. This, then, was a feminist theory that directly shaped men's lives, all the better, they believed, to reshape a new and better next generation.

Now, twenty years later, the media simultaneously declares feminism dead and victorious, dangerous, ludicrous, trivial, and commonsensical. Feminism has become normalized in many aspects of American thought, while the nation has changed in ways that feminism did not expect. My oversimplified, shorthand view for what has happened is that in these years feminism has won and the rich have won, and these are partially contradictory trends that increase class polarization; market emotions, genders, and sexualities; and unevenly increase some and decrease other opportunities for the gender-egalitarian life that second wave feminism promised. Traditional blue collar men's jobs are disappearing from the heartland; employment has become less secure; Americans work longer hours; and women have been massively integrated into the waged labor force. Many factors other than feminist theory, then, have cooperated to realign expectations and experiences of parenting in the United States today, but I want to trace one particular thread—Chodorow's claim that joint parenting is the key to feminist social transformation and subsequent discussions about today's perceived crisis of fatherhood. At the same time, this "crisis," with its disjunctions in men's lives, particularly the simultaneous intensification and erosion of fatherhood seen in noncustodial fathers like my friends, illuminates and helps modify feminist "mothering" theory.

In 1978, Chodorow posited that all children begin their emotional lives in primary relationship to a powerful and beloved mother, whom they also fear and from whom they do not originally distinguish themselves. Girls identify with their mothers and smoothly develop a secure sense of gender as female. They enjoy and come to need intimate, empathic emotional relationships, like those that they share with their mothers. Boys, in contrast, learn that they are not like their mothers and must form their masculine gender identity negatively, by separating from their mothers and developing a sense of self that is independent, autonomous, and individuated. They protect themselves against the desire to re-merge with the femininity of mothers through the negative reactions of misogyny, emotional withdrawal, and insistence on male superiority. Hence, according to Chodorow, women grow up to need an intimacy that men will fail to satisfy, a need that pushes women into motherhood and so renews the cycle. Her psychology of the two genders is asymmetrical: whereas women become mothers, men become masculine. "Masculine identification," she says, "is predominantly a gender role identification. By contrast, feminine identification is predominantly *parental*" (176). While girls develop flexible, personal identifications with their mothers, boys instead "develop a positional identification with aspects of the masculine role" and "appropriate those specific components of the masculinity of their father that they fear will be otherwise used against them," presumably in a judgmental, punitive, and demanding way (175, 176). One assumption of Chodorow's argument is that the modern Western families whose psychology she describes each consists of a mother devoted to childrearing and a single known father, who is away at work much of the time but idealized by the mother. Father absence accounts for a great deal in this theory. Because boys do not have their fathers as nearby models for positive identification, they must form their masculinity negatively. In contrast to the close relation between daughters and mothers, sons don't identify with their fathers as intimately-known persons, and they therefore appropriate the dominant "cultural images of masculinity" and so perpetuate sexism and patriarchy (176).

This theory has many advantages for women, and it therefore became quite popular among feminists. Not only does this theory celebrate female bonding, but its explanation of male dominance is at once universal and capable of social change. Despite its longevity and stability, male dominant society limits both sexes in a way that must be—and can be—changed. It limits women's opportunities by confining them to only one social role, and it limits men by making them rigid and insecure about their masculinity in ways that they take out on each other and on women. Furthermore, the theory describes how change will be generated: it will be generational. Better still, for women at least, its solution to patriarchal injustice does not require women to change. Women's nurturant and empathic personalities, that is, women's goodness, will remain, while women will lose the burden of total responsibility for children when men become equal parents. In one generation such joint paternal and maternal childcare will create androgynous, whole people. "My expectation is that equal parenting would leave people of both genders with the positive capacities each has," Chodorow says, "but without the destructive extremes these currently tend toward" (218). Men would gain capacities for love and nurturance; women would be more autonomous; and both genders' "sexual choices might become more flexible, less desperate" (219). Thus change would be better for society as well as individuals, and both women and men would welcome it because current strains in the sex-gender system have created widespread discomfort and resistance. Women are strained trying to work for wages and still be full time mothers, and, "in response to alienation and domination in the paid work world, many men are coming to regret their lack of extended connection with children" (213). A widespread movement toward joint parenting would therefore transform "the social organization of gender," eliminate inequality, and produce "a tremendous social advance" for all (219). Of course joint parenting would necessitate changes in U.S. economic structures. However, in the 1970s, many Americans thought the work week would continue to shorten and leisure and affluence would spread throughout society, so that these changes would be possible for and welcomed by all.

One of the advantages of Chodorow's theories for U.S. feminism in the 1970s and 1980s was its positive evaluation of women's traditional characteristics. It emphasized female bonding as fulfilling, rather than as antagonistic, as it had been portrayed in Freudian theory and much popular culture. It defended women from the Freudian imputation of being fundamentally lacking in anatomy, character, and morals, and instead found men lacking in the abilities to love and nurture, although it did not characterize men as violent brutes, as some radical feminist theories do. In Chodorow's view, masculinity causes social injustice and bad personal relationships for both men and women. Masculinity is a problem for men. Attaining it is difficult and anxious; the accomplishment is never secure. Masculinity is also a problem for women, since men's deficiencies prevent heterosexual relationships from satisfying women and so cause women to idealize men, grant them superiority, demean themselves, and seek intimacy through their children. Reversing another sexist Freudian commonplace, Chodorow sees men as the narcissistic sex who don't truly love others. Nonetheless, her theory optimistically showed how the change to a better society could be accomplished, through one comprehensible alteration—involving men in child care—and this was a change that allowed women to stay as they had been in terms of character while expanding their opportunities and choices. However, *men* would have to change their characters and assume tasks they had previously shunned as boring and onerous. As extended by other theorists like psychologist Carol Gilligan, such cultural feminist theories redeemed women's morality—their "different voices"—from the charge of ethical inferiority.

Although Chodorow's 1978 book is usually considered as a contribution to "mothering" theory, it makes fathers central to changing polarized gender as it now exists, less by changing their minds than by changing their practice. As we have seen, Chodorow argued that boys who identify their masculinity with individually known fathers will be more flexible than those who have only cultural stereotypes to rely on, a view now made problematic when Chodorow cites studies that claim fathers gender children more traditionally than mothers do, so that presumably mother-raised children would be less gender-polarized. Fathers collude, she says, with the dominant culture in preferring their sons to their daughters, in forming more intense bonds with sons, and in representing themselves to their children as more special, powerful, and exciting than mothers are (Femininities 58). Would more father time, then, mean firmer gendering along the old lines, which is what some of the new men's movement leaders seem to want? Are there advantages for women, as sociologist Miriam Johnson believes, in father absence?

Chodorow's 1978 theories drew criticism from some other feminists. It was not clear if the mother-present, father-distant family that Chodorow presumes as her model always produced the same effects of male dominance or did so only when the mother and the larger society colluded with this ideology. Should feminists be working toward more egalitarian male and female roles in all spheres or would involving more fathers in childrearing in itself transform all other social institutions? Historian Joan Scott complained that Chodorow's "interpretation limits the concept of gender to family and household experience and, for the historian, leaves no way to connect the concept (or the individual) to other social systems of economics, politics, or power" (38). According to Chodorow, changing male dominance in the future required changing men's behavior now, through shared parenting; however, men who are good parents are already unlike her stereotype of cold, rigid masculinity, and the stereotypical macho men, on the other hand, would presumably not be likely to agree to fifty percent childcare and would not do it empathically, even if all their jobs could be rearranged to make it possible. Radical feminist Pauline Bart, for example, used to say that Chodorow described men as so emotionally unfit for parenting that no reasonable mother would want to turn her children over to them.

Despite these criticisms, Chodorow's theories were very powerful, and many men attempted to understand their implications and implement their precepts. Isaac Balbus's 1982 book, *Marxism and Domination: A Neo-Hegelian, Feminist, Psychoanalytic Theory of Sexual, Political, and Technological Liberation*, focused on the damaging effects of "mother-monopolized" childrearing to men and to society and took to heart the prescription for joint parenting. The theories of Sigmund Freud and Karl Marx, Balbus decided, were inferior for understanding the injustices of patriarchy in comparison to Chodorow's and Dorothy Dinnerstein's analysis, and he announced his commitment to use these feminists' theories for personal change and for the broader changes necessary to bring about a transformed society:

> As I became increasingly aware of the extent to which my own tendencies both to exercise and acquiesce in domination in my relationships with women, friends, and the "world" were rooted in the nature of my relationship with my mother, the plausibility of a theory that locates mother-dominated child rearing as a central source of sexual, political, and technological domination likewise increased. This theory, in turn, enhanced considerably my understanding of the roots of domination in my personal life and thus my struggle against it (xii).

Balbus declared that "the feminist, participatory democratic, and alternative technology struggles are, at bottom, one struggle, the struggle to establish simultaneously intimate and autonomous relationships between ourselves and our world" and that the way to implement this movement was to "replace mother-monopolized child rearing with forms of shared parenting that encourage" new, more egalitarian character structures in both men and women (354). He put the responsibility for change primarily on men: "in the short run, it is up to the male participants in ecology and participatory democracy who do pay lip service to feminist principles to do whatever they can to make their practice consistent with these principles. They must learn from the women . . ." (397). Although therapy and men's groups would help, he conceded, "we will never be able entirely to undo the misogynist effects of our mother-monopolized child rearing" and so must transform current childcare practices in order to "create authentic forms of shared parenting" (397). Balbus's expectations for the current generation of men were limited; he had much more enthusiasm for future generations. As in Chodorow, shared childrearing can replace the neurotic and sexist present with an androgynous future in which the absence of gender polarity will give each person the advantages of both current genders without their negative qualities. In Balbus's words, "the men and women who emerge from shared parenting, then, will be equally prepared emotionally" for intimacy and autonomy, that is, for participation both in public and in private life: "shared parenting thus holds the key to the liberation of the relations between the sexes" (312). More recently, Balbus has written persuasively of his efforts to put his theories into practice through co-parenting his own daughter (Balbus forthcoming).

In the years since Chodorow's and Balbus's first books, both facts and theories have changed, though the progressive transformations they urged may now seem farther away rather than closer to hand. Now, both fathers and mothers may well be absent and heavily involved in work outside the home, so that overinvolved mothers may be less frequent. Now only a small minority of U.S. families consist of working father, homemaker mother, and children at home. With about half of American marriages ending in divorce, it is also likely that many fathers will be so disparaged or distant as to be hard to idealize, and the isolated nuclear family on which these descriptions depend has expanded as well as fragmented to include stepparents, parents' lovers, grandparents, and babysitters, all complicating the emotional lives of children (Sidel 42–44). Fathers' situations have also become more diverse: at home unemployed or logged on to a home computer or working sporadically or swingshift; traditionally absent on the job but idealizable; long gone in situations provoking anger rather than idealization; or replaced by a stepfather or mother's male or female partners. Stepfathers now spend more time with their wives' children than with their own, so that fathering as well as romance appears to follow the tune, "if you can't be with the one you love, love the one you're with."

Chodorow's writings of the 1990s modify her earlier views, defining masculinities, femininities, and sexualities more multiply and seeing many possible responses by individuals to their early childrearing. Rather than having two master narratives of male and female development, Chodorow now agrees with the postmodernists that "we probably need a cultural and individual developmental story to account for" each and every person's erotic choices and the meanings they give to gender (Femininities 37). Yet Chodorow's earlier ideas, like those of Dinnerstein on the baleful social effects of mother-dominated childrearing, continue to be influential, with feminist women and men often regarding gender-egalitarian parenting as an ideal to which they aspire, despite practical difficulties, and some actually trying to put it into practice.

Many other male theorists continue to accept Chodorow's 1978 views about the complementarity of male and female personality structures and the necessity for men to break the female monopoly on childrearing. For example, in a 1986 book entitled *How Men Feel*, Anthony Astrachan chronicled men's increasing support for "active fathering," though he admits that patriarchy remains intact: "we're still a long way, however, from the change that will mark the real victory of the revolution: the day when men do half the work of child raising" (401). In 1996 Michael Kimmel and Michael Kaufman were explicit about their feminist sources: "following Chodorow, Dinnerstein, Rubin, Benjamin and others," they wrote, "we think that the core psychological problem of gender formation for men is, in a sense, not too little separation from mother but too much" (26). They believe that manhood is currently defined to men's detriment as the flight from femininity, compassion, nurturance, affection, and dependence, and that men's rage at their own dependence and weakness results in antagonism to women and gay men and in high-risk behavior to themselves. They contrast themselves with the mythopoetic men's movement of Robert Bly who, they think, sees the "root psychological problem" of men as the failure to "cut our psychic umbilical cord," whereas they believe, with Chodorow, that the solution is "equal and shared parenting" and also sharing women's other traditional tasks. Men's lost emotions are not to be found playing drums in the woods, they say, but in the "simple drudgery of everyday life in the home": "we need more Ironing Johns, not more Iron Johns," they quip (27).

Other male profeminists justify their predilection toward joint parenting less on separation from the mother and more on the absence of the father in boys' lives, an absence that haunts the mythopoetic men's movement and about which a significant empirical literature has now accumulated. Most of this social science literature correlates negative outcomes like criminality, early school leaving, and low lifetime income with boy's childhoods in father-absent families—not the middle class white family Chodorow described where father is in the office all day while mom stays home, but more frequently the poor family of color headed by an unmarried mother. Here researchers are becoming more specific about their claims. Much research confirms father-absence as one of the variables that correlates with psychological, academic, and behavioral difficulties among boys in the United States and elsewhere, along with such demographic factors as minority and low socioeconomic status (Beaty, Lavigne, Mott). Using data from the National Survey of Youth, F. S. Wade found that white fathers are less likely to leave a home if they sons rather than daughters and that female-headed households disadvantage boys. Father absence in national U.S. data is consistently associated with the impoverishment of children (Piroggood, Sidel). On the other hand, current studies of African-American youth in single-mother households challenge the assumptions that nonresident fathers have no significant relationship with their children (Zimmerman, Wade) and find that positive relationships with the mother attenuate the risks associated with father absence (Mason). Radical profeminist John Stoltenberg says that social prejudice against single mothers is unjustified and that fathers are only necessary for instilling a kind of manhood in boys that they are better off without, because the only things men can teach their sons better than mothers can are the "gendered survival skills" of avoiding the dangers posed by other men (81). Instead, true affirming of the boy's self can be provided—in his words—by "any concerned and present grownup—someone born penised as well as the human who gave the child birth" (81). In 1985 James Q. Wilson and Richard J. Herrnstein judged that the data on father absence was contradictory and that it confused many variables. For example, father-absent children living with aunts and grandmothers as well as mothers did better than children living with mothers alone, so that maternal overload rather than paternal absence may have been the problem. They concluded that "the role of the father in raising children has been the subject of so little systematic inquiry that we have little more than guesswork" (252). Ten years later, Ruth Sidel critiques the biased treatment of father-absent families in academic and popular discourse, asking, "why should single-parent families be compared only to ideal two-parent families?" (47).

Not surprisingly, profeminist men use theories and empirical studies about mother-dominated childrearing in a manner more amenable to feminist thought than do the mythopoetic men's movement or conservative social scientists. Those who build on Chodorow's premises broaden their prescriptions from joint childrearing to institutional and social change. For example, Michael Messner says it doesn't matter "which parent parents" so long as every child gets adequate loving attention, and he cites studies of dual career families that focus not on their psychological structures but on the "rational and constant negotiations" necessary to maintain careers and family simultaneously (101). He points out that such dual careers are often a class privilege of the wealthy, who resort to paid childcare provided by poor women, often immigrants and women of color, rather than dividing it equally between husband and wife. Thus the so-called egalitaritan family is "premised on the continued existence of *social inequality*" (101). He is also skeptical about some claims that changing the configuration of masculinity will strike down patriarchy, particularly the idea that making men more emotionally expressive will solve social injustice. He thinks it naive to assume that men who express their feelings openly will refrain from dominating women and children: "the idea that men's 'need' to dominate others is the result of an emotional deficit overly psychologizes a reality that is largely structural" (105), he avers, and describes the televised Gulf War general shedding tears for those killed in battle—and continuing the battle. "We are witnessing . . . a shift in personal styles and lifestyles of privileged men" who want an emotionally fuller life and greater closeness to their children, he believes, not a divestiture of male power (101).

Kenneth Clatterbaugh says that men's rights and mythopoetic men's movements both stress the importance of fathers and decry their absence but "never explore the possibility that low income or failure of the father to visit or pay support is a major cause of troubles that beset children in single parent homes" (55). Bob Connell also relates the psychological results of family structure to a larger social and economic context. To transform the emotional structures of masculinity, he says, "is inherently a collective project" that must involve social action and the transformation of institutions. Citing feminist psychoanalytic and "mothering" theorists, he agrees that the emotional tensions of masculinity grow from particular family structures but proposes a "modest agenda" for change that includes not only shared childcare but also men's support for women's control over their own bodies, pay equity, equal job and educational opportunities, the discrediting of male violence, and the redistribution of wealth—in other words, a major social revolution (87). Such a political agenda, he believes, would eventually resolve the emotional contradictions of contemporary masculinity but be "highly stressful" for men in the short run (88). It would require heterosexual men to act against their own immediate interests and so face internal guilt, fatigue, women's suspicions, and men's hostilities, which he acknowledges may not be a very inviting prospect to them.

Thus a popular consensus has developed around the idea that American fatherhood is in crisis, with alarmed reports about irresponsible and abandoning fathers of every race and class. Johnson finds the decline of the father-headed household a potentially progressive tendency that decreases patriarchal power, but many other observers decry absent fathers and see impaired relations between fathers and, particularly, their sons as widespread and destructive. Men's movements such as the Christian traditionalist Promise Keepers and the 1995 African-American Million Man March to Washington pledge to reform men's behavior to women and children as a step toward enhancing their own self esteem as well as toward fighting injustice and inequality.

Some male advocates of shared parenting seek to give fathers more importance in order to make men's lives more fulfilling and to distribute tasks, and ultimately personality structures, more equitably. Other advocates use the same feminist psychological premises to reassert the value of traditional masculinity or to inveigh against feminism. So former profeminist Warren Farrell contends that eighty percent of men tell him they would choose to parent full time up to a year after the birth of a child if their wives and incomes didn't suffer, but that now male hard work and time away from children deserve recompense in higher pay and more male privilege (34). Fathers' absence from their sons' lives also haunts the mythopoetic men's movement, which guides men toward older male mentors. Farrell, a men's movement spokesman against what he now sees as the errors of feminism, says, "for thousands of years, . . . the woman raised the children and the man raised the money" (21). He believes changes are necessary in the present, including giving fathers greater power over their children, and, especially, greater access in cases of divorce. Feminism, once a force for good, has become totalitarian, as far as Farrell is concerned: "like communism, feminism went from being revolutionary to dictating politically correct ideology," he claims (372). Current federal programs exclude men from the lives of poor women and children so that the "new nuclear family" consists of "woman, government, and child" (376). The result, he claims, is that "a father's absence in the family is the single biggest predictor of a child's deterioration. Why? a father's absence appears to damage what might be called the child's 'social immune system'" (376). At the other end of the social spectrum, the men's movement focuses on fathers' access to their children, and men's weekends explore "'the two Fs'—fathering and feelings. But as men discover they've been deprived *of* their fathers, they start asking if they are also being deprived of *being* fathers" (393). Farrell contends that "fathers today are often being taxed for their children without equal representation in their children's lives. They are experiencing their version of 'Taxation Without Representation'" (398). Clearly from this rhetoric, a revolutionary change is needed to restore the balance: "a father's first right—fathering" means "sharing child care while his wife does her financial share" (394).

The literature on fatherhood continues to be contradictory. Whereas Chodorow recommended increased paternal participation in child rearing and other authorities claim it is occurring, Kimmel reports that the time American fathers spend with their children has been continuously *decreasing*, declining from two hours daily between the wars to under twenty minutes a day in 1987 at the same time that fathers now indulge in "increasingly heated rhetoric about how much they want to be involved" with their children (306).

Ross D. Parke opens a recent handbook on *Fatherhood* by saying, "traditionally, fathers have been portrayed as uninvolved in child-care," but they are now more frequently "active partners" in parenting (1–2). However, he admits that the actual change is less than the popular images. Some of his reports on recent social science research confirm Chodorow's belief in the values to children of active fathering. Thus he says that the most powerful predictor of empathy in adults is "paternal child-rearing involvement at age five," and people who experienced "paternal warmth" as children reportedly had better adult social relationships than those who did not (146). However, the fathers who claimed to share parenting equitably did not usually succeed in following through. In one study of parents who attempted role sharing, only one fourth maintained the same balance after two years (238). Furthermore, Parke notes the drastic decrease in fathering that accompanies divorce. In the United States in the 1990s, sixty percent of divorces involve children, and only ten percent of these children live with their fathers (179). Negative effects on children, especially boys, after divorce are well documented. Parke believes that "boys suffered more than girls as a result of divorce and the accompanying loss of the father as a live-in parent" (185), and he summarizes the grim statistics on father-child loss of contact after divorce. In various studies of non-custodial fathers, only one-fifth continued regular visitation of their children after two years; half lessened their visits during this period; and up to a third had no contact at all (194). Parke concedes that it is difficult to improve men's level of involvement with their children when they do not live with them, and he thinks more men speak of the importance of fathering than perform it well. Nevertheless, he concludes that "children need their fathers, but fathers need their children, too" (257).

The need of fathers for their children is at the center of Edward Kruk's surprising book, *Divorce and Disengagement: Patterns of Fatherhood Within and Beyond Marriage*, 1993, based on interviews with divorced Canadian and British fathers who were not the custodians of the children from their dissolved marriages. Kruk cites studies showing that men's psychological involvement with their families is now greater than with their work and that men are increasing their child care time and attention while married (12–13). His sample of fathers described themselves "as highly emotionally attached to their children during the marriage," whether or not they did primary child care (19). They claimed both they and their former wives esteemed them as good fathers while their marriages lasted. Kruk divided his noncustodial fathers into two groups. The first group was made up of those "androgynous" fathers who believed there should be no differences between the roles of father and mother in caring for children, a view closely conforming with the prescriptions by Chodorow and other feminist theorists in favor of joint parenting. The second group included "traditional" fathers who saw fathering as different from mothering—more distant and authoritarian, less concerned with the daily feeding, diaper-changing, and caretaking of children. Kruk's startling finding was that the traditional fathers fared better as noncustodial fathers than the egalitarian ones did. The traditional fathers adapted reasonably well to being "visiting fathers," often at first as "Santa Claus" fathers bringing presents, then settling into a new, more avuncular role with their children (27). These fathers often developed closer relationships with their children after divorce than they had during marriage because they were forced to be more fully responsible for their children in the time allocated to them. In contrast, those fathers who had been more egalitarian and more involved with their children during their marriages were the most bereaved at the loss of their children when the marriages dissolved. Despite their claims of closeness with their children, they were more likely than the traditional fathers to lose contact with their children entirely after the divorce. For these men, the sense of being deprived of their father role lead to further distance from their children. Kruk explains that these fathers were "overwhelmed by feelings of loss for their children and by a sense of devaluation as parents" (27). Many of them "reported that they could not tolerate the pain of only intermittently seeing their children" so they withdrew completely (28). Well over half reported pronounced symptoms of stress, including fatigue, alcohol abuse, and depression, but most of the men with severe symptoms sought no help and tried to achieve self-sufficiency and isolation instead (30). "In sum," says Kruk, "the most salient characteristic of the divorce experience of non-custodial fathers in general is the fact that the great majority of fathers ... experience a bereavement" that includes physical and mental health problems (49). Yet even more striking is his finding of "a strong *inverse* relationship" between closeness with the children before and after the divorce. Those "androgynous" fathers who consistently reported higher levels of "pre-divorce involvement with, attachment to, and influence on their children" than traditional fathers "were more likely to have *lost* contact with their children after divorce than fathers who had defined themselves in a more traditional manner" (60, 51).

Such loss of contact could not be explained by physical distance, money, or work schedules. Nor, according to the fathers, to indifference, since they manifested the symptoms of unresolved bereavement and "chronic grief" (67). These "disengaged fathers" felt "devalued as parents," "rootless ... anxious, helpless, and depressed" (87). Kruk quotes one father as saying, "I feel numb, I don't feel anything anymore" (88), yet one hundred percent of these "disengaged" fathers said they wanted "a lot more" contact with their children than they actually had; the "disengaged fathers yearned for the children with whom they were no longer in contact" (81). Kruk prescribes joint custody as a remedy for these fathers and as preferable for their children. "For these fathers," he claims, a visiting relationship or "limited access does not allow sufficient opportunity for the variety and richness of contact that is necessary to sustain complex family relationships" (125). That is, like Chodorow, he proselytizes for the benefits to children of joint parenting, though in this case fathering would be serial rather than simultaneous with mothering attention. Kruk also suggests a number of social remedies, including publically funded child care and education for fatherhood, to improve fathers' contacts with their children.

These current studies of fathering, then, return me to the contradictions and criticisms originally leveled against Chodorow. A few feminists faulted her prescription for joint parenting, we saw, for being isolated from other social forces and thus impractical, and for depending on untransformed men to behave toward their children in a nurturant manner alien to their masculine personalities. I interpret the current reports about divorced fathers, as well as the evidence I've seen in my male friends' lives, as indicating both some of the limitations implicit in feminist mothering theory and some of the strengths that indicate the theory should still be built upon rather than abandoned.

Kruk's more involved dads, those who shared parenting and believed mothering and fathering were the same thing, were devastated by separation from their children, like some of my male friends. Chodorow speaks of the benefits to children of shared parenting, and she details the satisfactions that women derive from infant care through reliving their unconscious early bonds with their own mothers. In her theory, men don't "mother" children because their psychological structures have formed in differentiation from their mothers and in fear and resentment of dependency. Chodorow asks fathers to parent but doesn't say much about the psychological effects on those who do. I suspect several things. First, I think male disinclination to parent is often a fear, not just of identifying and merging with the remembered mother but of identifying and merging with the infant's frightening dependency. It may also be a fear of being inadequate to deal with the child's demands and needs. That is, today's American fathers may take on an array of traditionally feminine competences and demands but don't subtract the traditionally masculine ones. Now they're supposed to be intimate and engaged with their infants, and infants are indeed engaging. The fathers who do daily care, changing diapers and feeding their children, feel themselves relied on, not merely as occasional exciting visitors, and they become intimately attached to their children. Their feelings that they are good fathers, reflected by Kruk's interviews, may enhance their own esteem and sense of accomplishment. These days being an involved dad is nothing to be ashamed of, and the father seen pushing a stroller through the park or taking a toddler to the doctor's office is likely to attract admiration, not condemnation, from others.

Given today's fragile job structure, polarizing economy, distance from kin, and increasing isolation from coworkers and neighbors, it is likely that many men are putting more of their emotional eggs in the children's bassinette, becoming deeply if inarticulately attached to their children at the same time that they preserve the sense that their duty is to protect the children, not to depend on them emotionally. Yet when separated from the children, apparently this all goes into reverse. By definition the men who had been good fathers have become bad fathers, unable to protect their children from the pain of separation that they themselves feel. They also cannot protect themselves from the loss of their most precious self-extensions and their main sources of nonsexual, physical warmth and pleasure, generous and sensous delight. These may be men for whom the only intimate ties are with women and children. Separated from women's warmth and approval, they often become angry and lash out, a response society will condemn but understand. However, they can't usually allow themselves to get mad at their children, at least not the youngest ones. Their suppressed anger becomes depression; they feel self-doubt and failure as they lose both their own sense of competence and their new emotional closeness to their children. These men were more deeply attached to their children than feminist "mothering" theories predicted, yet they were not, despite Kruk's label, "androgynous" people themselves. Instead, these fathers retained many features of traditional masculinity—not the fixed ego boundaries and competitiveness Chodorow mentioned but inexpressivity to adults and an unwillingness to seek help or admit weakness or failure. Thus there were profound disjunctions among their interdependence with their infants, their own reawakened dependency needs, and their inability to show or fulfill these needs when deprived of intimate access to their children and of the social sanction of marriage or custody. Legally losing claim to their children, they felt roleless, childless, less manly, grieving, and depressed, but tried to keep up the calm demeanors that led their ex-wives, officials, and perhaps their children to feel that they were cold and indifferent about their children.

Chodorow's critics were correct in seeing that today's men would have difficulties being fully co-parenting fathers. Yet many men have succeeded in becoming involved fathers as long as their role is supported by the women and children in their lives as well. When these positive sanctions are withdrawn, when ex-wives are hostile, when their children question their authority or lash out against them or wallow in the misery the fathers themselves feel, many of these men withdraw rather than persist. Then anti-feminist men's movements pick up these men's anger and blame women for depriving men of their children.

Thus feminist "mothering" theories might be modified to fit current situations. Shared parenting for children in families defined by traditional, stable heterosexual relationships is fine, but there are lots of other possibilities. Many forces other than feminism helped achieve the feminist goals of disrupting traditional marriage and the patriarchal nuclear family, although without providing the substitutes pioneered by my commune-dwelling friends, and we feminists have sometimes joined others in condemning those men who broke off ties to their children, seeing them exclusively as perpetrators of harm to children without challenging their facades of independence, indifference, or anger.

Feminism has consistently rejected the premise that women are like children, dependents needing governance. Conservatives, in contrast, continue to see women as similar to children in needing patriarchal authority and protection. Now may be a good time for feminists to move from the recognition of women's and men's adult autonomy to a reconsideration of the special status of children. I think my communard friends were right in trying to provide alternatives to the nuclear family and traditional marriage, but as contemporary American society continues to privatize, we may need to reconsider the responsibilities to children of their parents, other concerned adults, and the society at large. Such responsibilities will entail supporting public and private institutions like childcare facilities but also rethinking practical ideals and standards for single as well as coupled parenting.

The Second Wave feminist revaluation of mothering has been valuable, and it has validated and inspired more active fathering. However, Chodorow's feminist critics were also correct in seeing contradictions in a parenting theory that assumed today's men could smoothly bring up tomorrow's nonsexist children. Feminist mothering theory helped inspire a change in many men's lives that has enriched their emotional experience and that may lead to a more egalitarian future. Those skeptics about the new fatherhood who say most men want personal enrichment, not the overthrow of patriarchy, are probably right, but shared parenting is still likely to be good for women and children as well, and feminists are discovering that it is hard to motivate change if it appears solely to take men's privileges away without providing alternative compensations. Shared parenting is a feminist goal that can also reward men. Feminist mothering theory plotted out the first stage of this transformation, but it has not yet fully developed its proposals in the light of what men are currently finding in their own lives as fathers, single and married, custodial and separated, gay and straight.

Shared parenting is unlikely to be the one change that precipitates all other changes in the construction of gender, particularly since it cannot occur unless jobs, families, and people's minds and priorities are also changed, and the complexities of contemporary adult sexual life also render both parents' relationships to their children and to each other complicated. However, an increased emphasis on fathers' roles need not demean mothers' capacities to bring up children but rather stress the advantages to fathers as well as their children of more stable and affectionate contact, whatever their relationship to the children's mothers. I think that feminists were right to want increased men's participation in infant and child care, for daughters as well as sons, even if such child-care practices will not solve all social ills. Moreover, I suggest that time and money should not be allowed to substitute for one another: children deserve both from both parents, and they deserve continuing relationships with all living stepparents and extended family who take on their care. Conversely, although some men's movement spokesmen unfairly blame feminists for all failures in men's fathering, I agree with them that women have a reciprocal obligation to allow children continuing access to all non-abusive fathers and stepfathers. Child support might be enforced independently from custody, and separated parents should not triangulate their own needs and angers through their children. In short, to stop the patriarchal reproduction of mothering, I suggest, we need to assist a new feminist future for fathering.

Acknowledgments

This essay is part of a manuscript on "Masculinity in Feminist Theory," which has been supported by the Institute for the Humanities at the University of Illinois at Chicago and by a research residency in Bellagio, Italy, sponsored by the Rockefeller Foundation. For helpful responses to this project, I wish to thank Jonathan Arac, Isaac Balbus, Tom Digby, Leah Marcus, Sonya Michel, Marianne Novy, and audiences at the Universities of Illinois at Chicago, Illinois at Urbana, Pittsburgh, and Texas, at Northwestern University, and at conferences of the American Men's Studies Association and the Radical Philosophy Association.

Bibliography

Astrachan, Anthony. 1986. *How Men Feel: Their Response to Women's Demands for Equality and Power*. Garden City NY: Anchor Books/Doubleday.

Balbus, Isaac D. 1982. *Marxism and Domination: A Neo-Hegelian, Feminist, Psychoanalytic Theory of Sexual, Political, and Technological Liberation*. Princeton: Princeton University Press.

Balbus, Isaac D. Forthcoming 1998. *Emotional Rescue: A Story of the Theory and Practice of Parenting*. New York: Routledge.

Bart, Pauline. Personal communication. Also see her 1984 "Review of Chodorow's *The Reproduction of Mothering: Essays in Feminist Theory*. Ed by Joyce Trebilcot. Totowa, New Jersey: Rowman & Allanheld. 147–52.

Beaty, L. A. "Effects of Paternal Absence on Male Adolescents' Peer Relations and Self-Image," *Adolescence*. 30.120 (Winter 1995), 873–80.

Bly, Robert. 1990. *Iron John: A Book About Men*. Reading, Mass.: Addison-Wesley.

Chodorow, Nancy. 1994. *Femininities, Masculinities, Sexualities: Freud and Beyond*. Lexington: University Press of Kentucky.

Chodorow, Nancy. 1978. *The Reproduction of Mothering: Psychoanalysis and the Sociology of Gender*, Berkeley and Los Angeles: University of California Press.

Christian, Harry. 1994. *The Making of Anti-Sexist Men*. New York and London: Routledge.

Clatterbaugh, Kenneth. 1995. "Mythopoetic Foundations and New Age Patriarchy," in Michael S. Kimmel, ed. *The Politics of Manhood: Profeminist Men Respond to the Mythopoetic Men's Movement (and the Mythopoetic Leaders Answer)*. Philadelphia: Temple University Press, pp. 44–63.

Connell, Bob. 1996. "Men at Bay: The "Men's Movement" and Its Newest Best-Sellers," in Kimmel, pp. 75–88.

Dinnerstein, Dorothy, 1976. *The Mermaid and the Minotaur: Sexual Arrangements and Human Malaise*. New York: Harper and Row.

Farrell, Warren. 1996, c. 1993. *The Myth of Male Power*. New York: Berkley Books.

Gilligan, Carol. 1982. *In a Different Voice: Psychological Theory and Women's Development*. Cambridge, Mass.: Harvard University Press.

Johnson, Miriam. 1988. *Strong Mothers/ Weak Wives: The Search for Gender Equality*. Berkeley: University of California Press.

Kimmel, Michael S., and Michael Kaufman. 1995. "Weekend Warriors: The New Men's Movement," in Michael S. Kimmel, ed. *The Politics of Manhood: Profeminist Men Respond to the Mythopoetic Men's Movement (and the Mythopoetic Leaders Answer)*. Philadelphia: Temple University Press, pp. 16–43.

Kimmel, Michael S. 1996. *Manhood in America: A Cultural History*. New York: Free Press.

Kruk, Edward. 1993. *Divorce and Disengagement*. Halifax: Fernwood Publishing.

Lavigne, J. V., et al., "Prevalence Rates and Correlates of Psychiatric Disorders among Preschool Children," *Journal of the American Academy of Child and Adolescent Psychiatry*. 35.2 (Feb. 1996), 204–14.

Mason, C. A. *et al*. "The Effect of Peers and the Moderating Role of Father Absence and the Mother-Child Relationship," *American Journal of Community Psychology*. 22.6 (Dec. 1994), 723–43.

Messner, Michael A. 1996. "'Changing Men' and Feminist Politics in the United States," in Kimmel, pp. 97–111.

Mott, F. L. "Sons, Daughters, and Fathers' Absence: Differentials in Father-Leaving Probabilities and in Home Environments," *Journal of Family Issues*. 15.1 (March 1994), 97–128.

Parke, Ross D. 1996. *Fatherhood*. Cambridge, Mass and London: Harvard University Press.

Piroggood, M.A., and D. H. Good. "Child Support Enforcement for Teenage Fathers: Problems and Prospects," *Journal of Policy Analysis and Management*. 14.1 (Winter 1995), 25–42.

Scott, Joan Wallach. 1988. *Gender and the Politics of History*. New York: Columbia University Press.

Sidel, Ruth. 1996. *Keeping Women and Children Last: America's War on the Poor*. New York: Penguin Books.

Stoltenberg, John. 1989. *Refusing to Be a Man: Essays on Sex and Justice*. Portland: Breitenbush Books.

Wade, J. C. "African American Fathers and Sons—Social, Historical, and Psychological Considerations," *Families in Society: The Journal of Contemporary Human Services*. 75.9 (Nov. 1994), 561–70.

Wilson, James Q., and Richard J. Herrnstein. 1985. *Crime and Human Nature*. New York: Touchstone/ Simon and Schuster.

Zimmerman, M. A., D. A. Salem, K. I. Maton, "Family Structure and Psychosocial Correlates among Urban African-American Adolescent Males," *Child Development*. 66.6 (Dec. 1995), 1598–1613.

Chapter 14

A New Response to "Angry Black (Anti)Feminists": Reclaiming Feminist Forefathers, Becoming Womanist Sons

Gary Lemons

Revisiting "The Black Sexism Debate"

Since 1979, when *The Black Scholar* published "The Black Sexism Debate," controversy continues to rage around the idea of *black* feminism. Black antifeminist men have charged black women feminists with creating a racial/gender rift between black men and women, arising from the feminist positionality they have claimed. Thus, black feminist women have been accused of such Machiavellian plots as conspiring with white feminists against black men, with promoting lesbianism, and selling out black struggle against racism (a move tantamount to black cultural genocide). Stated another way, the single most virulent critique of black women in feminist movement has come with the perception by some black men that "feminism" is itself a racist ideology solely fixed in a man-hating ideology ultimately leading to the castration and "feminization" of all black men.

It was Robert Staples' "The Myth of Black Macho: A Response to Angry Black Feminists," appearing in the March/April 1979 issue of *The Black Scholar*, which declared a black male antifeminist stance that framed the parameters for a "debate on black sexism" (published in the following issue of the same journal). The Staples article, nothing short of a diatribe against Michele Wallace and Ntozake Shange, couched itself as a "response to angry black feminists"—stating that:

> Since white feminists could not marshal an all-out attack on black males, and well-known black female activists such as Joyce Ladner and Angela

Davis would not, how could they be put in their place. Enter Ntozake Shange and Michele Wallace. (24)

This statement, in tandem with those that defined Staples' anti-feminist position, prompted (upon the essay's publication) an outpouring of response to Staples from black women and men. In reaction, *The Black Scholar* reconstructed these responses in the form of a "Reader Forum" under the aforementioned title. Bringing together commentaries of twenty-three respondents[1] (and a rejoinder by Staples) on the essay's polemics, the editors stated:

> We are now entering a phase in which the oppression of women by men, and all aspects of that sexism, is the subject of considerable criticism and analysis by the women's movement. Black feminists have raised just criticisms of black male sexism, and this has strengthened the understanding of conscientious black men and women who seek to improve not only the collective black human condition, but the quality of their lives in terms of their individual personal relationships. We believe that the effort to clarify the nature of black male/female relationships is an important step in the process of re-uniting our people and revitalizing the struggle against oppression. (Quoted from the editorial statement, "The Black Sexism Debate.")

Considering the continued sexual abuse, exploitation, racist, and sexist oppression of black women in the U.S.—"conscientious" black women in feminist movement have confronted sexism and sexist practice in and outside black communities. Those black men in the 1979 "debate" who wrote in solidarity with black women against black antifeminist ideology must today be joined by those of us black men who declare ourselves in feminist alliance with black women—writing, speaking, and acting in comradeship against women's oppression. We must critique sexism perpetrated by black men (as well as other men)—calling out sexism and misogynist behavior wherever we encounter it.

While my objective here is not to give a full reading to the commentary of the Reader Forum respondents, I believe it necessary to reclaim the courageous words of one black male respondent—Kalamu ya Salaam who wrote:

> The facts of life are that African-American women are more economically exploited than our men, white women/or white men. Additionally, our women face a sexist discrimination, exploitation and harassment which our men do not. To deny these facts only aids in perpetuating sexism as we can not eradicate it or its effects and influences until we face and fight sexism head on.

Acknowledging the often complicitous relation between black sexism and white supremacy in the oppression of black women, Salaam resists the idea that black men cannot be sexist because we have no power to institutionalize sexism.

> It is equally inappropriate and down-right reactionary to resist the criticism that we African-American men have generally adopted a sexist outlook and behavior vis-à-vis our women. Our lack of the power to institutionalize sexism means little because *sexism is already embedded into nearly every institution in America. Regardless of our lack of power, the fact is that we routinely act our sexist behavior* (my emphasis) and the controllers of society at large condone, seldom punish and even sometimes reward such sexist behavior. . . . (21)

I respond to Salaam's words as a contemporary call for black men to recognize and resist sexism as a misogynist weapon employed to dehumanize all women. I hear his words as an echo of W.E.B. DuBois' exhortation to black men of his time to take up the cause of woman suffrage and women's rights. For those of us black men already committed to feminist movement, we must begin a more vocal and demonstrative declaration of a "pro-womanist" stand (a term I will use interchangeably with the phrase "black [male] feminist positionality" throughout this study to name a relationship of women's rights advocacy articulated by black men in the first, second, and present stage of U.S. feminist movement). I do, however, view the term "womanism" in nuanced relationship to "feminism." Evoking Alice Walker's name for the self-autonomized position occupied by black women and other women of color (see *In Search of Our Mothers' Gardens*), I apply it to the pro-woman writings of W.E.B. DuBois. As a race-specific representation of feminism, I believe "womanism" more closely approximates the Africanist vision of womanhood he defended.

Whether we name ourselves in solidarity with "feminism" or "womanism," collectively, black men must—as did black men in the woman suffrage movement—actively combat antifeminist thinking that privileges anti-racist work over women's struggle to end sexual oppression. As we know, sexism in the black power movement of the 1960s represented itself as a political move to "regain black manhood" to the exclusion of black *women's* struggle in the cause of black liberation. The movement reduced the place of black women in the struggle to the identical position they occupy in white supremacist capitalist patriarchy. Toward a new gender/race politic in black communities, we must work to eradicate the notion that black women (and men) active in feminism is synonymous with the emasculation of black men. Only when we begin to acknowledge the dehumanizing effects of sexism and misogyny on women, children, and ourselves can we participate in a life-affirming dialogue with black women to strategize an end to female oppression. Coming to recognize, as Kalamu Ya Salaam maintained, that—even as we struggle against our racial oppression—we possess power as *men* in a culture driven by patriarchal hegemony.

Contrary to popular black antifeminist belief, feminism conceived by black women has never been rooted in anti-male rhetoric, theory, or practice—nor has it ever been antithetical to the struggle against racism. Black men acknowledging this enables transformed thinking, where the narrow identity politics of male-centered black nationalism is displaced and disavowed. When we begin strategizing ways to end sexism, we bring about a form of self-healing that promotes a liberatory gender healing that affects all (black) women and men.

I employ the stated objectives of "The Black Sexism Debate" as the central premise upon which this study rests—that "[b]lack feminists have raised just criticisms of black male sexism . . . to improve . . . the collective black human condition . . . to clarify the nature of black male/female relationships . . . in the process of re-uniting our people and revitalizing the struggle against oppression." Today, nearly twenty years after "The Debate," the need still exists (perhaps more than before)—not just to discuss black sexism, but to create a dialogue of intervention. We need to return to the debate—critically dialoguing on the necessity of feminist agency in black communities and the primacy of feminist movement in the liberation of all black people.

Thinking about the editorial commentary *The Black Scholar* set in place to frame "The Black Sexism Debate," during the second wave of U.S. feminist movement, I am compelled to ponder its contemporary implications. Anti-racist activism conceived by many black men in the nineteenth century fostered the idea that the eradication of racism could not be fought solely in terms of racial stratagems. Along with Frederick Douglass, many other black men (including Martin Delany, Charles Lenox Redmond, James Forten, Jr. and Sr., Robert Purvis, William Whipper, Alonzo Ranzier, William Henry Johnson, and Alexander Crummell) perceived black women's issues in the black liberation movement to be a priority, believing that they too had to rally around them, understanding the fact that black women had to battle both racism and sexism. In 1910, as editor of *The Crisis*, W.E.B. DuBois ran a forum on woman suffrage. "[I]t was," he declared, "to be regarded as one of the strongest cumulative attacks on sex and race discrimination in politics ever written" (vol. 10, 177). Representing black men of distinction in religion, law, government, politics, and literature, pro-woman suffragists included Bishop John Hurst, Reverend Francis J. Grimke (who officiated in the wedding of Frederick Douglass and Helen Pitts), Benjamin Brawley (then Dean of Morehouse College), J.W. Johnson (the foreign U.S. Consul to Nicaragua), Robert H. Terrell (prominent judge in Washington, D.C., and husband of Mary Church Terrell), and noted novelist and short story writer Charles Chesnutt.

Documenting the History of Black Men in the Woman Suffrage Movement

Black men in the woman suffrage movement during the nineteenth and early twentieth centuries proved to be significant allies in women's struggle for voting rights. Black men advocating woman suffrage, almost from the movement's inception, believed strategically that a battle against racism linked to the campaign for female voting rights would create a stronger political power base. The African- and Anglo-American women and men who worked for a gender/race coalition believed abolitionism and feminism combined the principles that would lead to race and gender liberation. The woman suffrage movement formed in the North during the 1850s framed its emerging agenda around an anti-sexist, anti-racist platform.

From the alliance formed between abolitionists and feminists came one of the nineteenth century's most outspoken, black male advocates of woman suffrage—Frederick Douglass. Moreover, in the early twentieth century W.E.B. DuBois would become a leading spokesperson, not only for woman suffrage but for black women's rights. As woman suffrage activists, however, both Douglass and Du Bois discoursed extensively on the necessity of women's voting rights and issues of race/gender equality. What marks the distinctiveness of their "pro-woman texts" is what I choose to identify as a *black (male) feminist positionality*.

Chiefly, this study embarks upon an interrogation of Douglass, and DuBois' pro-woman writings, along with activist expressions by other black male advocates of woman suffrage, to ascertain the discursive features and particularities of an historic black male standpoint located in a theoretical and pragmatic alliance with feminism. I employ an analytical perspective that draws upon contemporary black feminist thought asserting the notion that gender, in and of itself, cannot be an exclusive analytical category in the critique of women's oppression—that sex oppression interrelates with racism and classism to form a system of triadic domination.

I aim to figure ways black male resistance against racism in the nineteenth and early twentieth centuries coalesced with, diverged from, and made further complex the already complex race/gender relationship between white and black women—whose struggle for voting rights never solely cohered around gender. Mapping the contours and production of black men's profeminist discourse during the woman suffrage movement brings forth an analysis that seeks to delineate the gender politics that men like Frederick Douglass and W.E.B. DuBois hoped to achieve, in light of the position each held as a "race" man. I argue precisely that from the early writings and actions of black men advocating race and gender rights that a black men's profeminist position came into being.

In pronouncing an historic relation between African-American men and feminism, I displace (as earlier stated) the myth, originating with the rise of the black power movement that black men are inherently anti-feminist. Counter to prevailing black nationalist rhetoric, all black men do not view our resistance to racism as a more urgent priority than fem-inist struggle to end patriarchal sexist domination, oppression, and exploitation of women. The aim of this study is to (en)gender a "race talk" among black men that seriously acknowledges the pervasiveness of sexism in black communities, as much as it is to establish Frederick Douglass and W.E.B. DuBois as proto-feminist black men. In recon-structing the history of each man in the woman suffrage movement, I replicate the move by contemporary black feminist scholars to reclaim their pivotal place in U.S. women's movement. I read the various discur-sive forms (speeches, autobiographies, formal essays, newspaper articles, and fiction) black men engaged to represent their personal and political commitment to women's rights.

Rather than writing a vindication of black men in which profeminist men like Douglass and Du Bois obtain the status of idealized icons of radically progressive gender politics, I examine them in the context of complex public and private lives where their theory and praxis sometimes failed to convey the idea(l)s they at other times maintained about the equality of women. In reality, neither Douglass nor Du Bois ever com-pletely freed themselves from the trappings of patriarchal thinking about women, gender, masculinity, and manhood. Encoded in their feminist dis-course is a race/gender "two-ness." On the one hand, it represented itself as liberatory in tone and sentiment. On the other, it reinforced a pater-nalistic and traditionally male-centered ethos that privileged their power as men (despite the racial inequality they experienced). I argue that in pro-woman writings by Douglass and Du Bois there surfaces at times a race/gender anxiety having to with their own ambivalence toward a sus-tained coalition struggle in which racism and sexism figure coterminately. The desire to legitimate black manhood, in a culture where manhood and masculinity were racially inscribed in "whiteness," drives a competing (race/gender) agenda in both men's writings—to such an extent that the lines between "blackness" and patriarchy blurs.

A black (male) feminist impulse generated in pro-woman writings by Douglass and DuBois registered in a race/gender expression that was always already given to masculine bias. Yet it signaled each man's attempt

to assert his identity as an exemplary figure of black manhood—as a
master rhetorician, a "spokes(man) for the race," and a man of progressive gender politics. Even while struggling to represent themselves as
"manly" men against white supremacist denial of their right to manhood,
both Douglass and DuBois resisted patriarchal ideas that labeled women
the weaker sex. And in spite of the patriarchal position each occupied in
his lifetime, he articulated an impassioned and liberatory vision of equality between the sexes. In so doing, he transformed the meanings of (black)
manhood, one linked to the empowerment of women. Considering the
status of race and sex in the U.S. during the time in which each lived, his
progressive race/gender ideas certainly generated controversy (See Davis
and Giddings). What did it mean for a black man to support women's
rights when black women and men had not been enfranchised as American citizens, who during slavery had been commodified as chattel to be
bought and sold? What did it mean for a black man to assert himself as
a "man" who embraced feminist ideas in a culture of white supremacist
patriarchy where he was perceived as a threat to white womanhood?
What did it mean for a black man to ally himself in the cause of black
women's rights in particular when black women were excluded from the
category "woman"—sexually, physically, and psychologically brutalized
in a system of enslavement that reduced them to exoticized objects of
white male capitalist consumption, their bodies forced into labor as
breeding machines?

In the dehumanized space that names the racialized/gendered history
of African-American women and men, ap(praising) the history of black
men in feminist movement, I work to revalue the political imperatives
that inform the nature of black (male) profeminism. Frederick Douglass
and W.E.B. DuBois, among other black men, claimed it as a standpoint
for black liberation understanding that the status of all women in the
U.S. (determined differently according to their relation to white ruling
class patriarchy). Douglass and DuBois "moved" incisively to empower
themselves as *black men* in feminist terms. Demystifying black men's relation to feminism and reclaiming the history of black male support of
woman suffrage, can be a powerful means to engage contemporary black
men in dialogue about the viability of feminist movement focused on the
liberation of all black people. Black men reading and talking about our
legacy in the woman suffrage movement carries with it transformative
possibilities related to gender, race, and sexual oppression. A concept of
black manhood and masculinity linked personally and politically to progressive antiracist-feminist thinking calls for a radical reordering of black
male and female relationship. Remembering our feminist past enables the
potential for liberatory thinking that supports coalition struggle across
race and gender, advocates resistance to black male sexist and misogynist

behavior, and embraces notions of sexual difference where heterosexism and homophobia are actively contested.

"Re-member(ing)" Not to Forget and the Idea of a Usable Past: Feminism and a Transformed Vision of Black Liberation: Lesson #1

> Our histories may be irretrievable, but they invite imaginative reconstruction.
> —Henry Louis Gates (231)

Restating my opening assertion that black men (and women)—across economic, sexual, class, and religious borders—hold on to a distorted belief that feminism is about middle class white women and manhating/castrating black women, in contest to this representation, I assert that black people must begin a critical reassessment of liberation struggle. Many black men (particularly those with nationalist and/or religious notions of black liberation) continue to situate anti-racist work in opposition to anti-sexist activism. Similarly, many black women have rejected feminism privileging racial solidarity over the need to combat gender inequality. We must envision black liberation as a radical space of transformation where domination is opposed—whether rooted in gender oppression, (hetero)sexist discrimination, class bias, and/or any other form of treatment that denies the basic humanity of the individual.

We can create a progressive agenda for emancipatory struggle based on a space of negotiation in which issues of race, gender, sexuality, and class are not filtered through a patriarchal hierarchy. Moving freely within a liberatory framework where black women and men operate in a partnership of mutual respect and recognition—we give rise to a visionary consciousness that is genuinely revolutionary. Progressive black men working toward a liberated consciousness no longer invest in ideas of manhood and masculinity in patriarchy and the subjugation of women. We must fully realize the meaning of our battle as black men resisting the dehumanization of racism when we begin divesting ourselves of *male* supremacist power. Reciting black men's pro-active stance in the woman suffrage movement, I rely upon the concept of a usable feminist past in service to a contemporary vision of unity among difference(s) in black communities as sites of individual and collective empowerment.

Black men supporting women's rights in the past serves as a model for their place in contemporary black liberation struggle. Black male profeminist activism in political solidarity with black women obtains as a powerful legacy for a new vision of unity in black communities. Contemporary black women and men struggling together against racism and sexism challenges the dogma of male-centered nationalism. When gender oppression is again placed on the agenda of black liberation as a crucial location for resistance, we invoke the past as an empowering force for change. Calling black men and women into critical remembrance of liberatory moments in history, such as the woman suffrage movement and its relation to abolitionism, serves as a complex but necessary lesson in the effectiveness of coalition strategizing. bell hooks calls us to a transformative "re-member(ing)" each other. Such a process may be employed as a political strategy to oppose sexism, as well as sexist and misogynist behavior in black communities. It means, in hooks' words, coming to

> the point of connection between black women and men [that is the] space of recognition and understanding, where we know one another so well, our histories, that we can take the bits and pieces, the fragments of who we are, *and put them back together, re-member them* (my emphasis). (19)

Recollecting the history of black women and men working together for women's voting rights evokes a powerful image of political solidarity. Remembering the past, serving as an active agent in the creation of spaces where "we can take the bits and pieces, the fragments of who we are" enables progressive dialogues to happen around issues of race and gender. Black feminist women and men need to create spaces in our communities where we can talk openly about sexism and its particular manifestations in the lives of black people. More importantly, we need to establish locations where antisexist activism can take place, illustrating the integral role political work opposing gender oppression plays in the liberation of black people.

The goal of any movement to end oppression should have as a priority the welfare of all those oppressed within its ranks—whether by race, gender, class, sexuality, or any other form of domination that seeks to devalue life. Black people in the U.S. possess a history of shared struggle across borders. Yet today many black men and women find ourselves battling each other, having internalized racist and sexist myths that perpetuate a gulf between us. In black communities, sexism continues to be a battle ground where black women must defend themselves, opposing black men who deny that sexism is less a problem than racism and that feminism has no place in work opposing racial oppression. Progressive black men disrupt antifeminist sentiment when we claim a profeminist relationship. Reclaiming the history of black men as advocates of women's rights, black male feminists establish a politic of remembrance in which the past intervenes powerfully on the present toward a new vision of black liberation.

My desire to situate a history of black male support of women's rights in relation to the present is generated by the lack of a sustained, vocal presence in the contemporary period of black men speaking in opposition to sexist and misogynist behavior—especially that perpetuated by many of us. As a feminist black man, I am particularly concerned about how we begin to educate black men about the hurtful effects of male supremacy. As rap has become a pervasive signifier of popular black youth culture, we have witnessed a young, black male-dominated mode of expression whose ladder of success, for the most part, has been placed on the backs of black women. Black female sexual denigration and misogynist objectification played out in gangsta rap is a prime example. In its anti-woman lyrics, black females occupy the status of "bitch" and "ho"—served up in a sexist minstrel show of black male supremacist, masturbatory fantasy. Supported by a white male-dominated sexist and racist music industry, colonized black men exploit black women and female sexuality for self-advancement in a system based on the capitalist exploitation of the black body. "Feminist critiques of the sexism and misogyny in gangsta rap, and in all aspects of popular culture," hooks asserts, "must continue to be bold and fierce" (123). Contemporary black men need to know that the early history of black liberation movement represented itself in coalition strategy where men like Frederick Douglass and W.E.B. DuBois envisioned the struggle for racial equality successfully won when women gained political freedom.

In the Cause of Women's Rights: Frederick Douglass and W.E.B. DuBois as Woman Suffragists: Lesson #2

Politicizing pro-woman speeches, essays, autobiographical narratives, and journalistic media by black men in the woman suffrage movement, contemporary profeminist black men become important allies to women fighting to end sexism. As "pro-woman" black men, our speaking and acting in feminist alliance not only challenge antifeminism in black communities but contests the myth of black macho that all black men endorse patriarchy and sexism.

Paula Giddings acknowledges Frederick Douglass and W.E.B. DuBois as the leading black male feminists of their times. As advocates of woman suffrage, each man crafted his own version of pro-woman discourse. On the one hand, Douglass viewed the subjugated status of (white) women as comparable to the condition of the (male and female) slave. Along with woman suffrage leaders Elizabeth Cady Stanton and Susan B. Anthony, among others, he strategized the idea of a joint movement based on the interrelation of race and sex oppression. The same strategy informed the feminist ideas of DuBois. However, he conceived women's liberation in a specifically racialized manner. Comparing the pro-womanist texts of these men reveals a particular race/gender problematic located in the very idea of "male" feminism. What does it mean for a man to occupy a feminist position—to speak and write from a feminist standpoint? What is at stake for the feminist man? What if anything must he give up? What are the benefits being a (male) feminist? These questions take on more resonance when asked in relation to black men.

Understanding the rhetorical tactics Douglass and DuBois crafted as black male woman suffragists means examining the political relationship between gender and race in their pro-woman writings. To show the discursive strategy each man employed to put forth a radical discourse of women's rights and racial liberation, I engage Houston Baker's discussion of the subversive nature of the black discursive tradition. Baker theorizes a history of black textuality formulated in two modes of literary discourse known as the "mastery of form" and the "deformation of mastery." In *Modernism and the Harlem Renaissance* (1987) he suggests, for example, that the writing styles of Booker T. Washington and W.E.B. DuBois displayed a conscious play of rhetorical subversion where the writing act established black (author)ity. Illustrating the skillful manner in which Washington conveyed the merits of his political program for black progress to white benefactors, Baker argues that his deceptively humble style bore the signs of a sophisticated command of Western literary convention. DuBois, on the other hand, by infusing certain "Africanisms" into his writings on race, purposely undermined the cultural hegemony of the West. Baker maintains that the insurgent stylistics of Washington and DuBois operate as models for the beginning of "black modernism."

Thinking about the established tradition of black men's writing on racial progress, I argue for the importance of establishing a history of black men writing pro-woman texts. The emergence of black modernism and the rise of black male profeminism bare a striking relation when viewed through the model Baker proposes. As mentioned earlier, I apply it to the problematics of DuBois and Douglass writing feminist texts to clarify the complex relationship between race and gender in them, as it informed the men's conception of women's rights.

Frederick Douglass' assertion of manhood (through his woman suffrage writings) is accomplished in a "mastery of form," or a *mastery* of the "master's forms" (to play on Baker's subversive intent, as I will go on to illustrate). DuBois, on the other hand, collapses traditional discursive categories to create a *black* feminist discourse to address the specific historical condition of black women. Troping on DuBois' radical departure from conventional form, Baker refers to his mode of writing as a "deformation of mastery"—a conscious subversion of Eurocentricity. It is achieved by the "(mask)ing" of form. Baker's mask trope, connotatively connected to his definition of form, acts as the illustrating device to convey his theory of the source for the modern black writer's "literary" agency. It is the *minstrel mask,* "a governing object in a ritual of *non-sense*" (21) that Baker establishes as the initial site of modern African-American literary form-"ing" (form in the active, moving sense). The minstrel mask is a space of habitation not only for repressed spirits of sexuality, ludic play, id satisfaction, castration anxiety, and a mirror stage of development, but also for that deep-seated denial of the indisputable humanity of inhabitants of and descendants from the continent of Africa. *And it is first and foremost, the master of the minstrel mask by blacks that constitutes a primary move in Afro-American discursive modernism* [my emphasis]. (17)

The minstrel mask, the historical embodiment of the black's non-human, objectified figuration in the minstrel show was, Baker states, "designed to remind white consciousness that black men and women are *mis-speakers* bereft of humanity—carefree devils strumming and humming all day—unless, in a gaslight misidentification, they are violent devils fit for lynching, a final exorcism that will leave whites alone" (21). As black men, Douglass and DuBois "played" within the minstrel mask for different reasons—the former manipulating its interior to advance his claim to manhood as a "self-made" man, the latter "Africanizing" it to empower black women (and men). Further defining the minstrel mask as prime device for black discursive legitimation, Baker insists that:

Obviously, an Afro-American spokesperson who wished to engage in a *masterful* (my emphasis) and empowering play within the minstrel spirit house needed the uncanny ability to manipulate bizarre phonic legacies. For he or she had the task of transforming the mask and its sounds into negotiable discursive currency. In effect, the task was the production of a manual of black speaking, a book of speaking "back and black." (24)

I draw on the minstrel mask's "formative" premise to suggest that both Douglass and DuBois wrote pro-woman texts that represented themselves as "manual(s) of black speaking" to talk "back and black" to white supremacy and sexism, but where the two men diverged in motive had to do with the audience they looked to for support. Douglass wrote mainly for a white middle class, female educated constituency; DuBois composed primarily for its emerging black counterpart. And the writing strategies each employed to advocate woman suffrage reflected his particular relationship to the race of the women to whom they appealed.

As I have already argued, Douglass' woman suffrage discourse affirmed his participation and status in a predominately white woman suffrage movement. Long-time personal friends of Douglass, Elizabeth Cady Stanton, and Susan B. Anthony, (as well as many other Northern white women feminists of the day) heralded him for his support. DuBois' womanist stance enabled a race/gender movement counter to the dominant culture—affecting his personal/political vision of black liberation through the revaluation and celebration of black womanhood. His pro-woman texts subverted the power and privilege of a Eurocentric view of "woman" to reveal the beauty of black women. On the other hand, the women's rights discourse of Douglass worked implicitly to erase a personal and political association with black women, though he on occasion assisted in black women's political organizing.

It may be seen that discursively Douglass and DuBois stood at opposite poles. Rhetorically, the politics of their writing strategies mirror the difference in the ideological positions each occupied in feminism. Located in Afrocentric nationalism, DuBois' womanist stance constructs a "literary" black female subjectivity figured in African mythology (focused on an eternal black feminine). He resituates it within the existing (author)ized tradition of the white Western imagination. In this way, he performs a "deforming" mastery. Rather than a manipulation of the position of the writer's voice inside the "minstrel mask"—as Douglass had done—DuBois radically re(forms) it, to speak beyond its racialized boundaries. Frankly speaking, DuBoisian black feminist nationalism opposes the assimilationist woman suffrage politics Douglass avowed.

(Re)writing *gender,* as a political category into the discourse of race (from a nationalist feminist standpoint), DuBois, I argue, works out a mastery of subversion. It functions not only to subvert the power of white supremacy but to disrupt the domination of patriarchy in the lives of (black) women. He seizes the minstrel mask and transforms it into a more authentically gendered, African one. The most performative text representing this oppositional gesture is exemplified in *The Quest of the Silver Fleece* (1911), his first novel.

The novel's protagonist, Zora Creswell is purposely imaged as *dark-skinned* black woman. Figuring her in "blackness," DuBois goes against the grain of African-American literary tradition, in which there exists a long history of "light-skinned" female representation. Zora, however, is the first black female hero in black literature. Troping on black female dark skin color, the author embodies her as the literal and "figurative" representative of an African goddess, mythic supernatural power. The "deformation of the mask" Baker claims DuBois affects in *The Souls of Black Folk* is ultimately realized in the image of Zora. Fittingly wearing the ancestral mask, she "distinguishes rather than conceals" (51) the particular attributes of a dark-skinned black female subjectivity. Defining them through Zora, DuBois achieves a discursive mastery that was (he believed) indigenous to Africa and the *African*-American. Baker observes:

> The deformation of mastery refuses a master's *nonsense*. It returns—often transmuting "standard" syllables—to the common sense of the tribe. Its relationship to masks is radically different from the mastery of form. The spirit house occupying the deformer is not minstrelsy, but the sound and

space of an African ancestral past. For the Afro-American spokesperson, the most engaging repository for deformation's sounding work is the fluid and multiform mask of African ancestry. (56–57)

As Douglass constructs himself as a "master of form"; DuBois (as Baker suggests) stood at the beginning of the twentieth century as its "most articulate adherent of African sound" (57). I agree with Baker that *The Souls of Black Folk* is the prototypic textual illustration of the "mask of African ancestry," but there can be no doubt that it exists in a precursorial relation to *The Quest*—DuBois' most sophisticated realization and most provocative display of deformative ancestralism.

Looking for Feminist Fathers, Becoming Womanist Sons: Lesson #3

In 1920, DuBois published "The Damnation of Women"—his most pronounced statement of women's rights support. Ten years before its publication, he had emphatically stated in "Votes for Women: A Symposium By Leading Thinkers of Colored America" that *"votes for women, means votes for black women"* (my emphasis). In his womanist prose, there obtains an unequivocal advocacy of woman suffrage even as he promoted himself as personal arbiter of black culture. And while his ideas of black manhood were rooted in patriarchal tradition, he constructed a self-image in which his nationalist agenda for black progress remained integrally linked to the liberation of black women as represented in "The Damnation of Women." Written over seventy years ago, as it spoke to the urgent need for black men to support the woman suffrage movement, its message of radical gender alliance speaks to black men today as a wo(man)ist manifesto. It calls for a new generation of black men to take up the cause of women's rights as comrades in feminist struggle.

Black men conscious of the relation between sexist domination and racial oppression in the lives of black women come to understand the necessity of joint resistance. We can no longer strategize a movement for black empowerment solely in terms of race. Insisting that white people divest themselves of the power of white supremacy, we should demand that black men rid ourselves of the hegemony of male supremacy. As profeminist black men wrote in support of feminist black women in 1979 who opposed Robert Staples' invective against Michele Wallace and Ntozake Shange, today we must write more and speak louder with (black) women who refuse to be sexually exploited, objectified, and devalued for misogynist pleasure. The moment has come for us to "remember." When black men begin to reclaim our feminist inheritance, carrying on the legacy of Frederick Douglass and W.E.B. DuBois, we share in a brotherhood founded not on a flawed quest for lost manhood (driven by a fear of masculine inferiority) but one anchored in the confidence that who we are as men does not depend upon our ability to subjugate, control, exploit, batter, dominate, and/or sexually violate women.

Contemporary feminist black men, like our pro-woman predecessors, can offer a transformed vision of black manhood—one in which we disclaim the need for patriarchy to affirm our masculinity. At this particular historical moment when the rhetoric of the Million Man March compels black men to atone for not having lived up to the patriarchal, capitalist ideas voiced by Louis Farrakhan—a progressive counter movement is needed that defies narrow (hetero)sexist notions of blackness and offers gender and sexual freedom for all black people. The need for black men's feminist alliance has not changed since the days of Douglass and DuBois. As profeminist black men, we must continue to wage war against sexual oppression as vigorously as we fight against racism. Only then will we sense the full meaning of a unified movement for black empowerment. Only then will we be able to assume fully our inheritance as "womanist sons" of Frederick Douglass and W.E.B. DuBois, our "feminist forefathers."

Note

1. The respondents in the Readers Forum included the following persons: Robert Allen, S.E. Anderson, Bonnie M. Daniels, Harry Edwards, Sarah Fabio, Chidi Ikonne, Terry Jones, June Jordan, M. Ron Karenga, Audre Lorde, Julianne Malveaux, Mark D. Matthews, Rosemary Mealy, E. Ethelbert Miller, George Mosby, Jr., Alvin F. Poussant, Kalamu Ya Salaam, Andrew Salkey, Ntozake Shange, Sabrina Sojourner, Robert Staples, Pauline T. Stone, Askia Toure, and Sherley Williams.

Bibiography

Baker, Houston. 1987. *Modernism and the Harlem Renaissance.* Chicago: University of Chicago Press.

DuBois, W. E. B. 1910. "Votes for Women: A Symposium by Leading Thinkers of Colored America." *The Crisis* 10, p. 177.

Gates, Henry L. 1993. "The Black Man's Burden" in *Fear of a Queer Planet: Queer Politics and Social Theory.* ed. Michael Warner. Minneapolis: University of Minnesota Press.

hooks, bell. 1994. *Outlaw Culture.* New York: Routledge.

Staples, Robert. 1979. "The Myth of Black Macho: A Response to Angry Black Feminists." *The Black Scholar: Journal of Black Studies and Research* 10, Nos. 6, 7 (March/April).

"The Black Sexism Debate." Editorial. *The Black Scholar: Journal of Black Studies and Research* 10, Nos. 8, 9 (May/June 1979).

Ya Salaam, Kalamu. 1979. "Revolutionary Struggle/Revolutionary Love." *The Black Scholar: Journal of Black Studies and Research* 10, Nos. 8–9 (May/June).

Chapter 15

Is Feminism Good for Men and Are Men Good for Feminism?

James P. Sterba

If feminism is good for men, there should be many ways that men are good for feminism. On the other hand, if feminism is not good for men, there will probably not be very many ways that men are good for feminism either. Before we can answer and explore the relationship between these two questions, however, we first must get clear about what we mean, or better, what we should mean, by feminism.

Feminism: The Ideal of a Gender-free or Androgynous Society

Now contemporary feminists almost by definition seek to put an end to male domination and to secure women's liberation. To achieve these goals, many contemporary feminists want a gender-free society where basic rights and duties are not assigned on the basis of a person's biological sex. In such a society, being male or female is not the grounds for determining a person's basic rights and duties. However, this only characterizes the feminist ideal negatively. It tells us what we need to get rid of, not what we need to put in its place. A more positive characterization is provided by the ideal of androgyny.[1] But how should the ideal of androgyny be interpreted? In a well-known article, Joyce Trebilcot distinguishes two forms of androgyny.[2] The first form postulates the same ideal for everyone. According to this form of androgyny, the ideal person "combines characteristics usually attributed to men with characteristics usually attributed to women." Thus, we should expect both nurturance and mastery, openness and objectivity, compassion and competitiveness from each and every person who has the capacities for these traits.

By contrast, the second form of androgyny does not advocate the same ideal for everyone but rather a variety of options from "pure" femininity to "pure" masculinity. As Trebilcot points out, this form of androgyny shares with the first the view that biological sex should not be the basis for determining the appropriateness of gender characterization. It differs in that it holds that "all alternatives with respect to gender should be equally available to and equally approved for everyone, regardless of sex."

It would be a mistake, however, to distinguish sharply between these two forms of androgyny. Properly understood, they are simply two different facets of a single ideal. For, as Mary Ann Warren has argued, the second form of androgyny is appropriate only "with respect to feminine and masculine traits which are largely matters of personal style and preference and which have little direct moral significance."[3] However, when we consider so-called feminine and masculine virtues, it is the first form of androgyny that is required because, then, other things being equal, the same virtues are appropriate for everyone.

We can even formulate the ideal of androgyny more abstractly so that it is no longer specified in terms of so-called feminine and masculine traits. We can specify the ideal as requiring no more than that the traits that are truly desirable in society be equally open to both women and men, or in the case of virtues, equally expected of both women and men, other things being equal.

So characterized the ideal of androgyny represents neither a revolt against so-called feminine virtues and traits nor their exaltation over so-called masculine virtues and traits.[4] Accordingly, the ideal of androgyny does not view women's liberation as simply the freeing of women from the confines of traditional roles thus making it possible for them to develop in ways heretofore reserved for men. Nor does the ideal view women's liberation as simply the revaluation and glorification of so-called feminine activities like housekeeping or mothering or so-called feminine modes of thinking as reflected in an ethic of caring. The first perspective ignores or devalues genuine virtues and desirable traits traditionally associated with women while the second ignores or devalues genuine virtues and desirable traits traditionally associated with men. By contrast, the ideal of androgyny seeks a broader-based ideal for both women and men that combines virtues and desirable traits traditionally associated with women with virtues and desirable traits traditionally associated with men. Nevertheless, the ideal of androgyny will clearly reject any so-called virtues or desirable traits traditionally associated with women or men that have been supportive of discrimination or oppression against women or men. In general, the ideal of androgyny substitutes a socialization based on natural ability, reasonable expectation, and choice for a socialization based on sexual difference.

One locus for the radical restructuring required by the ideal of a gender-free or androgynous society is the family. Here two fundamental changes are needed. First, all children, irrespective of their sex, must be given the same type of upbringing consistent with their native capabilities. Second, normally there must be an equal sharing of childrearing and housekeeping tasks within families, which, in turn, will necessitate flexible work schedules (typically part-time) that allow parents to be with their children for a significant period every day. A recent estimate shows that married full-time career women still do almost as much of the housework chores—70 percent—as the average full-time housewife—who does 83 percent of the housework.[5] Obviously, this will have to change if we are to achieve the ideal of a gender-free or androgynous society.

A second locus of change required by the ideal of a gender-free or androgynous society is the distribution of economic power. In the United States, the percentage of women in the labor force has risen steadily for three decades, from 35 percent (of those aged sixteen or more) in 1960 to 58 percent in 1993. Roughly 72 percent of women were employed in 1990 including more than 58 percent of mothers with children under the age of six and 53 percent of mothers with children under the age of one.[6]

Yet in 1992 women employed full-time still earned seventy-one cents for every dollar men earned, up from the sixty cents for every dollar that held from the 1960s through the 1980s. Earnings do increase with education for all workers, but all women as well as men of color earn less than white men at every level of education. For example, women with four years of college education earn less on average than men who have not completed high school.[7]

Sometimes women and men working in the same job category have different incomes. For example, while female secretaries earned a median wage of $278 per week in 1985, the median wage for male secretaries was $365.[8] More frequently, however, women and men tend to be employed in different job categories that are paid differently. According to one study done a few years ago in the state of Washington, women employed as clerk-typists earned less than men employed as truck drivers or warehouse workers. In another study done in Denver, women employed as nurses earned less than men employed as tree cutters. While in each of these cases, the women earned about 20 percent less than the men, the women's jobs when evaluated in terms of skill, responsibility, effort, and working conditions were given equal or higher scores than the men's jobs with which they were compared. Clearly, denying women the opportunity to earn the same as men do for equal or comparable work is a basic injustice in our society, and it will be a very costly one to correct.[9]

It is sometimes assumed that the problem of unequal pay for comparable work will be solved once women move into male-dominated occupations.[10] Unfortunately, as women move into occupations that men are beginning to abandon, we are seeing a subsequent drop in pay for the men who remain in those occupations. For example, as the percentage of women bartenders increased 23 points, men's pay dropped 16 percent and as the percentage of women pharmacists increased 12 points, men's pay fell 11 percent.[11] So the discrimination against women in the economic arena is a far more entrenched problem than is sometimes thought.

To remedy these inequalities suffered by women in the economic arena will require programs of affirmative action and comparable worth. Affirmative action is needed to place qualified women in positions they deserve to occupy because of past discrimination. Without affirmative action, the structural violence of past discrimination will not be rectified. Only with affirmative action can the competition for desirable jobs and positions be made fair again given our history of past discrimination. There are even cases where affirmative action candidates are clearly the most qualified, but those in charge of hiring, because of their prejudice, could only see the candidates as simply qualified, but not as the most qualified candidates.[12]

Comparable worth is also needed because, without it, women will not receive the salaries they deserve. They will do work that is judged equal or comparable to the work that men are doing in male-dominated occupations, but, without comparable worth, they will be paid less than the men are being paid. Paying for comparable worth programs will not be easy, but it can be done. The state of Washington spent $115 million over seven years on a comparable worth program, and the state of Iowa spent almost 9 percent of its payroll over a three year period to achieve comparable worth.[13]

A third locus of change required by the ideal of a gender-free or androgynous society is the overt violence perpetrated against women in our society. According to former Surgeon General, Antonia Novello, "The home is actually a more dangerous place for the American woman than the city streets." "One-third of the women slain in the U.S.," she continues, "die at the hands of husbands and boyfriends."[14] In addition, women in the U.S. live in fear of rape. Forty-six percent of women are either subjected to rape or attempted rape at some point during their lives, according to one study, and almost 50 percent of male college students say they would commit rape if they were certain that they could get away with it.[15] Not infrequently, women are beaten by their own husbands and lovers (between one quarter and one third of women are battered in their homes by husbands and lovers).[16] Women also experience sexual harassment (85 percent of women in the federal workplace are sexually harassed, and two-thirds of women in the military, according to recent studies) and not infrequently they are beaten by their own husbands and lovers (between a quarter and a third of women are battered in their homes by husbands and lovers).[17] One-third of all women who require emergency-room hospital treatment are there as a result of domestic violence.[18] Thirty-eight percent of little girls are sexually molested inside or outside the family.[19] Since most of these crimes are minimally prosecuted in our society, women in our society can be raped, battered, sexually harassed, or sexually abused as a child and little, if anything, will be done about it. What this shows is that the condition of women in our society is actually that of being subordinate to men by force.[20]

Feminism requires that we put an end to the overt violence against women that takes the distinctive form of rape, battery, and sexual abuse. This overt violence is in every way as destructive as the other forms of violence we oppose. So we cannot in consistency fail to oppose this form of violence done to women in our society. According to one cross-cultural study of ninety-five societies, 47 percent of them were free of rape.[21] What this shows is that it is possible to eliminate or, at least, drastically reduce overt violence against women.

One way to help bring about this result is to ban hardcore pornography that celebrates and legitimizes rape, battery, and the sexual abuse of children, as the Supreme Court of Canada has recently done.[22] Catharine MacKinnon has argued that pornography of this sort causes harm to women by increasing discriminatory attitudes and behavior in men toward women that takes both violent and nonviolent forms.[23]

Another way to decrease violence against women is to de-emphasize violent sports like boxing and football. To see why this would help, all one needs to do is consider the evidence. For example, an exhaustive study of heavyweight prizefights held between 1973 and 1978 and subsequent homicide statistics showed that homicides in the United States increased by over 12 percent directly after heavyweight championship prizefights. In fact, the increase was greatest after heavily publicized prizefights.[24] In addition, a study of twenty-four cases of campus gang rapes indicated that nine of them were by athletes, and in an investigation of sexual assaults on college campuses that included interviewing over 150 campus police, it turned out that football and basketball players were involved in 38 percent of the reported cases.[25] There is also a significant increase in batteries by husbands and boyfriends associated with the yearly Superbowl football game.[26] In the Chicago area, a local radio station went so far as to recommend that women "take a walk" during the game in order to avoid being assaulted in their homes.[27]

A third way to help reduce violence against women is to teach conflict resolution, childcare, and the history of peacemaking in our schools. Several schools have experimented with teaching conflict resolution and childcare to elementary and high school children with impressive results, especially for boys.[28] The history of peacemaking could also provide our children with a new and better set of models than the history of war-making has done.

Thus, feminism requires a number of important changes in our society. It requires the changes in the family, particularly, equal socialization for girls and boys and equal sharing of childrearing and housekeeping tasks between mothers and fathers. It requires changes in the distribution of economic power in our society through programs of affirmative action and comparable work. It requires changes that are necessary to put an end to the overt violence against women that takes the form of rape, battering, sexual harassment, and sexual abuse. All of these changes and more are required if we are to achieve feminism's ideal of a gender-free or androgynous society.

Is Feminism Good For Men?

Using this characterization of feminism, we are now in a position to answer the questions with which we began. Concerning the question of whether feminism is good for men, there is obviously much that men can gain from feminism's ideal of a gender-free or androgynous society. First of all, men would no longer be discouraged from acquiring those truly virtuous or desirable traits traditionally associated with women like being nurturant, compassionate, and cooperative. Secondly, men would have the chance to benefit from women acquiring those truly virtuous or desirable traits traditionally associated with men like being independent, decisive, and competitive.

But while men have much to gain from feminism, they seemingly have much to lose as well. After all, sexist practices and institutions have long favored men over women through unequal family structures, unequal economic structures, and overt violence against women. Yet Warren Farrell has argued that the benefits of sexist practices and institutions for men have been overrated, especially by feminists.[29] Farrell notes, for example, that when families break up, men are more likely to have their children involuntarily taken away from them than women, that the economic advantages men enjoy in society need to be balanced against their greater spending obligations, and that while women are undeniably victims of violence in society, men are more likely than women to be victims of violent crimes.

Clearly, Farrell is right that there are ways that men are disadvantaged in society. But these disadvantages for men appear to be a consequence of the very same sexist practices and institutions that also disadvantage women, and so they can be removed by simply ridding society of those same sexist practices and institutions that also disadvantage women. For example, once men begin to equally share childrearing and housekeeping tasks within families, they will surely be perceived as having equally viable claims in child custody cases, and once men lose their economic advantages over women, they will no longer be regarded as having greater spending obligations either, and once men begin to control their use of violence against women, they will most likely begin to control their use of violence against other men as well. Farrell further observes that men, not women, must fight in wars, and that men are the unpaid body-guards of the women they are with, but this too will change once feminism's ideal of a gender-free or androgynous society were established.[30]

It also should be noted that the disadvantages that men suffer from sexist practices and institutions significantly differ from those that women suffer from those same practices and institutions. Given that men retain greater political and social power in society, the disadvantages that they suffer from sexist practices and institutions are clearly more self-imposed than those that women suffer from those same practices and institutions. In addition, the only way to account for the slow rate at which sexist practices and institutions are being eliminated from society is by assuming that the disadvantages suffered by men are part of a political and social system that substantially advantages men overall.

But if sexist practices and institutions substantially advantage men over women, how could feminism, which aims to rid society of such practices and institutions, be good for men? One way that we have of determining what is good for a person is by noting what the person values or identifies with. Of course, this introduces a certain relativity into the notion of what is good for a person. In each case, the person's good is determined by what that specific person happens to value or identify with, but it does suggest a way that feminism can be good for men: It can be good for men if they happen to value and identify with feminism's ideal of a gender-free or androgynous society. Accordingly, if we were ever able to change most men so that they valued and identified with feminism's ideal of a gender-free or androgynous society, feminism would then be good for most men. Nevertheless, the relativism implicit in this understanding of what is for a person's good is somewhat unsettling given that it follows from it that feminism is not good for men as long as they continue to value and identify with sexist practices and institutions. On this account, feminism would not be good for many men today.

Fortunately, there is another way that we can understand what is for a person's good that need not have these relativistic implications. What is for a person's good can be understood as what is morally good or morally right for that person. So to ask whether feminism is good for men is to ask whether it is morally good or morally right for men to endorse feminism. Yet in the light of our characterization of feminism as seeking to put an end to male domination and to secure women's liberation by bringing about a gender-free or androgynous society, we can surely say that feminism is morally good and morally right for men to endorse. So in this sense feminism is good for men. Feminism is morally good and morally right for men even if accepting its practical requirements necessitates giving up certain advantages that men have over women, thus making it worse off for them overall. Clearly, giving up the advantages of unfair gains and ill-gotten goods is bad for men in one sense—it clearly disadvantages them, but it is also good for them in another—it makes them morally good.

Are Men Good for Feminism?

Given then the relativistic and nonrelativistic senses in which feminism is good for men, there should be ways in which men are good for feminism as well. And there are. Of course, there is also reason to be somewhat skeptical and critical of men's claims to be good for feminism. This is because we still live in a sexist society that significantly advantages men over women. Consequently, men who have enjoyed these advantages in the past usually remain conflicted, despite their best resolve, with respect to their willingness to give up these advantages in the present. This is not to say that there are not advantages to men, as we have noted, from being feminists. It is just that there also remain advantages to men, as we have also noted, from not being feminists. As a result, men are tempted to try to have it both ways. For example, men are tempted to endorse the changes in women's roles that encourage women to become more trained and educated and to take on higher paying jobs in the male-dominated occupations, particularly when these women happen to be their spouses. At the same time, men tend to resist changes in their own roles that require them to assume more childcare and housekeeping responsibilities, even when their spouses would like them to do so. An analogous problem exists in environmental ethics with respect to those who claim to have changed from an anthropocentric perspective that sees nonhuman living beings as simply having instrumental value for humans to a biocentric perspective that recognizes the intrinsic value of all living beings. Those who have made this change in their environmental ethics can also be tempted to have it both ways. For many who claim to hold the biocentric perspective and thus are committed to a vegetarian diet and to minimize their impact on the living earth, the taste of meat and the luxuries that modern technology can provide still hold their attractions.

Yet despite this general worry about men's claims to be good for feminism, there are still many contexts in which men are good for feminism, that is, many contexts in which men can make useful contributions to the cause of feminism. This seems be particularly true where feminist views are widely attacked and there are few women committed to feminism around to respond to such attacks. For example, many philosophy departments presently have no senior women and few, if any, junior women, and the areas of expertise of these women may or may not include feminism. So, in these contexts, if feminist views are not defended by men, they may not be defended at all.

There is also an enriching effect that comes from women and men defending feminist views together. Sexists have come to expect that women might endorse feminist views, but when women and men endorse such views together, it is particularly unsettling, given the advantages that accrue to men in a sexist society.

It is also unsettling to sexists to see philosophers who are trained and recognized as competent in mainline areas of philosophy, particularly mainline areas of ethics and social and political philosophy, demanding the inclusion and infusion of feminist views in these areas of philosophy. Accordingly, this is another context where men who have established themselves in mainline areas of philosophy can be particularly useful to the cause of feminism. There is an analogous benefit when those who have established themselves in mainline areas of philosophy, particularly mainline areas of ethics and social and political philosophy, demand the rejection of an anthropocentric environmental ethics in favor of a bio-centric environmental ethics. In fact, ecological feminists have argued that these two perspectives are interconnected: They claim that rejecting an androcentric social and political philosophy requires rejecting an anthropocentric environmental ethics as well.

Furthermore, there are contexts where men because of their past involvement with sexist practices and institutions can be helpful in exposing and critiquing those same practices and institutions. One such practice is that of hardcore pornography, which Catharine MacKinnon has argued causes harm to women by increasing discriminatory attitudes and behavior in men toward women that takes both violent and nonviolent forms.[31] Now men who participate in this practice learn through the pleasures of masturbation to enjoy depictions of the forceful subordination of women. Accordingly, those who think that the practice of hardcore pornography does not harm women must think that it is possible to enjoy depictions of the forceful subordination of women without in any way desiring to actually forcefully subordinate women in real life. But given that the enjoyment of hardcore pornography comes from vicariously experiencing and identifying with the activity of forcefully subordinating women, it difficult to see how men can experience such enjoyment, culminating in organism, without desiring to actually forcefully subordinate women in real life.

To see how difficult it would be for people not to be moved to desire in such contexts suppose we inhabited a world in which in all the fiction we encounter the morally bad characters, who always look attractive, triumph over the morally good characters, who always look unattractive. In such a world, how could we think that the fiction to which people are exposed would not move them to desire to act like the morally bad characters? Moreover, can you imagine what strong measures people would want to take if the poetic justice of all the fiction we encountered were reversed in this fashion? And would not the reason that is given for taking these strong measures be that this reversal of poetic justice would lead people to behave similarly in real life?

Why then could not a similar justification be given for banning hardcore pornography, since it involves a similar reversal of poetic justice with the morally bad characters (in this case, men), who appear strong and dominant, forcefully triumphing over the morally good characters (in this case, women) who appear weak and submissive? It might be argued that the difference between my imaginary world where there is a need for some corrective action to restore poetic justice and the real world in which we live where hardcore pornography is not banned is that in the real world there are competitors to the message of hardcore pornography that serve to undercut its practical impact on people's actions. Now to some degree this is true. There are competitors, specifically, what MacKinnon calls "erotica" or sexually explicit materials that are premised on equality.[32] The problem is that in the real world these competitors tend to be overwhelmed by the multi-billion dollar pornography industry, which is now probably the dominant educator of boys and young men with respect to how to engage in intimate sexual relations.[33]

What this suggests is that what is important is not whether some message is classified as speech or not, but rather what is the impact the message will have on people's lives. In my example of a complete reversal of poetic justice, the impact of such a message on people's lives would be clearly destructive enough to justify a coercive corrective. Since, in the real world, hardcore pornography depicts a complete reversal of poetic justice with respect to women and men's sexual relations, it should follow that once the destructive impact of this message on people's lives is similarly recognized, a coercive corrective will be seen to be required.

Given the plausibility of this argument, one might wonder then why hardcore pornography has not been banned in most Western countries. Well, of course, it has been banned in some places; Canada's Supreme Court recently has banned hardcore pornography explicitly on the grounds that it is harmful to women.[34] But most other Western countries have not followed Canada's lead in this regard. One explanation is the difficulty of separating hardcore pornography, which is arguably harmful to women from forms of softcore pornography, which are arguably not harmful to women. But the line here does not need to be drawn with any high degree of precision. It suffices if the law is used to prosecute the worse cases of hardcore pornography characterized as being sexually explicit, violent, and sexist in order to begin to undercut hardcore pornography's grip on the male psyche.

Yet another explanation of why hardcore pornography has not been banned appears to be that many people do not see it for what it is. For many people, hardcore pornography represents either acceptable or even desirable sexual relations between women and men, and so they have basically no problem with its spillover into practice. In addition, many women who are feminists may tend to underestimate the harmfulness of hardcore pornography to women. This is because these women may sample hardcore pornography and find that they have little difficulty renouncing the submissive and degraded images of the women that it displays. These women may then mistakenly infer from their own reactions to hardcore pornography that men should have little difficulty doing likewise.[35]

It is here where men can explain how their reactions to hardcore pornography are typically different from those of women. Men can explain how hardcore pornography when combined with the pleasures of masturbation can enter their psyches and structure their sexual tastes in ways that may be quite difficult to resist. This happens when the sexual images drawn from hardcore pornography impose themselves on men's real-life encounters demanding to be re-enacted as the price of sexual pleasure. Men can easily find themselves in a situation where they cannot achieve orgasm without somehow incorporating the sexual images of hardcore pornography into their lives, leading them either to impose or to try to impose hardcore pornographic roles on the women who come into their lives, with more or less harmful effects. It is just here that men can well serve the cause of feminism by testifying to the destructive impact hardcore pornography has had on their relations with women, and, thereby help demonstrate the necessity for banning it.

In so many contexts, women are in a much better position than men to expose and argue against the harmful effects of sexist practices. Generally, nothing succeeds better at sharpening one's perception of the injustice of sexist practices or at developing one's argumentative skills to oppose such practices than actually having suffered from sexist practices oneself. That is why men's role in combating sexist practices should be generally supportive and subordinate to that of women who rightfully should be leading the fight for feminism's ideal of a gender-free or androgynous society. Nevertheless, I have argued that there are a number of contexts where men are in a particularly good position to be good for feminism. Of these, possibly none are more important than the role men can play in exposing the harmful effects that hardcore pornography can have on their own lives and on the lives of the women with whom they come in contact.

In conclusion, we have seen that feminism is good for men if they identify with feminism's ideal of a gender-free or androgynous society, and morally good for them even if they do not. We have also seen that there are a variety of ways that men can be good for feminism ranging from defending feminism when no women can or will defend it to contributing their own special insights to the overturning of sexist practices and institutions. So properly understood, feminism is good for men and men are good for feminism.

Notes

1. See, for example, Ann Ferguson, "Androgyny as an Ideal for Human Development," in *Feminism and Philosophy* edited by Mary Vetterling-Braggin and others (Totowa, 1977) pp. 45–69; Mary Ann Warren, "Is Androgyny the Answer to Sexual Stereotyping?" in *Femininity, Masculinity, and Androgyny,* edited by Mary Vetterling-Braggin (Totowa, 1982) pp. 170–86; A. G. Kaplan and J. Bean, eds., *Beyond Sex-Role Stereotypes: Reading Toward a Psychology of Androgyny* (Totowa, 1976). Andrea Dworkin, *Women Hating* (New York, 1974) Part IV; Carol Gould, "Privacy Rights and Public Virtues: Women, the Family and Democracy," in Carol Gould, *Beyond Domination* (Totowa, 1983) pp. 3–18; Carol Gould, "Women and Freedom," *The Journal of Social Philosophy* (1984) 20–34; Linda Lindsey, *Gender Roles* (Englewood Cliffs, 1990); Marilyn Friedman, "Does Sommers like Women?" *Journal of Social Philosophy* (1991) pp. 75–90. For some feminists who oppose the ideal of androgyny, see Mary Daly, *Gyn-Ecology: The Meta-Ethics of Radical Feminism* (Boston, 1978); Kathryn Paula Morgan, "Androgyny: A Conceptual Critique," *Social Theory and Practice* (1982); Jean Bethke Elshtain, "Against Androgyny," *Telos* 47 (1981).

2. Joyce Trebilcot, "Two Forms of Androgynism" reprinted in *Feminism and Philosophy*, Mary Vetterling-Braggin, Frederick Ellison and Jane English, eds. (Totowa, 1977) pp. 70–78.

3. Ibid., pp. 178–79.

4. For a valuable discussion and critique of these two viewpoints, see Iris Young, "Humanism, Gynocentrism and Feminist Politics," *Women's Studies International Forum* (1985) Vol. 8, no. 3, pp. 173–83.

5. Women's Action Coalition, *WAC Stats: the Facts About Women* (New York: The New Press, 1993), p. 60. According to another study, wives employed in the labor force do approximately 29 hours of domestic labor a week, in addition to their labor market jobs. Wives not in the labor force do between 32 and 56 hours of domestic labor a week, with the differences largely due to the presence of young children. Overall, husbands spend approximately 11 hours a week in domestic labor, regardless of whether or not their wives are in the labor force. See Shelley Coverman, "Women's Work is Never Done," in

Women: A Feminist Perspective, 4th ed. Ed. Jo Freeman (Mayfield Publishing Co., 1989), pp. 356–68.

6. *Statistical Abstracts of the United States* 1994 (Washington, D.C.: U.S. Governmental Printing Office, 1994).

7. See *The New York Times*, October 6, 18, and 19, 1992; See also Phyllis Moen, *Women's Roles* (New York, 1992); Elaine Sorensen, "The Comparable Worth Debate," in *Morality in Practice*, ed. James P. Sterba (Belmont: Wadsworth Publishing Co. 1994), pp. 293–94.

8. See Susan Okin, *Justice, Gender and the Family*. (New York, 1989), Chapter 7.

9. See Jerry Jacobs and Ronnie Steinberg, "Compensating Differentials and the Male-Female Wage Gap." *Social Forces*, Vol. 69, No. 2 (December, 1990)

10. Clifford Hackett, "Comparable Worth: Better From a Distance," *Commonweal* May 31, 1985.

11. *Rapid City Journal*, October 20, 1992.

12. Gertrude Ezorsky, *Racism and Justice* (Ithaca: Cornell University Press, 1991)

13. Elaine Sorenson, *Comparable Worth* (Princeton: Princeton University Press, 1994), pp. 88–89. See also Ellen Paul, *Equity and Gender* (New Brunswick, 1989) and Mary Ann Mason, "Beyond Equal Opportunity: A New Vision for Women Workers," *Notre Dame Journal of Law, Ethics and Public Policy* (1992).

14. *The New York Times*, October 17, 1991. See also Elizabeth Schneider, "The Violence of Privacy," *The Connecticut Law Review* 23 (1991) pp. 973–99.

15. See Diana Russell and Nancy Howell, "The Prevalence of Rape in the United States Revisited," *Signs*, vol. 8 (1983), pp. 688–95 and Bert Young, "Masculinity and Violence," presented at the Second World Congress on Violence and Human Coexistence, Montreal, July 12–17, 1992.

16. R. Emerson Dobash and Russell Dobash, *Violence Against Wives* (1979); R. Langley and R. Levy, *Wife-Beating* (1977); D. Martin, *Battered Wives* (1981).

17. Catharine MacKinnon, *Feminism Unmodified* (Cambridge: Harvard University Press, 1987), Chapter 14 and Women's Legal Defense Fund, "Sexual Harassment in the Workplace" (1991).

18. Dierdre English, "Through the Glass Ceiling," *Mother Jones*, November, 1992.

19. Diana Russell, "The Incidence and Prevalence of Intrafamilial and Extrafamilial Sexual Abuse of Female Children," *Child Abuse and Neglect: The International Journal*, vol. 7, no.2 (1983).

20. On this point, see Catharine MacKinnon, Op. cit., pp. 169–71.

21. Myriam Miedzian, *Boys Will Be Boys*, (New York, 1991), p. 74.

22. Donald Victor Butler v. Her Majesty The Queen (1992).

23. Catharine MacKinnon, Op.cit., Chapter 14.

24. David Phillips, "The Impact of Mass Media Violence on U.S. Homicides," *American Sociological Review*, (1983), pp. 560–68. See also Ron Thorn-Finch, *Ending the Silence: The Origins and Treatment of Male Violence Against Women* (Toronto: University of Toronto Press, 1992).

25. Myriam Miedzian, *Boys Will Be Boys* (New York: Anchor Books, 1991), pp. 203–204. According to a recent survey reported on CNN (November 12, 1994), student athletes who represent about 10 percent of college students are involved in 30 percent of sexual assaults.

26. Christina Sommers has also challenged this claim, but responses to her challenge have, I think, discredited it unless she is simply objecting to a more

particular version of this claim that maintains that there is a 40 percent increase in batteries by husbands and boyfriends associated with the yearly Superbowl football game. For Sommers's challenge and responses to that challenge, *Who Stole Feminism*, Chapter 9, the special issue of *Democratic Culture*, and Laura Flanders, "The 'Stolen Feminism' Hoax."

27. WBBM, January 31, 1993. Playing football also impacts negatively on the life expectancies of football players themselves. The average life expectancy of National Football League players in the United States is fifty-four, nearly two decades below the overall male mean. See Don Sabo, "Sport, Patriarchy and Male Identity," *The Arena Review* (1985), pp. 1–30.

28. Miedzian., Op.cit., Chapters 6 and 7.

29. Warren Farrell, *The Myth of Male Power* (New York: Berkeley Books, 1993).

30. Ibid.

31. Catharine MacKinnon, Op.cit., Chapter 14.

32. Ibid.

33. Susan Dwyer, *The Problem of Pornography*, (Belmont, Wadsworth Publishing Co., 1995), p. 2.

34. Donald Victor Butler v. Her Majesty The Queen.

35. For this kind of feminist reaction to hardcore pornography, see Stephanie Bauer, "Pornography, Language and Identity," presented at the 13th International Social Philosophy Conference held in De Pere, Wisconsin, August 15–18, 1996 and forthcoming in the Proceedings of the Conference.

Chapter 16

Reading Like a (Transsexual) Man

Henry S. Rubin

The title of this essay is meant to evoke a genre of scholarship that flourished in the late 1980s, one which found its niche among literary critics who applied these terms to ask if men can be, should be, or would be able to read like (or as) women. This type of writing can be found in the pages of a volume entitled *Men in Feminism* (1987). Of all the contested terms in that book, the conjunctive "in" carried the greatest burden. Many of the contributors to that book, both men and women, commented on the troublesome "in" with its possible innuendoes of penetration and rape. "Feminism" was construed as a territory at risk from plunderers and conquest. The contributors pointed out that even feminist men might recapitulate their cultural role as aggressors with a vested interest in retaining their power and that they might use (literary) violence to maintain that position within the space of feminism. So it is a sign of our times that the present collection is alternatively titled *Men Doing Feminism*. What shift in epistemology is reflected by this change?

The earlier collection of essays asked (among other things) whether or not a man could read as a woman in order to ask a larger question about the possibilities for male feminists. To read as/like a woman implied that feminist knowledge was generated out of female-bodied experience. For a man to read like/as a woman meant that a man could get into the skin of a woman and therefore generate feminist knowledge. The logic of this claim is a kind of literary transsexualism, where men can be women and knowing is not tied to biology.

In the intervening ten years, it has been pointed out (with greatest clarity by Diana Fuss) that the essays in the collection *Men in Feminism* assumed that a feminist subject position could only be inhabited by a woman. This foundationalist assumption was the linchpin of identity politics. This paradigm of politics, derived from Marxism, required a stable, coherent, group identity that all political actors acknowledged as their own. It was further assumed that all of these actors would have the same interests because of their similar location within the dominant culture. The assumptions of this identity-paradigm were challenged first by women of color in the 1980s (hooks 1981, Anzaldúa 1987, Moraga and Anzaldúa 1981) who introduced an analysis of race to feminism and questioned the homogeneity of the category "Woman." When the category "Woman" was fractured along racial axes, it became apparent that feminist subjects could be as different from each other as men are from women. The dream of an unfragmented identity politics took a further blow from Judith Butler's work (1989), which pointed out the fallacy of organizing around a (gendered, sexed) subject who supposedly stood prior to or innocent of those structures of power that produced her (Butler 1989, 2).

The title of this volume, *Men Doing Feminism*, foregrounds a paradigm shift, which resulted from these critiques of identity politics. The verb "do" puts action in place of the notion of identity implicit in the title *Men in Feminism*. We have moved from a paradigm that emphasizes identity to one that is action or practice oriented. "Womanhood" is no longer a necessary, nor sufficient qualification for feminist identity. A feminist is one who acts in concert with feminist ideals. This new conception accounts for women who are anti-feminist and might open the door for male feminism. What matters now, at least in some minds, is not whether one can read like/as a woman, but rather like a feminist. And if Fuss is correct that the essence of feminism and of feminist identity is politics (Fuss 1990, 37), then male feminism is possible. What counts is one's political actions.

Nonetheless, this is an incomplete revolution. The old questions about male feminists hang like ghosts in the air. Can we be trusted? How can female feminists trust that proclaimed male feminists are not penetrating female space for our own purposes? Will we take away the few jobs, books, and opportunities that have been the province of women in the scarcity economy? We have read the new canon of feminist theory, but how do women know that we are not going to twist it to undermine what voice women have managed to gain? We might offer to do childcare while women march and rally, but how can we be trusted not to perpetrate sex crimes on those children?

Into this fray steps the female-to-male transsexual (FTM). Me. Even though I am just one transsexual man, with my own history of becoming a man and my own relations with feminism, I have noticed that feminists who are partial to the identity paradigm have imagined three different transsexual *types,* based on archetypal stories about transsexuals, which they use to make sense of me. In the first story, feminists are eager to have me, a new man, a hybrid, a mix, the "best of both worlds," stand with them as a feminist. I have, they say, lived as a woman and can carry my experience, my knowledge, my reading and writing skills across the gender divide. I can be that thing that is impossible, a male feminist.[1] This story preserves some measure of my masculinity, but rewrites my pre-transition life as that of a woman. I reply: Though I had a female body, I never lived as a woman or girl.[2]

Identity-paradigm feminists have a second story about me: I have appropriated male technologies of war to transform myself in order to obtain the opportunities and freedoms all women deserve.[3] This is a story about the progress of women. Progress narratives like this one attribute a feminist motive to transsexuals who change their sex. I must *really* be a women masquerading as man. My worldly accomplishments are claimed by feminists as the achievements of a woman in a man's world. The trouble with this progress narrative is that it does little to validate my manhood. According to this story, I am a wily woman strategically passing in order to be successful. It preserves my feminist status but only by misrecognizing me as a woman.[4]

In the last story that identity-paradigm feminists tell about FTMs I am worse than a male (read pseudo) feminist. I am a traitor. Either I was a spy, a man among feminists, or I was a woman who gave up my womanhood in a mistaken bid for male power. Instead, I should be working alongside my sisters for the emancipation of all women. This interpretation concedes my masculinity, but I must turn in my feminist badge at the door.

These three ideal types of FTM transsexuals preserve the paradigmatic claim that a feminist must be a woman first. She must either be embodied as a woman, embrace womanhood, or have life experiences as a woman. The identity-paradigm that produced these three stories about FTMs grants or denies me feminist status according to the first principle: Is "it" a woman? Aside from the fact that there are some folks who do not identify as either a man or a woman, this paradigm wrestles away from an FTM the power to self-define as a man. In these stories, I am either a woman and a feminist or I am a man and not a feminist. Ultimately, in this paradigm gender identity establishes political identity.

Although the identity-paradigm has been challenged by the action-paradigm, its three stories about FTMs continue to inform day-to-day events. The competition between these paradigms was clearest to me during my first year on the academic job market. I applied for several Women's Studies jobs as an "out" transsexual. My vita reflected my graduate school concentration in gender and sexuality studies, including teaching in the Women's Studies program at my graduate institution, my committee work reviewing curricula and initiating a feminist studies unit in a survey course on social theory, and my dissertation, which focused on the experiences of FTM transsexuals. Nonetheless, I was unsurprised by my lack of success given the flooded job market and the scarcity of jobs. What did surprise me was the reaction of many of my colleagues and friends to my "hubris" at applying for these jobs at all. In one upsetting conversation, a female feminist friend said that although I had the obvious qualifications to teach in such programs, she would prefer to "learn her women's studies from a woman."

What I am highlighting here is not that I (or any man) deserve these opportunities. I am suggesting that these questions are still as contested as they were ten years ago. We are in a period of deep conflict between the identity-paradigm, which argues that women are the subject that grounds feminism, and the action-paradigm, which makes political practice the essence of feminism. The tension between these paradigms is not restricted to two discreet "camps"; it is just as often embodied in a single person who may favor one framework in her hiring practices and the other in her theoretical work. Even the terms I have chosen reflect the internal inconsistencies of each paradigm. No one operating within the identity-paradigm believes that identity without action is a useful strategy, nor can the action-oriented paradigm function without reference to a person's position within the gender order. The tension between these paradigms creates ambivalence even as it demands consistency. Indeed, as I write these words I know my own ambivalences structure them.

Still, I have faith in the action-paradigm with its emphasis on political commitment as the essence of feminism. I believe that there is a way of knowing that can provide me(n) with a feminist viewpoint, and that is not generated out of a woman's experience of her body. Instead, it is generated out of subjectively located struggle. To show the limits of the identity paradigm, I will return to the three feminist ideal types of transsexual

Identity Paradigm	Action Paradigm
gender identity=feminist identity	action is the essence of feminism
Ideal type #1: female-bodied and feminist	FTM Ideal type #4 ?
Ideal type #2: woman passing as a man and feminist	
Ideal type #3: spy or traitor, not feminist	

Figure 1: Identity Paradigm and Action Paradigm

men that I outlined above. After closely examining these three feminist constructions of transsexuals, I will introduce another model of a transsexual that can provide evidence for the value of the action-paradigm.

The first feminist construction of transsexual men depends upon embodiment as the ground of all knowledge. Because I was born with female equipment, I am assumed to have a range of experiences that are eminently female. These experiences of bleeding monthly, of limits placed on my physical and mental activities, of vulnerability (to penetration, to aggression on the streets or in my own bed), are said to give me a common bond with other women, or at least those of my class and race. These common experiences, if properly mined in consciousness-raising sessions, could provide me with a feminist consciousness not unlike that of women.

But the lens of subjectivity, which focuses on the experiences generated by bodies, is missing from this interpretation. Joan W. Scott has written that "experience," as a category of evidence, is an obfuscating term (Scott 1993). She claims that "experience" is often viewed as an unmediated and uncontestable set of truth claims. Common sense tells us that "experience" is something that already constituted subjects have. Contrary to this received wisdom, Scott claims that experience *constructs* the subject. This is a very strong claim and it has analytic power, but Scott only hints at the dialectics between subjectivity and embodied experience. "Subjects are constituted discursively and experience is a linguistic event (it doesn't happen outside established meanings), but neither is it confined to a fixed order of meanings" (Scott 1993, 409). I would add: Experience constructs the knowing subject, and new experiences are, in turn, focused through the lens of the subjectively located knower. Experience constitutes subjects who then have experiences that they interpret subjectively and that contribute to the dialectic of subjective construction.

As I wrote above, I say now that I never lived as a girl or a woman. The hegemonic narrative construction of transsexuals (co-produced by sexologists and transsexuals, both MTF and FTM) is that we experience our identities as gender-neutral or gender-dysphoric at very early ages.[5] Transsexuals do not interpret their bodies like other female-bodied people. Instead transsexuals develop subjectivities that are specifically transgendered. With or without a name for what we feel as children, transsexuals are conscious of our difference from others of our birth sex and this difference gets constructed as evidence of our transsexual status. Scott might say that experience constitutes us as transsexual subjects. Reified in a transsexual subjectivity, these experiences act as a filter through which we organize further embodied experience. For example, an FTM may have experiences quite different from a woman walking down the same dark street in an urban neighborhood: A woman may look over her shoulder, anticipate the sound of footsteps with keys clenched between fingers, cross the street to the lit side. An FTM, similarly embodied but with a transsexual subjectivity, may become aware of a woman crossing the street in fear that the FTM is a potential attacker. Alternatively, the FTM may also feel vulnerable. His fear comes from different reasons: fear of being read and then attacked for being a gender-freak. In this situation, I have crossed the street to the *darker* side in order to avoid detection. Same bodies, different vulnerabilities, different courses of action.

An epistemological equation that factors in embodied experience but not subjectivity will perforce fail to take account of differences between subjects. It will render all experiences of similar bodies the same and it will prescribe set strategies for differently located individuals. The implication of such an epistemology is that it may reserve a feminist identity for "special" men, like FTMs, but it maintains that other men cannot be feminist. On the other hand, feminist analyses that incorporate a dialectical notion of embodiment, subjectivity, and experience, can take account of differently located bodies that appear similar in form. Using this more complex epistemological framework recognizes a transsexual man's subjectivity qua man, but this does not automatically make all FTMs into feminists. (Transsexual) men may refuse to generate feminist insights out of their *own* location.

The second construction of FTMs in the feminist imagination depends upon a similar logic that homogenizes female bodies and their attendant motivations. The main difference between these two ideal types is that for the second a feminist motive is provided for an FTM's transition. The story goes that FTMs, like "other" women, experience the limits of their bodies and attached social meanings in the same way. The transsexual desire to live as a man is only a feminist dream taken to its illogical extreme. If as a female bodied person I cannot *further my ambitions,* then I will take on a male mask and succeed this way. I am not really a man, but only doing a plausible impersonation.[6] Whereas in the first story, FTMs have formerly female bodies and female experiences that qualify them as feminist, in this story FTMs never rescind their female membership. FTMs are women pretending to be men to attain privilege or power. A generous feminist might consider this an heroic feminist strategy, albeit somewhat misguided: "S/he" wanted _____ (her music, her education, her lover . . .) so much that she sacrificed her identity as a woman for it."

This analysis does not grasp what is essential to the subjective understandings of the FTMs themselves; our bodies do not reflect our internal sense of who we really are. FTMs are not motivated to enact body modifications to realize our worldly dreams and goals, though these are often attenuated by our suffering in bodies that do not conform to our self-image. FTMs are motivated to alter our bodies in order to express a deeply felt, internal sense of the men we are.

These first two constructions of FTMs as either "the best of both worlds" or as tragic "feminist heroes" have the potential to incorporate transsexual men into a feminist subject position, but at a cost to transsexual self-understandings. Subjectively mediated experiences of female bodies are discounted. FTMs regularly resist the idea that they were ever women/girls or that they are impersonating men. Rather, most FTMs self-define as men. Emphasizing their subjectivity throws a wrench in the simple machine that inputs female bodies and churns out feminist knowledge.

The third construction of transsexual men by the feminist imagination takes seriously the claim that these men are really men like all other men. They are therefore disqualified as feminists. Again, in the identity-paradigm gender identity is the necessary criteria for a feminist identity. Being a woman and having a female body generates female experiences that serve as the basis for feminist knowledge. Obviously, men do not that female bodies. This third construction of FTMs rests on a notion of (male) subjectivity that cannot attain feminist consciousness because of a lack of the embodied experiences that structure a woman's struggle. Men of all kinds are not able to access a feminist identity because they have no experience of these *particular* struggles. In this story, all men are equally invested and located in the hegemonic social order. All male bodies produce a worldview that obscures or protects male power.

Either FTMs are really women and therefore potential feminists or they are really men and therefore not candidates for feminist citizenship. In these three ideal types, produced within an identity-paradigm that requires a female subject for feminism, male feminism is still impossible. Is there a way for transsexual men to be feminist and still be men? What embodied experiences and subjective self-understandings do these men have that would promote a feminist consciousness? Standpoint feminist theorist Sandra Harding poses a similar series of questions about non-transsexual men:

> But how can our male students and colleagues who intend to be anti-sexist—to be feminist?—activate their identities to generate analyses about gender codes? We certainly don't want them pretending to "read as women" when they cannot have the lives or the experiences that would enable them to do so. How can they use their different identities to generate their own distinctive (feminist?) analyses? (Harding 1991, 103).

These questions begin to move us away from the identity-paradigm and open the door to the action-paradigm where politics is the heart of feminism. Within this paradigm, men of all kinds have the potential to be feminist. In the next section, Harding provides the material for constructing a fourth transsexual in the feminist imagination: a transsexual man who might be able to generate feminist knowledge.

Activating Perverse Identities

Harding borrows, from Bonnie Zimmerman, the phrase "perverse identity" to refer to those who choose their own marginality; those who are "willfully refusing to do what the culture of the center expects them to do." (Harding 1991, 107). Some FTMs could be said to be perverse men in this sense. These men, like all men, are faced with the persistent temptations of cultural, economic, and political power at the everyday level, which are reinforced by pressures from systemic structures and maintained through violence. Yet we, like some non-transsexual men, can engage in a neverending series of refusals to these pressures and temptations. "Opting out" of these privileges and opportunities is not a one-time decision, but a string of regular and continuous challenges that are met with varying degrees of success. These challenges are always negotiated between two oppositional belief systems—a desire to be a "real" man and a desire for social justice.

"Real men" are typically defined by their willingness to participate in the cultural, economic, and political circulation of power. Real men do not activate their perverse identities. Real men are not gay, not black or brown or yellow. If they are, then they try to pass as real men. They are straight-acting gays or passing as white (if they are light-skinned enough) or they hold corporate jobs where the clothes they wear make them respectable citizens, not gangsta rappers. Or they are gangsta rappers who menace women with lyrical violence. Real men drum on the weekends. There are so many ways to participate in the economy of realness, even if your body is not white or your sexuality is deviant or your size does not measure up or you cannot afford to keep your wife at home. But are there ways of being a real man that do not conflict with feminist ideals? Is my desire to be real synonymous with the desire to be accorded male power? Are these the same meaning of real?

The paradox of being an FTM and trying to activate a perverse identity is in assuming a centered position (with the requisite pressures, both internal and external) while straining against the cultural and political demands of that position. Because we are not born male our move from the margins to the center make the more general pressures on all men to be real even more intense. At the same time, activating a perverse identity entails refusing the political and cultural benefits of that position to which we have aspired.

Though she has non-transsexual men in mind, Alice Jardine suggests that one strategy for negotiating this paradox is to "talk your body" (Jardine 1987, 61). This means getting specific about our lives as men:

> There's men's relationship *after feminism*, to death, scopophilia, fetishism, ... the penis and balls, erection, ejaculation (not to mention the phallus), madness, paranoia, homosexuality, blood, tactile pleasure, pleasure in general, desire ... voyeurism, etc. (Jardine 1987, 61)

Jardine's comments are purposely provocative. She appeals to our prurient interests and catches our attention by stringing together a series of unspoken terms—bodily fluids, body parts, and perversions. Having done so, she makes a significant distinction between talking our bodies and talking about our bodies. Though she leaves this underdeveloped, I interpret her suggestion as a call to subjectivize our bodily experience and to refuse to stand outside our bodies as if they were only objects that we do not inhabit. The objectification of our bodies allows us to remove ourselves from the strengths (power) and vulnerabilities that come from being a male body. I wonder what it would mean to speak such things from the specificity of a transman's body? In the following pages, I will try to talk my embodiment and subjectively mediated experience, both pre- and post-transition—in other words, to activate my perverse identity in order to cultivate a sense of struggle with my new location within the hegemonic order. Activating a perverse identity, I argue, can be the basis of a male feminism.

Feminist Training

Not unlike many FTMs, I took a roundabout route to my transsexual identity. It began at the Santa Cruz campus of the University of California where I took courses on the sociology and the politics of gender in the Women's Studies program. I worked in a coffeeshop on campus, which was a mixed bag of gay men, lesbians, and other perverted characters. I admired several notable lesbian/feminist theorists on campus and eventually identified myself with them, especially the few butches who dared to make themselves visible. After undergraduate school I moved to Berkeley, another town with more of a lesbian population than nearby San Francisco. During my brief stay there I worked in a lesbian-feminist construction company and at the infamous Brick Hut restaurant, a brunch spot owned and operated collectively by lesbians. I was in the thick of it. The feminists at the Hut provided me with the flesh-and-blood figures who inhabited the pages of history in my coursework at UCSC. Several of the women there were active in the Olivia Music company during its formative years and I served eggs to the stars.[7] In the kitchen we discussed feminist theory and practice while I washed dishes. At meetings, I was educated in the process of feminist decision-making. My evenings were spent with a crowd of proto-Queer Nationales, intent on shaking the foundations of the lesbian-feminist community I served during the day. The contrast between them made me increasingly aware that I was unlike either crowd of lesbians.

In graduate school, I got a reputation for being aggressively dykey. Although there were several dykes in my department, I stood "out." I cropped my hair, came out in my classes and wore my "Silence=Death" T-shirts around campus. Gradually, this uniform was replaced by a standard tie and jacket. When the professor of the Introduction to Women's Studies class asked if anyone ever felt genderless or even wanted to be a man, I found myself confessing to this class of nascent feminists that their teaching assistant was transgendered. I think I was surprised that none of the other members of the class raised their hands to answer her question. Embarrassed, I scuttled out of the room.

These details of my pre-transition life suggest that I, like many FTMs, went through a trajectory that includes rigorous feminist training. Obviously, this "training" was in a particular school of feminist thought. Like "training" in the martial arts, there are several schools of feminism each with its own inflections and interpretations arising out of geographic, historical, and individual conditions. The feminist training I received emphasized a rejection of the power differentials between men and women and the cultural signs that represented this balance of power. It also put forth an ideology of women's power that was generated out of some mystical source, usually women's bodily connection to the spirit. While rejecting the hegemonic power of men and those cultural signs, which denoted that power, I had a much harder time embracing my own female body and the spiritual power invested in the female body.

The point here is not that I went through this kind of training and am therefore qualified to be a feminist, but rather that feminism enabled my eventual identification as a transsexual man. My feminism said men and women were not all that different, at least not after you dismissed biology. It said I could be and do whatever I could dream: automechanic, writer, or chef. Feminism said I could style myself however I wanted. I could reject makeup, highheels, curling irons, and blowdryers. Hell, I could even stop shaving my legs. Feminism said I could wear a jacket and a tie, and throw away those dresses. On a daily basis, feminism brought me closer to the line that divides men from women.

On the other hand, my feminism eventually came between me and my transsexual desires. I developed that feminist imagination that could only see transsexual men as women, misguided heros, or traitors. One of the overriding limits this feminism posed to my transition was a prohibition against bodily mutilation. Guarding against centuries of patriarchal fetishistic gazes that constructed Woman or coerced her into constructing herself for men's hungry eyes (and other body parts), I fought fat phobia, plastic surgery, the cosmetics industry, and genital mutilation ritual abuse. But what, I thought, is sexual reassignment surgery (double mastectomies, phalloplasties) if not body mutilation? How could I hold the line against female objectification and mutilation, while going to the plastic surgeon? This feminism, which had carried me so far, seemed unable to take me all the way home.

Eventually I turned to the new feminist/queer work that followed Judith Butler's *Gender Trouble*. This took me closer still to the edge of gender, but seemed to deny me permission to cross over. In this paradigm, outlaws who juxtaposed ambiguous gender cues and revealed the seams of gender were subversive. FTMs who claim an essential identity as men were not. This was part of my daily struggle before transition—trying to think differently through questions that generations of feminisms had raised but whose answers left me stranded in a female body.

Feminism gave me a language for analyzing gender. But I have come to believe that what I took from my experiences with it was that part of feminism that is concerned with gender theory. By this I mean the theory that accounts for how we become gendered (and sexed) bodies. I was less drawn to the parts of feminism that documented the injustices committed against those gendered bodies. Perhaps these two aspects of feminism seem cut from a whole cloth to others, but for me these were two distinct branches of feminism—gender feminism and social justice feminism. This is the hardest thing to admit: that I was always drawn to the theory that analyzed the social construction of gender, while skirting (so to speak) the huge bodies of feminist knowledge about how gender constructions enabled differential and unequal treatment of women. I was drawn to the theories of gender construction during a time in my life when I was personally constructing my own gendered identity. At the same time, I was repelled by the work that theorized social injustice because these highlighted my continued vulnerabilities in a gender order that presumed I was a woman.

I would venture a guess that this is not an uncommon experience of academic feminism for FTMs, or even for some non-transsexual men. Paradoxically, I have noticed a new ability to be open to those feminist texts that make connections between the mechanisms by which people are gendered and the harms and injustices that accrue to those people who inhabit those constructed subject positions. I have become a better feminist in my post-transition life as a man. I am not constantly defending against an erroneous identification with women. I find myself wanting to remind transsexual and non-transsexual men alike that feminism is different from (if grounded in) theories of gender construction, that as we theorize "masculinities" we have to stay attuned to questions of power and justice.

You've Got to Be Real

I have been living full-time as a man for a little over a year now. I have had my chest reconstructed and I inject hormones bi-monthly. My name and birth certificate are legally changed to reflect my social status. The tensions with feminism that structured my pre-transition life remain unresolved and there are new questions that I have to negotiate now. More than anything else, I wonder if I am doing it right. Being a man is uncertain terrain, even as I know that I am one. I do not think I am so different from non-transsexual men in this respect.

In general, I want to be unambiguously recognized as an authentic man even though I was not born with a male body. When addressed by my new name or the pronoun "he" I want the speaker to mean what she says. I do not want people to think of me as a woman first and then have to translate it in their heads, the way that you do when you learn a new language. I want to respond naturally to her address, not to look around to see if she meant me. I want to live manhood with the same authenticity as a man born with a male body. I want this so much more than I want a penis. I will be fifty-nine years old before I will have lived more of my life as a man than that other way. I wonder if I will ever be accorded my authenticity or if it is forever out of my grasp.

"Real men" are heterosexual and sometimes obnoxiously homophobic. I try to maintain my heterosexuality while avoiding homophobia. It is a struggle. My desire for women makes me an upwardly-mobile, white, heterosexual guy. Some straight FTMs I know resist this hegemony by calling themselves "queer." Some have even found out that they are gay men. Their desires may have always been for other men, or their sex change also brings a change in their desires—lesbians who become fags (can I even use this word now that I am straight?). Strangely, I am often read as a gay man. Perhaps it comes from the sweet softness still in my face or the way that I lend a good deal of affect to my voice. Lately, I think that there is an overlap between an FTM aesthetic and a gay look. I am obsessed with male bodies, like so many gay guys. I fetishize chests, dicks, side burns, muscles. I vainly worry about my hairline creeping and the few strands that have appeared on my shoulders. I joke that I will be buying Rogaine and signing up for electrolysis or waxing. I like (gay) men's magazines like *GQ* and *Details*. I learn how to buff my shoes to a mirror-shine from the columns—things my father should have taught me. I like going to parties thrown by my gorgeous hunk of a gay male friend; I get cruised there. It makes me feel like I am authentic. Sometimes though, I worry that I am giving off some sign that will reveal my past or that will (more frighteningly) mean that I am gay. Like most heterosexual guys, I have a panic response, one that verges on homophobia. I go home from parties disturbed by, as much as I took pleasure in, those cruisy eyes. Uncertainty about my status produces a defensive stance. Again, this overlaps with the dilemma that most heterosexual men face. Unlike the FTMs who have claimed a gay identity or even a queer identity, I have tried to embrace my new heterosexual status and tried to theorize heterosexuality. I have asked whether heterosexuality is synonymous with hegemony. I have started to keep track of heterosexualities, in the plural. I have made friends with heterosexual men and women who distance themselves from the culture of their parents as much as they distance themselves from queer culture. I take pleasure in our/their rituals. I have been surprised by their politics and their dreams. Yet, I am always struck by my new status in this heterosexist culture that welcomes me as a full-fledged man.

As a friend of mine pointed out, the tension between a desire for gender authenticity or realness and a desire for male feminism is not only experienced by men. Women are also caught in this paradox. Some heterosexual women want feminist husbands, fathers, and sons. They encourage men to refuse the power that comes with their embodied subject positions. On the other hand, these same women want "real men" as husbands, fathers, and sons. They are critical of SNAGS (Sensitive New Age Guys)—too passive, bad clothes, bad hair, bad taste in music. These men are sexually unattractive and psychologically draining. They mooch off women. They are boring conversationalists. They want to "help out" with the housework, but they don't take any initiative. It seems women, as much as men, are fearful that feminist men can not be real men.

Transsexual Bodies

We read an article about a boy who was morphologically male, didn't know that he was intersexed until puberty at which time he began to menstruate through his penis and I just remember the men in the class were absolutely mortified. They were really upset by it. Many of them being clinicians, psychologists in training, they were really empathetic. "Oh how horrible he must've felt. Oh that must've been the most humiliating thing. Oh I feel for this . . . oh my god!" They really just felt like it was something really tragic and horrible. Like they wanted to feel this boy's pain. I just remembered thinking that's exactly how I experienced it. And at first I was really just pissed. . . . I felt [like these men were saying] maybe it's bad if you're a girl, but if you're a boy it's like how tragic! And I experienced it how these men expressed they imagined this boy must feel. Something almost beyond words, something so shameful and humiliating.

(Julian 1995, FTM interview)

Like other men, FTMs have difficulty talking our bodies. Even among themselves, FTMs withhold the details. I have even managed to put it off in this essay for pages and pages. Perhaps it is different from non-transsexuals because we harbor intense shame. Our bodies are scarred. Our bodies are "incomplete": most FTMs do not have reconstructive "lower" surgeries. The costs are prohibitive and the results are often unsatisfactory (sexual pleasure is reduced, aesthetics are not pleasing, functions are compromised). Some FTMs have noted that the poor quality of our genital surgeries compared with the analogous procedures for MTFs is a kind of sexism: a case of nominal "females" being denied the phallus. Our bodies are uncooperative; FTMs report "shut down" in sexual encounters. We have to perform an immense amount of "head work" to transport our bodies from the imaginary into the real. I suppose all people have to do this work; it is hard for me to judge. Sometimes, it is not worth the effort. Sometimes even our best efforts fail to effect the real. Sex is supposed to be raw, animalistic, unmediated. Thinking interferes with the naturalized notions we all have of sex.

This is made tragically frustrating by the increase in my sexual drive, which results directly from the testosterone injected into my muscles. Four days into the two-week cycle of hormone fluctuation (a new cycle to keep track of), it is almost unbearable. This peaks out around the eighth or ninth day and I get some relief until the next shot. What does it mean for a social constructionist to follow this cycle, to believe it is a direct result of this manmade hormone? How can I acknowledge these changes without justifying, or at least understanding, men's sexual aggression? What should I do with the knowledge that this hormone has stopped my monthly bleeding? ("Breakthrough" spotting still occurs occasionally. What is "breaking through"? Through what is it "breaking"?) The rollercoaster ride of emotions has also ceased. How do I theorize the difficulty I have producing tears now? Sobbing was a daily occurrence for me during the last days before I jumped across the gender divide. Did I just cry myself out? How can I account for biology without being a determinist?

I lie awake at night, erect and full of desire. Where can I put this? Sublimation takes me only so far. Besides, how can I have a theory of sublimation which explains my hyperproductivity since transition does not simultaneously assume that men have been able to produce more art, theory, architecture, poetry, etc. because they have more "drive" to sublimate than women? My nights are full of questions that I fear I will never be able to answer: what does it feel like to penetrate someone, to be inside another body, to ejaculate on or in somebody? Am I wrong to want to know the answers? Is this a symptom of my/men's desires to possess? To put my mark on someone, in someone? Is this yet another example of the incompatibility of my desire to be authentic and my desire to be feminist?

I am alone. When I mark that box, "single," on those forms that are everywhere in this bureaucratic society, it has new meaning now. When I tried to live as a lesbian, I had no investment in checking "single" (or any other box) because the question of my status was foreclosed by the law that would not recognize a commitment I made to a partner. Now those boxes are an economy I participate in. Changing my birth certificate means that I am legally able to marry. The politics of this bureaucratic process are driven by heterosexism and a reproductive imperative. I had to prove to the state of my birth that I was incapable of conceiving a child. The criteria for a legal change of sex insist upon a traditional interpretation of marriage: a partnership between a man and a woman for the purposes of reproduction.

I worry about asking a woman out. First, I worry that she will not take me seriously because I look like an adolescent boy, about nineteen years old. The women I want to date are not nineteen. Then I worry that I will have to explain to her about my life, my body. Then I fret over the possibility that she will not have the courage to walk with me. It is a fear of my own vulnerability, of laying myself open for someone. Asking someone out as a transsexual is like walking around in grade school with a "kick me" sign taped to my back. And what of the vulnerabilities that await me when she says "yes"? On the street, nobody can see what I lack. In the bedroom, my body is incomplete and I quake at the idea of producing my prosthetic for a first-timer to see. Or of offering my cock, my flesh-and-blood organ, grown too from testosterone, for her to see, touch, taste. How are these vulnerabilities like those of every man? Like or unlike women's vulnerabilities? Which do I overcompensate for? How does this affect my ability to be feminist?

Grief is a first response to these and other bodily limits. Sadness over the loss of a body I never had and never will have. I will never have the basic human experience of being physically inside the person I love, nor will I contribute to the making of a new life. And more than the body, I mourn the history I never had and never will have. I will never have been sixteen and out with my buddies playing hoops on a hot day with my shirt off and the sun burning my back. I try and push this away because I know that there is nothing that can be done in this lifetime to give me back the twenty-plus years of my life that were sacrificed between my boyhood and my manhood in service to a body that was foreign and a culture that would not recognize me apart from that body. Still, when I think about the mortal limits of this life, of the eighty odd years that we are given to make something of it, I go limp with anguish over the loss of a full quarter of my life spent so thoroughly disassociated that I can hardly remember it. And more, that despite the new condition of my body, I will never have the naturalized, unconscious experience of it that other men have. This is what makes me the most dejected: that I will forever be conscious of my body in a way that others fully take for granted. Some might say that this is something to be thankful for, something we should all aspire to, but that is easy to say when you have never rubbed your hand over your chest and wondered what it felt like not to encounter the strange sensation of numbness from scars acquired in the process of making myself whole.

If I start to think about these things I am lost and so I quickly shift gears. Rage follows my grief. I am angry to have been fated to this life. I wonder if I am suffering a cosmic punishment for having assaulted someone in a past life. Is this another feminist interpretation of transsexualism? I try to transform "transsexualism as punishment" into "transsexualism as blessing" but my rage interferes. There are experiences I am forever denied that I feel are rightly mine to have. I am haunted by the images of dwarfs and young boys. Even they must have bigger penises than I. I envy and resent adolescent boys. They are carefree in their bodies, to a fault. Undoubtedly they have abused their bodies and those around them. I am not proud of these emotions, but I claim them. I watch them to see how they affect my potential to be feminist. Being a "real man" in a sexist society can cut too many ways against too many bodies.

I am full of rage at my invisibilities. Prior to my transition, I was tormented by the world's inability to see me as a man. There was no reason why they should have, of course. Our culture remains tied to its system of materialist references. My body was female and that implied that I was a woman. I made every attempt to have it otherwise, using all my resources to signify my masculinity: my hair, my clothes, my demeanor, my handshake, my walk, my speech patterns, all to no avail. Now that I have transitioned, I am distraught at my invisibility as a transsexual. Unlike most MTFs, who remain legible because of their large hands, feet, stature, and adam's apples (not to mention the incredible scrutiny that all women are subjected to in this culture), most FTMs are thoroughly illegible as transsexuals. We pass as men, undistinguished and undistinguishable, in our everyday lives. It is something I looked forward to and still treasure. Nonetheless, I have a transsexual consciousness forged from years of living a non-normative life. I am discouraged by my invisibility to others who automatically assume that I have never questioned the world.

One thing I miss from my life among lesbians is the knowing wink of the wise in the supermarket, dinner party, or classroom. I find myself looking at queer folks and giving the wink and waiting for the return glance that says "I know you. Stay strong. Be safe." But I am invisible. Lesbians look offended. Gay men think I am one of them or flirting or both. I have stopped winking. It is a small loss, but one for which I grieve. I am frustrated by the lack of respect that I now command, especially among feminists. This is just par for the course for women in other settings, so I smile a sad smile and accept this as payment I must make for the power that I have been accorded just because I walk the earth in male form. Just something all men must be willing to accept: we are not the authority on this subject. I think it teaches me some humility. I am not the authority here, I may not be an authority in other spheres also. Still, I wish I had some other way, besides wearing a T-shirt or a button, that could signal to others that I have a history at an angle to the subject position I inhabit so smoothly now.

Voice is one potential signifier. Coming out in unexpected places is one strategy for visibility. I have exercised my voice in forums where I thought it would make a difference. It is a hard choice and I do not want this to be my only option. Honestly, I resent this strategy because it undermines my lifelong desire to be seen as a man, to be real. Coming out as transsexual puts question marks in the air about my authenticity as a man. It also makes people wonder if I am fraudulent by nature about other things. Instead of being viewed as a sincere gesture, this "coming out" can be taken as a corruption of trust.

I also rage against FTM invisibility in forums that are explicitly dedicated to transsexuals. Recently a panel at the Society for the Study of Social Problems (a sociological association) included activists and academics and psychiatrists, but no one was asked to speak from an FTM perspective. This is a kind of sexism that renders female-bodied experiences invisible. FTMs are the forgotten transsexuals.

Invisibility results in an odd consequence. Most folks assume that I have not struggled to become this white, heterosexual, upper-middle class guy. If there is anything that can provide the basis for male feminism it is this kind of grappling with the world. My struggle to become a white, heterosexual, upper-middle class man is not the same as a woman's struggle for justice, but having had to struggle has provided me with a measure of consciousness about the gendered order. It helps me empathize, but more than that my struggle has taught me about refusal—the refusals of the world to recognize me and the refusals I return to the world that hoped to crush me. The refusals of the world infused me with utopic vision. I learned to see that the world as it is was not the only possibility. To sustain my struggle, I imagined something else, a future, an otherwise. I called it into being myself. I planned and organized. My refusal to accept my body as it was and to allow the world to define me have prepared me to refuse the structural demands and daily temptations of privilege that are now accorded to me as a man. It has given me strength to question how my desire to be authentic dovetails with the cultural pressures to be a real man, and how this conflicts with my feminist ideals.

How does this notion of struggle lend itself to other men who want to be feminist? It offers a possibility for all those men who do not automatically fall into the category of "real man": in other words, practically all men. Almost all men are constantly threatened by this standard. In his analysis of hegemonic masculinity, Robert Connell has suggested that cultural versions of masculinity are differentiated along two axes: in a relationship of dominance over women and in relationships of legitimated authority of some men over others: "'Hegemonic masculinity' is always constructed in relation to various subordinated masculinities as well as in relation to women" (Connell 1995, 183). He argues that hegemonic masculinity cannot do without the existence of other marginalized forms of masculinity. The hegemonic form does not seek to eliminate the other versions. Rather, hegemonic masculinity is an ideal type, not necessarily a lived experience (or lived only by a small fraction of men), one that requires the subordination of other men and other cultural forms of masculinity. Connell has also pointed out that "[n]ormative definitions of masculinity ... face the problem that not many men actually meet the normative standards. This point applies to hegemonic masculinity. The number of men rigorously practising the hegemonic pattern in its entirety may be quite small" (Connell 1995, 79). The fact that most men are already outside of the hegemonic construction of masculinity means that they are engaged, as I am and as other FTMs are, with some kind of struggle. Not all men will want to or be able to abstract from their own struggles to refuse the power that is accorded to them by the gender order. Some of these men will be seduced by their desires to be real. But the specific struggles that men have can serve as a catalyst for activating perverse identifications and for refusing their gendered power.

Activating a perverse identity, struggling, talking one's body—these all belong to the action-paradigm that does not depend on a female-bodied experience in order to be feminist. Through talking our bodies we acknowledge our own location as inhabitants of male bodies each with its orifices and protrusions, its strengths and vulnerabilities. Our bodies are both our point of view on the world and objects for others. The form we inhabit constructs and is constructed by our subjectivity and places us in relation to other bodies/subjectivities. We cannot be women and we cannot know the world as embodied females know it, but our own positions as embodied (male) subjects are implicated in the webs of power that constitute this culture. Our task as action-feminists is to take account of ourselves as bodies. This cannot be done from a position that draws an analogy between women's struggle for justice and our own struggle for justice in their name. We benefit from this unjust system and many men will continue to make investments in this injustice because they are its beneficiaries.[8] Our struggle is not the same as a woman's struggle. We do not have the same stakes in the outcome of the struggle. We can, however, draw on our own struggles with hegemonic masculinity to refuse the political privileges accorded to hegemonic men. We can refuse the cultural pressures to participate in the continued webs of power that we have inherited. We can imagine it otherwise and act accordingly.

Occasionally, during the days while I was writing this essay, I felt a nagging doubt about the position I have been taking. To my mind, living in a period of conflict between paradigms is the cause of this ambivalence. The creeping doubt is an indicator of the social fact that the shift is incomplete. Feminism is still torn by these questions and no clear resolution is forthcoming. It is likely that these two paradigms will co-exist and feminist knowledges will be created by each in their different registers with different implications. From my perspective within the action-paradigm, drawing on embodied experiences for feminist knowledge will be a limited strategy if we do not acknowledge the importance of subjectivity, which is constructed and constructs that experience. Embodied experience refracted through subjectivity can beget male feminism if men are willing to talk their own bodies and learn to refuse the power that we are offered because we inhabit male bodies. Activating my perverse identity and talking my body provide me with a rich source of material that adds to the counter-hegemonic discourse that men, women, and others need for struggle.

Notes

1. Stephen Heath's opening essay in *Men in Feminism* (Jardine and Smith, 1987) makes the argument that male feminism is an impossible contradiction.
2. I acknowledge that this is a revisionist account of my history and that in my past I have made claims to womanhood. I have made such revisions consciously and with intent because they substantiate my claims to be a real man. Realness has significant valence to people, like myself, who have had to face the world with a body that serves as a mask to our authentic selves. I also believe that such revisions trouble an easy feminist accommodation of FTMs.
3. Forthcoming work in trans-studies will make the argument that some transsexual technologies were originally developed in response to phallic war injuries sustained by veterans. See Donna Haraway's cyborg manifesto for the theoretical logic behind these claims.
4. Marjorie Garber dissects this progress narrative in her book *Vested Interests: Cross-Dressing and Cultural Anxiety*. For example: the jazz musician Billy Tipton has been claimed as a feminist hero who cross-dressed and cross-lived in order to be heard in a time when female musicians were an anomaly. Trans-historians and cultural critics are reclaiming Tipton as an FTM who had a male subjectivity. This interpretation has been justified on the basis that Tipton did not reveal his birth sex to his wife and family.
5. Some trans-scholars are documenting non-hegemonic narratives among FTMs that do not posit "boyhoods" or do so only with retrospective perspectives that reflexively acknowledge the constructedness of their histories [Cf. Nakamura, forthcoming].
6. This interpretation takes the literary debates about reading as a women/man to

a whole new place. FTMs are male impersonators. The concept of "impersonation" provided one logic for male feminism. But in this case, "impersonation" is used to maintain the female status of FTMs and by extension, grant feminist status to FTMs.

7. Little did I know at the time, of Sandy Stone's transsexual battle with Olivia. Stone is an MTF who played a crucial role as a sound engineer at many of Olivia's early recording sessions and concerts. She was the subject of a witch hunt when her transsexual status was revealed [Cf. Stone].

8. See David Kahane's essay in this volume.

Bibliography

Anzaldúa, Gloria. 1987. *Borderlands/La Frontera: The New Mestiza.* San Francisco: Spinsters/Aunt Lute.

Bordo, Susan. 1993. *Unbearable Weight: Feminism, Western Culture and the Body.* Berkeley: University of California Press.

Fuss, Diana. 1990. *Essentially Speaking: Feminism, Nature, and Difference.* New York: Routledge.

Garber, Marjorie. 1992. *Vested Interests: Cross-dressing and Cultural Anxiety.* New York: Routledge.

Harding, Sandra. 1991. "Who Knows? Identities and Feminist Epistemology" in *(En)Gendering Knowledge: Feminist in Academe.* eds. Joan Hartman and Ellen Messer-Davidow. Knoxville: University of Tennessee Press.

Haraway, Donna. 1991. "A Cyborg Manifesto: Science, Technology, and Socialist-Feminism in the Late Twentieth Century" in *Simians, Cyborgs, and Women: The Reinvention of Nature.* New York: Routledge.

hooks, bell. 1981. *Ain't I a Woman: Black Women and Feminism.* Boston: South End Press.

———. 1984. *Feminist Theory: From Margin to Center.* Boston: South End Press.

Jardine, Alice. 1987. "Men in Feminism: Odor di Uomo or Compagnous de Route?" in *Men in Feminism.* Alice Jardine and Paul Smith, eds. New York: Methuen.

Julian. 1995. Interviewed by Henry S. Rubin. Tape recording. Cambridge, MA., July 19.

Nakamura. Forthcoming. "Unsutured Narratives" in *GLQ* (special issue on Trans Studies).

———. Forthcoming. "Radical Transsexuality and the Ineffability of Being: SM and Foucault's Escape."

Moraga, Cherríe and Gloria Anzaldúa. 1981. *This Bridge Called My Back.* Watertown: Persephone Press.

Scott, Joan W. 1993. "The Evidence of Experience" in *The Lesbian and Gay Studies Reader.* eds. Henry Abelove, Michèle Aina Barale, David M. Halperin. New York: Routledge.

Stone, Sandy. 1991. "The *Empire* Strikes Back: A Post-Transsexual Manifesto" in *Body Guards: The Cultural Politics of Gender Ambiguity.* eds. Julia Epstein and Kristina Straub. New York: Routledge.

Chapter 17

Feminist Ambiguity in Heterosexual Lives: Reflections on Andrea Dworkin

Laurence Mordekhai Thomas

If everyone wants sexual equality, then it is something of a mystery why this equality has not yet been realized in our lives. Of course, it is obviously false that everyone wants sexual equality. Yet, even among those who sincerely seem to be committed to this ideal, something seems to be amiss. I want to offer some remarks about that, drawing upon Andrea Dworkin's book *Right-Wing Women*. I conclude this essay with a call to courage.

There is a significant number of individuals who are not collectively unified in any way, save that they sincerely hold the belief that, in theory, there are no substantial differences between the sexes with respect to intellectual and emotional capacities. These individuals, who call themselves sexual egalitarians, would be the first to point out that we all know that women can be very strong and intellectually incisive, and we all know that men can cry over personal matters and be intellectually impotent. Whatever differences there are in nature between women and men along these dimensions—there is no need to insist that there are none at all—sexual egalitarians would argue there is no reason for society to codify them. That is, the sexual egalitarians would assert there is no reason to suppose that society would be better off if social institutions were arranged so as to reflect these differences, such as they might be, between women and men. Indeed, they would maintain exactly the opposite, namely that society would be worse-off if this were the case.

Let me be clear here that sexual egalitarians are not pan-bisexualists. They do not hold that everyone is or should be bisexual. Not everyone has the same tastes with respect to many significant things in life, so why suppose that everyone should have the same sexual tastes, though most sexual egalitarians might insist that pure heterosexuals or pure lesbians/homosexuals are rather rare. Just so, there are reasons (monogamy, for example) why, in practice, a person might live an entirely heterosexual or lesbian/homosexual lifestyle.

Now, without calling into question the sincerity of sexual egalitarians, I am struck by just how much female and male behavior among sexual egalitarians accords with traditional female and male behavior, setting aside the ultra-feminine woman and the ultra-macho man. In particular, the ways in which women are emotionally supportive of one another and the ways in which men are emotionally supportive of one another do not seem to have changed much at all. To be sure, men now display a level of affection between one another that did not take place in times past, even in some instances between members of the same family. But a brief display of public affection is one thing, being emotionally supportive is quite another. We do not have the latter in virtue of having the former. Besides, the male display of affection, which is often now valorized, has a very masculine quality to it: each male leans slightly forward engaging in upper shoulder-to-shoulder frontal contact, while refraining from any facial contact. During this shoulder-to-shoulder frontal contact each gives the other several short pats on the back. Women are much less likely to act like that while displaying public affection toward one another, which is not to say that all women are comfortable with traditional displays of affection between women. If I am right in the claim that when it comes to emotional support not much has changed in the behavior of women and men, even among sexual egalitarians, one naturally wonders why? It is to this question that I want to provide at least a partial answer.

Before proceeding a caveat is in order. My focus in this essay is not the world, or even Western culture at large, but the United States Other cultures and countries often have expressions of public affection that are gender neutral. Thus, while *la bise,* the kiss on each cheek, is on the decline in France between men, it nonetheless remains a significantly rich part of French culture that two males, even so-called rough guys, can perform this greeting—*faire la bise*—in public without incurring any suspicion of being homosexual or otherwise calling attention to themselves. Certainly, no one would think to call two men "sissies" simply because they greeted one another in this way. In numerous Arabic countries, men walk hand-in-hand as a show of affection and touch between them is often sensual but not erotic. As far as I can tell, there are no gender neutral expressions of public affection in the United States Certainly not between adults. Unfortunately, both in the case of France and Arabic countries, these forms of affection between men are diminishing as people from these countries succumb to the influence of American imagery.

Holding on to Oppression?

In her provocative book *Right-Wing Women*, Andrea Dworkin maintains that conservative women are not being nearly as irrational as it might seem in resisting feminism. Contrary to all appearances, these women are not in love with being subordinate to men. She argues that conservative women are well aware that, notwithstanding the enormous power that men have in society, there is one aspect of life in which women have a most formidable measure of power, namely that through sexual intercourse women provide a profound affirmation of manhood that a man cannot otherwise attain. Accordingly, conservative women sense that it would be foolish for them to relinquish this power without any assurances of anything in return. It can never be rational to knowingly make oneself worse-off, the case of altruism aside. As a trade-off, this would be utterly irrational, as traditional game-theoretic considerations show.

In the end, I believe that it must be conceded that Dworkin has a point that has withstood the test of time. To be sure, women may, as the song says, want "it" just as much as men do; and there is no doubt that there are sexually aggressive women who are as proud of their sexual prowess as any man might be. And on the other side, there are men these days who are choosing to be virgins, who are willing to admit it publicly, and who insist that the spectre of AIDS is not what inclines them to make this choice. But none of these considerations counts against Dworkin's point, which is that there is an asymmetry between womanhood and manhood; that sex ushers a man into manhood in a way that it does not usher a woman into womanhood; and that men do not suppose that their manhood can be secured in any other way. The familiar theme of the wife sending the husband to sleep on the couch is hardly about the wife not wanting to share the bed with her husband. The not so subtle message is that he will not be having any sex with her tonight. That is, he will not be participating in that rite-of-manhood tonight. Presumably, if he does not, then neither does she. But the reply on the man sent to the couch is never, "You are not getting any either." And to this day, I have not heard of the wife being sent to the couch by her husband. Presumably, this is because a man who passes up sex with his wife cannot quite be all man; whereas a woman who sends her husband out to the living room couch is not, thereby, any less of a woman. One reason for this asymmetry is that while it is true that not all woman either have children or can have children, the fact remains that giving birth is far more decisive an affirmation of womanhood than is sexual intercourse with a man. The male's contribution of the sperm fails to have the same magnitude.

Let me be clear that I do not hold that there is one single component to either womanhood or manhood, as we have typically conceived of these social constructs. On the other hand, the fact that both are multi-faceted is compatible with some components being more central than others or one being more decisive than others.

I believe that sexual egalitarians have travelled quite far in their thinking about sexual equality. I also believe, though, that they have not yet parted company—at least not fully—with that conception of women and men that inclined Andrea Dworkin to put forward the thesis that I mentioned above. It is not only that women play this indispensable role in affirming a man's manhood, but they remain the seat of emotional support for men. In terms of such support, being rocked in the bosom of a woman has a resonance for men that has no equal. Together, we have what may be referred to as the sexual-nurturing role of the traditional female. And while I hardly want to deny that finding a strong man has had, and still does have in many cases, no small amount of resonance for some women, all the available evidence shows that in general women play an emotionally supportive role in the lives of one another that far exceeds anything that men generally play in the lives of one another.

Before proceeding any further, a preemptive response is in order. An apparent drawback with Dworkin's position is that it would seem to have the vice of blaming the victim. Likewise for me if I concur with her. Sexism oppresses women; and if Dworkin is right, then some women have a hand in their oppression by holding dearly to the traditional role of woman as sexual-nurturer. I do not know whether in the end Dworkin would so go far as to blame conservative women for not embracing feminism in order to hold on to their manhood-affirming power. But I take offering an explanation for why an individual does something to be fundamentally different from blaming that individual for why she so behaves. Furthermore, it may be a characteristic feature of all forms of oppression that it is most effective when those being oppressed have a hand in their oppression. The best slave, after all, was not one who labored for the master only under pain of death, but, rather, one who saw this to be his role in life. And as difficult as it might be for us to wrap our mind around the idea, given the extent to which we valorize freedom in present day American society with all of its amenities, some slaves were ambivalent about having their freedom precisely because it meant that they would then have to forge for themselves in a society that provided no form of economic floor. Slave owners, in turn, took this as evidence that slavery was a just order after all. We should no more blame these slaves than we should blame women who hold on to the sexual-nurturing role as a power basis; for it is on account of their having been victimized that they embrace a morally untenable viewpoint. On the other hand, we should be mindful of the fact that oppression is most effective when the oppressed are to some extent rendered complicitous in their own oppression. I offer a few more comments about this in the conclusion of this essay.

From the standpoint of rational choice theory, we are understandably ambivalent about trading a significant good that we firmly possess for the mere possibility of attaining a much greater good, however much we might desire that good. Notice that fraudulent vacation offers work because they generally masquerade as a guarantee rather than the mere possibility of attaining an extraordinary good. By contrast, lotteries work precisely because they play upon the hope of becoming rich for virtually nothing: a mere one dollar ticket. Unfortunately, in the hopes of increasing their odds of winning, poor people buy a great many tickets. In any event, I read Dworkin to mean that lots of women hold on to the sexual-nurturing role as a power basis out of understandable ambivalence, as they endeavor to secure a meaningful romantic relationship with a man. This role gives women at least one formidable bargaining chip. On the one hand, heterosexual men have despised lesbian women on the grounds that these women refuse to play the sexual-nurturing role in the lives of men. On the other, heterosexual women have despised gay men because these men play the sexual-nurturing role in the lives of men, thus depriving women of the one formidable bargaining chip that they have with men in a heterosexually oriented society.

Negotiating Ambiguity

In relationships, especially in the beginning, getting clear about what the other wants is of enormous importance. And often enough, the way we express our own wants is a function of what we take our partners wants to be, given that love is thought to involve having a deep interest in the wants of one's partner. Thus, to take a silly example, whereas we might really want to go to the movies, we might express that desire to our partner far less forcefully, because we do not know what our partner wants to do; and we do not want to seem either inflexible in terms of our own wants or indifferent to the wants of our partner. A desire expressed too forcefully is tantamount to expressing a non-negotiable preference. In actuality, we and our partner could very much want to do the same thing, but arriving at that realization could involve negotiating a few layers of ambiguity. We might begin with, "I would like to see such-and-such film, but we don't have to go tonight." Our partner, testing the waters, responds with, "What else might you want to do?" We respond with, "You know, we could also go dancing. But what would you like to do?" This could continue with our partner responding, "Either dancing or the movies would be nice." The ball back in our court, we then have to figure out whether our partner is really indifferent between the two or actually has a preference for one over the other, since our partner may not have wanted to be adamant in the expression of a preference. Accordingly, in many cases, it would be a mistake simply to assume indifference. A conversation such as this is about negotiating ambiguity.

We negotiate ambiguity in many aspects of our lives. Gender roles is one of them. In a society, such as ours, that privileges heterosexuality over lesbianism/homosexuality, it is of considerable relevance whether this or that behavior casts doubt upon one's heterosexuality. In a society such as ours, most people do not only want to be heterosexual; they want to appear to be so in the eyes of others. In fact, there is considerable evidence that there are many men who want the appearance of being strictly heterosexual all the while living a life that is replete with homosexual experiences. The harsh, anonymous, public restroom sex that society so deplores often takes place between a straight male, ever so anxious to be anonymous, and a gay male. Interestingly, society blames gay males here, but not their "straight" clientele; and this is analogous to the way in which society blames women for getting pregnant, as if men were merely innocent bystanders in the matter. Between females showing rich emotional support of one another and males showing rich emotional support of one another, the latter far more readily calls into question the assumption of heterosexuality than does the former—not only in the eyes of men, but women as well. Surely one of the reasons why many straight males, having cold, anonymous, public restroom sex, do not suppose that they are having anything but straight sex is precisely because no emotional attachment is involved.

Everyone knows that, in theory, touch is of great significance in offering emotional support. And sexual egalitarians would further insist that, in theory, the emotional needs of women and men do not substantially differ from one another. Yet, many sexual egalitarian men would be most uncomfortable crying in the arms of another man, although women do so, whether they are feminist or not. It is significant that we have the asymmetry to which I have just called attention, even among many sexual egalitarians of great sincerity and integrity. This shows that even sincerity and integrity often bow to the reality of social pressures.

But the problem becomes even more vexing, if you will. Heterosexuality is not just a preference on the order of mere tastes. It is generally regarded as a deep feature of our self-identity, and so of the way in which the erotic plays itself out in our lives. But if Dworkin is right, having sex with a woman is for men more than a confirmation of their heterosexual preference. Doing so is ineluctably an affirmation of their manhood via the nurturing-sexual role of women. So, we have an emotional need that is tied to the way in which manhood has been configured. Both women and men have a need for sex. And we can allow that heterosexual sex affirms womanhood as well as manhood. However, let us not forget the observation made earlier that for woman what is far more decisive in this regard is giving birth rather than having sexual intercourse with a man. Thus, woman's emotional need for womanhood affirmation through sexual intercourse is not on par with man's emotional need for manhood affirmation through sexual intercourse. If talk-shows are any indication of what might be true, it is common enough to hear of young girls seeking sex in order to become a mother; whereas it is very rare to hear of young boys seeking sex in order to become a father. For males the affirmation is in the sex. Sex and sports are the only two contexts in society where men can allow themselves to be fully taken over by the passion of the moment. And I have deliberately used the word "allow." It will take a very long and convoluted argument to show that as sports spectators men are owing to the way in which they are biologically wired. So even if we made the concession that it is owing to biology that men give themselves over to passion in the sex act, it does not follow that men cannot be this way in other areas of life, as in the case of a sports show. But if in the case of sports, it is not biology, but social acculturation that explains why men express such emotion and passion, then we know that men could so behave in many areas of life, even if the hardwiring in this regard is only with respect to sex. I do not think that when it comes to displaying emotions and passion men are hardwired to do so only in the context of sex. I am merely pointing out that even if this claim were true, it would not get us very far in terms of explaining male behavior.

What I have done in the preceding two paragraphs is establish a connection between heterosexual men generally looking to women for emotional support by drawing attention to the reality of heterosexual men needing women emotionally to have their manhood affirmed. The affirmation of manhood constitutes a fundamental form of emotional support. If there is such a thing as a continuum of need for emotional support, then surely that continuum is put into place by the fundamental emotional need of manhood affirmation.

Someone might object to Dworkin's views because they regard her as recommending lesbianism. Perhaps. But a view considerably short of that is the following: if we are ever to achieve a non-sexist world, then we must de-couple manhood from heterosexuality; and women must be prepared to participate in bringing about that end. Although lesbianism may be sufficient to achieve this end, I do not think that lesbianism is necessary to bring about the realization of this end. On the other hand, I hold that along with men being willing to run the risk of being viewed as homosexuals because they turn to one another for emotional support, women must relinquish the view that the affirmation of manhood comes from a man having sex with a woman and the concomitant emotional support that this entails. Just as men, up to a certain point, are not presently threatened by women providing one another with rich emotional support, women must likewise not be threatened by men turning to one another in this way. If, when men turn to one another in this way, women feel threatened because they suppose that they have been replaced by a man, and regard a man that so behaves as less of a man, then heterosexual men who would so behave have a reason not to do so. If, when men turn to one another in this way, women are terribly ambivalent about men so behaving, then heterosexual men will more than likely pick up on that ambivalence and be ambivalent about turning to one another for emotional support.

One of the most majestic statements in John Rawls's contemporary classic, *A Theory of Justice*, is that by ourselves we are but part of what we might be. Perhaps in no context is this more true than with respect to the attainment of the ideal of sexual equality in a heterosexual world.

It is a commonplace for women to say that they want a more sensitive male, a male who is willing to share his emotions. And while John Gray's *Men are from Mars, Women are from Venus* would suggest that the reason why women and men have different emotions and reactions is that women and men are just constructed differently, I believe that a much better explanation is available. What we have here, between heterosexual women and men, is very much akin to a coordination problem regarding a set of expectations well in place: women have certain expectations concerning the emotional role that they play in the lives of men, and men know that women have these expectations; and women know that men know that women have these expectations. Not surprisingly, surely, heterosexual females and males are massively responsive to one another's expectations. The question is how might we change those expectations, which by so many, especially among sexual egalitarians, are deemed most undesirable. Lesbianism is not the only answer, although that would suffice. Lesbians would suffice because it constitutes a complete refusal to affirm the manhood of men through sexual intercourse. It is not a conceptual truth, however, that the only way this decoupling can take place is through women becoming lesbians. Certainly, a woman does not have to be a lesbian in order to appreciate that too much of a man's male identity is tied up with the sex act. A woman does not have to be a lesbian in order to believe that sex would be better if a man would stop trying to prove something in the bedroom.

My point is that insofar as women hold dearly to the view that they provide the emotional support of manhood affirmation through sex, then men will at least have a reason not to change. Or, insofar as women are ambivalent about playing this role in the lives of men—wanting to, but not wanting, and there is no telling when they want to or not—then men will undoubtedly be ambivalent about changing their behavior. It is worth pointing out that women are not just emotionally sensitive with men, but also with other women. The sensitivity that they bring to their encounters with men has been honed and refined through the emotionally rich interactions that they have with other women. Surely, it is just wishful thinking to suppose that men will be ultra-sensitive with women, but ever the macho-fellow with their buddies. This is to invite a kind of schizophrenia.

Unfortunately, so it seems to me, even sexual egalitarians are haunted by the spectre of homosexuality on the part of men. Suppose it suddenly became a fact about the world, or simply the United States, that the kind of man with whom women most wanted to have sex, the kind of man who made women lose their reserve, was one who was capable of crying in the arms of another man and shedding tears over sensitive issues. Need I point out that, given this supposition, there would be demonstrations of male crying the likes of which we have never before seen. The streets would be awash in male tears. Men who had no clue that they could cry, let alone cry over nothing, would be wailing in the streets. Handshakes between men would require handkerchiefs? Why, men would find themselves crying over the mere thought that another man was about to engage in a friendly touch. What is more, men would hardly be worried about whether anyone took them to be gay, since being emotional with men would be seen as the route to having sex with women. To be sure, as I have just told the story, men would also be looking over their shoulder to see just how many women were watching and being moved by it all. Yet, if women had this expectation of men and men knew that women had this expectation of men and this expectation were truly deep, crying would be as natural for men as we suppose it is for women nowadays. Where and when we cry is not entirely independent of the expectations in place. For the obvious reasons, were I held hostage by a group of neo-Nazis, I would not cry watching *Schindler's List*, though I have cried dearly the several times that I have seen the film. So while there is much talk of women wanting more sensitive men, the truth of the matter is that men doubt the sincerity of women here, and I dare say that they do so with good reason; for women are perhaps more than a little ambiguous in their feelings about wanting more sensitive men. Why? Because as I noted in the preceding paragraph, more sensitive men would be more sensitive not only with women but with other men as well. This means that women would no longer be the sole provider of emotional nurturance in the lives of men. In a sexist world, where men hold the balance of power, it is understandable that women are reluctant to give up this role, as Dworkin so perceptively observed.

I have claimed that women view themselves, and that men view women, as playing the primary sexual-nurturing role in the lives of men. The further claim is that if men ceased viewing women playing this role, while maintaining fully voluntary and non-coercive interactions with women, as they sought women for sexual partners, then that would bring about a change for the better in the elimination of sexist attitudes. Likewise, if women ceased viewing themselves as playing this role, as they sought fully voluntary and non-coercive interactions with men, then that would bring about a change for the better in the elimination of sexist attitudes. What I am not by any means claiming is that women should never play a nurturing role in the lives of men. Nor am I claiming that men should never play a nurturing role in the lives of women. The point, instead, is that this role should flow from the voluntary interactions between two people rather than from some socially constructed a priori role of womanhood and manhood.

What is required is a measure of moral courage on the side of both parties. Understandably, in a heterosexual society heterosexual men want not just to be heterosexual but to appear as heterosexual in the eyes of others, among these being heterosexual women. By contrast, heterosexual women understandably enjoy the power, however subtle it might be, of being the purveyor of emotional support and manhood affirmation. With these expectations still firmly in place, it is no wonder that things continue to look so much the same. And it is most unfortunate that the spectre of homosexuality has gotten in the way. We can all wait for the other to make the first move. If we do that, though, we may be waiting longer than we want. There is another option, though: we might exhibit the courage to move first, and in so doing, inspire the other to move. What makes the prisoner's dilemma so fascinating is that it shows that what is rationally better for all is not secured simply by individuals acting rationally independently of one another. The great good is obtained by an exercise of moral faith. Having seen that others desire that good, as do we, the most appropriate move we can make sometimes is not to wait for the good to come about as if there were yet another entity that might achieve for us the good that we both want. Rather, we might have the courage of our convictions. This is an appropriate moral response to a morally ambiguous situation. And if enough of us should have the courage of our convictions, then we thereby shift the character of our moral climate for the better.

Conclusion: A Call to Courage

I have hardly denied that men have created the sexist society in which we now live. Nor, certainly, have I denied that men need to abandon their sexist ways. Rather, I have drawn attention to the truth that the demise of sexism requires that both women and men change their ways of thinking about one another. Some would bristle at the idea of saying that women have power in being able to affirm the manhood of a male, preferring to say that in a sexist society women are completely powerless. I do not hold such a view of oppression, neither in the case of racism, including American slavery, nor in the case of sexism. I believe that in subtle ways it is possible for the oppressed to come to be complicitous in their own oppression. Indeed, as I said earlier, we have oppression at its most effective when this is so. If slave owners could not have trusted some black slaves, the nanny role would not have existed. This means that some blacks were trustworthy as slaves, and so to some extent complicitous in their own enslavement.

It may be that men created the role of women affirming the manhood of men. However, if women have internalized that role, then they are to some extent complicitous in their very own sexist oppression. What is more, if women have internalized this role, then in order to achieve a non-sexist society it is a fact of the matter that women must abandon that role. And if women are ambivalent about that, then that ambivalence reverberates across social interactions between the two sexes. I call for the courage of women to move beyond their ambivalence; I call for the courage of men to move beyond the internalized expectations of women that it is their role—and theirs alone—to affirm a man's manhood. I call for both to have the courage to put aside the roles of womanhood and manhood. I should like to think that in the ideal non-sexist world, there would be sexual preferences that did not come packaged as expressions of either manhood or womanhood, but simply as expressions of humanity with all of its richness and diversity. Some women might prefer men to women, and some men might prefer women to men. But none of this would be about the former expressing or realizing their womanhood and the latter their manhood. Rather, it would be about both women and men more fully realizing their humanity.

Many have taken the ideas in Dworkin's *Right-Wing Women* to be a call to lesbianism and so, for that reason, they have rejected her insights. I cannot, and do not, speak for her. Still, it is significant that we can recast her ideas as a call to be morally courageous. The problem, one might argue, is not that we have this or that sexual orientation; for as I noted earlier, human beings have a myriad of preferences in all walks of life. We should not behave as if things are any different in the sexual realm. The problem, then, is not that we have this or that sexual orientation or preference, but that we are hostage to it. Courage in this regard requires only that we not be hostage to our sexual orientation, and not that we pretend that we do not have a given sexual orientation. Arguably, only a world in which people are hostage to their sexual preference could it turn out that our sexual identity has metamorphised into the controlling phenomenon that it is. To use the immortal Kantian language, one might have thought that our sexual identity should be an expression of ourselves as free and rational creatures, thereby elevating the physical to the realm of the spiritual—not because the physical is necessarily morally sullied, but because when free and rational human beings act with purity of heart they necessarily transform the physical, no matter what form it takes.

Acknowledgments

In writing this essay, I am deeply indebted to the excellent philosophical writings of Sandra Bartky, *Feminity and Domination: Studies in the Phenomenology of Oppression* (New York: Routlege, 1990); Claudia Card, *Lesbian Choices* (New York: Columbia University Press, 1995); and *The Unnatural Lottery: Character and Moral Luck* (Philadelphia: Temple University Press, 1996). I would also like to thank John Stoltenberg for years of inspiration. The last section of this essay, especially the last paragraph, owes both its inspiration and expression to Nasri Abdel-Aziz.

Chapter 18

A Progressive Male Standpoint

Larry May

A progressive male standpoint is an egalitarian theoretical and practical position from which men can critically assess male experience and traditional male roles.[1] This standpoint is similar to feminist standpoint epistemologies that have been developed in the last decade.[2] As I use the term, "progressive standpoints"[3] are perspectives that intermix considerations of knowledge and politics in such a way that practical knowledge (or praxis) is created. People who attain a progressive standpoint come to understand how their participation in certain social arrangements may contribute to inequality and oppression. In the context of gender, progressive standpoints allow men and women to understand their roles in gender inequality. While progressive female standpoints on gender have proliferated, progressive male standpoints have not. The chief question asked is this: Can men get enough distance on their privileged position in society to assess it critically and attempt to create an egalitarian model of masculinity?

In this essay I describe a model of a progressive male standpoint. This model has four dimensions that overlap and collectively provide sufficient conditions for a progressive male standpoint. First, there is a striving for knowledge or understanding based on experience, especially personal experience of traditional male roles and activities. Second, there is a critical reflection on that experience in light of the possible harms to women, as well as men, of assuming traditional male roles and engaging in traditional male activities. Third, there is a moral motivation to change at least some aspects of traditional male roles and activities. And finally, there are practical proposals for changes in traditional male roles that are regarded as believable by other men. In what follows I devote a section to each of these four aspects (personal experience, critique, moral motivation to change, and believable practical proposals) of one version of a progressive male standpoint.

In the first section of the essay I consider to what extent personal experiences of men are crucial for developing a progressive knowledge or understanding of masculinity. I reject the often stated claim that personal experience is necessary for true understanding. But I explain why certain types of personal experience are quite valuable for a progressive orientation nonetheless.[4] In the second section of the essay I argue that a male viewpoint is not the same as a male standpoint, the latter but not the former requires most especially a *critical* appreciation of one's experience.[5] I argue that many but not all men will find it difficult to attain this perspective, and that women will find it easier to do so. Throughout the essay, I am especially concerned to discuss the claim raised by some feminists that a progressive standpoint, as opposed to a viewpoint, cannot be achieved unless one is a member of an oppressed group.

In the third section of the essay I take up the explicitly moral part of the progressive male standpoint. As with other moral standpoints, the progressive male standpoint is concerned with the sort of understanding that provides a motivation to change oneself, and ultimately one's society. If one comes to understand that rape is morally wrong, and one understands that one has contributed to a climate that makes rape more prevalent, then one should be motivated by this understanding to do something to change that environment.[6] I discuss the internal and external sanctions that make such motivation efficacious. In the fourth section of the essay I discuss the idea that men will take more seriously proposals for changing masculine roles when these comes from men rather than from women. The believability of a claim is sometimes as important as its justifiability, although believability cannot be a substitute for justifiability. I end with a discussion of what men and women each can bring to the progressive critique of male roles and experience.

Personal Experience

For most of recorded history, the voice of knowledge has been a male voice. When women theorists began to challenge that voice they seized upon the idea that there were certain subjects, such as pregnancy and childbearing, that men could not understand as well as women could.[7] If experience is intimately connected to understanding, then those who have not had a relevant experience will have to work harder to attain the understanding, in most cases, than those who have had the relevant experience. Any person should be able to gain understanding as long as he or she could at least imagine experiencing the relevant phenomena. But in most cases, the task of imagination needs to be guided by someone who has had the relevant experience. I will begin my inquiry into the components of a progressive male standpoint with a discussion of the importance of personal experience.

A progressive male standpoint is an epistemic standpoint that places personal experience at center stage.[8] By experience is simply meant a state of affairs, or a process, in which a person comes into contact with the world through the use of one's senses. Personal experience is experience based on having lived through a particular event (such as giving birth or having a vasectomy), having assumed a certain role (such as becoming a mother or a father), or having perceived a certain state of affairs (such as that one is an object of sex discrimination, or that one has contributed to the rape culture).[9] Personal experience can also involve observing someone else who is experiencing something (such as being present when someone else is giving birth to a child) or being told about someone's experience by someone who one has reason to trust (such as being told about a friend's experience of being the victim of sexual harassment).

It is a commonplace for people to say that they can only really understand a thing if they have lived through it.[10] Those who have had direct acquaintance with something seem to be better placed to understand that thing than someone who has not had this experience.[11] If one has not experienced something personally, one must rely on the accounts of others. Yet, there may be a gap between what others experience and what they report they have experienced. Such a gap may exist because of intentional distortion or because of unintended distortions. Even when undistorted we may not be able to comprehend what another person reports because of problems of communication, or lack of a common basis of shared experience. It seems that these problems of distortion and communication do not exist (at least to the same extent) when one learns something from one's own experience as opposed to learning from the reports of other persons who one does not know.

In some cases, "perceiving" is not a matter of sense perception; a moral "perceiver" relies on his or her value orderings and conceptions of moral saliency.[12] Value orderings and rules of saliency are not themselves infallible. Accounts of one's moral experience are difficult to justify as well as difficult to transmit to others so that others can judge the cogency of what one claims to have experienced. A person may morally misperceive a situation he or she is personally experiencing. Of course, when one is forced to rely solely on what others experience, this problem may be compounded since the possibility of misperceiving a situation may increase the further removed one is from the initial experience.

Consider two examples of assessing the degree of pain that a man experiences. In the first case the man suffers while undergoing a vasectomy. In the second case a man suffers when he is denied his paternal right to decide whether his biological child should be given up for adoption. Men who have had such experiences have a fairly straightforward way of assessing these types of suffering, namely, merely remembering what they felt when they went through it. But here distortion is possible on two levels. First, one's memory may be faulty or clouded by other experiences. Second, one's initial experience may have been influenced by painkillers or depression and not easily generalized. In order to generalize on the basis of one's personal experience, these men will also have to imagine what other men would experience. Because of this, one's ability to understand some general state, such as the degree of pain one is likely to suffer from having a vasectomy, is never based only on one's personal experience.

We cannot literally feel the pain or suffering of another person. We must reconstruct that pain or suffering on the basis of information that is problematical in several respects. Those who have not had the experience in question will often need to rely on people who have had the experience to help them test or check what they have imaginatively come up with. If one is having a direct experience of pain, a person can get what seems to be nearly immediate access to data that can confirm or deny that the pain is intense.[13] But of course, one can be deluded here, as in the case of the phantom limb, where people who have lost a limb yet still feel pain in that limb.

Many men who have not had a vasectomy, or been denied paternal rights, have had other operations, or denials of rights, on the basis of which they can extrapolate. And this is also true of many women, who, after all, are more likely to experience pain and discomfort in the groin area than are men, and also more likely to have been denied their rights. If one is going to have to extrapolate to come to an understanding of what others are experiencing, why should it matter whether one has had the relevant experience oneself or not? And if one has not had the experience, why would it matter whether one was male or female in being able to imagine the psychological pain of the man who does experience these things directly?

Can a woman imagine what it feels like to be repeatedly "kicked in the balls" (the account most men give of what it feels like to have a vasectomy)? Obviously she can at least partially imagine this by extrapolation from other intensely painful experiences she has had. But at least part of the psychological distress men feel in such events is wrapped up with the fear of castration or impotence. And the suffering involved in the loss of paternal rights is bound up with the idea of losing one's sense of manhood. In this respect most men who are trying to imagine what it is like to have a vasectomy, or to lose paternal rights, will be initially better placed than most women. For there is no psychologically stressful experience comparable for most women to the fear of castration and impotence or of losing one's manhood. It is true that some women have a fear of being rendered infertile, but this fear is not ordinarily associated with an intensely painful experience. Of course, this does not completely block women from imagining what men experience in vasectomy operations, but it does mean that they will find it more difficult than most men to engage in reconstructive imagination. For as one gets further and further removed from the actual experience, and as the pool of experiences upon which one draws is less and less analogous to the actual experience, the powers of imagination are more and more strained.

Why isn't imaginatively reconstructed or simulated experience close enough to direct experience to be as initially useful as direct experience? At least one reason is that people have limitations to their powers of imagination. A person who is able to use his legs to walk could imagine that this is not true and that he would have to use a wheelchair for mobility. But he would find it difficult to imagine what it would be like to have to use a wheelchair to get anywhere at all, that *every* time he needs to go somewhere, he would have to get there in his wheelchair. Our imagination can replicate certain kinds of temporally limited experiences, but it has trouble being sustained so as to replicate temporally extended experiences.[14]

The general point is that it is harder to achieve and to sustain an understanding of something if one has not experienced the thing oneself. The image fades more quickly if that image was not implanted through some kind of lively experience. And as we will see, some faint images don't motivate the way that more lively ones do. But it is not impossible to replicate a set of experiences through imagination. For this reason, all that can be concluded from the above is that having had personal experience of something makes it easier for a person initially to gain a certain kind of knowledge or understanding of that thing than if one has not had personal experience. But it cannot be said that such knowledge or understanding is blocked by lack of personal experience. Thus we have a reason for thinking that personal experience is initially valuable in attaining a progressive male standpoint, but not a reason for thinking that this standpoint is unattainable by those who lack certain personal experiences.

A Critical Point of View

There is more to the formation of a progressive standpoint than merely having a certain type of experience. We need to distinguish between merely having a viewpoint and attaining a progressive standpoint. As Nancy Hartsock has said, a standpoint is not merely something one assumes; rather it is an achievement.[15] To occupy a progressive standpoint a person has to see certain experiences as part of a larger whole, not merely as isolated events. One must critically reflect on these experiences in light of a certain kind of enlarged consciousness, namely, one that filters out certain individual biases that one might impose on the interpretation of these experiences.[16] More importantly, a person must somehow come to an understanding of what it means to be oppressed, to be powerless rather than to be wielding power.

Consider the claim that women can understand the morality of abortion, because of their personal experiences, better than men can. A progressive female (or feminist) standpoint takes account of women's personal experiences in two respects. First, there is the experience of having had an abortion or having gone though, or at least feared, pregnancy. Second there is the experience of being able to reflect critically on the dominant institutions and roles that influence women's lives. It is the latter experience that turns the viewpoint of some women on their own personal experiences into a progressive standpoint. Not all women can achieve the progressive standpoint on gender issues because not all women can attain a critical view of their own position in the world. But, by virtue of being a member of an oppressed group women are better placed initially to be able to achieve a progressive standpoint than is generally true for men.

Members of oppressed groups, on this view, are thought to have fewer biases in the maintenance of a certain status quo since their powerlessness allows fewer clear-cut interests in the continuation of the status quo than members of oppressor groups. In this sense the members of oppressed groups can potentially attain an account of social reality that is more accurate than that attainable by members of oppressor groups. But members of oppressed groups also have interests, and those interests can block them from discovering certain kinds of social knowledge or understanding. Just as the oppressors often have an interest in maintaining the social status quo, so the oppressed often have an interest in overturning that social status quo. So, there is also a sense in which oppressed group members will have trouble attaining a more accurate account of social reality than that attainable by members of an oppressor group, although it remains true that members of oppressed groups have fewer hurdles to overcome than do members of oppressor groups in attaining a progressive standpoint.

Many men have traditionally had a viewpoint that could be called "a male viewpoint" based largely on the privileges and powers they have enjoyed. The traditional male perspective has also virtually excluded the perspective of women, at least in certain domains. Can there be an alternative male viewpoint that does not merely replicate the existing position of privilege and power that men have traditionally occupied? Does the fact that men are not systematically oppressed diminish the value of, or perhaps even make it impossible for them to attain, a standpoint from which critically to assess their lives? What are the unique practical problems faced by men who try to achieve a progressive male standpoint? Is it necessary that a person be a member of an oppressed group in order to attain the enlarged consciousness that is central to the formation of a standpoint?

In order to provide answers to these questions, I will first construct, and critically assess, an argument in support of the view that being oppressed is necessary for the achievement of a progressive standpoint. Perhaps the most obvious and commonsensical position would be that those who are not oppressed lack the motivation to challenge their own privileges and biases, since these contribute to the self-interest of the unoppressed. Hartsock argues that the viewpoint of those who are in an oppressor class is both partial and perverse.[17] It is partial because it cannot get beyond the self-interest of the oppressor group, and it is perverse because it seeks to nullify the interests of the oppressed group, thereby failing to afford women equal treatment and respect.

Can some men attain enough critical distance to be able to step outside the dominant position of their gender group to be able to approximate the standpoint of the oppressed gender group, namely women? This is not to suggest that men must become women in order to achieve a progressive male standpoint on gender. Rather the question can be rephrased as follows: can men attain a critical distance from their own positions of power and dominance over women, which would be like the position that women, as a group, occupy? The answer I wish to offer is a qualified "yes." The qualification is that not many men will be likely to achieve this, and that they will no doubt only be able to approximate the progressive standpoint that some women can occupy.

As a first step, men need to be able to become critical of their roles in society, to see how the roles of husband and father, for instance, contain elements that contribute to the inequality of women and to sex discrimination. This is a necessary first step because otherwise men will be too likely to mistake what appears to be the normal functioning of a social role for the way that role should function morally. Men who are fathers and husbands will be inclined to see their roles in the narrow terms of whether they are successful at occupying certain roles, without recognizing that the successful fulfillment of these roles can, and often does, curtail the ability of women as wives and daughters to be afforded equal treatment and respect. Not only will men be inclined not to be self-critical because they are focused on conforming to the expectations of the role, but they will also be inclined to misunderstand the harmful effects of the role because it will be in their interests to have a positive public view of these defining roles for men. For these reasons it is important that men engage in critical thought and discussion about their roles, even though this will be quite difficult for most men.

Such critical thought and reflection, however, is probably not sufficient to afford some men the chance to achieve a progressive standpoint on their male roles and experiences. In addition they will need to spend time interacting with women in non-dominating ways to learn from them what it is like to be oppressed. Here is a legitimate role for imaginative reconstruction, especially in the context of role reversal. The critical perspective men need to achieve on their masculine roles is dependent on imagining the position of those who lack privilege and power that can be attained more easily by women since women normally in fact lack privilege and power. Men need to think about their own masculinity from a position where their interests are not so bound up with the maintenance of male privilege. In this sense men cannot attain a progressive male standpoint unless they imagine and then come to understand the position of the oppressed, in this case the position of women.

Why not think that women are better able to reflect critically on masculinity and male experience than men since they do not need to imagine the perspective of the oppressed? I think there is a lot to be said for this position. Just as men are in a better position for data gathering about male experience and roles because of being directly acquainted with them; so women have a better position for critically assessing male experience since they are not as likely to be biased in favor of that experience.[18] Men will be better at certain aspects of the study of male experience and roles and women will be better at other aspects.[19] But in both cases, these are only initial advantages for some members of these groups. Other members of the group will still have difficulty attaining a progressive standpoint, and no one is completely blocked from attaining this standpoint just because he or she lacks certain experience.

Since men are generally not discriminated against on grounds of sex, and do not suffer from unequal treatment merely because they are male, it is not easy for them to take on the critical standpoint of one who has been adversely affected by a set of discriminatory roles and practices. Nonetheless, some men can potentially approximate such a stance either by engaging in role reversal or by extrapolating from other experiences they have, for instance as members of a marginalized sub-group of the larger group of men (as is true of men who are homosexual or bisexual, or of men who are non-white). In general men need to be able to become critical of the privileged position of men, while at the same time realizing that they will never be able completely to distance themselves critically from such privilege because they will continue to benefit from being male in ways that they are often not conscious of, such as the way all men benefit from the rape culture.[20]

Moral Understanding

In addition to experiential and critical components, there is also a normative and motivational component in a progressive male standpoint. This third part of the progressive male standpoint involves that curious mixture of understanding and motivation to change that is characteristic of moral standpoints generally. What is the source of the motivation to change? Is the increased understanding of the harmfulness of rape and of a man's contribution to the environment that makes rape prevalent enough to spark a man to act in ways that would change that environment? Is the motivation to change merely internal to the understanding, or is there something added that brings about the motivational impetus?[21]

When a man comes to gain a critical understanding of why it is wrong to contribute to the rape culture, what causes him to be motivated to respond by changing his behavior? In answering this question it is interesting to note that there are humans, most commonly referred to as sociopaths, who are unmoved even when they seemingly understand their role in producing harm. If one thinks that there is a necessary (internal) relationship between knowing what is right and doing it, there are at least two strategies that one can adopt to explain the sociopath. First, one can attempt to deny that sociopaths actually understand that others are harmed or that they have caused this harm. Secondly, one can admit that there are sociopaths but deny that there are very many of them, thereby downplaying the significance of this fact. Normal people are not sociopaths; normal people are moved by their moral understandings. There is a third strategy for taking account of the sociopath that would call into question the necessary (internal) relationship between knowing what is right and doing it. This third strategy admits that there are sociopaths, and argues that moral understanding does not motivate without an additional element being present, for instance the threat of sanction or the hope of reward. Or even more basically, it might be claimed that understanding alone is not sufficient to motivate without some kind of caring disposition already in place,[22] and that this is precisely what the sociopath lacks.

Let us first consider the strategy of denying the relevance of sociopaths because normal people are not sufficiently like sociopaths. This strategy runs into trouble whenever otherwise normal men, who have come to see that they are causing harm, display the same complete lack of motivation as shown by sociopaths. Normal men often seemingly fail to react to stimulations in their environment due to lack of sensitivity or empathy. As a result of traditional socialization patterns, men have been less prone to display empathy and sympathy than have women.[23] Many heterosexual men in Western cultures are emotionally stunted and as a result have a harder time than women in changing their behavior even when they realize that they are causing or contributing to harm.

The second strategy, which claims that there are simply very few people like the sociopath, runs into similar difficulties. Whether due to weakness of will, or indifference, or self-interestedness, many people in my experience do not do what they themselves think they morally should do. Of course many of these people are not sociopaths: they care about the fact that they cause harm. The problem is that they also care about many other things, and so their caring about the harm they cause is not sufficient to motivate them to change their behavior. It is thus the third strategy that I am inclined to accept since I find it implausible to deny the existence, indeed the prevalence, of sociopaths and others like them.

Would achieving a progressive male standpoint make it more likely that men would work to reduce sexual violence in their own lives and communities? This is a hard question to assess. While the example of the sociopath shows that people do not always act on their normative understandings, this example tells us nothing about whether there is necessarily some motivational pull associated with normative understanding. I believe that normative understanding of such things as men's complicity in the prevalence of rape will, under certain conditions, make it more likely, but not necessary, that men will be motivated to act to change the environment that contributes to the prevalence of rape.

Moral understanding, unlike other forms of understanding, is infused with understanding of how we should live our lives. Those who achieve a progressive male standpoint attain heightened moral understanding of male experience and roles that will correspondingly heighten their motivation to change their own behavior and to affect the behavior of other men and the social institutions in their societies. But having heightened motivation to change does not guarantee that change will occur. Motivations can be offset by other motivations and hence fail to result in action. For moral motivation to result in action without additional sanctions or rewards, men must come to feel that changing themselves is a desirable thing.

Motivational change occurs due to some felt compulsion to act on what one already understands. When external sanctions are threatened, a person comes to *feel* motivated to change behavior in a deeper sense than occurs when one merely *believes* that one should change. Externally imposed sanctions add an extra impetus to change that often tips the scales so that other motivations pulling us away from change can be overridden. Socialization can also act as a kind of added sanction, although its force is felt as if it were internal rather than external. Emotions can perform the function of inner sanctions in that they motivate in a way that mere belief does not.[24] Socialized feelings of guilt and shame for instance can be as powerful a motivator as fear of punishment.

For a progressive male standpoint to motivate men to change their behavior it must generate emotions, such as shame and guilt as well as compassion and caring, in addition to beliefs. One way this can occur is when men socialize boys to feel shame for sexual aggression. Then, later in life, when men criticize other men the earlier socialization is reinforced in a way that motivates men to change. In the case of complicity for rape, there is often a profound sense of shame that motivates some men to try to distance themselves from the rest of the group of men by speaking out or attempting to raise their sons in a way that will break the spiraling pattern of male socialization that results in the increasingly violent rape culture. Men need to help motivate one another to change socialization patterns.

Women also can help emotionally motivate men to act on their normative understandings. It is important that women, especially mothers, aunts, grandmothers, and neighbors contribute to the effort to bring about change in male socialization and motivation to change. Because of the central role played by many women in early childhood socialization, women can contribute quite a bit to the progressive socialization of boys. So there is nothing in my view to support the contention that women should be marginalized in motivating men to change. But men may be better placed to affect these changes in adult men than are women because these are largely male problems and because, regrettably, men are more likely to listen to other men than to women, as we will see in the next section.

Men are the perpetrators of rape and sexual harassment, they are the impregnators and the predominant buyers of pornography, they are the sexual aggressors and those most likely to exclude and diminish the status of women. But many men are also enraged, saddened, guilt-ridden, and ashamed of their position in society. Mostly, though, many men are confused about the alternatives that are available to them that would be more socially acceptable and yet not merely a pale reflection of the other gender group. And it is for this reason that men need to assume a progressive male standpoint and speak to their fellow men about methods to change patterns of male socialization in ways that are believable and plausible.[25]

Convincing Ourselves

In this final section I turn from discussions of how one acquires knowledge or understanding to questions of how that information is best conveyed. A progressive male standpoint that seeks change in traditional male behavior will need to provide analyses and proposals for change that men will find believable for them to be motivated by these propos-als. Whether someone is regarded as believable is often as important as whether his or her ideas are theoretically justifiable. Believability is affected by many factors that are not properly germane to justifiability, although the two are not completely separate. In this section I will briefly address this aspect of a progressive male standpoint, recognizing that it is frought with problems.

The distinction between justifiability and believability is important in many contexts. A person who has just looked through a telescope may be quite justified epistemically in saying that what appears to be a shooting star is really a fast moving plane. Yet, this person may not be believable to others unless it is known that the person is an astronomer, or it is known that she has just looked through a telescope, or until someone else looks through the telescope and publicly confirms the observation. Similarly, men often are more likely to believe other men than to believe women, even when the two are saying the same things. Believability is often a function of appearances, especially public appearances, rather than a matter of theoretical justification.

There is an obvious difficulty with this type of believability. When men give greater uptake to fellow men than to women concerning the critique of male roles, this sounds suspiciously like men's historical distrust of women as thinkers and scholars. We should not give credibility to men's discriminatory attitudes. If men were more likely to believe other men because of contemptuous attitudes toward women scholars, then this type of believability should not count for much. But if men tend to trust other men more than women because they believe that men will be better positioned to understand both the positive and negative aspects of male experience, then this is a type of believability that may be legitimately given some weight.

Here is an example. I have attended conferences where male speakers have made jokes or statements that are blatantly sexist. If this is pointed out by a woman in the audience, many men will roll their eyes or chuckle, often saying to one another, "she has too thin a skin," or "she can't take a joke." But when I or another man point out the sexist nature of the joke or statement, men in the audience, as well as the speaker, often look sheepish or guilty. There is no room for a conspiratorial nod or chuckle toward other men since it is not clear whether these other men will side with the speaker or with the man who has challenged the speaker. In addition, men cannot easily dismiss the criticism since it emanates from a position where it is assumed that male experience is taken seriously. For these reasons, criticism of male behavior will sometimes be more believ-able if it is issued by men rather than by women.

It is a regrettable fact that men generally take other men more seriously than they take women. But the regrettable nature of such a state of affairs can be overcome in some cases if the male voice of authority is used as an effective critical tool. Believability is not a substitute for justifiability. If a person lacks justifiability for a claim he has made, merely being believed counts for very little. But if a person has a reasonable degree of justifiability, then being believable can enhance his claim enough to make it preferable to other justifiable claims that lack this believability. The preference for the male critical voice of course is practical rather than theoretical: the truth of the claims themselves is not affected by believability.

At least part of the explanation for the greater believability that men have with other men is that many men see the criticism of their experiences and roles by women as an affront to their manliness. If other men are critically calling for the change, then it is harder to dismiss the call for change as an affront to one's manliness. I must confess that I don't think much of the affront to manliness charge, but if it is taken seriously by many other men, then I am inclined to take it seriously. It is for this reason that I have sought to provide positive suggestions about what men can do to build on the strengths they already have, rather than merely providing negative criticisms of male experience and traditional conceptions of masculinity.[26]

Another part of the puzzle of believability is now becoming clear. Men have more trust in men than in women not to discount the positive aspects of male experience and roles. Of course men can demonstrate that this trust was misplaced, as can be seen in the negative reaction by many men to certain writers in the men's movement. Such criticisms are not nearly as common as those directed at women who write about men. Indeed, the current backlash against feminism is fueled by this general charge of male bashing,[27] whereas there are few similar criticisms of male writers. This is because one does not expect a person to "bash" himself or his own group since such bashing seems so clearly self-hurtful. So men are afforded more trust than women not to be overly critical of the experiences of males and of masculinity more generally.

There is a serious political problem here, though, that has epistemic ramifications. If men need to be perceived as not overly critical of male experience and roles in order to be believable, then this may put a constraint on their critical writings and this would jeopardize the justifiability of those writings. Purists who insist on providing a thoroughgoing critique of male experience and traditional roles will find that their message will not be taken as seriously by the very people that they want most to affect, namely other men. But then a fine line needs to be walked between doing respectable philosophical work that calls for a healthy dose of critique, and not losing the trust of those to whom the critique is addressed.

A similar problem occurs in the fields of medical and business ethics. In order to be taken seriously by the practitioners in business and medicine, philosophers have found that they cannot be perceived as critical of the whole enterprise of business or medicine. But this has sometimes meant that philosophers have shied away from systemic critiques of these disciplines so as to make sure that they do not lose the trust of the members of these fields. The integrity of the philosophical investigations is difficult, although not impossible, to maintain under these circumstances. Just the right balance needs to be struck between searchingly critical inquiry and sympathetic attempts to understand a person's or group's point of view.[28]

I have argued that for some men it is possible to attain a progressive male standpoint. Such a position involves observing male experience and traditional roles with a critical eye, being motivated to try to change certain traditional ways of behaving and thinking, and constructing believable proposals for change for other men. I have not argued that such a standpoint is blocked for women. But I have argued that generally men are better placed than women in two ways: they have better access to certain data because of their direct acquaintance with certain male experiences, and their criticisms are more believable by other men because it is presumed that they will not be excessively critical of those experiences. I have also argued that women are more likely to have a distanced, critical perspective on male experience and roles, and that women are often better placed to contribute to changing early socialization patterns so as to motivate change. Thus, men and women can each bring different resources and expertise to a progressive standpoint on masculinity.

A male standpoint that is progressive and morally responsive can be achieved. One of the obstacles to such an achievement is that men currently feel under siege. They are being asked to give up a lot—for instance, roles that they previously felt quite comfortable filling; and it is not yet clear to many of them what they will gain in return. Male philosophical writing about male experience and traditional roles needs to provide not only critical arguments but a new vision of what men can become.[29] There is no reason to think that men and women must become alike: there is the option that men could still be distinctively men, but different from how they now are. A progressive male standpoint on male experience and traditional roles needs both to make that point clear and also to make a concerted effort to go beyond merely sketching out what the alternative conception of masculinity would be like.[30]

I have previously made a start in this direction. My discussions of male anger, paternity, sexuality, pornography, rape, sexual harassment, and the exclusion of women have all had a strong morally critical dimension.[31]

But these discussions have also tried to indicate avenues for positive reconceptualization of male roles, building on some of the traditional strengths of those roles. In this way, I have tried to illustrate how the progressive male standpoint can produce reasonable critiques of male roles and yet still be believable enough to motivate men to change their lives. In this essay, I have tried to lend some support to the growing, but still relatively small, number of men trying to provide a moral reconceptualization of masculinity.[32]

Notes

1. Unlike some in the feminist standpoint movement, I will use the term standpoint in a fairly broad way to cover both considerations of knowledge and practice. Indeed, I use the term standpoint to be a rough equivalent to situated knowledge, contrary to some of the main adherents of feminist standpoint epistemology.

2. Sandra Harding has developed what she calls a feminist standpoint epistemology that specifically shares many features with the view I will articulate. Among the many things she has written on this topic, I would recommend the recent piece, "Rethinking Standpoint Epistemology: 'What is Strong Objectivity?'" in *Feminist Epistemologies*, edited by Linda Alcoff and Elizabeth Potter (New York: Routledge, 1993). The first essay in this anthology, Linda Alcoff and Elizabeth Potter's "Introduction: When Feminism Intersects Epistemology," ibid., especially pp. 1–4, gives a good, brief overview of the general projects that fall under the label of feminist epistemology.

3. Many women who are feminists wish to reserve the label "feminist" for women's progressive views of gender, whereas some other women are willing to use the label "feminist" in a broader way to describe progressive views of gender by both women and men. Without wanting to enter into the merits of the positions in this debate, I have chosen simply to use the label "progressive" rather than "feminist" for the view of masculinity I will here describe. But I believe that my view could also legitimately be called "feminist."

4. In this respect I follow twenty years of feminist theorizing. I would cite two essays that help locate my own views. First, Bat-Ami Bar On has a good account of why feminists have generally privileged certain kinds of personal experience in her essay "Marginality and Epistemic Privilege," in *Feminist Epistemologies*, op. cit. Second, Joan W. Scott has argued that the privileging of personal experience is highly problematic for feminists in her essay "Experience," in *Feminists Theorize the Political*, edited by Judith Butler and Joan W. Scott (New York: Routledge, 1992). My views are closer to Bar On's than to Scott's, although I recognize a number of problems with personal experience in what follows.

5. I use the term critical here to refer to a position in which people have a healthy skepticism about the dominant ideologies and perspectives that are held by the majority of people, especially by those who hold power in a given society. I am influenced here by contemporary critical social theorists, although my use of the term critical is not as highly specialized as is theirs. For a discussion of this

issue, see chapters two and three of my book, *The Socially Responsive Self* (Chicago: University of Chicago Press, 1996).

6. See Larry May and Robert Strikwerda, "Men in Groups: Collective Responsibility for Rape," *Hypatia*, vol. 9, no. 2, Spring 1994.

7. One of my personal favorites is Iris Young's *Throwing Like a Girl and Other Essays in Feminist Philosophy and Social Theory* (Bloomington, IN: Indiana University Press, 1990), which has wonderful essays on being pregnant, having breasts, and throwing like a girl.

8. A progressive male standpoint also here has some features in common with what feminists mean by standpoint epistemology, where the standpoint of the knower, his or her experiences and biases, are crucial for the status of the knowledge alleged.

9. I use the expression "the rape culture" to refer to the way that many of the roles and activities of men contribute to the increased prevalence of rape in contemporary society.

10. In some cases, personal knowledge can blind one to what is really going on, as when one regards one's experiences as self-certifying. A man who has been discriminated against may feel that this experience gives him an insight into all forms of discrimination. As I will explain later, there is always a need for critical reflection on this experiential base before experience can be a legitimate source of knowledge.

11. One of the best and most accessible accounts of this view is put forth by Bertrand Russell in his book *The Problems of Philosophy* (Oxford: Oxford University Press, [1912] 1970).

12. For a good discussion of moral saliency see Barbara Herman's essay "The Practice of Moral Judgment," in her book *The Practice of Moral Judgment* (Cambridge, MA: Harvard University Press, 1993).

13. W.V. Quine, an otherwise model behaviorist, allows that introspection is an important source of data. See Roger Gibson, *The Philosophy of W.V. Quine* (Tampa, FL: University of South Florida Press, 1986), pp. 195–96.

14. At least in part this has to do with limits on our attention spans. But also it has to do with limitations on sustaining an idea that was itself based on something not very vivid.

15. Nancy Hartsock, "The Feminist Standpoint: Developing the Ground for a Specifically Feminist Historical Materialism," in Sandra Harding, editor, *Feminism and Methodology* (Bloomington, IN: Indiana University Press, 1987).

16. In a later section I argue that a person who has been subject to oppression may have an easier time achieving a progressive standpoint than someone who has not had this experience. On first sight, this might appear to be a bias that one must have, as opposed to what I have just said about eliminating biases. But as will become clear, being a member of an oppressed group does not give one a bias so much as it eliminates various biases.

17. See Nancy Hartsock, op. cit.

18. I here assume that women will not be biased against male experience more than men are biased in favor of it. Men have a clear self-interested basis for favoring their own experience. Women do not have a correspondingly strong interest in disfavoring male experience.

19. I am grateful to Ed Soule for help with this point.

20. See my discussion of this point at the end of "Men in Groups: Collective Responsibility for Rape," *Hypatia*, op. cit.

21. For a good discussion of the motivational dimension in morality, and the debate between those who think that motivation is internal and those who think it is external to moral judgments, see David Brink, *Moral Realism and the Foundation of Ethics* (Cambridge: Cambridge University Press, 1989), chapter 3.

22. I am grateful to Tom Digby for help on this point.

23. Indeed, many studies show that men have trouble expressing their feelings and sustaining intimate relationships even though they want to do so. See Robert Strikwerda and Larry May, "Male Intimacy and Friendship," *Hypatia*, vol. 7, no. 3 (Summer 1992).

24. See Patricia Greenspan, *Practical Guilt* (Oxford: Oxford University Press, 1995), especially chapters 1 and 6.

25. There will also be other things that are necessary to end traditional patterns of male socialization. Various collective and institutional efforts will have to go hand-in-hand with individual men choosing to educate their sons differently. I discuss some of these collective and institutional changes in my book, *Masculinity and Morality*, (Ithaca, NY: Cornell University Press, 1988).

26. See especially Larry May and Robert Strikwerda, "Fatherhood and Nurturance," *Journal of Social Philosophy*, vol. 22, no. 2, Fall 1991.

27. See Susan Faludi, *Backlash* (New York: Crown Publishing, 1991).

28. Some of these points are discussed at greater length in the collection of essays edited by David M. Rosenthal and Fadlou Shehadi, *Applied Ethics and Ethical Theory* (Salt Lake City: University of Utah Press, 1988).

29. There are already a few good books in this domain. John Stoltenberg's book, *Refusing To Be A Man* (New York: Meridian Books, 1989), is a good example. A new journal, *masculinities*, is also proving to be a good source of scholarship by men taking a progressive male standpoint. It is interesting though that even in this journal there are as many women as men writing. Indeed, in a recent issue, vol. 3, no. 2 (Summer 1995), all of the articles were written by women.

30. Also see *Rethinking Masculinity*, second edition, edited by Larry May, Robert Strikwerda, and Patrick Hopkins (Lanham, MD: Rowman and Littlefield Publishers, 1996), for a number of attempts, in their own small ways, to fill out such a sketch.

31. These are each the subject of chapter length treatment in my book manuscript, *Masculinity and Morality*, op. cit.

32. I am grateful to Tom Digby for motivating me to begin thinking about this issue by inviting me to a panel discussion on "Men do Feminism" at the APA Eastern division meetings in 1994. I am also grateful to Tom in addition to Ed Soule, Elvia Herrera, Marilyn Friedman, James Bohman, Roger Gibson, Iris Young, Carl Wellman, Richard Hiskes, and Margaret Walker, as well as the students in my graduate seminar in moral epistemology in the spring of 1996, for critical discussions of, and suggestions about, these issues. A slightly revised version of this paper will appear as the final chapter of *Masculinity and Morality*, op. cit.

Contributor Notes

Michael Awkward is professor of English and Afro-American Studies at the University of Michigan. He is author of *Negotiating Difference: Race, Gender, and the Politics of Positionality* (1995) and of *Inspiriting Influences: Tradition, Revision, and Afro-American Women's Novels* (1989) and editor of *New Essays on Their Eyes Were Watching God* (1990). He is currently completing an autobiographical narrative exploring the genesis of his relationship to feminism, and doing research for a study of contemporary black representations of slavery.

Sandra Bartky is professor of philosophy and women's studies at the University of Illinois at Chicago. She is the author of *Femininity and Domination: Studies in the Phenomenology of Oppression* (1990) and co-editor (with Nancy Fraser) of *Revaluing French Feminism: Essays on Difference, Agency, and Culture* (1992). She has written numerous journal articles, anthology chapters, and book reviews, and has lectured widely.

Susan Bordo is professor of philosophy and holds the Singletary Chair of Humanities at the University of Kentucky. She is the author of *The Flight to Objectivity: Essays on Cartesianism and Culture* (1987) and *Unbearable Weight: Feminism, Western Culture, and the Body* (1993); the latter was named a New York Times Notable Book in 1993. Her forthcoming books are *Twilight Zones: The Hidden Life of Cultural Images from Plato to O.J.* and *My Father's Body and Other Unexplored Regions of Sex, Masculinity, and the Male Body*.

Harry Brod teaches in the philosophy department and in the women's studies, Jewish studies, and honors programs at the University of Delaware. He is the editor of *The Making of Masculinities: The New Men's Studies, A Mensche Among Men: Explorations in Jewish Masculinity*, and (with Michael Kaufman) *Theorizing Masculinities*, and the author of *Hegel's Philosophy of Politics: Idealism, Identity, and Modernity*.

Tom Digby teaches philosophy and feminist theory at Springfield College. His articles on feminism and a wide range of other subjects have appeared in numerous journals. A recent article, "No *One* Is Guilty: Crime, Patriarchy, and Individualism," appeared in the *Journal of Social Philosophy*. "Do Feminists Hate Men?: Feminism, Antifeminism, and Gender Oppositionality," is forthcoming in the same journal. He serves on the Executive Board of the Society for the Study of Women Philosophers and has also been active in the Society for Women in Philosophy.

Judith Kegan Gardiner is professor of English and women's studies at the University of Illinois at Chicago. She is the author of *Rhys, Stead, Lessing, and the Politics of Empathy* (Bloomington: Indiana University Press, 1989), the editor of *Provoking Agents: Gender and Agency in Theory and Practice*, (University of Illinois Press, 1995), and an editor of the interdisciplinary journal *Feminist Studies*, with essays on feminist and psychoanalytic theory and on women writers in *Critical Inquiry*, *Feminist Studies*, *Signs*, *Tulsa Studies in Women's Literature*, and other journals. She is currently working on a book about masculinity in feminist theory.

C. Jacob Hale is an associate professor of philosophy at California State University, Northridge, where he recently co-founded, with Donald E. Hall, LesBiGayTrS (The Institute for Lesbian, Bisexual, Gay, and Transgender Studies). He has scholarly articles, written from an explicitly genderqueer sex radical subject position, in *Hypatia*, *The Journal of Homosexuality* and *GLQ: A Gay and Lesbian Quarterly*. Hale's primary theoretical and political concern is to create broader conditions of possibility for genderqueer discursive agency. He co-directs the National Coalition for GID (Gender Identity Disorder) Reform with Susan Stryker and Riki Anne Wilchins, recently started Genderqueer Boyzzz, a Southern California social group primarily for and about people assigned female at birth or in childhood and raised girl-to-woman who have masculine self-identifications some or all of the time, and occasionally writes for *TNT: Transsexual News Telegraph*.

Sandra Harding is professor of women's studies, education, and philosophy at the University of California at Los Angeles, where she also directs the Center for the Study of Women. She is the author or editor of seven books, including *Discovering Reality: Feminist Perspectives on Epistemology, Metaphysics, Methodology and Philosophy of Science* (1983), *The Science Question in Feminism* (1986), *Sex and Scientific Inquiry* (1987), *Feminism and Methodology* (1987), *Whose Science? Whose Knowledge? Thinking From Women's Lives* (1991), and *The 'Racial' Economy of Science: Toward a Democratic Future* (1993). Due out in

1998 is her most recent book, *Is Science Multicultural? Postcolonialism, Feminism and Epistemology.*

Patrick D. Hopkins teaches philosophy at the University of Colorado at Boulder. He has edited a text in gender studies and technology studies entitled *Sex/Machine: A Reader in Gender, Culture and Technology* (Indiana University Press, forthcoming), has co-edited *Rethinking Masculinity: Philosophical Explorations in Light of Feminism*, 2nd ed. (1996), and is currently writing a book on technology and the nature/culture distinction provisionally entitled *Un/Natural: "Nature," "Culture," and "Technology" in Moral and Political Discourse.*

Joy James teaches political and feminist theory in the Department of Ethnic Studies at the University of Colorado at Boulder. She is the author of *Transcending the Talented Tenth: Black Leaders and American Intellectuals* (1997), and *Resisting State Violence: Radicalism, Gender and Race in U.S. Culture* (1996), and editor of the *Angela Y. Davis Reader* (1997). Currently, she is working on issues of prisoners' rights.

David J. Kahane is assistant professor of philosophy at the University of Alberta. He writes about the complex ways in which group memberships shape identity, and about how democratic deliberations should take group memberships into account. He is completing a book called *Democratic Deliberation and Social Diversity*, and has published articles and reviews in *The American Political Science Review, The Canadian Journal of Political Science*, and *Constellations.*

Michael S. Kimmel is professor of sociology at State University of New York, Stony Brook. His books include *Changing Men* (1987), *Men's Lives* (3rd edition, 1995), *Men Confront Pornography* (1990), *Against the Tide: Profeminist Men in the United States, 1776–1990* (1992), *The Politics of Manhood* (1996), and *Manhood in America: A Cultural History* (1996). He edits *Masculinities*, an interdisciplinary scholarly journal, and a book series on Men and Masculinity at University of California Press. He is the National Spokesperson for the National Organization for Men Against Sexism (NOMAS) and lectures extensively on campuses here and abroad.

Gary Lemons teaches African-American literature and feminist studies at Eugene Lang College at the New School University. In 1995 he received a Rockefeller Post-Doctoral Fellowship at the Womanist Consortium of the University of Georgia to begin research on the history of black women in U.S. fashion design. His most recent publications include

"Teaching the (Bi)Racial Space That Has No Name: Reflections of a Black Male Feminist Teacher," in *Everyday Acts Against Racism*, ed. Maureen T. Reddy; "Young Man, Tell Our Stories of How We Made It Over: Beyond the Politics of Identity," in *Teaching What You're Not: Identity Politics in Higher Education*, ed. Katherine J. Mayberry; "To Be Black, Male, and Feminist: Making Womanist Space for Black Men," in the *International Journal of Sociology and Social Policy*. Another essay, "'When and Where We Enter': Reclaiming the Legacy of Black (Male) Feminism—W.E.B. DuBois and My Search for a Womanist Forefather," is forthcoming in *Traps: Black Men on Gender and Sexuality*, ed. Beverly Guy-Sheftall and Rudolph Byrd.

Larry May is professor of philosophy at Washington University in St. Louis. He is the author of four books: *The Morality of Groups* (1987), *Sharing Responsibility* (1992), *The Socially Responsive Self* (1996), and *Masculinity and Morality* (1997). He has also co-edited six books, including *Rethinking Masculinity* (2nd edition, 1996). Currently he is writing a book on moral sensitivity and guilt.

Brian Pronger is the author of the *Arena of Masculinity: Sports, Homosexuality, and the Meaning of Sex*. He has written numerous articles on sexuality, gender, and sport as well as on philosophies of postmodernism, the body, and science. He teaches philosophy at the School of Physical and Health Education at the University of Toronto.

Henry S. Rubin is a lecturer in the Committee on Degrees in Social Studies at Harvard University. His forthcoming book, *Transformations* (University of Chicago Press), brings together a genealogy of FTM transsexual identity and an ethnographic account of FTMs becoming who they always were all along.

Richard Schmitt has written books and articles about topics in existentialism and Marxist theory. His recent *Beyond Separateness* (1995) criticizes dominant conceptions of autonomy, knowledge, and power from the perspective of feminist theory. The present paper is one of a series of papers about the hidden roots of the oppression of women. An earlier one about male fears of impotence, co-authored with Lucy Candib, appears in *Rethinking Masculinities: Philosophical Explorations in Light of Feminism*, 2nd edition (1996), edited by May, Strikwerda, and Hopkins.

James P. Sterba is professor of philosophy at the University of Notre Dame, where he teaches ethics and political philosophy. He has written books, including *How to Make People Just, Contemporary Ethics, Feminist Philosophies, Earth Ethics, Morality in Practice* (5th Edition), and *Contemporary Social and Political Philosophy*. His most recent book, *Justice for Here and Now*, is forthcoming from Cambridge University Press. He has served as president of the North American Society for Social Philosophy, president of Concerned Philosophers for Peace, and president of the International Society for Philosophy of Law and Social Philosophy (American Section). Sterba has lectured widely in the United States and Europe.

Laurence Mordekhai Thomas is professor in the departments of philosophy and political science, and a member of the Judaic Studies Program, at Syracuse University. He is the author of *Vessels of Evil: American Slavery and the Holocaust* (1993) and *Living Morally: A Psychology of Moral Character* (1989), as well as articles on a wide range of subjects, including feminism. His essay, "Erogenous Zones and Ambiguity: Sexuality and the Bodies of Women and Men," appeared in *Rethinking Masculinities: Philosophical Explorations in Light of Feminism*, 2nd edition, (1996) edited by May, Strikwerda, and Hopkins.

Thomas E. Wartenberg is professor of philosophy and chair of film studies at Mount Holyoke College. He is the author of *The Forms of Power* (1990) and has edited *Rethinking Power* (1992) and, with Cynthia Freeland, *Philosophy and Film* (1995). He has published widely on topics in the history of philosophy and social theory as well as the philosophy of film.